BY THE EDITORS OF CONSUMER GUIDE®

Porsche

A Tradition of Greatness

RICHARD M. LANGWORTH

BEEKMAN HOUSE
New York

CONTENTS

Louis Weber, President
Publications International, Ltd.
3841 West Oakton Street
Skokie, Illinois 60076

Manufactured in the United States of America
10 9 8 7 6 5 4 3

Library of Congress Catalog Card Number: 83-60704

ISBN: 0-517-40496-6

This edition published by:
Beekman House
Distributed by Crown Publishers, Inc.
One Park Avenue
New York, New York 10016

Acknowledgements and Bibliographic Notes

The editors wish to extend special thanks to Gene Babow, Porsche expert *extraordinaire*, for checking the advance manuscript and advising us throughout. Equal thanks to Fred Heyler and Porsche+Audi of America for their invaluable help in research and photographs, and for their encouragement. Gene Babow contributed Chapters 6 ("The Coachbuilt Porsche") and 20 ("Connoisseur's Choice"), while Chapter 12 ("From Glöckler Spyder to RS61") was adapted from an article by the same title by Craig Bozorth in *The Milestone Car* #17, (Autumn 1976), © Dragonwyck Publishing Inc.

Principal photography for the color section was supplied by Bud Juneau. Selected plates were provided courtesy of Dean Batchelor and David Gooley and Associates. To all, our sincere appreciation. Besides the aforementioned, additional black-and-white photography was contributed by Gene Babow, William L. Bailey, Richard M. Langworth, and the Sports Car Club of America.

The editors welcome comments and additional information pertinent to future editions of *Porsche: A Tradition of Greatness*. Address Automotive Editor, CONSUMER GUIDE® Publications, 3841 W. Oakton St., Skokie, Illinois 60076, USA.

AN INTRODUCTION BY KEN PURDY

The following is excerpted from The Porsche Story *(1964), a Porsche company publication written by the late Ken W. Purdy (1913-1972). Once described by former* Automobile Quarterly *editor Don Vorderman as "the godfather of us all," Purdy is generally regarded as the pioneer of the human-interest approach to automotive journalism, as opposed to the strictly nut-and-bolts style that prevailed before World War II. Perhaps best known for his magazine articles in the '50s, Purdy was also the author of eight major books. One of these was* All But My Life, *a 1963 biography of race driver Stirling Moss, which earned the distinction of being the most popular automotive book ever published up to that time.*

People who own Porsches may be anything from industrial tycoons to freelance artists, but they all have two things in common: (1) When they want to go, they want to *go*; they don't want temperament, delays or fussiness in their automobiles; (2) They don't live in ugly houses, they don't wear ugly clothing, and they won't drive ugly automobiles.

Driving the ordinary automobile is essentially boring. That's why you see so many people sitting sideways to the wheel, or steering with the wrist, the hand draped over the rim of the wheel, or running with the left hand dangling out of the window or plastered to the roof. They're bored. And why not? Most automobiles are boring, so driving them can't be anything else.

But you almost never see a Porsche driver who looks bored. There are two big reasons: (1) The Porsche is so fast, so cat-quick and responsive that driving it is a constant amusement, a diversion, a recreation, a pleasure; it makes driving the average car feel like steering a house with wheels; (2) The Porsche driver is not piloting some dreamboat, sporting a model-name cooked up a few months back. He's driving an aristocrat, a thoroughbred machine with a lineage that runs back eight decades and more, almost to the invention of the automobile. Behind the PORSCHE badge stand hundreds of men who have proved the car in competitions around the world, from Ferdinand Porsche himself, setting a new record for the Semmering hillclimb on September 23rd, 1900, to someone who ran a Porsche in a race last weekend a few miles from you, wherever that may be.

Bigness is best? Nonsense. I know a man who had eleven children. For a family car he bought a so-called "airport conversion"—a big sedan that had been cut in two and lengthened by about six feet. If a family of that size is your problem, I recommend his solution. It's practical, although it's not a lot of fun. It's almost axiomatic that the bigger a vehicle, the less fun it is to handle. The sailor at the helm of the *Queen Elizabeth II* may know a surging sense of power, but he does not feel that he's *steering* anything. That's *work*, what he's doing. Driving an automobile shouldn't be boring and it shouldn't be work — it should be recreation. With a Porsche, it is.

Too small is no good, either. Below a certain size, an automobile lacks one or both of two essentials: comfort and power. There are on the market some small cars, very small cars, that will stun the average driver with their speed, say 110 miles an hour—and stun him with their boiler-factory noise level, too. Then there are the very small cars that are reasonably comfortable and quiet, but can't get up enough speed to get out of their own way.

How big should a car be to be comfortable, safe, powerful, and a pleasure to handle? It should be big enough to accept a six-foot driver, one tall friend, and their luggage. It should have enough power to move itself and the cargo aforesaid at a reasonable speed—say 100 miles an hour—and it should handle impeccably and move sure-footedly over any road between here and Hong Kong. If it's that big, it's big enough...just the size of the Porsche.

Changes in classics are made when they have shown themselves to be necessary, and not before — and certainly not afterward. Often they are imperceptible except under careful scrutiny. The Type 356B Porsche, for example, had a different muffler system than the Type 356A; a heated, mist-proof rear window; a compression ratio .5 higher—all changes that improved the car but not noticeable as it stands at the curb. Close examination of the two cars side by side will show a very slight difference in the shape of the body, slightly higher headlights, and two openings in front leading cooling air to the brakes. The Porsche company made no particular effort to call these changes to the attention of its clients. Porsche owners knew that the essential design of the 356 Porsche, like that of the Rolls-Royce, was timeless; that it didn't really change because it didn't need to change. (And, since the factory has never been able to produce enough Porsches to meet the world demand, it's not necessary to change the design in order to con buyers.) Truly beautiful and functional design rarely changes. Who could improve the essential form of the teaspoon?

A radical departure, for Porsche, was the change to disc brakes in place of drums, on the 1964 models. Invented in 1902, the disc brake came into wide use in aircraft after World War II, and, beginning in the Fifties, in racing and sports cars, and fast touring cars. Its great virtue is that the disc stands clear of the wheel, not shrouded, as are drum brakes, and thus is quickly and easily cooled by air rushing past. Disc brakes do not heat and fade, as some drum brakes will after repeated use. Early disc brakes had disadvantages, too: they required heavy pedal pressure, they wore fast, they squealed, their hand braking was inadequate; and some manufacturers who rushed to install them for publicity value lived to regret it. Porsche had disc brakes under investigation from 1957. Porsche disc brakes don't squeal, they last a long time, they don't need power assistance and Porsche has added an efficient drum hand brake to the rear discs. Except in the $100,000 racecar category, most manufacturers have compromised by putting disc brakes only on front wheels. Porsche put them on all four. Longtime Porsche drivers, confident that the famous Porsche drum brakes could not be improved upon, will be surprised, the first time they use them.

A good deal of hand-fitting and hand-assembly work goes into a Porsche; in the early days of the company, each engine was put together by one man, who stamped it with his initials—in effect, signed it—when he'd finished. The practice had to be abandoned as unfair to the other workers—what about the man who paints the body, where can *he* sign his name?—but the spirit that produced it is still strong. When Porsche *grand prix* cars hit a losing streak in 1961-62, racing department mechanics took an oath not to shave until it was over.

Racing is in the background of most of the world's great cars, the classic, connoisseur's motorcars. Even the Rolls-Royce was a competition car before World War I. Oddly, the automobile that is founded on racing may or may not be very fast, but it will invariably be very sturdy, long-lived, trouble-free. Racing is an extremely severe form of testing. A manufacturer cannot find a car tester who will, for hire, drive a car as hard as a race driver will. No salary can offer that much inducement. To take an automobile to the outermost limits of its performance and hold it there, hour after hour, at the risk of his life—for this a man must be paid in more than money. To do this, he must be offered a chance for fortune, for renown. *Then,* he'll take your car and if it's going to break, he'll break it.

What does all this mean to the man or woman who wants to go out and buy a Porsche? It means that if one feels like a spot of racing a reasonable expenditure will give one a much-better-than-reasonable chance of winning. If one doesn't want to race but to use the Porsche in its other guise, that of elegant personal transportation, there's the satisfaction of knowing that everything in the car, from the engine itself to the screws holding the rear-view mirror has been tested thousands upon thousands of times, through the mill, through the toughest, most brutal testing process known: flat-out racing, and not just racing on a track, but racing over the roads and in the mountains, from the borders of the Sahara to as far north in Canada as you can drive without needing a snowknife and your supply of pemmican.

There's no such thing as a really great *new* automobile.

The automobiles that are universally rated best by the world's experts have all been many decades in development: Rolls-Royce, in continuous production since 1904; Peugeot, winner of a race in 1894, and the company still wholly owned by descendants of the founder; Cadillac, winner of the Dewar Trophy in 1908 for demonstrating the principle of interchangeability of parts; Rover, made by a firm that went into business in 1868; Mercedes-Benz, product of Daimler-Benz, a company joining the names of the two men generally held to have invented the automobile. And Porsche, the first of which was designed wholly by one man, Ferdinand Porsche, an innovator of extraordinary range and power; a Porsche-designed car was the sensation of the 1900 World Exhibition in Paris.

The design of a successful automobile is a shatteringly difficult task. The really great car comes into being *only* when a design that is absolutely *right* to begin with, has been given years to mature, to develop, years of modification, minute change, and refinement. Three conditions are essential: A designer of the first rank, a near genius, one destined for immortality, a Royce, a Ford, a Lyons, a Bugatti; very early commercial success, to provide money for development; and few models, forbidding change merely for the sake of change.

All really superb automobiles meet these conditions, but none more precisely than the Porsche. Ferdinand Porsche satisfied most of the definitions of genius: He could do things that he had not been taught to do; his capacity for taking pains, for detail, was fantastic; original ideas spilled out of his mind like water from a fountain.

Dr. Ferdinand Porsche died on January 30th, 1951, a full life, rich in creation, behind him. Direction of the firm Dr. Ing. h.c. F. Porsche K. G., then came to his son, Ferry Porsche, holder, among other honors, of the Elmer A. Sperry medal, one of the highest U.S. engineering awards. Brilliant in his own right, he is an extension of his father, and it is as likely as such things can be that the developments in the car that have been made since the elder Porsche's death—the great *Carrera* model, for example, the 911 and the 924/944, and 928—would not have been differently done had he lived.

What *is* all this Porsche talk? What makes Porsche owners act such a special breed of cat? Why do so many of them say that their next car will be another Porsche, and the one after that, and the one after *that*, too? Because they do say so: no other car in the market commands a greater customer loyalty than the Porsche. And that, when you stop to think about it, almost ends the discussion, doesn't it? Because *nothing* says more for a product, any product, than an owner's sworn oath, hand-on-heart, that all he wants for Christmas is another one.

Why? After all, a man can drive only one Porsche at a time. *That's* an answer? He can wear only one Lesly & Roberts suit at a time, too, only one pair of shoes by Kember of Montpelier Street. His jacket may appear, casually, to be much like any other jacket—but he knows it isn't. It doesn't *feel* like another jacket. His shoes may look like other shoes—they aren't: they fit *his* foot—only. And a Porsche *feels* like no other car. It steers like a wish, it brakes as if the great brown hand of legend had appeared from the sky to hold it like a toy, and it runs through corners as a train is supposed to—a train with its wheels flanged to the steel track—as a train is supposed to do, and doesn't, because it can't, bucking and swerving as the steel rims of the wheels whack against the steel of the rails. A 356 just sticks, and goes on around, far faster than you'd have believed possible.

What's the magic answer? Why does this car, of which so few, comparatively, have been made, not the biggest, not the fastest, not the most expensive automobile in the world, still do things that no other car will do? What's the magic answer?

There *is* no magic answer. What did Ferdinand Porsche put into his car that no one else could put into another? Something secret, strange and wonderful? No. All right, it had torsion-bar suspension, which meant that the wheels were held tight to the road, where they are supposed to be, where they do their work, rather than being allowed to bounce around and goof off, as most springing systems let them do; it had the best synchromesh gear system then known, the best, probably, that could, in the then state of the art, be devised; the engine was in the rear, and was air-cooled, which is merely intelligent. Right, it was as comfortable a vehicle as runs on the roads today, and it was over-safe, over-sturdy, over-strong.

But magic? No. Just genius, the simple, inexorable application of intelligence over a period of many years, intelligence intent upon bringing into being the best thing of its kind in the world.

Dr. Ferdinand Porsche, circa 1923

FERDINAND PORSCHE: THE ARTISTIC GENIUS

To use his full title, he was *Herr Professor Doktor Ingenieur* Ferdinand Porsche. He was a tremendously complicated man, a master engineer who was more artist than theoretician, more maestro than composer. He was not a body designer, though the bodies of Porsche automobiles have been admired for two generations. He was not a chassis engineer, though the chassis of Porsche automobiles have always been technically superb expressions of the chassis designer's art. No, Ferdinand Porsche's greatest skill was in engine design; yet even here he wasn't always right. Like many great auto pioneers he had the loyal assistance of unsung heroes. His chief assistant, Karl Rabe, wrote Leonard Setright, was "scarcely known for his own ideas, but [his] eventual claim to fame was that he made so many of Porsche's ideas work. If it were not Rabe, then it might have been his aerodynamicist Mickl who wielded the slide rule: when Porsche wielded it publicly, it seems to have been mainly for effect."

Whatever else one may say of Ferdinand Porsche, one fact is indisputable. He was a man of single-minded purpose, "one of those creatively fecund individuals," as Setright put it, "whose vision penetrated the obscurantist orthodoxy of more than mere cars." Today's Porsche company owes its existence to his drive and lifelong concepts about sports cars. Thus, the story of Porsche automobiles must begin with an account of Ferdinand Porsche's career.

He was born in 1875 in the tiny village of Maffersdorf, Bohemia, near what is today the Czechoslovakian town of Liberec. It was the heyday of the Austrian Empire, which stretched from The Carpathian Mountains to the Alps and embraced scores of nationalities among its 50 million people. Porsche's father was a master metalsmith and, when the eldest son Anton died following an accident, young Ferdinand became his father's heir apparent and apprentice. Metalworking proved to be Ferdinand's first failure: he didn't like it, and he was no good at it. His father was furious.

Ferdinand was in his mid-teens when he became fascinated by electricity. Soon, he had set himself up in the family attic with batteries and wires, experimenting with a form of power that Bohemia as a whole had hardly heard of. His father considered this hobby a frivolous waste of time and on several occasions destroyed the batteries and circuits, but the son persisted. When the elder Porsche came home one evening to find the house ablaze with electric lights —from a system Ferdinand had designed and built himself—he realized that there was perhaps more here than met the eye. Ferdinand was sent to Vienna to look for work, and his younger brother Oskar became the apprentice metalsmith.

Ferdinand's professional education was rudimentary. He'd done poorly in a technical school near home and could not afford, nor qualify for, university training. Working as a handyman for an electric company in Vienna, Porsche demonstrated an enthusiasm that gained him admittance to university classes; but he was not matriculated and so could not take the examinations.

In 1898, Porsche signed on as an engine designer with Viennese coachbuilder Jackob Lohner, who had just launched his own automobile. Lohner wanted to build an electric. Ferdinand Porsche designed one for him. Built on the *Radnabenmotor* principle, it had an electric motor at each front wheel, dispensing with a transmission. Trying to avoid heavy batteries, Porsche later developed what we would now call a hybrid power system, whereby the electric motors were fed from a generator powered by a small gas engine. The Lohner was, incidentally, the first front-wheel-drive car—Ferdinand's first "first." But Lohner sold his patents to Emil Jellinek in 1906, and young Porsche looked for new horizons.

Joining Austro-Daimler in 1906, Porsche completely redesigned that firm's large four-cylinder engine and created the "Maja" model (named after one of Jellinek's daughters, the sister of Mercedes Jellinek, a name with which Ferdinand would soon become familiar). In 1909 a trio of racing cars was developed for the Prince Henry

Below: Dr. Porsche's first car, the 1900 Lohner electric with front drive

Above: Another Lohner-Porsche, circa 1902, with rear hub drive

This page: An early-1900s Lohner built for Englishman E.W. Hart (left), with four-wheel drive and two tons of batteries. Porsche's first light-car design, the 1.0-liter "Sascha" (below) of the '20s. Opposite page: Early Porsche-designed military vehicles, the "Big Bertha" mortar tractor (above) and the Skoda "train."

Trials. They were unsuccessful, but provided lots of new ideas for the following year. Sure enough, in 1910 the Prinz Heinrich Austro-Daimlers were the cars to beat, finishing 1-2-3 overall. Despite its small size for the day (5.7 liters/348 cubic inches) the Prinz Heinrich engine produced 95 bhp, and Porsche took pains to make the car it powered as light as possible, making up for the brute force of the heavy, plus-20.0-liter (1220-cid) competition. Porsche's concern with aerodynamics was apparent in the body shaping (called *tulpenform*, after the tulip): round at the front, tapering to the rear, the sides curving upward and outward. There weren't any wind tunnels in those days, but the Austro-Daimler racers were astonishingly slippery. Their top speed was nearly 90 mph, remarkable for 1910.

That year proved the high point for the Austro-Daimler racing team. Indeed it was one of the last times in history that the old Hapsburg Empire of Franz Josef would receive any kind of acclaim. Big power rivalries—commencing with the Kaiser's decision to build a navy to rival Britain's, and France's alliance with Russia in the early 20th Century—were about to plunge the world into a cataclysm that would sweep away the old royal houses and redraw the map of Europe. The war came in August 1914, but long before that the Great Powers were preparing—Britain and Germany by a naval race, France, Russia, and Austria-Hungary by piling up armaments.

In those days, what is now Czechoslovakia still belonged to Franz Josef. The great armaments company of Skoda was assigned to provide army artillery—and Ferdinand Porsche was assigned to Skoda. His task was to find a way to move Skoda's big guns. Drawing on his past

experience, Porsche designed a four-wheel-drive tractor along the Lohner mixed-drive principle, with hub motors driven by electricity. A monster 305mm mortar, hauled into position by a Porsche tractor, leveled the fortress of Naumur, helping the Central Powers roll through Belgium in August and September of 1914. Porsche also built an incredible train of self-steering electric carriages. Coupled together they were a conventional train; uncoupled each could proceed under its own power over tracks not adequate to handle the full train. The same concept was applied to Skoda's 26-ton mortar, which fired a one-ton shell—one of the most devastating weapons of the First World War. Ferdinand Porsche achieved great success in these years; he was given an honorary doctorate (hence the title) from Vienna Technical University in 1917, and a year later became managing director of Austro-Daimler.

But the walls came tumbling down around Austria-Hungary in 1919, when the Treaty of Versailles carved the former empire up into several new nations. Porsche found himself the boss of a car company without business—and in the wrong country to boot: his native Bohemia had been taken away from Austria and was now part of the Czech Republic.

Ferdinand was never a man obsessed with politics and—despite a notorious impatience with sloppy engineering, accompanied by a vicious temper when he encountered it—he was not averse to new political ideas. In the postwar world he saw that, in place of the mighty, there were young, new, but poor nations throughout Europe. These countries needed not luxury cars but small, affordable ones. Ferdinand Porsche began to have new ideas.

An opportunity came when a wealthy Austrian filmmaker, Count Sascha Kolowrat, said he'd stake Porsche to designing a 1.0-liter (61-cid) car with a lightweight body. Naturally enough, Porsche called this car the "Sascha." A two-seater, it had a single-overhead-camshaft four in a light two-seater body, and it was capable of an astounding 90 mph. Alfred Neubauer, later the great racing manager of Daimler-Benz, drove a Sascha to

This page: Ferdinand Porsche's early racers, the 1921 Sascha (left) and 1924 Mercedes GP car, both Targa Florio competitors. Opposite page: Porsche-designed Mercedes (from top) included 1923 and '25 K-Types, mighty SSK, and "Stuttgart" small car.

seventh-in-class in the 1921 Targa Florio.

Porsche's next design used a 2.0-liter engine good for over 100 mph. It was well on its way to production when Austro-Daimler cut off development funds. Never one to suffer fools gladly, Porsche hurled a gold cigarette lighter at the directors and stormed out of the boardroom. He was probably right to do so: Austro-Daimler was wedded to big automobiles and *luxus* clients. Though Porsche's later righthand man, Karl Rabe, replaced him at Austro-Daimler, the firm was out of business within 10 years. Porsche, meanwhile, had gone to Germany and Daimler in Stuttgart. He chose wisely and well.

There's argument over how much Porsche actually contributed to his first project at Daimler. Before he arrived, the company had built a new supercharged 2.0-liter engine with competition in mind. David Owen has written that Porsche spent nine solid months improving it to the point where it was transformed from an also-ran (at the 1923 Indy 500) to a class champion (1-2-3 at the 1924 Targa Florio). But Leonard Setright says Porsche really inherited this engine. In any case, the Technical University of Stuttgart awarded him his second honorary degree at about this time, which says something. But there is less argument about the huge supercharged sixes Porsche built for the K- and S-series Mercedes in the middle Twenties. They were among the greatest feats of engineering in the history of the automobile.

Of these great Mercedes, Michael Frostick wrote that "brute force and bloody ignorance is hardly a fair description," yet there was some of both in the formula. The engine was a masterpiece in light alloy, 6.0 liters in displacement and supercharged — a veritable King Kong among Twenties powerplants. Yet the blower was its Achilles heel, for driving even a few miles with it engaged could destroy that brilliant engine with ease. Connie Bouchard, a distinguished collector and owner of a magnificent 540K, still keeps the bits of engine he found laying on Woodward Avenue when he decided to take up the challenge of a village hot rod one afternoon in Detroit. It has been said that the blower was never intended to run on gasoline. If you wanted to use it you had best fill it with benzol — and to be fair, the owner's manual advised against prolonged use of the thing. Even with its assistance, the Porsche-designed K/S/SS/SSK/SSKLs tended to be more sluggish than their spectacular styling suggested, mainly because the bodies and chassis were ponderously weighty. Setright wrote that on the basis of these cars' handling, Porsche "was utterly hopeless on chassis design." But even Setright was at pains to note that "occasional errors can be forgiven in anybody; even though man might be a divine creation, his design has shown the need for some developmental work ... let us at least give [Porsche] the credit for having been, in an admittedly special sense, an artist."

At this point it would be worthwhile to sort out the Porsche-designed Mercedes models. The initial one was the Model 24/100/140, a huge touring car of relatively little aesthetic appeal. This evolved quickly into the K (for *kurz* or short, i.e.

wheelbase), also known as Model 24/110/160. Arriving in 1926, the K packed 160 bhp at 3000 rpm and was capable of 90 mph. In 1927 came the Model S, with an engine bored out to 6.79 liters for 180 bhp and a 100-mph capability. The SS of 1928 saw displacement boosted to 7.02 liters, horsepower to 225, and top speed to nearly 100 mph—quite impressive considering its body size. The SSK, with a shorter wheelbase and lighter body, was commensurately faster. The final development, in 1931, was the fabulous SSKL (*sehr schnell, kurz, leicht*—very fast, short-wheelbase, light). This car produced 300 bhp at 3200 rpm with supercharger, and was good for an unprecedented 140-150 mph.

In any list of, let us say, the world's 10 greatest cars, the Mercedes SSK simply must be included. It makes no difference that it was a handful to drive, that it delivered only 5 mpg with all the stops out, that its cable brakes were useless against the mighty forces generated by that unbelievable engine. Nor did it matter that a mere handful of people could afford them. The SSK and SSKL were otherworldly beasts, part of the razmatazz that was the Roaring Twenties. And did they ever roar, on road and track, to the astonishment and delight of all who appreciated things mechanical. The Model S won the 1926 German Grand Prix. The SS won the 1928 German Grand Prix. The SSKL won everything in sight.

Great as they were, however, these mighty Mercs were a long way from the people's car, the *volkswagen*, that Ferdinand Porsche continued to think about and plan. And since the unexpected demise of the Sascha, he had been waiting for a chance to try the idea again. But Daimler-Benz was unlikely to build such a car, and Porsche was looked upon as something of a dreamer. Company managers were ironically hostile to the creator of the SSK. The nearest thing to his dream car they would allow was a proposal for a medium-priced model known as the "Stuttgart." In 1929, management asked Porsche to prove that he'd finally licked the prototype's cold-starting problems by starting any one of 15 that had been left outside overnight. Porsche failed, flew into a fury, told them all to go to the devil, and resigned on the spot. Nobody offered to coax him back.

After this, Porsche worked for a time at Steyr in Vienna on concepts similar to the Stuttgart. But when he learned of an intended merger between Steyr and his old firm Austro-Daimler, he quickly left. The last thing he needed was another bout with *that* company.

As a matter of fact, why put up with bosses of any kind? Porsche set himself up back in Stuttgart as managing director of his own company, *Dr.Ing. h.c. Ferdinand Porsche, G.m.b.H., Konstruktionsburo für Motoren-, Fahrzeug-, Luftfahrzeug- und Wasserfahrzeugbau,* "Doctor Engineer (honoris causa) F. Porsche, Incorporated, Design Office for Motors, Motor Vehicles, Aircraft and Ships." He brought over Karl Rabe from Austro-Daimler and added Adolf Rosenberger, a financier who liked motor racing; Joseph Kales, a specialist in aircooled engines, with experience at Tatra and Skoda in Czechoslovakia; body designer Erwin Komenda, who later would design the first Porsche car; son Ferdinand (Ferry), a skilled technician in his own right; gearbox expert Karl Frohlich; and other engineers from Steyr and Austro-Daimler who admired Porsche and wanted to work with him. The company opened its doors on December 1, 1930, with the Depression in full swing and a politician named Adolf Hitler telling Germans he had the solutions to their miseries.

So too, in his way, did Ferdinand Porsche. He would build Germans a car, one they could afford to buy new. It would have a rear engine to avoid a long driveshaft and allow plentiful interior and luggage space, it would be aircooled to avoid the need for a heavy water-cooling system, and it would be made of light alloy to prevent a severe rear-end weight bias. The car would also have a platform chassis with a central backbone to avoid the heavy conventional frame, and a swing-axle rear suspension, with torsion bars located transversely both front and rear. The engine, he decided, should be a horizontally opposed four, which was compact and thus well suited to the small body size envisioned and would also hook up easily to Frohlich's proposed aluminum-cased transaxle. Certainly it was overdue, this *Wagen für das Volk*: in America at that time there was a car for every six people; in Germany there was a car for every 200. Porsche called the emerging concept "Project 12."

The first commercial opportunity for Project 12 came through Zündapp, the motorcycle company in Nuremburg, which was considering a move into small economy cars. Porsche built three prototypes along Project 12 lines as proposals for Zündapp. But instead of the flat four he proposed a water-cooled radial five-cylinder engine, a contradiction in terms for a simple people's car, though maybe Zündapp had something to do with this. In any event, the prototypes did not look promising, and Zündapp lost interest.

The Project 12 proposal for Zundapp, Dr. Porsche's early "people's car."

Porsche then discarded the radial-five and developed a similar car with the flat four for NSU, which expressed interest. An arrangement for further development was concluded in late 1933, and the prototypes built looked quite feasible for production. (The final one, Type 32, was discovered in Germany by an NSU employee in 1945, and is presently owned by Volkswagenwerk.) But NSU's agreement with Fiat, under which the Italian company would handle NSU's auto development while the German firm concentrated on motorcycles, put an end to the relationship by 1935.

Porsche's dream for a people's car might have ended right there had it not been for the aforementioned Herr Hitler. Rising from obscure mediocrity, Hitler came to power in 1933 on a wave of optimistic sloganeering and theories for building Germany out of the Depression. As part of the latter, he envisioned a network of *Autobahnen* — the first of the superhighways — plus an affordable people's car with which the average German family could travel them. Hitler asked his advisors which engineers might be best qualified to design such a car. "Somebody foolish got up and mentioned three names," wrote Erik Eckermann: "Joseph Ganz, Edmund Rumpler, and Ferdinand Porsche. There followed an icy silence, because Ganz was a Jew, and so was Rumpler. That left Porsche."

Dr. Porsche (above) with the pre-production VW Beetle prototype of 1938 (also shown top and left).

Ferdinand Porsche was apolitical, and Hitler's racist notions didn't concern him. When Jakob Werlin, one of *Der Führer's* inner circle, asked Porsche to visit Hitler in Berlin in the autumn of 1933, Porsche was encouraged. At this crucial meeting Hitler outlined what he wanted: a roomy rear-engine car providing a 100-kph (62-mph) cruising speed, 30 miles to the gallon, and low maintenance costs. It must be aircooled, he said, because most Germans didn't own a garage and the winters were harsh. It must seat four people because, Hitler said, "we can't separate the children from their parents... And one thing more, Herr Doktor," Hitler is recorded as adding: "The car must not cost more than 1000 Reichsmarks."

It is easy in retrospect to dismiss Hitler's specifications as the ravings of a lunatic—especially that price ($250 U.S. at the time). We now know that these requirements were not met until Germany was prostrate after the war she started. But to so dismiss them would not do history justice. The fact is that Hitler knew something about automobiles. He personally attended every Berlin auto show, and he was the single reason why the Mercedes-Benz and Auto-Union racing cars of the Thirties came to dominate the world's Grand Prix circuits. As a politician, he knew his proposal for a RM1000 *volkswagen* would be well received. As a dictator, he knew he could subsidize the price down to that level even if Porsche couldn't design the car such that it could be built for so little. As in most of Hitler's industrial recovery programs, there was a degree of reason behind the airy rhetoric. Indeed, Dan R. Post has recorded that in mid-1934, when Porsche said he couldn't get the price below RM1500, Werlin told him that Hitler would solve the cost problem in "an administrative way."

In making his people's car a reality Porsche had certain advantages—his Zündapp experience, the NSU prototypes on which he retained full rights—and some disadvantages—an impatient Hitler, a doubtful if not unbelieving German Society of Automakers. Hitler even went so far as to tell the Society to sponsor what all Germany was now calling the Volkswagen, but the $50,000 budget it offered Porsche was faintly ludicrous. At this level all he could do was revise what he had already developed. But tests of three Series 3 prototypes, built at Porsche's home in late 1936, proved the design well up to claims. The Society admitted that the Volkswagen deserved further study and development.

It was also apparent that nobody within the Society wanted to help back the project. Obviously, a successful small car selling for even RM1500 would be a serious competitor to the economy models on which most German car companies had been working since the Depression. Accordingly, the government organized a state-owned corporation with Dr. Porsche as its head, and testing went forward from 1937. Porsche visited the United States in 1936, talked to rear-engine exponents like John Tjaarda, visited the Fords in Dearborn, and toured Franklin in Syracuse. He returned with several production experts—of carefully selected Aryan stock—to help set up the Volkswagen factory in Wolfsburg, Lower Saxony. The factory site having been selected, the Nazis promptly confiscated the property, and Hitler himself attended the dedication ceremonies in May 1938.

Tests continued with unlimited government backing on the Type 60, which became the VW Series 30 and, in due course, the VW Series 38. The latter was the final prototype for the production Volkswagen, typified by a beetle-shaped body with a high beltline and a tiny divided rear window. Hitler had wanted to call the car the KdF—for *Kraft durch Freude* (strength through joy)—but even Josef Goebbels couldn't sell that one. Volkswagen, the people called it; Volkswagen it became. The *Deutsche Arbeitsfront* (government labor organization) issued booklets, into which prospective buyers pasted stamps, buying them weekly for RM5 minimum, creditable toward the purchase price. All the stamp money, of course, went into the war effort from mid-1939. The stamp collectors never did take delivery, as nothing but pilot models were produced through 1945. But Volkswagenwerk did honor the stamps, to the tune of 600 Deutschemarks credit or DM100 cash, through 1961.

Ironically it was the British, then the dominant car exporting people, who got Wolfsburg into serious production after the war. They picked Heinz Nordhoff (formerly of Opel) to run the place, and Nordhoff put VW firmly on its feet. It would take 10 years, but the lowly Beetle

overwhelmed Austin and Morris in export markets. Thus Germany accomplished in the auto field what it had failed to do in the war —industrial supremacy over the hated plutocrats of France and Britain.

Porsche's accomplishments on the sporting side of motoring are less known, but are a vital part of his story. Having conceived a rear-engine racing car for Wanderer (which, by 1933, was part of the Auto-Union along with Audi, DKW and Horch), he met with Hitler to request the same $250,000 racing subsidy the Chancellor had just granted Daimler-Benz. Hitler told Porsche that when it came to racing cars, only Daimler-Benz could provide Germany with a champion. Porsche turned five shades of red before the startled Chancellor. Before Hitler could stop him, writes David Owen, "he launched into a typical flood of technical argument, explaining just what his new racing car was, what it could do, and why no other car could do it. Hitler tried to interrupt, but for once in his life he was forced to listen... At first astonished, finally he was impressed. He changed his mind completely and signed an order

Left: A Porsche-designed Auto-Union 3.0-liter racer from 1938 (left), with 500 bhp DIN. Below: A modified version of this 12-cylinder GP car in action in the late '30s.

awarding Auto-Union the same government subsidy."

Porsche finished his first Auto-Union Grand Prix car, the 295-bhp A-type, in late 1933. Hans Stück drove it to win the Grands Prix of Germany and Switzerland in 1934, where the Auto-Unions generally demolished the factory Alfas and even the GP Mercedes. A Mercedes onslaught gave D-B the Manufacturer's Cup for 1935, but Auto-Union's squirrelly but blindingly fast monsters still managed to win the Italian and Tunisian GPs, with Stück and Bernd Rosemeyer starring. Rosemeyer was particularly adept at using the car's awesome oversteer to advantage. With the 520-bhp 6.0-liter Type C in 1936, he placed first in three Grands Prix. In 1937 he won Germany's *Eifelrennen* against the best Mercedes could throw at him. Before Hitler rang down the curtain on peace, Auto-Unions won the Rumanian GP (Stück), the French GP (Müller) and the Yugoslav GP (Nuvolari). The last would be the last Grand Prix for the duration, and was actually run while the Germans were beating down the Poles on September 3, 1939.

The Auto-Union racers were also impressive high-speed record breakers. In October 1937, Bernd Rosemeyer broke 17 marks, including the flying kilometer at 252.47 mph, on the Frankfurt-Darmstadt autobahn. He alternated between a 6.3-liter V-16 R-type (which did the 252 mph) and a smaller-engine car for the 3000-5000cc class. In January 1938, Rosemeyer attempted to better Rudi Caracciola's new 270-mph record in a Mercedes. The devilishly tricky R-type was caught in a crosswind, and the great Rosemeyer was killed.

There are very few who won't admit that the 1930s was the golden age of motor racing—and indeed of the German Grand Prix racing cars. Driven by men like Caracciola, Tazio Nuvolari, Lang, Dick Seaman, and Von Brauchitsch, these silver behemoths ruled the GP circuits for a decade. Anyone who wasn't there missed something wildly beautiful. But it isn't hard to recall them in the mind's eye today, drifting the fast, sweeping bends of Tripoli at 180 mph, screaming along the tree-lined straight at Berne—first a stream of Mercedes, then the Auto-Unions, then the other way round. We can imagine the harsh scream of Caracciola's great beast of a Mercedes as it howled past the grandstands at Le Mans, or Hans Stück's twitchy, rear-engine Auto-Union manhandling the corners at the *Eifelrennen*. It is a heady thought, but you could say that all these immortal cars—the Auto-Unions directly and the Mercedes at least tangentially—owed their concept to the same gifted man.

Yet Ferdinand Porsche's years at the pinnacle would be short-lived. With the coming of World War II, Wolfsburg was given over to military manufacturing. One of its first tasks was producing stoves, to keep the *Wehrmacht* warm during the invasion of Russia. The Volkswagen project was shunted

Opposite page: the 16-cylinder R-Type Auto-Union GP car. This page: Dr. Ferry Porsche (above), and Dr. Ferdinand Porsche (circa 1949).

aside; the few cars that were built went to the Army for staff use. But Porsche was, of course, too talented to be left idle. His first wartime project was the *Kübelwagen* (bucket car), a go-anywhere version of the VW that carried Rommel's *Afrika-Korps* across North Africa. In due course, Porsche rendered the *Schwimmwagen*, an amphibious version with four-wheel-drive and auxiliary (detachable) propellor. Porsche also designed the Tiger tank, which spearheaded the invasion of France and the Low Countries in 1940, staved off the advancing Russians for months, and fought the Americans to a standstill at the Bulge until the Germans ran out of gasoline in late 1944. He also had a hand in some of Hitler's "secret weapons," notably the 20-foot-high *Maus* (Mouse), which was supposed to be a sort of motorized fort, impregnable and far ranging. In practice, it was almost immobile in any kind of soft terrain, and only three prototypes were built before the Third Reich collapsed in 1945.

Herr Doktor Porsche was saved from immediate imprisonment after the war by Albrecht Speer, the architect who had interpreted Hitler's grandiose plans for a new Berlin. Speer told the British forces who had arrested Porsche that this plain-bolts engineer knew or cared nothing about politics, and was not a Nazi.

Porsche was released — only to be picked up by the French in November 1945. The French Minister for Industry wanted to know if he would help them design a "people's car" of their own. Porsche said he would, but before anything further could happen he and his son were thrown into jail. Porsche was marched through Dijon in chains by the all-conquering French, who nevertheless had the presence of mind to tap his brain at the Renault factory, obtaining suggestions that ultimately led to the Renault 4CV. Then they locked the 72-year-old man in an unheated Dijon dungeon and demanded one million francs "bail."

Ferry Porsche, previously released, raised the money by signing a design contract with Cisitalia. The old man was finally brought home. Later he was tried and acquitted by a French court—but he never got back the million francs.

In the few years remaining to him, Ferdinand Porsche continued to work. But war, politics and betrayals had broken the once-indomitable spirit that had survived countless setbacks, that had enabled him to stand up even to Adolf Hitler. He approved Ferry's design for a supercharged Cisitalia Grand Prix car, yet its suspension, writes Leonard Setright, "set at nought the experience garnered in the 1938-9 Grand Prix Auto-Unions... The Cisitalia reverted to a form of independent rear suspension that once again imposed camber variations and toe-in aberrations without any means for controlling them."

Dr. Ing. Ferdinand Porsche died on January 30, 1951, just as the first sports cars bearing his name were making exciting impressions on the motoring press. He had a great deal to do with their design, starting with the prewar Type 114 F-wagen, conceived with his son as a sporting evolution of the Volkswagen. In spirit, too, he was truly the founder of the Porsche marque. He brought the rear-engine layout to its ultimate expression in his time. He attracted superbly talented men to produce it. His artistry would be present in every rear-engine Porsche ever built, and his spirit lives on in all of them.

As a man, he was mercurial, subject to violent temper. He would not tolerate slipshod engineering—or engineers. When he disliked something he said so, in the bluntest of language. "Politically," as David Owen wrote, "he was a child." He saw Adolf Hitler only as a sponsor, and a useful one at that. He was never a Nazi, and the evidence is that Nazi practices abhorred him. (It was Ferdinand Porsche who prevented the Gestapo from arresting and probably killing Jean-Pierre Peugeot, after the French Resistance bombed the occupied Peugeot factory. After the war, Peugeot responded by naming Porsche a "collaborator" — and getting him arrested.)

Ferdinand Porsche's two greatest dreams — an efficient small car that everyone could afford, and an unbeatable racing sports car — were realized in his lifetime. In September 1950, Ferry took the old man to Wolfsburg. "On the way [they] passed shoals of VWs crowding the *autobahns*," Owen recorded. "For Porsche, coming at the end of his captivity and illness, it was too much. He broke down and wept. Yet if Porsche was an artist —and he was—he was unusually fortunate. Not many artists are lucky enough to see their work valued at its true worth before they die."

THE GMÜND YEARS: ORIGIN OF THE SPECIES

The Porsche family estate at Zell am See, Austria today

The Nazis ordered Ferdinand Porsche's design firm to vacate its offices in the Zuffenhausen district of Stuttgart in late 1944, when Allied bombing became intense. By May 1945, the company seemed to have vanished, perhaps because it was a high priority target for Allied forces as they fanned out over Bavaria. The Berghof, Hitler's getaway nest at Berchtesgaden near Salzburg, was blown up by an American troop detachment. To the south, British troops were combing the pastoral countryside, finding little of significance. But in the sleepy Austrian village of Gmünd, they were startled to discover the emergency headquarters of the Porsche firm, including most of its top engineers.

Gmünd was a useful, out of the way place for the refugees from Zuffenhausen. Ferry Porsche had thought it would do better than Berlin's alternative suggestion in Czechoslovakia, a country growing ever more restless as the Germans fell back. Some machine tools were shipped there, but not all—Porsche decided that they could no longer chance a single repository for their valuable equipment. Some tools and files were stored at Zuffenhausen and at the Porsche family estate at Zell am See, Austria.

Ferry Porsche was released from prison in mid-1946, though his father would remain incarcerated for another 15 months. Ferry began to prepare at Gmünd for reactivation and new projects. The company had been held together by his sister, Louise Piëch, and the faithful Karl Rabe was on hand to lend his expertise.

Karl Ludvigsen has written that early progress was brisk despite the circumstances: "By December of 1946 the works employed 222 people, 64 more than it had a year earlier...Their total 1946 business volume was 1,319,000 Reichsmarks, only 17 percent less than it had been in 1938." Ferry contracted with Piero Dusio of Cisitalia to build a rear-engine Grand Prix car, and on the strength of this and other projects paid his father's bail. The elder Porsche was released from confinement in Dijon on August 1, 1947.

The Porsche-Cisitalia GP car was stillborn, despite strong enthusiasm from Tazio Nuvolari — by then aching to race again, especially in something designed by the father of the prewar Auto-Unions. The reason it didn't get off the ground was that Dusio saw more profit in street sports cars, in this case based on off-the-shelf Fiat components. In this he was hardly original: Ferdinand Porsche had had a similar idea back in the 1920s.

His father had always wanted to build a sports car under his own name, Ferry Porsche has said, but had never had the money. Ferdinand's decision to join Mercedes in 1923 was based on this realization. By 1937, when he *did* have the money (courtesy of the VW project), Dr. Porsche was again thinking about a sports car.

His first project to this end was the Type 64, built around stock Volkswagen components with a special body and a hotter engine. Unfortunately it was done in by its very concept. When Porsche applied to the *Deutsche Arbeitsfront* to supply the necessary VW hardware, he was told that as a state-owned firm, VW could not sell anything to a private company. Porsche accepted this, but not for long. His next sports car took shape as the Type 114 in 1938, and this was the direct forerunner of the Porsche car.

The Type 114 was an astounding technical achievement, largely finalized by gearbox expert Karl Frohlich and completed in terms of chassis design by early 1939. Like the great Auto-Union racers, its engine was placed ahead of the rear axle, with Frohlich's transmission dangling out behind. The engine was a V-10 displacing 1493cc, with a bore and stroke 58.0 × 56.5mm. It was a complex affair, with an aluminum block and cylinder heads, six main bearings, domed pistons, and hemispherical combustion chambers. Magneto ignition was provided for each bank of cylinders, driven off the inlet camshaft, and carburetion was via three single-barrel downdraft instruments squeezed between the banks, which were set at a 72-degree included angle. Frohlich's transaxle contained a five-speed gearbox. Suspension was VW-like — swing axles, trailing arms, and torsion bars at the rear, parallel trailing arms

The prewar Type 60K10 experimental displays aerodynamic styling ideas only now coming into widespread use. All glass was flush-mounted—in 1939!

and transverse torsion bars at the front—sprouting from a tubular chassis. The engine was, however, watercooled; the radiator and cooling tubes were initially mounted up front, later transferred to the rear. In plan view the car looked like an evolution of one of Paul Jaray's streamliners, with a smooth, rounded nose and a flowing two-passenger cockpit, tapering to a ground-hugging tail end. The wheelbase was initially 106.3 inches, later 108.3, and the track 53.2 inches front and rear. Three of these Type 116 racing coupes, designated Type 60K10, were built using the 114's technology, and received the blessing of *Korpsführer* Huhnlein of the Nazi Motoring Corps (NSKK). Ferdinand Porsche even sold Huhnlein on an 800-mile Berlin-to-Rome road race to prove the car's mettle. But by September 1939, when the race was scheduled, Germany was at war. Porsche used a street-modified version to commute back and forth during the early war years, and Karl Ludvigsen has noted that he once traveled from the VW factory to Berlin at an average of 85 mph over ordinary roads, driven by his capable chauffeur Josef Goldinger.

We can see that the idea of using ordinary componentry to produce a truly remarkable sporting machine was not a new one for the Porsche firm in 1947, the year when Ferry and Karl Rabe began again to develop ideas for a Volkswagen-based two-seater. When Ferdinand Porsche rejoined them in August, the concept had already been put down on paper: a smooth, aerodynamic, open body on an 85-inch wheelbase, a tubular space frame, aircooled rear-mounted engine, and a dry weight of about 1300 pounds. The tubular frame was a sturdy affair, anchored by bulkheads in the cowl and behind the seats, turned inward front and rear, and connected by hefty transverse tubes at each end.

Frohlich's Auto-Union concepts, rather than those of the production VW, influenced the drivetrain. The engine was located nearly amidships, behind the seats but ahead of the rear axle centerline. VW's swing-axle/trailing-arm rear suspension was reversed so that the transverse torsion bar tube was mounted at the rear of the chassis and the trailing arms became leading arms. Theoretically, this would result in considerable oversteer, but this tendency was reduced to manageable proportions by very even front-to-rear weight distribution and an ultra-low center of gravity. The front suspension was stock VW. So, too,

were the steering and the 9-inch, cable-actuated drum brakes. Brake horsepower of the VW flat four was increased by special Porsche-modified VW heads with larger inlet valves and ports, by raising compression ratio from the standard 5.8:1 to an alleged 7.0:1 and, ultimately, by providing twin carburetors. From the stock Volkswagen's 25 brake horsepower, these changes raised output to close to 40 bhp at 4000 rpm despite no increase in displacement, which remained the same as the Beetle's at 1131cc on a 75 × 64mm bore and stroke.

The running chassis was first tested in March 1948 by Ferry Porsche and Robert Eberan von Eberhorst, a bright young engineer. The made-to-order testing ground was not 20 miles from Gmünd: the daunting, 32-percent grade of the Katshberg Pass. The prototype passed every test easily, proving that the VW components would hold up under the most difficult conditions.

In April, roadster bodywork was added, and by May the first prototype Porsche was ready—smooth and low, with a two-piece unframed windshield. Unlike familiar production 356s, there were no air grilles on the engine lid, which was forward hinged for optimum access. It lifted in one long unit, not as a hatch as on later production cars. Behind the engine was room for the spare wheel, a six-volt battery, and a

Center spread and opposite page: The mid-engine cabriolet prototype, the first Porsche. This page: Gmünd coupe from July 1948.

small amount of luggage. Inside was a rudimentary, semi-contoured seat. The only instrumentation was a speedometer, though there was a clock built into the glovebox at the driver's right. The "Porsche" name at the front of the car was spelled out in letters not much different in style from those used today. Altogether, the 356 roadster prototype was a good-looking affair, obviously constructed with attention to detail and aerodynamics, and different from anything else on the road.

Ferry Porsche and one of the engineers drove the finished prototype to Zell am See on a shakedown cruise, and found only one fault. During a terrific pounding over the rugged pavement of the Grossglockner Pass, one of the rear frame tubes bent. They limped into Grossglockner, where they fashioned a two-piece metal sleeve over the weakened nub. Similar reinforcements were later made to the production cars. By July, the Porsche roadster was being shown at Berne, Switzerland, and was receiving good reviews from the European and British press. Porsche recorded its first competition victory when the prototype won a 1000-1200cc-class road race at Innsbrück.

The next development was designated 356/2 which, Ludvigsen determined, "was developed in parallel with the space-framed roadster and not as a successor to it, as has often been maintained. Planned in both coupe and cabriolet models, the Type 356/2 Porsches differed sharply in design from the mid-engined roadster. They had a new frame construction, body style and engine position."

There was little heard about the original prototype once the 356/2 appeared. The engine was now set much farther back in the chassis. This encouraged severe oversteer, which was only partially alleviated by returning to conventional trailing-arm rear suspension. The 356/2 was much closer to the production Type 356 with which all of us are familiar, and established the inimitable Porsche style, contributed by perfectionist body engineer Erwin Komenda. Backed by good-faith orders from two Swiss enthusiast-businessmen, R. von Senger and Bernhard Blank, *Porsche Konstruktionen GmbH* planned to build 50 Type 356/2 chassis and 10 coupe bodies. It was March 1948: the Porsche sports car had been born.

Initial publicity brochures pegged the coupe at $3750 U.S. and the cabriolet at $4250—hardly small change at the time—and in all just 50 production examples were built for 1948-50. The coupe/cabriolet breakdown has been variously quoted as 45/5 and 42/8. Most of these early cars were sold by the intrepid Bernhard Blank, a successful Zurich car dealer. A few were equipped with a 73.5mm bore instead of 75mm to hold displacement under 1100cc for class racing purposes. Historians doubt the published 7.0:1 compression ratio really was the actual figure; it was more like 6.5:1. But the interesting thing is that the Porsche was at least as economical as the Volkswagen, perhaps more so. Despite its piddling 40 (DIN) horsepower, its 1300-pound weight and slippery body meant that the car would approach 90 mph while delivering, according to road tests, no less than 27 mpg—and usually closer to 35. At a 70-mph cruise, testers commonly reported 30 mpg. This high-speed frugality, which would remain a Porsche characteristic, would perplex the bureaucrats responsible for today's 55-mph U.S. national speed limit.

The cabriolet models were initially built up from bare chassis supplied by Gmünd to the Beutler coachworks in Thun, near Berne, Switzerland. They had slightly different, more elongated shapes, undoubtedly inspired by Beutler, and sold for around $4000. Beutler delivered the last one in August 1949, and the total built was between five and eight, out of the 50 Porsches constructed through the end of 1950. The official total may be low. Serial number 57 is known, but some earlier numbers could have been skipped.

As the months passed and word about the Porsche spread, a minor demand developed. Karl Rabe had enthusiastically promised 150 units by the end of 1948, a figure twelve times the actual number delivered. Things at Gmünd moved pretty slowly in those days. The aluminum bodies, for instance, were hammered out by hand over wooden forms. Engines varied from car to car, not because of engineering doubts, but because everything was in such short supply. Still, the financial ledgers were in the black, if just barely. Porsche's survival in those days depended to a great extent on Volkswagen. With the advent of the Marshall Plan the German economy had begun to revive. The canny Porsche family reestablished its old consultancy relationship with Heinz Nordhoff, whom the British had put in charge at VW.

One of the problems in making Porsche's car business viable was Gmünd itself. It was too small, too remote, and completely removed from the car-building heart of industrial Germany. Designing and building cars there made about as much sense then as General Motors setting up car production in upstate Vermont today. Porsche clearly needed to return to Zuffenhausen, but the Americans had been using its old premises as a military motor pool and weren't eager to give it up.

Ultimately, the GIs agreed to vacate in mid-1950. Porsche accordingly made plans to close up shop at Gmünd and move back

An all-around look at one of the 42-45 Gmünd cars built in 1948-49. Door wing vents, wheel arch shapes, and more bulbous rear contours distinguish these first Porsches from later 356s.

home. This decision was not, however, taken lightly. The VW relationship was Porsche's most profitable line of work at that time; the sports car was but a hobby by comparison. Conceivably, Porsche looked at reopening Zuffenhausen as a tax write-off, to counterbalance the payments it was beginning to receive from VW as Nordhoff and company started their drive to success among economy cars. But sports cars were more fun than people's cars, and of course there was no question of building tanks or any other military hardware. The one fly in this ointment was a big one: the actual costs of getting serious production started at Zuffenhausen were relatively astronomical, considerably higher than Porsche's income from VW.

The problem was solved when Ferry's wily business manager, Alfred Prinzing, took a Porsche coupe on a tour of Germany's main VW distributors. It was a veritable door-to-door sales job, and Prinzing was a born salesman. He returned with orders totaling DM200,000. That, added to the receipts from VW, gave Porsche at least a fighting start. Plans were made to use part of Reutter's Stuttgart coachworks for chassis assembly, and Porsche began moving out of Gmünd in early 1950. In April, the first of a long and distinguished line rolled out of Zuffenhausen — the first of the German-made Porsches.

TYPE 356 1950~55: BIRTH OF A LEGEND

An early, 1950 Type 356 Cabriolet, bodywork by Reutter

In late 1949, Porsche commissioned Reutter of Stuttgart to build 500 bodies. In preparation for this unprecedented volume, Erwin Komenda cleaned up the lines of the 1948-50 Gmünd-built cars, creating the now-familiar shape known to generations of enthusiasts. Windshield area was increased (though two-piece construction was retained), side window area was decreased via a higher beltline, wing vents were eliminated, an oil temperature gauge was added, and the clock moved over from the glovebox to flank the speedometer. There was still no gas gauge, Porsche relying for the time being on VW's reserve-tank system and a thoroughly un-Porsche-like measuring device, a wooden dipstick. The engine remained the Porsche Type 369 unit, still Volkswagen-based with special Porsche heads, but its twin Solex carburetors were now the type 32PBI. Suspension development followed that of VW, which in 1950 introduced hydraulic shock absorbers, mounted in steel towers in the chassis platform, and hydraulic drum brakes. By 1951, Porsche had replaced the inadequate VW brakes with twin-leading-shoe Lockheed front drums supplied by Ate in Germany, and also had replaced the lever-arm rear shocks with more up-to-date tubular types.

Ferdinand Porsche barely lived to see this further development of the car bearing his name. His health had been broken during his imprisonment in France, and had gone steadily downhill after his release. He was felled by a stroke in November 1950, two months after celebrating his 75th birthday. He died on January 30, 1951.

At the time of his death, the factory was already claiming an output of 60 cars per month, and Porsches were gradually getting into the hands of reviewers outside Germany from whom, presumably, the harshest critiques would come. A 356 was made available to the British automotive weekly *The Autocar* in April 1951, but its thoroughly approving article quickly dispelled any fears of censure the factory may have had.

"Even a short run serves to give the characteristic impression of a really well streamlined car. The acceleration above 50 mph is quite beyond what would normally be expected from the engine size, and is achieved in extraordinary quietness. About 60 mph is available in third gear ... It is a rare car these days on which the designer has gone all out for certain great qualities with the limited means at hand and has accepted certain accompanying disadvantages instead of trying to achieve a well-balanced mediocrity.

"It is not a car for everyone's taste, but it offers a unique combination of comfort, performance and economy, for which some people will pay a very good price."

At the Frankfurt Automobile Show, held the same month that *The Autocar* was testing its first Porsche, Zuffenhausen introduced the Types 356/1 and 356/3, its first 1300cc models.

The new engine—precisely, 1286cc (78.5 cid), 80.0 × 64mm (3.14 × 2.52 inches)—was a bored out Type 369 unit with aluminum rather than cast-iron cylinders, chrome-plated on their wearing surfaces for greater durability. Whether or not the Type 369 had 6.5:1 or 7.0:1 compression, this new Type 506 derivative definitely had a 6.5:1 ratio, and this plus greater displacement allowed Porsche to claim 44 bhp (DIN). The modest compression made contemporary European fuel a bit more palatable than it had been for the 1100 engine, and brought with it a slight gain in performance. Factory records quote the 1300's top speed at 92 mph, marginally better than the 1100's. Also introduced at Frankfurt as across-the-board changes were improved defrosting provisions, optional tachometer, and the new VW-based suspension, tubular shock absorbers, and Lockheed-Ate brakes. The 1300 was a definite improvement for the breed, and was well received by the press.

Production started taking off in 1951. The 1000th German Porsche was completed on August 28, and output for the year totaled 1103 units for a profit of $3 million. Part of that revenue, though admittedly a small part, had come from America, home of hard currency and seemingly innumerable buyers. Max Hoffman, the veritable godfather of import car sales in America, agreed to add Porsche to the select nameplates at his Park Avenue showroom in New York City in 1950. Initially, Hoffman had some doubts about the car, which many Americans thought curious because it looked like a well-worn bar of soap and cost as much as a Lincoln. But he also had a weakness for Porsches, being Austrian-born and a great admirer of Ferry and his father. Hoffman had also introduced the Volkswagen to America, selling two of them in 1949, but eventually giving up the franchise. Later he admitted that was one of his great mistakes. But he did sell Porsches, slowly at first, rising to 10 a week by 1954. Hoffman said sales—and his own approval rating—picked up considerably in 1953, after Porsche dumped the VW-based crashbox for its own four-speed synchromesh transmission.

That gearbox was developed from a design Dr. Porsche had conceived for the racing Cisitalias and which he had patented in 1947. Its most unique aspect was its method of gear synchronization, accomplished through an intermediate servo-synchronizing ring rather than conventional cones. A servo ring revolved with each pinion at equal speed. When the clutch ring was moved towards the gear by the gearchange linkage, its rate of rotation was slowed or speeded up by the servo ring, thus equalizing its speed to that of the gearbox's rear output shaft. The result was quicker shifts than the cone system allowed, because gear braking/acceleration took less time. The servo ring arrangement was also more compact. According to Porsche, the new transmission was no larger than the old non-synchro crashbox. Synchromesh was eventually extended to all Porsche models, but the factory regretted that a retrofit arrangement for earlier cars was not possible.

As America's stock car drivers are fond of saying, there's no substitute for cubic inches. If the 1100 and 1300 models could perform as well as they did while sipping tiny amounts of fuel, a 1500cc version should do even better. Porsche began work on this larger power unit in mid-1950. The displacement was chosen because it was the upper limit of several contemporary competition classes, thus ideal for a small, light sports car. Since Porsche had already bored out its flat four to get 1300cc, it was only logical to lengthen stroke to get 1500. The Hirth company of Stuttgart designed a connecting rod compact enough to allow a 10mm stroke increase, to 74mm giving 1488cc with the 80mm bore. Hirth also supplied the 1500's roller-bearing crankshaft, which soon had people like Max Hoffman complaining about durability. Prolonged engine lugging or failure to change the oil regularly almost always led to early crankshaft failure. All one had to do to avoid trouble was read the owner's manual, but of course not everyone did—a lesson for those seeking the highly collectible 1500 today.

The initial 1500s were fitted with an engine designated Type 502, which had small, 32BPI Solex carburetors and developed 55 bhp (DIN) at 4500 rpm. Only 66 were built before Porsche switched to the Type 527 powerplant with 40BPI Solexes and 60 bhp (it was possible to fit smaller carburetors if desired). The early use of the Solex 32s indicated Porsche's caution rather than an error in specification. The company was concerned about the gearbox's ability to handle the extra power, but its new all-synchromesh transmission ended that worry.

A squad of both 1100s and 1500s was brought to Monthléry, France's huge banked oval track, for some speed record attempts in September 1951. All performed brilliantly. The 1100s set three new marks, averaging better than 100 mph for distances of 500 miles and 1000km and for six hours running. The 1500s, including a mildly modified car from Volkswagen dealer Walter Glöckler, broke no fewer than 14 records. The factory 1500 raised official averages to over 97 mph for 3000, 4000, and 5000km; 2000, 3000, and 4000 miles; and 24 and 48 hours; it also averaged 95.75 mph for 10,000km and 94.60 mph for 72 hours. The Glöcker, a smoothly streamlined roadster, ran 500 and 1000km and the six-hour period at speeds of 114-116 mph, breaking three more records. The 72-hour mark came despite a disabled top gear that forced drivers to run in third at 90 mph, with the engine churning at a busy 4500 rpm. It was a tremendous performance that proved the 1500.

Dr. Porsche once said, "it makes

Below: A late-1952 Type 356 Cabriolet. Note revised bumpers and slotted wheels. Bottom: the VW Beetle-like Type 356 coupe from 1950, one of the early cars built in Stuttgart following Porsche's return to Germany from Austria. Note oblong and round taillamps.

no difference where in a car the engine is located, so long as it's light." The 1500 power unit weighed only 160 pounds, and the entire car rarely exceeded 1750 pounds at the curb. Weight distribution was approximately 780 pounds front and 970 pounds rear, but this wasn't as great a difference as it seems. During tests conducted unofficially by an unnamed Southern California aircraft company, it was learned that the Type 356 design produced a 175-pound downward air pressure on the front wheels at 60 mph, thus effectively equalizing weight balance.

Dick von Osten tested a Porsche 1500 for the U.S. magazine *Auto*, and his report is interesting. "The top speed runs were made with two different drivers on a level, measured, quarter mile at sea level. I expected to clock slightly over 100 mph, so it was quite a shock when [I] reached that figure with no apparent effort and kept on going. [We] both managed to hit the maximum speed of 111.11 mph on both an east and west run. Five mph were probably added to the top speed by perfect wheel balance, a typical detail of this car: all Porsches come from the factory with the wheels and tires in a perfect state of dynamic and static balance. Dr. Porsche once said that improper wheel balance can add or subtract 500 engine rpm at top speed." Interestingly, that 111 mph maximum was 15 mph higher than the official factory claim.

Fuel mileage proved hardly affected by the more powerful engine. Von Osten covered 329 miles (75 in city traffic) on one tankful, including top speed, acceleration and braking tests and a highway average of 70-75 mph. This required 11 gallons of gas for an overall average of close to 33 mpg. Somehow, test results like these make you wonder what we've learned in the intervening 30 years.

Auto's editor noted: "...the most frequent comment I have heard about the car is its unmistakable quality. From the gentle 'click' of the door to the smooth paint, from the handling ease to the engine's performance, the Porsche reflects genius in design and pride in craftsmanship... Although it is not a low-priced car (approximately $4284 for the coupe and $4560 for the convertible), it is a car to which every owner can point with pride, one of the rare sports cars that makes the owner feel that he has cheated the factory by paying so low a price."

Above: An example of the very rare 356 America roadster, photographed recently at a Porsche club meet.

The process of detail refinement went on during the 1500's production run, and naturally spilled over to the 1100 and 1300cc cars as well. By mid-summer 1952, the two-piece windshield had given way to one-piece glass, perforated disc wheels were being used, and the bodywork was wrapped well down under the bumpers. A large, 6000-rpm tachometer became a standard fitting, replacing the clock, and both tach and speedometer were hooded to prevent windshield reflections at night.

The ultimate developments of the original Type 356 series were the Supers, the 1500S and 1300S introduced in 1952 and 1953 respectively. The 1500S, developed specifically for production-class competition, was announced in October, 1952. Its heart was a new Type 528 powerplant, unchanged in displacement from the Type 502/527 unit but now running an 8.2:1 compression ratio for a rated output of 70 DIN horsepower and 80 pounds-feet of torque at 3600 rpm. The high torque peak was a clue to Porsche's racing inclinations. In fact, below 3500 rpm the "S" was less sudsy than the basic 1500 engine. Both 1500S and 1300S (same CR but 60 bhp) benefited from a new camshaft designed by Ernst Fuhrmann, one of the original engineers at Gmünd and one involved with the Cisitalia project. The factory assigned the 1300S an "official" top speed of 100 mph, 105 mph for the 1500S, but the evidence is that these were conservative

Right: An early, 1951-52 Type 356 Cabriolet with body by Reutter. Below and opposite page: All 1955-model Porsches bound for the U.S. carried the 1500cc engine and the name "Continental" on the front fenders. This was the only year the name would be used, mostly because of Ford Motor Company's prestigious Continental Mark II, which would be introduced the following year. Despite the fancy name, the Porsche Continental differed little from previous models in trim or mechanicals.

figures, especially given a careful tuneup.

Among the early 1500 Supers was a rakish roadster with an ultra-low-swept beltline, the America. This aluminum bodied sportster with coachwork by Gläser was almost unknown in Europe and was hardly common in the U.S., perhaps because it sold for a lofty $4600. It was the progenitor of what has become one of the most beloved of all Porsches, the immortal Speedster.

Like many of the more interesting European imports of the '50s, the America was an idea from the fertile mind of Max Hoffman, who wanted a light, open Porsche without the heavy top and side windows of the normal 356 Cabriolet. Purpose: mainly competition. Everything about this car was designed to save weight, which did not exceed 1600 pounds. There were light, aluminum-supported seats, Plexiglas side curtains, a thin snap-on roof canvas, an open hole in the dash instead of a glovebox, and a divided windshield that could be replaced by a racing screen. Coupled with the 1500cc Type 528 Super engine, the end product was exciting—and an exciting performer. *Auto Age* magazine's test produced a top speed of 110 mph, 0-60 mph in 9.3 seconds, and the standing-start quarter-mile in 17.9 seconds. Only a handful of Americas were built. Sources in Stuttgart gave a figure of 15 in 1970, but this has since proven low. Today, one Porsche expert puts the total at 20, another at 50. Whatever its number, the America remains an important and highly desirable car.

Perhaps the most symbolically noteworthy change for 1953 was the addition of the now-famous Porsche crest, quickly sketched by Ferry Porsche at the suggestion of

Max Hoffman. It places the Stuttgart coat of arms, a prancing horse, over the background arms of the state of Baden-Württemberg. Like Ferrari's, the Porsche stallion is black on a yellow field. Enzo Ferrari, it is said, took his design from the emblem of the World War I air squadron commanded by Italian pilot Francesco Baracca, an insignia connected with Stuttgart's, in Ferry Porsche's opinion.

Other changes introduced at the same time were repositioned parking lights, now under the headlamps instead of inboard, and circular instead of oblong and circular pairs of taillamps. All three engine sizes were continued as were the Super versions of the 1300 and 1500 powerplants. The Type 528 engine now acquired a forged-steel crankshaft, replacing the previous Hirth crank. This was made possible by Karl Rabe, who was able to shorten the original rod design by making a diagonal cut across the big end, thus providing adequate clearance for the longer stroke. The standard 1500 model, the Normal, had 6.5:1 compression and packed only 55 bhp at 4400 rpm, but that was good for a top speed of 96 mph, according to the factory. It was an ideal foil to the 1500 Super, more tractable at lower speeds and smoother for all-purpose work. This model lineup — 1300 and 1500 Normal and Super, coupe and cabriolet — continued through 1955, while the 1100s disappeared after 1954.

In the United States the base 1500 was called the 1500 America, and was impressively priced at the lowest figure yet seen on a Porsche: $3445 for the coupe, $3695 for the cabriolet. The pricing was another piece of Hoffman's work. (One is reminded that Max brought the first BMW 1600 2-doors into the U.S. for under $2500 some 12 years later.) To get the America's price down to that level, however (the upmarket Supers sold for $4284/$4584), Hoffman had Porsche delete the reclining seatbacks, the wheel trims, the fold-down provision for the vestigial back seat, the radio, the passenger-side sunvisor, and the tachometer, equipment ordinarily found on equivalent European models.

The last batch of running changes for the original Type 356 design were instituted in early 1954, just a few weeks after Porsche had turned out its 5000th car. Flanking the parking lights were tiny grilles that despite their size, efficiently channeled cooling air to the brakes and opened up hooting-space for the new twin Bosch horns. Inside, there was a semi-circular horn ring, a passenger grab handle, and a rheostat for instrument lighting. Standard equipment also now included a windshield washer and an oil filter.

The Autocar summed up the essence of Porsche motoring in those days with its test of a 1500 in November 1953: "By virtue of its very low build and fine aerodynamic lines it attracts immediate attention and interest from young and old. It is so obviously a car that was designed by men who knew what they wanted and were able to carry out their ideas. Its very appearance suggests speed, and as soon as one is seated in the car any desire to loiter is quickly dispelled. The Porsche [holds the road] in no uncertain manner, the soft torsion bar springing allowing it to hurry round main road corners without roll, while the rather direct steering gives the driver exact control over the front wheels."

The editors even went so far as to admit that they had extended their customary test period, simply because the 1500 was so much fun: "The high top gear makes cruising effortless, with an indicated 75-80 on the speedometer. One can imagine the car being thoroughly at home storming Alpine passes, where the admirable third gear and also second could be used to advantage. At night there is the impression of being in an aircraft cockpit, with the close curved windscreen and discreet lighting from the fascia, the suspension ironing out any sudden undulations in the road surface and no squeal being evident from the tyres when cornering fast. There is a feeling of rushing through space with the road disappearing rapidly immediately in front and the subdued beat of the engine from the rear."

That was about as lyrical a comment as ever appeared in the conservative British weekly. But it summed up better than most the essence of Porsche sport. The 356 taught many American enthusiasts in the '50s what serious driving was all about, taught them what a true sports car was and should be. And for many of these people, the class is still happily in session.

THE SPEEDSTER AND NEW ENGINES

An early 1955 production Speedster in its element

The Porsche Speedster has an enormous following. If one were pressed to name the single most desirable Type 356 model, the Speedster would probably be it. Lately, we have even seen a couple of very good Speedster replicas on the market—proof that demand for the original far exceeds the supply. The Speedster wasn't the quintessential early Porsche—that would have to be a coupe—but it ccrtainly was one of the most interesting.

The first series-built Porsche roadster was the limited-production America of 1952. The Reutter coachbuilding factory in Stuttgart sent rolling chassis to the Gläser coachworks in the town of Ullersricht, north of Munich. There, artisans hand-hammered the America's aluminum body and welded it to the frame. The semi-finished cars were then trucked back to Zuffenhausen for final assembly. In 1952, only four Americas were sold in the U.S. and production ended the following year. A seemingly limited market and high production costs, including transportation expenses, were the main reasons for its demise.

One Porsche dealer who didn't think the roadster market was limited was that wizard of the import car business, Max Hoffman. He believed that an inexpensive roadster should be a permanent part of the Porsche inventory. His arguments were sound. The American market had become a crucial one for the German company, hc told Ferry Porsche. The factory was producing an average of nine cars per day. America was buying four of them—and Hoffman was selling about two of the four: 22 percent of production. Americans had also discovered sports cars enthusiastically. MG and Jaguar had opened up the market; Triumph, Austin-Healey, and Fiat were getting into it fast; and by 1953 even Detroit was chiming in with production two-seaters like the Chevrolet Corvette and the Anglo-American Nash-Healey.

Hoffman was a confirmed believer in the saleability of open sports cars. In the early '50s he also made suggestions to Daimler-Benz that resulted in the Mercedes-Benz 190SL, another car he would sell in good numbers. But the Mercedes had to sell at upwards of $4000. Hoffman wanted a Porsche that could be priced under $3000. Max knew his market, and Porsche listened.

What emerged was an evolution of the Porsche America, bearing the same type number (540) and designed by

Above: The Speedster's stubby proportions are evident even when seen from above, as in this contemporary 1955 factory photograph.

Reutter with an eye to keeping production costs to the bare minimum. It started with the ordinary cabriolet bodyshell but had none of its ordinary accoutrements. Like the America, it had a light, removable canvas top and side curtains instead of a built-in cabriolet top and roll-up windows. For an extra dash of raffishness, the windshield was about 3½ inches shorter than on other Porsches. The interior was as spartan as that of a Triumph TR2, with minimal instrumentation (speedometer, tachometer, temperature gauge), a painted dash, and simple bucket seats with no rake adjustment. On the outside were all the regular Porsche appearance features plus a neat strip of bright metal encompassing the door handles along the bodysides. From a styling viewpoint the brightwork was absolutely essential. Even so, the new Speedster was often compared to an upside-down bathtub, and with weather equipment in place it looked particularly bizarre. Technically the tachometer and heater were options; both were usually part of the package, pushing the as-delivered cost over $3000. But the target base price was realized: Hoffman sold the Speedster for $2995, plus options and delivery, f.o.b. New York City.

The standard Speedster engine was the 1500 Normal powerplant, but one could order the Super specification for $500 extra. Not immediately available in Europe, the Speedster enjoyed good sales success in the U.S. After a cautious initial run of 200 units in 1954 the factory increased production, and by the time the last Speedster had been delivered in 1958 the total exceeded 4900.

Visually, the 1954 and '55 Speedsters were quite similar. The most distinguishing features were the dashboard gauges, bonnet handle, and emblems. In 1956, 15-inch wheels were offered as an alternative to the standard 16-inchers, which were phased out later that year, though they continued to be available on the lightweight Spyder models.

More readily identifiable than the 1954-55 Speedsters, the 1956-59 cars had new high-bow canvas top frames and, from 1957 on, teardrop-style taillights instead of the earlier "beehive" units. Except for dashboard gauge placement, other visual changes for 1956-59 were negligible. The 1959 models were "works" specials, built to customer order only, usually for competition.

The Speedster was a natural for the race track because of its light weight, nearly 200 pounds lighter than the 1500 coupe. As a result, the base model was about a second faster in the 0-60 mph sprint, though at about 80 mph the coupe would pull away thanks to its superior aerodynamics. The 1500S Speedster was commensurately faster, though again deficient at the top end compared to its coupe counterpart. Compared to the normal 1500 Speedster, the S version would do 0-60 mph in 10.0 seconds vs. 14, and would see the quarter-mile post in 17.5 seconds at 100 mph against 19 seconds at 95 mph.

Opposite page and above: A late 1955 A-series Speedster as photographed in Germany by the factory. Though very well built (coachwork by Reutter), the Speedster had few amenities in keeping with Max Hoffman's idea of a no-frills price-leader model for the U.S. Trunk space and weather protection weren't the best, but there was nothing like the Speedster for top-down, sunny-days motoring. Left: Subtle fender script identifies this as one of the rare Carrera Speedsters.

Walt Woron tested an early Speedster for the July 1955 issue of *Motor Trend* magazine, and waxed enthusiastic. "Its size, power, easy shift and steering make it fun to drive..." Woron wrote. "The brakes are extremely good. They have a servo action [and] are very positive; they get you out of situations where you may have delayed too long... For a sports car, and especially such a small one, the Porsche Speedster has a very smooth ride. It recovers quickly after a dip or bump, which seems to be inherent in torsion-sprung cars. There's absolutely no wallowing when it comes out of a dip; you've always got it under control."

Woron felt slightly claustrophobic inside the Speedster, as did most drivers. "With the top up...you have to jacknife in; the top is extremely low, and if you're over 6 feet, your head is going to touch. [The car's overall height was a mere 48 inches with the top down, with an extra 2 inches added from mid-1955.] It doesn't leave much room between the top and doors for seeing out; and with the side curtains on, you may as well be content with just looking forward."

Although the Speedster's top was rudimentary compared to that of the Porsche cabriolet, it was veritable space-age stuff next to the build-it-yourself mechanisms on contemporary British sports cars. "Putting up the soft top is absurdly easy," Woron continued. "You reach behind you, grab the top's forward bow, pull forward so it reaches the windshield, and snap the two locks in place." He also noted that Reutter had found it possible to insert a little padding in the top, an advance unknown in darkest Coventry.

Speedsters were raced with considerable distinction. John von

This page: Higher windshield marked Speedsters from 1956 (above and top). Factory hardtop (right) was a rarity for '55. Opposite page: 1600 Supers from '58 (top) and early '57 (center). The 1960-61 356B Roadster (bottom).

Neumann, Porsche's west coast counterpart of Max Hoffman, often entered them in California SCCA events. His first performance in a Speedster was with a 1500S at the Torrey Pines six-hour enduro in November 1954. The car finished a respectable eighth overall, and won its class the following day. The F-Production SCCA championship was won by a Speedster in 1955, driven by Bengt Soderstrom. Speedsters have continued to race throughout the years, nowadays in vintage events mainly, although a few still compete—and win—in production classes against rivals many years newer. Never was there a better expression of the dual-purpose, race-and-ride sports car.

Although popular, the Speedster was apparently not popular enough. At the behest of Max Hoffman, who often brought in new cars at bargain rates and

raised prices later, Porsche decided to move upmarket. Reutter, the firm's exclusive body builder through 1960, was hard pressed for space by that time, and was finding it increasingly difficult to satisfy demand for regular Porsche models, let alone the Speedster. Ultimately Porsche decided to offer the Speedster D, later the Convertible D, with body construction farmed out to Drauz in Heilbronn, 20 miles from Stuttgart.

Walt Woron neatly summed up the appeal of the well-loved Speedster: "Where else are you going to get a sports car that has the performance, the ride, and the workmanship of this one? There are few cars in its price class or above that can compete with it in an across-the-board comparison. Sure, it lacks certain features like roll-up windows, but if you want an open-air car you'd have no complaints on this score. If you drive for the fun of driving, you'll *love* this one."

Shortly after the Speedster's debut, Porsche completed a wholesale revision of its powerplants, which saw the designation "/2" added to engine type numbers on the 1300/1300S and 1500/1500S units and the end of the 1100 displacement. On the 1500 models, for example, engine types were 546/2 for the 1500 and 528/2 for the Super. The most significant engineering aspect of this change was in valve gear and crankcases, the latter now built in three pieces instead of two, using aluminum instead of magnesium alloy. Oil capacity was increased, castings were strengthened. The 1300's bore and stroke dimensions now became virtually square at 74.5 × 74.0mm. The "/2" engines put further distance between Porsche and VW engineering, being designed for easier servicing and for quicker camshaft swapping under racing conditions. Porsche did not make much of these changes in its advertising, and they are listed only in official documents. But they are indicative of the quest for improvement that is still a fact of life at Zuffenhausen.

As the last of the original Type 356s came off the line, Porsche was celebrating its 25th anniversary. The company had successfully covered much ground, met and mastered many problems. Production for calendar year 1955 had been 2952 cars, and on December 1st of that year, Porsche's old Zuffenhausen buildings were returned by the government. As difficult as it may have been to believe then, greater things lay ahead.

TYPE 356A/B/C 1955~65: THE PATH TO PERFECTION

The factory's portrait of the 1956 Type 356A 1600 Cabriolet

To the casual observer, the new Porsches introduced in time for the 1956 model year were little changed. But to the more discerning, they represented a change in approach, one important enough for Porsche to add the suffix "A" to their type designation. The Type 356A series would see the last of the 1300/1300S models, which disappeared after 1957, and the first of the fabulous Carreras—the fastest "street" Porsches to date, capable of 125 mph in normal touring trim (Chapter 7).

Few differences were immediately apparent outside. The main ones were rub rails on the rocker panels of coupes and cabriolets as well as Speedsters, a new curved windshield to replace the earlier creased version, and heftier tires. Porsche had adopted a "super-wide" 4½-inch rim and decreased wheel diameter from 16 to 15 inches, fitting 5.60 × 15 tires instead of the previous 5.00 × 16s. This, it was discovered, was the key to improved roadholding.

More obvious alterations were made inside the 356A. The driver now confronted a flat-face instrument panel with a padded top instead of the center-bulge, all-metal dash of previous years. Visible through the steering wheel were three large gauges, tachometer prominently placed in the middle, flanked by speedometer and a combination fuel and oil temperature gauge. A trip odometer had joined the total mileage recorder in 1953. The handbrake was relocated. Cockpit entry was improved slightly with a floor lowered by 1½ inches. The ignition switch now incorporated a starter detent, and (except on Speedsters) there was a built-in dash mounting slot for a radio. Standard lighting was comprehensive, with courtesy lights, self-cancelling directionals, and headlamp flasher. Car for car, the 356A was quieter than the 356, thanks to thorough sound insulation in strategic places.

The by-now familiar Porsche chassis was heavily revised for the A, based on a prototype (nicknamed "Ferdinand" after the elder Porsche) that had been used for testing since 1954. Besides the chunkier tires, rear suspension was modified for increased travel and a softer ride, and correspondingly higher-capacity shocks were specified, now mounted vertically instead of at an angle. Up front, suspension mountings were beefed up, shocks repositioned, and the stabilizer bar was of larger diameter and thus stiffer. Outer suspension arm bearings were now of the needle-roller type. Steering

Above: A little oom-pah-pah with the 1955 (right) and 1956 356A cabriolets. Below: One-piece curved windshield marked the new 356A series.

geometry was altered, and a small hydraulic damper was added to absorb shocks and reduce steering wheel kickback. The overall aim of the chassis tuning was a softer ride with no loss in roadability. Consequently, the feel of a 356A is considerably more "modern" than that of a 356.

Avid Porschephile John Bentley said the updated chassis gave the 356A "a brand-new handling and riding personality. If the steering lost its feather-lightness, it also shed that alarming front-end tendency to 'float' and wander at high speed. Then too, the traditional oversteer gave way to neutral steering; and although the car offered a slightly 'softer' ride than before, it became as tractable as a front-engined machine and could be driven in much the same way."

There were also important improvements in Porsche's flat-four, even to the fast-fading 1300 versions. Almost immediately they received heavier flywheels and, for the S-type, cast rather than fabricated inlet manifolds. All engines after December 1955 had forged crankshafts; all had thermostatically controlled warm air nozzles designed to direct heat up toward the carburetors from below the engine. But it was the new 1.6-liter powerplant that engaged most of Porsche's attention on the 356A. With the FIA's new 1600cc competition limit in mind, Porsche fitted larger cylinder barrels to the 1500 engine to up bore by 2.5 mm. Bore and stroke was thus 82.5 × 74.0mm, which raised displacement to 1582cc. Increased compression gave 60 bhp (DIN) (70 SAE) at 4500 rpm for the new Type 616/1 1600 Normal unit. The Type 616/2 1600 Super developed 76 bhp (DIN) (88 SAE) at 5000 rpm. Both units had improved low-speed torque, which made the car more tractable at moderate speeds and less dependent on its gears. The transaxle, by the way, received new mounts to improve longevity, and the clutch was also redesigned.

Although the 1300/1300S were limited to the coupe and cabriolet both styles, the 1600s could also be had in a new version of the two-seat Speedster, redesignated Convertible 'D' from 1958. In late 1957, a detachable steel hardtop became a new option for the cabriolet, which then took on the appearance of a notchback coupe. Prices continued to range in the mid $4000s for coupe and

Opposite page: Twin horn grilles distinguish 356A models from earlier 356s. This page: The Cabriolet's top was bulky when lowered, but gave superb weather protection and a snug cockpit when raised. On the right is a late 1957 model as shown at that year's Frankfurt Auto Show. Full-width bumper bar (above) was a popular accessory for U.S. Porsches, shown here on a 1956-model 356A coupe.

cabriolet, with the Speedster remaining the line leader at around $3200.

Magazine reviews of the early 1600s generally agreed that the 356A was altogether better behaved. It responded, as *The Autocar* told British enthusiasts, "more like an orthodox high-performance sports car, although a certain skittishness at the rear, attributable partly to the swing-axle rear suspension, can still be felt... Stability remains very good indeed, and the design as a whole gives a liveliness to the controls of which the skilled

A look inside the Porsche secton of the Reutter works in Stuttgart in the early '50s. Left: 356 coupes move on hand-pushed carts toward completion. Above: Finished cars await delivery just off the line.

driver can take advantage."

The editors noted that even German *autobahnen* had curves and rough sections, yet a 1600 Normal pegging 4500 rpm could take such tricky stretches with no need to slow down: "Off these main highways the car is even more enjoyable, for its modestly sized engine does so much without fuss, provided that the driver expends on the gear box energy equivalent to a housewife cutting soft butter... As the car will so willingly cruise at 90 mph, it is made to do so by most drivers when traffic conditions permit, making the mpg range of 29-36 [Imperial] all the more creditable ... At under 1500 rpm the characteristics of the flat-four engine and the transmission result in a reduction in response and a slight feeling of snatching." But who would routinely drive a Porsche at under 1500 rpm?

Although Porsche had increased its workforce, it had also increased its output per employee. Yet there had been no compromise in the by-now famous Porsche quality. The Germans' painstaking attention to detail must have been as mind-boggling to the British as it was to Americans, probably more so. For example, all steering mechanisms were run-in "on the bench," from full lock to full lock, for the equivalent of 5000km on the road. The quality of trim, upholstery and paintwork was a cut above the norm, even for Porsche's price class.

"The superbly controllable Porsche brings back to motoring some of the joy that those priviledged to drive sports cars in the earlier spacious days must have experienced," *The Autocar* concluded. "At the wheel one feels to be one up on the other fellow in all the things that matter in driving for its own sake. The imposition of duty and purchase tax make the total price formidable for British buyers [£1891 or $5300 U.S. for the 1600 at the time], but the car remains, none the less, highly desirable."

In what was, by now, standard Porsche practice, running refinements continued throughout the 356A's lifespan. These included, but were not limited to, one-piece oval taillights, transposition of speedometer and combination gauge, improved door locks, one-piece aluminum transaxle in place of the cast-magnesium unit and, for the 1600 Normal engine, offset-wristpin pistons (to eliminate cold-engine piston slap) and (1957) aluminum instead of fiber camshaft gears. Later came FIA-homologated gear ratios with 5.17:1 final drive, cast-iron cylinders for Normals (providing strength and quietness on the largely roadgoing 1600), deletion of the roller-bearing Hirth crank on the 1600S unit, redesigned oil coolers, new timing cases (except on Speedsters), Zenith instead of Solex carburetors, rerouted exhaust outlets (through the lower portion of the rear bumper guards), diaphragm spring clutch, and a revised shift linkage. Convenience and appearance alterations comprised repositioned heater controls, new door handles and window winding levers, revised rear package shelf, optional gasoline heater, slim-back bucket seats, larger-diameter steering wheel, front wing vents (optional on coupe, standard on cabriolet), a wider rear window for the cabriolet, and new hubcaps bearing the Porsche crest. The most controversial change on this series of 356As, which were designated T-2, were the Cadillac-type bumper-guard exhausts. But Porsche had adopted this for practical reasons: better protection and more ground clearance.

A change in sales tactics was apparent in the 1958 replacement of the Speedster by the Speedster "D"—soon rechristened "Convertible D." The D stood for Drauz of Heilbronn, which built the body (see Chapters 5 and 6). Rationale behind this upgrading—the Convertible D cost $500 more than the Speedster—was simple: Ferry Porsche had never liked the Speedster. He thought a "stripper" really didn't fit the Porsche image, and pointed to its low sales to make a case against it on cost grounds as well. Compared to the Speedster, the Convertible D offered a higher windshield (thus more headroom), roll-up windows, an easily raised non-detachable convertible top, and reclining bucket seats. One Speedster feature was retained: a unique dashboard, with the instruments grouped under a hooded bulge in front of the

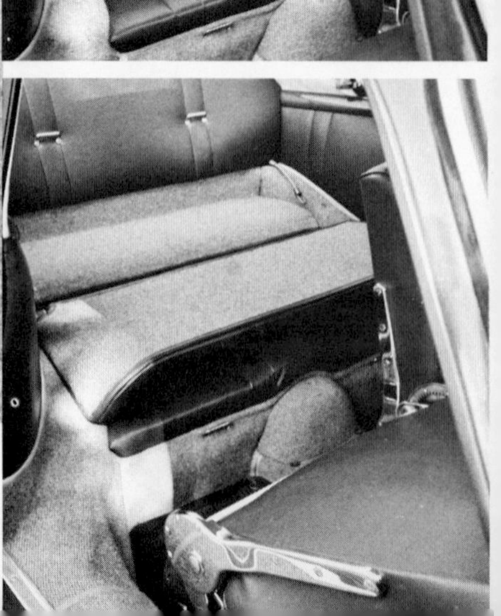

driver, and no flanking glovebox (map pockets were provided instead).

Press reports praised the Convertible D. *Road & Track* magazine called it the best buy in the Porsche line, and *Motor Trend* took the unorthodox approach of comparison-testing it with a 1959 Corvette. While insisting that both cars were great buys for the money, writer Wayne Thoms kept admitting throughout his review that the Porsche was superior: in fit and finish, handling, braking, low-speed tractability, passenger comfort, fuel economy. About the only areas were the Corvette had the edge were acceleration (the fuel-injected test car did 0-60 mph in 7.8 seconds against the Convertible D's 15.2) and wider availability of service.

The new Type 356B, introduced at the Frankfurt Automobile Show in late 1959, was the nearest Porsche ever came to a GM-style facelift. Indeed, General Motors itself could have come up with the cowl-forward rehash, which to old Porsche hands was pretty frightening. Erwin Komenda, still an active company designer, had conjured up a massive front bumper with jumbo bumper guards, riding about four inches higher than before for better body protection. The headlamps were propped more upright, and announced prominent, almost straight-edged front fenders instead of the flowing fenders of the 356A. There was a garish chrome handle on the hood and phallic parking lights sprouting from the

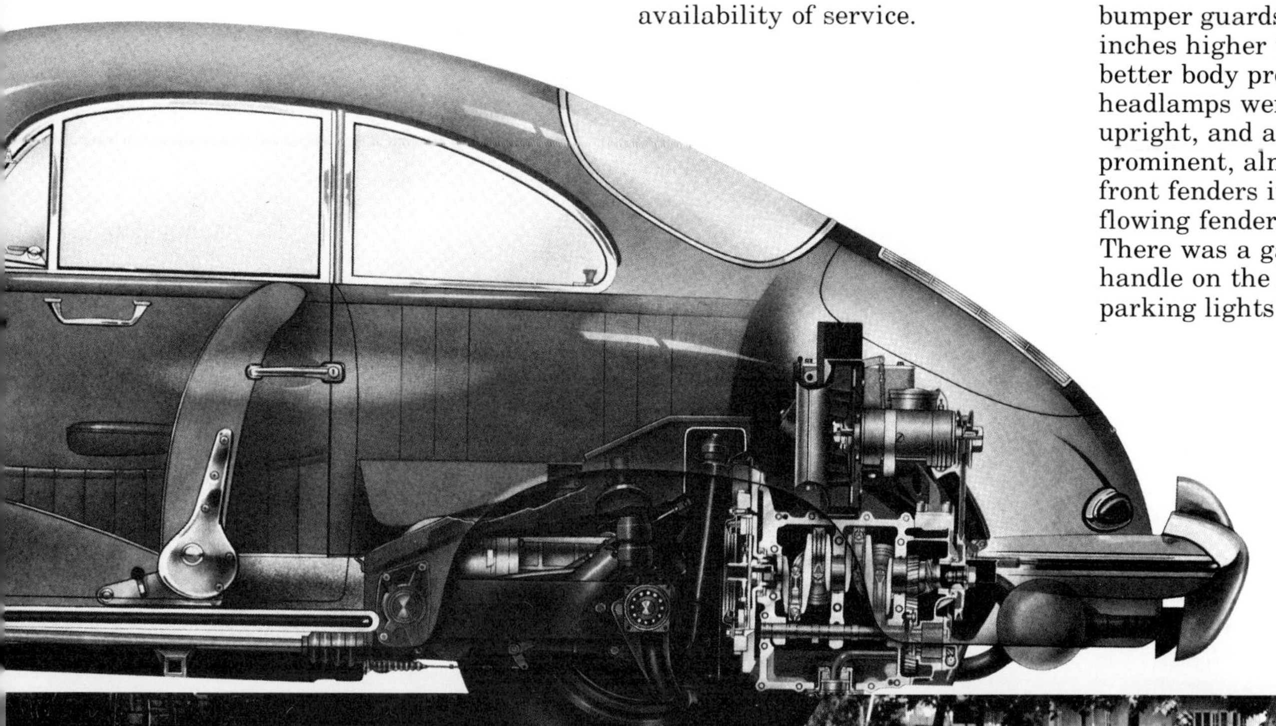

Center spread: An X-ray view of the 356C's efficient body and mechanical package. Opposite page: The 1957 Type 356A coupe and its tiny fold-down back seat. This page, clockwise from lower left: The 1959 Type 356A Convertible D, the 1960-61 Type 356B coupe, and '57 356A Cabriolet with optional detachable hardtop.

outboard ends of the front air vents. The more fervid carped about Porsche's having "done a Detroit," but like most factory changes the 356B's were soon accepted as part of the Porsche style. As Karl Ludvigsen has pointed out, people were inclined to think that if Porsche did something it *must* be alright, no matter how it looked.

The engine lineup, now shorn of the 1300cc versions, consisted of a triumvirate, each representing a designated state of tune: the 1600 Normal, with 60 bhp (DIN) at 4500 rpm and a top speed of 100 mph; the 1600 Super (often called Super 75), with 75 bhp (DIN) at 5000 rpm and 110 mph; and the Super 90, with 90 bhp (DIN) at 5500 rpm and an official top end of 116 mph. Body styles were carried over from the last of the 356A line—coupe, cabriolet (with or without hardtop), and Convertible D, which was renamed the Roadster from 1960 on. All were available with each engine for a total of nine separate models. (There were also the Carreras, which are treated elsewhere.) Aside from the more blatant changes already mentioned, the "B" had a stubbier gearchange lever, greater glass area and, from 1961 on, twin rear deck grilles. Mechanical alterations were subtle but noteworthy. The new Porsche synchromesh, with an easier-to-engage first gear, had been added to late 356As and was carried over to the B. The brakes were still drums, their days numbered, but they were now stronger Al-Fin units and better sealed against moisture.

The Super 90 was a new ingredient in the model mix, developing its 90 horses through conventional techniques: higher-lift camshaft, improved carburetion and higher compression. The Super 90's Zenith carburetors gave way to Solex 40s with larger throats and venturis and high-performance jets. Compression ratio was 9.1:1 instead of the 75's 8.5:1.

This was basically minor, precision tuning—nothing exotic or beyond the limits of the car—which was Porsche's way. Nothing was lost in tractability, and *Sports Car Graphic* magazine suggested, in fact, that the Super 90 was "tamer in traffic and lower speed ranges than the 1600 Super. Getting off the mark fast from a standing start takes some practice, as the big carburetors can't be dumped open too fast. Once the biggest chunk of inertia is overcome, you can go to the floor with the pedal and start moving out very fast indeed. In fact one of the most impressive things about this engine is the feeling of torque—sheer push in the shoulders—that one gets on booting the throttle... there isn't the feeling of wild acceleration from a standing start, but once under way it comes on with increasing force [and] builds up faster than one would believe possible." Even so, acceleration

was quite quick enough: under 10 seconds in the 0-60 mph test.

Testers also noted that the stock Super 90's handling was somewhat different than expected, thanks to softer spring rates and, because of a standard camber compensator, stiffer roll-resistance. According to *SCG:* "Normal procedure... letting the front end plow to compensate for the rear coming out... will net you a trip through the tules [sic]. It must be set into a drift attitude before the corner and varying amounts of power applied." This was Super 90 behavior on German Dunlop Sports tires; with harder racing tires the handling was more like what Porsche drivers were used to.

Super 90s could be revved about 800 rpm higher than the 1600N or 1600S thanks to a special cooling layout that gathered more air, along with nitrided crank and cam bearing surfaces, a lighter flywheel, stiffer valve springs, light alloy rockers, 5mm-larger main bearing diameters and cylinder liners treated with

Opposite page: What appears to be an early 356C coupe wears non-production hubcaps perhaps intended for the 1963 disc-brake models (top). A 1962 356B fixed-roof hardtop ready for an afternoon "at hounds" (bottom). This page: The 1962-63 B-series Cabriolet shows right fender fuel filler adopted with the T-6 body modifications (left). The '62 Roadster (below).

Ferral, a steel coating spread over molybdenum. The Super 90 also had a unique oil pickup system, which allowed it to draw oil from the full side of the sump during hard cornering, thus ensuring proper lubrication at all times. This was an important advance that Porsche racing drivers had wanted for several years, and was especially welcome in the high-performance Super 90.

Last and, arguably, the best of the pushrod 356 Porsches was the Type 356C. It arrived at the end of 1963, and was available in diminishing quantitites through the autumn of 1965. There were few external alterations as the previous round of changes (designated T-6), involving the twin deck grilles and larger glass area, had been instituted only two years earlier, in 1961. Even so, it was apparent that constant improvement was still a watchword at Zuffenhausen. For instance, the clumsy VW-like heater knob was replaced by a lever (VW itself switched to levers a few years later), and more buckety seats with standard armrests adorned the interior. There was an even larger backlight on the coupe.

More important were the mechanical updates, starting with four-wheel disc brakes as used earlier on the Carrera 2 (see Chapter 7), identifiable at a glance by a new wheel/hubcap design. This was certainly a departure from long-standing tradition, but it was consistent with Porsche's philosophy and was, in the end, inevitable. The cars were getting faster; now they would stop with authority equal to their speed. The engine lineup was rationalized as follows. The

continued on page 65

The final development of the original 356 design was the 1963-65 C Series, displayed in this array of factory photographs. Note the flat-face hubcaps on both body types, a clue to the four-wheel disc brakes adopted with this series. The C coupe's deeper rear window is evident even in profile (bottom). The last of the 356s were built at Karmann alongside the first of the 911s.

1951 Type 356 coupe

PORSCHE

1949 Type 356 coupe, one of 50 production models constructed at the tiny Gmünd works in Austria. Note the distinguishing front chrome strips, the elliptical rear wheel openings, and the door ventwings that mark these early Porsche coupes.

A more detailed look at the Type 356 coupe pictured on the opening page of this section. Sometimes referred to as the "Stuttgart," these were the first production Porsches built in that city following the firm's relocation there from Austria. This car bears the crest of the Reutter coachworks, which would construct Porsche bodies for many years under contract in a designated area of its plant. Note the distinctive center-bulge dash with its unusual radio and the very low front and rear bumpers. Another spotter's point on 1950-52 models is the parking lights, placed slightly inboard of the headlamps. The windshield divider bar was deleted after '51.*

TELEFUNKEN

Above: U.S.-market Porsches for 1955 bore "Continental" fender script, but were mechanically identical with earlier models.

Opposite page top: A 1958 Type 356A built to European specifications. Note the wire mesh stone guards for the headlamps.

Below: a trio of great Porsches. Left to right, the 1957 Type 356A Speedster, 1962 Type 356B cabriolet hardtop, and 1959 Convertible D.

MLC 853

Introduced during 1958, the Convertible D replaced the low-slung Speedster in the Porsche lineup. Like its predecessor, it was a two-seater, and retained many of its features and most of its appeal in a less radical package compared with the normal Type 356A coupe and cabriolet. The model was initially cataloged as the Speedster D, the initial denoting the coachbuilder, Karosserie Drauz of Heilbronn. Compared to the Speedster, the Convertible D featured a higher windshield and more conventional folding top that was built into the body, plus roll-up windows, and was thus more practical for everyday use. This particular car, built in 1959, carries the 1600 Normal engine, but was also offered with the Type 616/2 Super engine.

Two late examples of the 356B series. On the left is a 1962 1600N cabriolet with optional liftoff hardtop. Shown right is a 1963 cabriolet with the top-line Super 90 powerplant.

CALIFORNIA
779 YJV

Opposite page, bottom: Though not much different outside from other 356Bs, the Carrera 2 packed a good deal more punch—130 DIN horsepower (152 SAE), which translated to more than one bhp per cubic inch. The car shown was built in 1963, and is equipped with optional sliding sunroof. This page and opposite top: Porsche's detachable hardtop, shown on this 1962 356B cabriolet, arrived late in 1957 as an option for the 356A. A fixed-roof version of this style was also offered.

CALIFORNIA
699 XGN

Introduced in late '61 as a 1962 model, the Carrera 2 was officially designated 2000GS. Its four-cam Type 587 engine was descended from the Type 547 unit used in the Type 550 Spyder.

continued from page 48

60-bhp Normal was dropped, the 75 was retained, and the Super 90 engine was pushed up to 95 bhp by virtue of higher compression. The 75- and 95-bhp models were now called, respectively, C and SC. The customary body styles—coupe and cabriolet—carried on for both engines, as did the detachable hardtop option for the cabriolet.

For the enthusiast interested in investing in a 356 Porsche (somehow "buying" seems inappropriate), a "C" will offer reliable transportation as well as an increase in capital worth. This most refined of the long 356 line was as near perfect as a car could be. Ludvigsen recorded that, in its last season, the C's average warranty repair cost was only $8.38 per car, "the lowest in history for Porsche and incredibly low for any car." The other side of the coin is that no 356 comes cheaply.

Production totals at the end of the 356 run are as follows:

type	**production**	**yearly avg.**
356	7,627	1,090
356A	21,045	5,261
356B	30,963	7,741
356C	16,668	8,334

These aren't figures to pop champagne over, at least not at General Motors. But for Porsche, which had started from ground zero just 15 years before, they tell a remarkable story, one of constant evolution and steady growth within the original 1947 concept. Of course, the Type 356C bore little similarity to the Gmünd cars or even the early 356s built at Zuffenhausen. *Road & Track* noted: "Gradually, and part by part, Porsche adopted bits, pieces and complete assemblies of its own. Today nothing remains in the way of VW parts, though there are many similarities in arrangement and construction. The modern Porsche is unique, it has had a tremendous success, and it deserves it."

Though considered an interim model by some, the 356C is highly prized today.

Crafting an early 356 (inset); the 1961 Beutler 356B coupe

CRAFTSMAN'S CREED: THE COACHBUILT PORSCHE

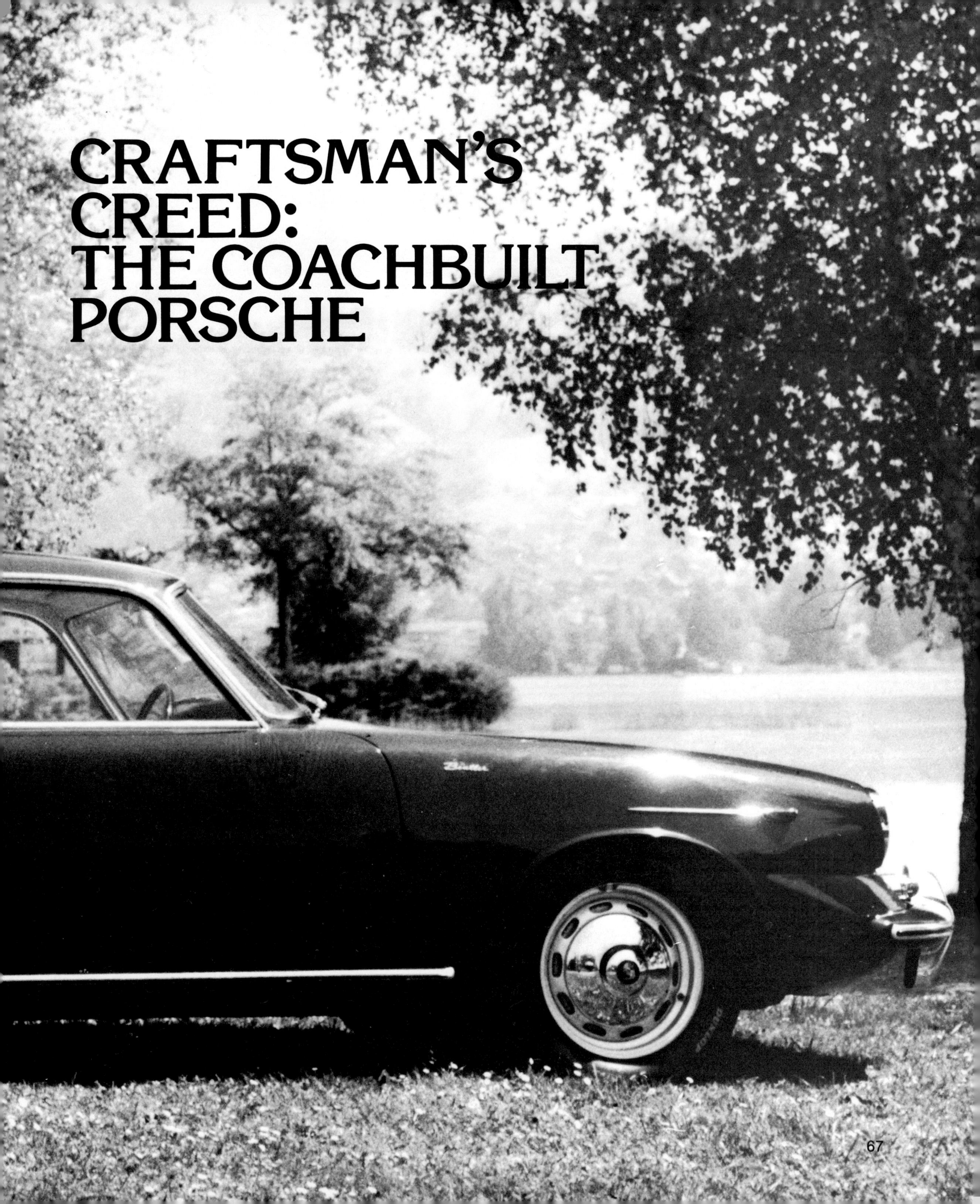

Reutter, Karmann, Beutler, D'Ieteren Freres, Gläser, Heuer, Wendler, Zagato, Bertone —coachbuilders all. And all have one thing in common: at one time or other, all have attached their nameplates to Porsche automobiles. Others, such as b+b, Carelli Design, Giugaro (ItalDesign), Glöckler, Weidenhausen, Ghia, and Frua have also put their mark on Porsches.

Coachbuilders are craftsmen, experts at translating dreams and drawings into solid reality. "Craftsman" is not a four-year degree; it is a learned skill—and an art. It involves all the senses: sight, smell, touch, hearing, even taste. To watch a craftsman take an ordinary piece of metal and form a body is an increasingly rare privilege. Today robots and machines are taking over from humans on most automobile assembly lines. But not at Porsche, where excellence has never been confused with mere technology.

Looking at a new Porsche or a well-maintained older model, one sees genuine craftsmanship. Seams are tight and equal. Gaps around every opening panel invariably—and precisely—measure 1.5 mm. The paint is mirror-smooth and lustrous, partly because of the body's uniformity and partly because of the quality and depth of the paint itself. Such surface appearances are not deceiving. Porsche doors close with a precision "click," and continue to do so for years. A Porsche body stays free from annoying rattles. It has been rightfully said that if a rattle develops in a Porsche, it is something the owner has done to the car.

The superb engineering and balance, the charisma and precision workmanship that are Porsche are reflected in such sensory characteristics, which almost everyone can appreciate. And these favorable first impressions are only reinforced when you actually drive a Porsche. The typical sports car of

Opposite page: The Reutter-bodied 356A Speedster is perhaps the most sought-after coachbuilt Porsche. Shown are an early 1956 (above) and '58 1600 Super (below). This page: The Speedster's successor, the Convertible D, at the Drauz factory (above). An earlier version of the 356B Beutler coupe (right).

the late Forties and Fifties was a cantankerous, noisy, rattling lash-up. The Type 356 virtually revolutionized our definition of how sports cars were supposed to be. Porsches would not be built down to a price, like most of their rivals. They were—and are—designed and built to exacting standards. Once these were met, then and only then was the appropriate price attached.

"Sticker shock," a common consumer malady these days, probably first appeared with the advent of the Porsche 356. How could such a little car with such a small engine cost so much, the average American wondered.

How indeed! It was worth every penny. It was also an investment. Other sports cars lost a third of their value as soon as they were driven off the showroom floor, while Porsches retained a large share of their original purchase price—and some actually started appreciating in value. Yet a Porsche was usually not an enthusiast's first sports car, for it was a bit unreal, unbelievable. As one delightful advertisement put it, "Porsche is an acquired taste."

Of course, the bodywork was not the most important factor in creating the Porsche mystique. The cars were meant primarily for driving, and it was this and their stirring performance that made them not just highly regarded but highly sought after as well. Still—if each time you get into your car the door goes "clank," if each bump causes squeaks and shakes, if drops of water join you inside when it rains, then your desire to keep the car can quite quickly lead to a "for sale" ad. In a Porsche, on the other hand, doors close with inherent integrity, bumps sound like a mallet striking a block of rubber, and the rain stays outside even on the cabriolet models. Actually, it's the liberal use of rubber, carefully placed between metal parts, that allows both car and driver to endure road shock. You'd never find that kind of structural solidity on a contemporary British sports car.

After his initial Volkswagen prototypes were finalized in the prewar years, Ferdinand Porsche moved to build a racing version. Despite opposition from Volkswagen's state-controlled management, he argued that a competition model would generate positive publicity for VW. In due course, the Type 60K10 emerged from the Karosserie Reutter works in Stuttgart.

Inspired by the efforts of Paul Jaray, the father of streamlining, the 60K10 took the shape of half a raindrop. Jaray stated that top speed could be increased measurably, without additional power, by using a "stream line" design. This was crucial to the design of the first production Type 356, because when you have an engine with only 1100cc and little money to render it exotic, you need all the help you can get. Streamlining employs curved lines. A soft curve is beautiful; it has character. A box is merely a box, as we can see by gazing at all the new little econoboxes on the highways. A straight line may be the shortest distance between two points, but it is inherently boring. A curve can take infinite shapes, each new and different.

When the first Porsches were built in the early postwar years aluminum became the expedient choice. Wooden bucks were used to shape the metal into body panels, each one hammered by hand. About 50 of the first coupes were made at the little factory in Gmünd, Austria. Karosserie Beutler in Switzerland then produced a handful of open models (see Chapter 2). About 10 years later, Beutler would produce a stretched, four-passenger Porsche coupe in very limited quantities.) Demand for the cars soon outstripped production capability and aluminum had its limitations for higher-volume production. Partly for these reasons, Porsche returned to Stuttgart, as mentioned, and its car bodies were made of steel from that point on.

Because of limited capital and facilities, Porsche contracted with the Reutter coachworks for a small area of its factory to be given over to Porsche body construction. Reutter was an

Below: The 1959 356A Convertible D, coachwork by Drauz. Right: The slow-paced assembly line at D'Ieteren Freres in Belgium, where the Convertible D/Roadster was built beginning in 1961.

obvious choice. Its work on the Type 60K10 body had proved that the firm could translate ideas to reality with a high degree of quality. Just as each Porsche engine bore the initials of the workman assigned to make it, each door and lid made by Reutter bore the serial number of the car to which it would be attached. The fit was letter-perfect. A factory film, "Made by Hand," told the story in great detail. Reutter's standards were high: after assembly, each car was disassembled and painted, one panel at a time. Almost everything was painted, inside and out. Then the car was reassembled. With all this, it should come as no surprise that there was no time for "holidays" at Reutter.

When Porsche began building its racing cars, it selected aluminum for the bodywork because of its inherent lightness. Karosserie Wendler, a small firm in Reutlingen, had a fine reputation in the aluminum-body field, and had built bodies for Dr. Wunibald Kamm, who would later become known for his ideas on aerodynamics. Kamm's trademark was the chopped tail, now known as the "Kamm-back" or Kamm tail, a styling element he considered more efficient than a pure teardrop shape. It was Wendler who built the bodies for the racing Porsche Spyder, designed by Erwin Komenda. Despite their strictly competition purpose, the Spyders were built with all the gem-like precision of the production Porsches—and, of course, they won races. The resultant publicity could hardly help but improve sales of the production 356s.

Volume picked up so

dramatically, in fact, that Reutter began having difficulty meeting Porsche's demand for bodies. The America roadsters (see Chapter 3) were accordingly produced by Karosserie Gläser, but that entailed costly shipping that ultimately limited that model's saleability. Later, the Heuer coachworks took up production of what would become the famous Porsche Speedster.

Designed as a no-frills model at the suggestion of Max Hoffman, the Speedster lacked the heavy padded, hand-sewn top and roll-up glass side windows of the normal 356 cabriolet. But the degree of quality that went into the car—thanks to the skilled hands of Heuer and Porsche craftsmen—belied its $2995 price, which was remarkable for what it bought. The Speedster, from a quality standpoint, suffers

only by comparison with the more expensive coupes and cabriolets. Next to an MG, it was a masterpiece of the coachbuilder's art, with the same precision fit and mirror-finish paint that were Porsche hallmarks even as early as the mid-'50s.

After 1958, the Speedster's place in the model lineup was taken by the more elaborate Convertible D (originally called Speedster D). The letter denoted Karosserie Drauz of Heilbronn, which made its reputation before the war as a builder of open cars. In the late '50s, Drauz was also under contract to Ford of Germany to supply truck bodies. Accordingly, it built a new addition for the Porsche work, and Drauz's efforts took some of the supply burden off of Reutter. Drauz would later sell the plant to NSU, and still later this plant would turn out bodies for the 924 and 944. It was the Ford business that ultimately ended production of the Convertible D (known as the Roadster after 1960). Ford gave Drauz an order for an extra 150 truck bodies a day, a big increase for the small company that was too good to pass up. While they lasted, however, the Drauz-built open Porsches were yet further testimony to the brilliant quality and craftsmanship of German coachbuilders.

The roadster production assignment then shifted to Belgium and the firm of D'Ieteren Freres, a company whose history stretched back to the days of horsedrawn carriages. Responsible for Porsche and VW sales in Belgium, the company also assembled some VWs in its plant. D'Ieteren produced about 725 Roadsters, of which 87 were the twin-rear-grille 1962 models.

Porsche needed still more capacity to meet rising sales in the early Sixties, and the logical choice was Wilhelm Karmann GmbH of Osnabrück. Already known by that time for its magnificently constructed VW Karmann-Ghia, the firm would produce some 50,000 bodies, both Type 356 and Type 911/912 models. Karmann later turned out about 119,000 bodies for the mid-engine Type 914. Even at these relatively high quantities, the quality of a Porsche body remained at an admirably high level.

In 1963, tail finally wagged dog, in a manner of speaking, and the once tiny car company that used to rent a portion of the Reutter coachworks bought out Reutter. For a short time, Porsche was so proud of the fact that it attached a special plaque to its cars reading "Porsche Karosserie."

The last metal-bodied racing Porsches were built in Italy by the house of Zagato, the Abarth-Carreras. Italian contracts pre-empted Zagato from using its trademark on the 20-odd cars constructed.

By now, aluminum, like steel before it, was considered too heavy for racing. Fiberglass was the thing. Porsche found a supplier in the Stuttgart firm of Ernst Heinkel Flugzeugbau, which among other things had built the famous Heinkel fighter aircraft for the wartime *Luftwaffe*. Heinkel had considerable expertise in fiberglass manufacturing, and was accordingly awarded the contract to supply bodies for the Carrera 904 GTS. This car was designed by the third-generation

Opposite page: Though the Abarth-Carrera GTL did not bear its coachbuilder's name, Carrozzeria Zagato executed this racing type's all-aluminum body. Left: Fiberglass was featured in the mid-engine Type 904 Carrera GTS body, which was constructed by the Heinkel Aircraft Company.

Ferdinand Porsche, known as Butzi, who would also design the ageless 911.

The 911, introduced as the Type 901 at the Frankfurt Auto Show in 1963, retained the familiar Porsche shape, but reinterpreted it with a view to more interior comfort. It proved at once that a rear-engine car can be beautiful, fresh and original. Even some 20 years later it still looks good, and in a world of ever-changing fashion that is high praise indeed.

Since the last of the potent 917s, most of Porsche's factory competition models have been designed around heavily reworked derivatives of the 911 bodyshell. The new, or nearly new, water-cooled cars were, however, designed by an American, Tony Lapine. Thus far, they have not met with the same enthusiasm enjoyed by the 356 and the 911/912—possibly because they represent in some ways a 180-degree shift in thinking and methodology and thus do not seem to be "true" Porsches in the tradition of the marque.

A few other coachbuilders have on occasion tried their hand at Porsche design over the years. In 1963, Ghia put a pretty cabriolet on its motor show stands. This car bore styling that closely prefigured the Karmann-Ghia, but was marred a bit by a dummy grille up front. Interestingly, Ghia's general lines were inspired by another American—Virgil Exner, father of Chrysler's tailfins. Exner had worked closely with Ghia since 1951, and the K-G itself was taken almost verbatim from an Exner show car, the Chrysler d'Elegance. During the years of the 914, Giorgetto Giugaro, whose work now appears under the ItalDesign label, created the lovely Tapiro. Most observers thought it a better 914 than the 914—perhaps this is what the car should have looked like all along. Bertone also got involved with a single 911 convertible, and in the USA Dick Troutman of Troutman-Barnes built a stretched four-door 911 sedan and a futuristic 910. Today,

Carelli Design of Costa Mesa, California offers a 928 convertible conversion worthy of the Porsche name. Back in Italy, Frua designed a special 914 body too, as did Eurostyle. B+B of Cologne, West Germany has produced many variations on the 911 and 928 themes, most of them quite exciting, and has also built up a sizeable business in personalizing Porsches for wealthy clients. But the majority of these exercises have been mere one-offs, plays for recognition. The style that endures is the coachbuilt 356 and

Left: Porsche built its own bodies beginning with the 911 ('69 models shown). Opposite page bottom: The Carelli Design 928 convertible conversion. Below: The Frua-designed 914 special, circa 1971. Bottom: Bertone executed this 911 roadster in the late '60s.

the 911. The Types 914 and 924/944 may have sold in excess of 100,000 units, but they are not the same in character.

Coachbuilt cars in the modern context are increasingly rare. The cost of the expensive and time-consuming processes that go into them continue to mount; even for such prestige marques as Porsche, the costs eventually prove formidable and uneconomical. The finest flowering of the coachbuilt Porsche came in the 356 era, and it is the 356 toward which collectors turn in the greatest numbers. It would be hard to come up with a finer example of modern art—or of an immensely desirable possession.

The Type 356A Carrera coupe for 1956

THE FIRST CARRERA: THE ULTIMATE TYPE 356

One of the more diffident critics of the early Type 356 was John Bentley, who owned six of them during the early Fifties. After spinning the sixth, in an airport race at 90 mph, Bentley vowed never to buy another: "They are front-end happy; they oversteer like mad; they are temperamental beasts—absolutely unbeatable when conditions are perfect, but morose and stubborn when temperature, barometric pressure, humidity or a combination of these three is not exactly to their liking."

In 1955, Bentley paid a visit to Zuffenhausen on behalf of *Foreign Cars Illustrated* magazine, and casually remarked to Spyder engine designer Dr. Ernst Fuhrmann, "Why don't you put that engine into a coupe? It would make quite a package." Fuhrmann astonished the journalist by replying, "Would you care to try the pilot car?" This turned out to be a gray coupe often used as a test bed by Ferry Porsche himself. Under the rear engine lid was Fuhrmann's lovely four-cam powerplant from the Type 550 Spyder. It was the first Carrera.

That first ride—and the Carrera Speedster he later bought—convinced Bentley anew that there was nothing to top a Porsche. The idea of slotting the Spyder's Type 547 engine into the 356 bodyshell was a natural, of course. They mated as if they were designed for each other—which, in a sense, they were.

The model name came from the *Carrera Panamericana,* the romantic Mexican Road Race where Porsche had distinguished itself in 1953-54. Factory nomenclature for the first version was 1500GS, the "G" signifying "Grand Touring." Few would argue that the standard line of 356s already provided plenty of that, but the Carrera was a cut above even this norm. There were few differences between the Carrera's powerplant, designated Type 547/1, and the engine fitted to the racing Spyders. Compression was initially lowered from the Spyder's 9.5:1 to

8.7:1, but was soon raised to 9.0:1, and the Carrera's distributor drive was placed at the opposite end of the inlet camshaft compared to that of the Spyder for easier accessibility in the 356 body. Power was rated at an even 100 DIN (115 bhp SAE) at 6200 rpm, but the four-cam unit was a well-known revver, so 7000-7500 rpm was attainable without serious concern.

A few minor changes were made to the 356 package for the Carrera, notably wider tires (5.90s), an 8000-rpm tachometer, and a 180-mph/250-kph speedometer. The typical specimen weighed about 100 pounds more than the corresponding pushrod model, due to the heavier engine. Dr. Fuhrmann summed up the Carrera succinctly as "a detuned version [of the Spyder] providing extra performance for high speed, Gran Turismo competition, with more power than the pushrod engine could produce."

Bentley recorded the 0-60 mph dash in under nine seconds and reached 100 mph in under 20 seconds with the gray prototype, but he admitted that the extra weight—most of it out back—created handling even more squirrely than that of his 356 slalom coupe. However, the production Carrera appeared with Type 356A specifications, which meant the improved suspension geometry mentioned earlier in Chapter 5.

The Carrera didn't come cheaply: $5995 in the United States. Alternately, you could take delivery in Stuttgart, drive the car while over there, then ship it home as a used car. This would save you about $1700, which would more than pay for the accompanying vacation in those days.

In mid-1957, Porsche produced a deluxe version of the Carrera, which meant mainly a heater that really heated instead of one that

At a glance, the Carrera version was difficult to pick out from a standard type 356, but there was no mistaking the difference once you put your foot down. These contemporary photos depict the 1956 356A coupe.

blew merely tepid air at your feet. At the same time a no-extra-cost GT option was announced, with an extra 10 bhp (and a higher 6500-rpm power peak), a 21- instead of 14-gallon fuel tank, Spyder front brakes with 128 square inches of lining area instead of 115, and Spyder worm-gear steering. The result was primarily a competition car, available in coupe or Speedster body types. Shorn of excess weight, it lacked the road cars' heater and undercoating; by 1958 it had acquired aluminum doors, hood, and engine lid and lighter bucket seats. Thus, a GT coupe weighed about 150 pounds less than a standard Carrera coupe, a GT Speedster about 100 pounds less than its roadgoing counterpart. It was one of the latter that John Bentley bought and tested in 1958, having had his mind changed. Not surprisingly, he specified a metallic silver-gray car like the prototype that had introduced him to Carrera motoring. Bentley's car had the latest running additions: new crankshaft distributor drive, a ram-type air intake (via engine lid louvers), built-in rollbar posts and Fren-do competition brake linings. He was too early for the Koni adjustable shock absorbers that were later made standard, but he installed a set post-purchase. His report is enough to stir your blood:

"Low gear [with the standard 5.17:1 U.S. final drive ratio] is a shade too low; but in second gear the GT leaps forward with a wild, exhilarating surge...The muffler is noisy, but that noise is music of a delightful kind. As the tach needle leaps to 5200 rpm and peak torque, the car seems to grab hold and a terrific surge of power becomes available. The savage bark of the exhaust levels off to a high-pitched snarl, and before you know it the tach is indicating 7500 rpm."

Another Carrera Speedster GT registered similar impressions on Jesse Alexander, who wrote in *Sports Cars Illustrated* magazine: "...the engine smooths out at about 4200, right where a pushrod Porsche would be getting rather wound up. At 5000 rpm... things start to happen, and from there on you've got that feeling of being pushed in the small of the back. The acceleration is accompanied by the most unholy snarl of power you ever heard...a shattering blast of sound that sends chills up the spine of the uninitiated. The range of speeds in the gears is amazing, 40 mph in first, 70 in second and 100 in third."

Everything hung on to the always-improving 356 worked beautifully on the Carrera. The all-synchro gearbox shifted like a knife through butter; the brakes were totally fadeproof and required only light pressure; the bucket seats, more rudimentary on the GT, provided plenty of support. The handling was, in Bentley's opinion, beyond criticism: "With 26 lbs in the front and 27 in the rear [tires] you can break the tail loose in the secure knowledge that the machine will respond to correction in the normal manner. There is no danger that the slide will become an uncontrollable spin, as in former years."

Most testers noted one serious Carrera failing: plug fouling. A week of around-town work was usually all it took to gum up the plugs completely, and changing them, Bentley said, required "the dexterity of a trained octopus and the tenacity of a leech."

But, all in all, almost everybody agreed that the Carrera in any form was one helluva car. "What an enthusiast's dream," Bentley summed up. "It is in a class by itself." (And now, *Motor Trend*, where did you lay that fuelie Corvette?)

As we bask in the memory of those great early Carreras, let us not forget that, in America, they were more often than not like fish out of water. A car that really didn't begin to come alive below 4000 rpm, that fouled its plugs after a few trips to the supermarket, was really in its element only on unlimited-speed highways like the German *autobahnen*—or on the race track. Since the Carrera was meant to sell as well as race, Porsche prescribed changes, developed under the firm's technical manager, Klaus von Rücker. He was responsible for the new distributor drive in Bentley's car. He also exchanged the Hirth roller-bearing crank for a plain-bearing version made by Alfing, and compensated for the

resultant higher oil temperatures by mounting twin oil radiators behind the tiny horn grilles. In this form the revised 1500 Carrera engine was designated Type 692/1; a roller-bearing version, Type 692/0, was used in competition. Von Rücker also designed in room for a bore increase, and the Type 692/2 Carrera unit duly arrived in 1958 with 1588cc (87.5 × 66.0mm) and 105 DIN horsepower (120 SAE). The GT version of this engine was Type 692/3, which had 9.8:1 compression, Weber 40DCM2 carburetors, free-flow muffler, and 12-volt ignition. It developed 115 bhp (141 SAE). This output, incidentally, represented over 1.4 horsepower per cubic inch. Consider that, at the same time, Chevrolet was pronouncing one horsepower per cubic inch from its fuel-injected 283 V-8 a new high in automotive engineering.

Even with these changes the Carrera did not prove as potent in the showroom as it did on the road. Sales from its introduction through December 31, 1959 totaled only 700, far below the factory's expectations. The problem seemed to be that the basic Porsche was a highly tuned beast already—nobody denied that—and rendering it yet more esoteric, which the Carrera undeniably was, only served to limit the car's appeal. Most monied clients able to part with the approximate $6000 it took to buy one, aside from the few who raced, were really not cut out for a Carrera. They lugged them around town, avoided using the gears, failed to exercise them when the (rare) opportunity

Below: The 2.0-liter Carrera 2 from 1962, based on the Type 356B platform. Four-wheel disc brakes were new for a Porsche road car.

permitted. Not surprisingly, many went back to the dealership unhappy with their cars' performance—about as unhappy, if they had feelings, as the Carreras must have been with them. No, it was much more rational to buy a pushrod model if you lived in America and didn't race. "There was really not much point in preferring the more sophisticated engine and its exacting demands on maintenance unless the superior performance in the upper speed range could be exploited." wrote Hansjoerg Bendel. "The pushrod units were cheaper to buy and to run, less noisy and, in daily use, just as fast."

Porsche recognized this situation, and during 1960-1961 restricted U.S. Carrera sales to GT models with the 692/3 engine. This unit evolved in 1961 to the Type 692/3A, a freer-revving unit with larger main-bearing journals, stronger con rods and a redesigned cam. The company also busied itself with new competitive derivations like the GTL Abarth-Carrera.

Meanwhile, plans were laid for one more series of street Carreras in the Type 356B series. These debuted at Frankfurt in late '61 as 1962 models: a new 1600GS, with a 110-bhp (DIN) version of the 1582cc engine, and the 2000GS, destined to be the most popular of its breed and better known as the Carrera 2. The latter featured new four-wheel disc brakes (by Dunlop), and both models had all the contemporary body mods except the Detroit-style bumper-guard exhaust outlets (there was an extra panel below the rear bumper that provided some exhaust pipe protection). The Carrera 2's big attraction was the engine, designated Type 587. An evolution/expansion of the Type 547 unit, it was decidedly oversquare at 92×74mm, displacing 1966cc and developing 130 DIN horsepower at 6200 rpm. In U.S. parlance, this translated into 152 SAE horsepower, close to 1.3 bhp per cubic inch. Peak torque was an impressive 131 pounds-feet at 4600 rpm and the torque curve was long and flat. Applying lessons learned in the marketplace, the Carrera 2 used plain rather than roller bearings and came with slightly shorter ratios in the top two gears for lazy Americans:

Above: The rare and highly desirable Type 356A Carrera Speedster.

gear ratios

	European	**American**
1st	3.090:1	3.090:1
2nd	1.765	1.765
3rd	1.130	1.227
4th	0.852	0.885

Above: Another view of the 356B Carrera 2. Again, differences from lesser Porsches were subtle, but note twin under-bumper exhaust tips.

This was not a major adjustment —few Porsche modifications ever seem to be more than incremental —but it had a desirable effect. The American Carrera 2 had that fraction of extra power that made the difference between lugging and pulling away at proper rpm. For this reason, and through its innate civility, it proved to be the most popular Carrera yet.

Civility—that was the key. Hansjoerg Bendel commented on the "notable innovation" of a combination fresh-air intake and heater fan (via the gasoline heater option), the comfortable Reutter seats, the quick gearchange and, above all, the unmistakable feel of a quality car built for the connoisseur. He also noted some chassis improvements: "The steering gave improved response with reduced vibration, the car seemed to stick better to the road and stay stuck during full hard acceleration, and the disc brakes, added late to the Carrera 2 specification, were more than adequate.

"The car's acceleration is exhilarating," said Bendel. "The clutch takes quite a bit of throttle without protest and when one finds that it is time for 2nd gear, down comes the stick in a flick, more acceleration, and other cars pass by as if in reverse. High up in the speed range, this is it—the effortless superiority of the true high-performance machine."

As for criticisms, Bendel had few. He thought the car was still too noisy inside—and for a luxury GT priced at $7595 it probably was—and that the engine had a "certain roughness well remembered from older Carreras." Also, and more telling perhaps, was the now almost 20-year-old basic design in the context of 1962: "Even the accustomed eye begins to notice some signs of age. The instrument panel, for example, is higher up than is usual nowadays, and visibility could only benefit from a lower waistline."

Bendel should have been more patient. The 911 was on its way.

TYPE 911/912 1964–66: GRANDER TOURING

Below: The immensely strong Type 901-series bodyshell.
Opposite page: Dr. Ferry Porsche and the 911 in 1968.

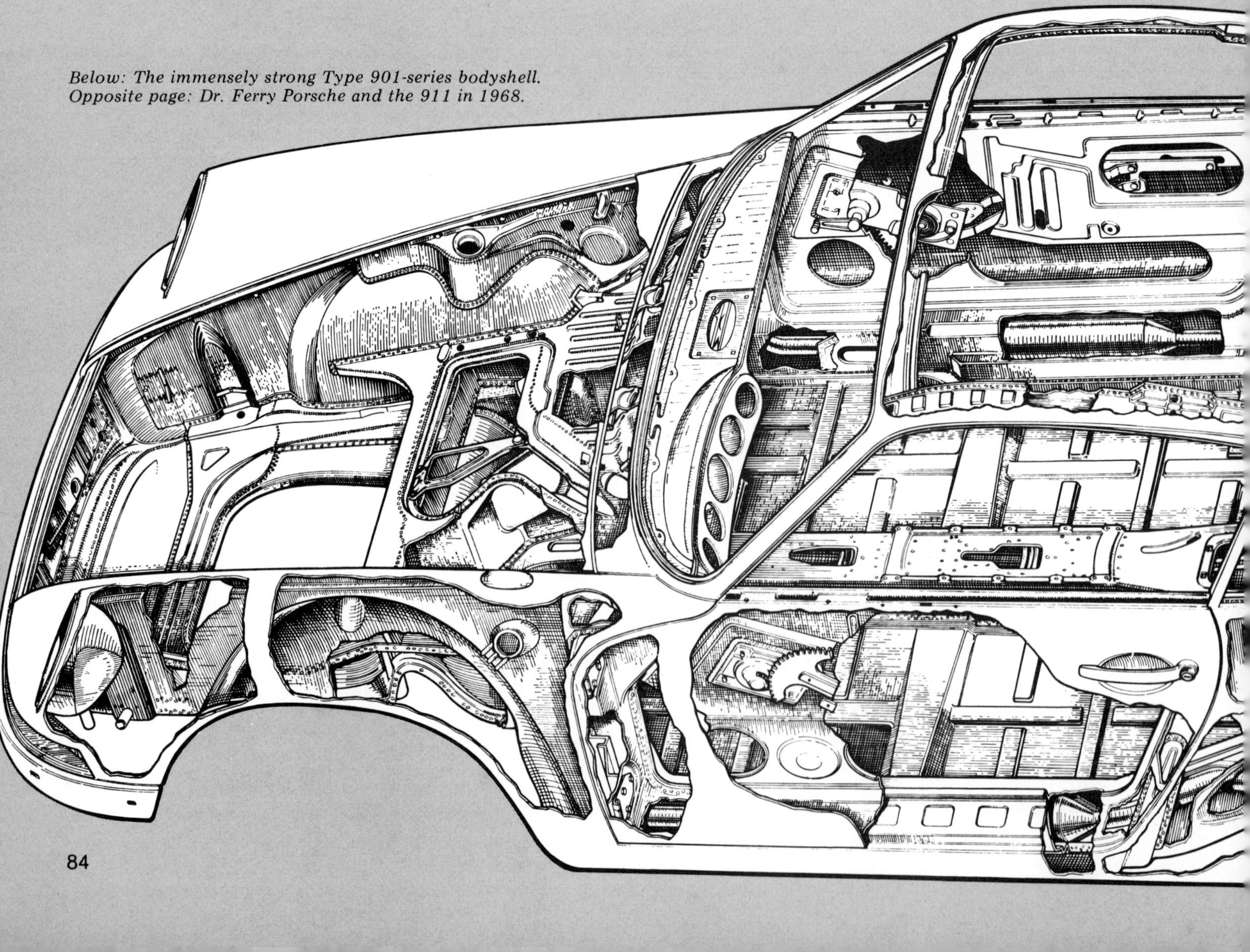

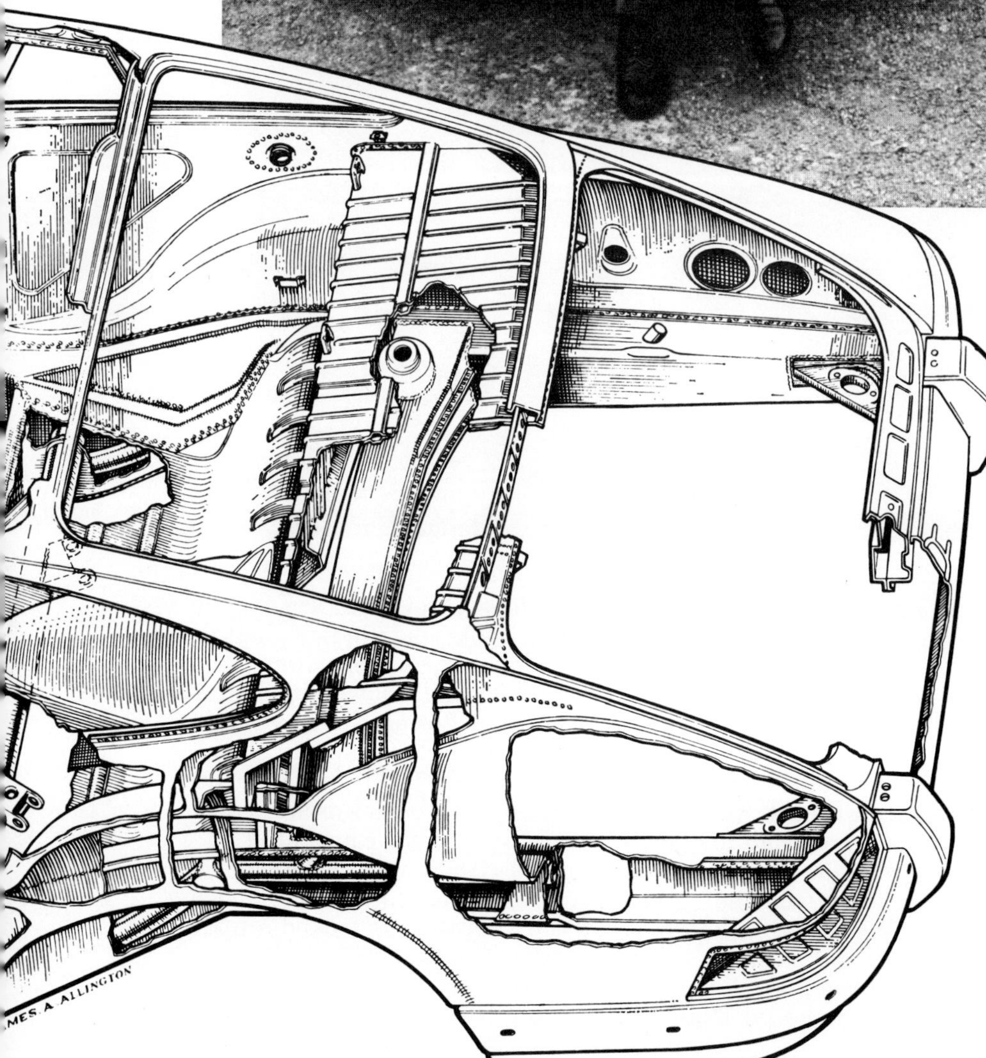

In late 1965, Denis Jenkinson, long-time contributor to Britain's *MotorSport* magazine, was asked by editor William Boddy to sample the new Porsche Type 911 and tell readers if it was any good or not. "Jenks" was highly qualified for this assignment. Not only was he the veteran of a quarter million Porsche miles, he had never been one to mince words, even at the expense of *MotorSport's* advertising revenue. Jenkinson's would be the acid test of the new car in Britain, and against his words a fair proportion of UK sales would be weighed.

His report was published in February 1966. "Jenks" surprised a lot of people with his assessment—including, probably, himself: "...it is the best car Porsche have yet built for normal road use," he wrote. And, "this is one of the best cars I have ever driven." We might add that there are Porschephiles today who would still agree with that, the 944 and 928 notwithstanding.

Why was the 911 so good? Mainly because it preserved the essence of earlier Porsches while setting an entirely new and higher standard of engineering and design excellence. Its shape was completely new, recognizeably Porsche yet sleek and modern—as it remains to this day. General Motors styling head Bill Mitchell once said the Type 356 looked like a loaf of bread. While not inclined to such an extreme view, a good many respectable critics would agree that, lovable though it was, the 356 was hardly beautiful. But the 911 *was*. It remains a stunning design, arguably one of the most handsome sports/GT road cars in history.

Mechanically, the 911 was a clean break in several ways. It was the first production Porsche to drop the swing-axle rear suspension and trailing-arm front suspension, though it retained the 356's torsion bars for springing. It was the first production Porsche with six cylinders, though the engine

This page: A scale model for a proposed notchback version of the Type 901 body (left), probably a prelude to the Targa convertible that Butzi Porsche wanted to have distinct rear-end sheetmetal. The vehicle under the shroud (below) remains a mystery is this 1968 peek into the Porsche design studio. Opposite page: 1968 was the last year for the original 87.0-inch wheelbase. Shown is that year's 911L, which replaced the S in the U.S. market.

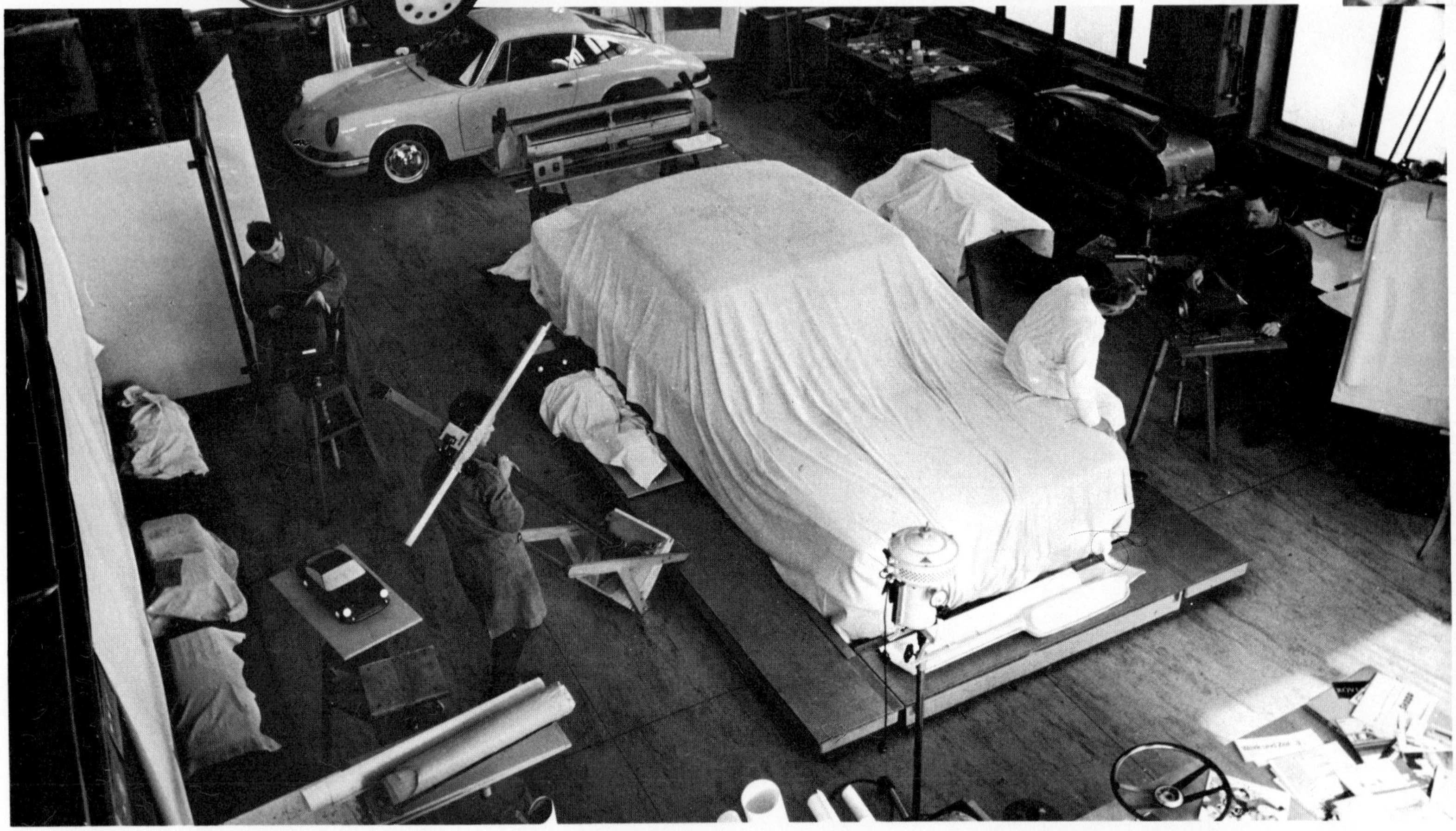

remained a horizontally opposed aircooled unit mounted at the rear, as per 356 practice, behind the rear axle centerline. Unlike the 356, however, it was supported at both ends—by the transaxle unit in front and a transverse mount in the back. Like previous Porsches the 911 had all-synchromesh transmission with an overdrive top gear, but now there were five ratios instead of four, providing greater flexibility than ever before.

The 911 had its origins in Type 695, the project that also produced Porsche's disc brakes. Its body, designed under Butzi Porsche's direction, was given the factory code designation T-7 (T-6 was the final development of the Type 356 that had appeared back in 1961). Butzi's assignment (from his father, who was not a body designer but knew what he wanted) was 2+2 seating, more cargo capacity, and a family resemblance to the 356. Without greatly extending the familiar wheelbase, Butzi did a remarkable job in blowing out the interior to 2+2 proportions. The Type 695 had a low beltline, lots of glass including a huge wrapped backlight, and a severely sloped front "hood." The front fenderline remained high and prominent, something Butzi considered a Porsche trademark. Because of its comparatively large greenhouse the 695 prototype looked a little unorthodox, but it was distinctively Porsche and its styling from the cowl forward

survived in the production 911 almost intact. Eventually, the 695 was redesignated Type 901. With smoother rear styling and ovoid rear side windows, both of which complimented the fastback roof treatment, it was displayed at the Frankfurt Automobile Show in the autumn of 1963.

It is widely believed that Porsche neatly arrived at its 901st project number in time to coincide with the appearance of the all-new road car. In fact, this isn't how it worked. Over the years, the factory has not been consistent or absolutely sequential in its numbering system, and quite a few numbers have been skipped. (Ferdinand Porsche's first was Type 7—he didn't want anybody to think he was just starting out.) The number 901 *was* chosen to suggest a fresh start and a new direction, but that's all there was to it. Ultimately 901 become 911 because of protests from Peugeot, which had been using three-digit numbers with middle zeros on a number of cars and promised to prevent Porsche from selling the 901 in France unless the number were changed. (Peugeot seems to have caused its share of problems for Porsche and the Porsche family over the years.) But Zuffenhausen had a last word of sorts by giving a half-dozen competition models middle-zero numbers, as in the case of the beautiful 904 GTS.

On the 901/911, a rear seat was retained as on the 356, though the seatbacks were individually hinged for greater cargo/passenger carrying versatility. Despite the production car's more streamlined rear compared to that of the Type 695 prototype, there was still room for an adult or two children to sit in back.

Porsche told everyone at Frankfurt that the new car was being shown a year early; production would not begin sooner than the summer of 1964. John Bond of *Road & Track* magazine reported: "there were so many rumors circulating that they were forced to show it."

However, that first chrome-yellow Type 901, Bond reported, was "not as much different from the 356 as appears in the photos; seen side by side the actual contours are almost the same. The big difference is elimination of the broad-beam hip effect that results in a trimmer, narrower look and a roof line that, in plan view, no longer tucks in at the rear. The net result of these appearance changes is a car 2.7-in. narrower, overall, and more head, shoulder and leg room for rear seat passengers." The 901 wheelbase was 86.8 inches, up 4.1 inches from the 356C, but Bond was glad Porsche did not call it a four-passenger model.

As mentioned, the 911's suspension was a complete departure for a Porsche. At the front were MacPherson struts—something new at the time—and wishbones connected to longitudinal torsion bars; rear suspension comprised transverse torsion bars and semi-trailing arms. "On all swing-axle Porsches, in spite of a very high degree of taming, the 'animal oversteer' could still be sensed," *Road & Track* would write later. "On the 911, the beast is out, and the car is neutral in behavior and perfectly controllable throughout the whole speed range and even on atrocious road surfaces. True, the suspension is on the firm (not to say harsh) side, but for a high-performance car like this, it appears a small price to pay for the ability to drive the car with an abandon and enjoyment that many other top class cars would not accept from any but the most wary, experienced pilots."

Another change on the 911 was steering, now ZF rack-and-pinion instead of the old VW-based worm gear mechanism. Thus vanished one of the last remnants of the original Porsche/VW kinship. The steering was light, shock-free (thanks, as usual, to provision of a hydraulic shock absorber in the linkage) and had plenty of surface feel. Incidentally, Porsche had taken pains to supply a really competent heating system. Now, air was taken from the cooling fan through a heat box and rammed into the cockpit via heater and defroster outlets. An option was a gasoline heater with an electric fan that forced more air into the heating boxes, though once the car was warmed up and moving the fan was rarely necessary. Porsche had also improved interior air flow by adding extractor vents above the backlight.

The pace of Porsche production didn't change much despite the 911/912's sales success. Compare these mid-'60s views with the early-'50s photos of the 356 assembly line on pp. 42-43.

The heart of the 911 was, of course, its new sohc 2.0-liter flat-six, with one camshaft per cylinder bank driven by a pair of double roller chains rather than the complicated multiple bevel gears of the four-cam flat-fours. The reasons for this change were explained by John Bond: "In an air-cooled engine it is very difficult to maintain constant valve-tappet clearances (cold to hot) with pushrods. Hydraulic valve lifters offer a solution but they are expensive, often troublesome, and they "pump up" or cease to function at high speed. In addition the sohc and its enclosure give the designer more latitude in providing for air flow and cooling

fins in the most critical area. The camshaft enclosure also forms a natural barrier for directing cooling air without the need for awkward sheet metal baffles to do it."

The 911's six-throw crankshaft had no fewer than eight main bearings. A countershaft was mounted underneath to carry impulses to twin chain sprockets at its rear end, each sprocket driving a camshaft. Ahead of the countershaft were two oil pumps, a large scavenger circulating oil from the dry sump to the tank and back and a smaller unit maintaining lubrication pressure. An oil cooler was fitted, and Porsche instructed that oil temperature should never rise above 130°. No tester ever recalled that it did.

Bond compared the 911's new powerplant to one of his domestic favorites, the Corvair flat-six, but the moderately tuned 110-bhp version really looked anemic against the Porsche engine. The Corvair Corsa's 180-bhp turbocharged unit, top of the line, is more directly comparable:

	Corsa	**911**
displacement (ci)	164.0	121.5
compression ratio	8.0:1	9.0:1
bhp (SAE)	180 @ 4000	150 @ 6200
torque (SAE)	232 @ 3200	119 @ 4600
bhp per ci	1.098	1.235
torque per ci	0.976	0.983
frontal area (sq ft)	19.6	18.2
top speed, mph (approx)	115	125

These figures suggest that the 911 was still a Porsche in that it was designed to give its best performance at relatively high rpm. By contrast, the Corsa showed excellent torque that peaked some 1400 rpm below that of the 911—"an obvious difference of opinion," wrote Bond, "if not basic design philosophy."

As was the case with every evolution of the 356 before it, the 911 received a somewhat mixed reception from confirmed Porsche fans, most of whom later grew to accept it—and inevitably to respect it. It would prove to be the most popular Porsche in history—a title it still holds despite the advent of the front-engine cars. One of those transformed from doubter to believer was Denis Jenkinson in his test for *MotorSport.*

Jenks termed his first acquaintance with the 911 "a little disappointing." Behind the wheel, one faced a dashboard that seemed relatively bland compared with the by-then almost classic 356 control board. On top was a molded full-width crash pad. Ahead of the steering wheel was an oblong binnacle housing five circular gauges. The largest was the tachometer (*not* the speedometer), mounted dead center, flanked on the left by combination dials for oil and fuel levels and oil pressure and temperature, and on the right by the speedometer and an electric clock. Below the cluster was a panel with teakwood trim containing various minor knobs and switches. There were the usual shapely bucket seats with adjustable backrests. Overall, though, the 911 cockpit left Jenkinson unmoved: "Driving quietly away this lack of character was even more noticeable, so that seasoned Porsche owners commented that it was all right, but hardly a Porsche, and in fact it could have been almost any sort of reasonable GT car."

Once he was familiar with the car, however, his impressions changed dramatically: "Out into the open country the whole car immediately became alive and was unmistakably a Porsche in all the true traditions of the Stuttgart firm. The more I drove it and the harder I made it work the more Porsche-like it became, so that by the end of the week I had no doubts at all that this was a car from the brains of Dr. Porsche and his men, and could not possibly have come from anywhere else." One attribute solidifying his impression was the traditional, all-of-a-piece Porsche feel to the body regardless of road surface or speed: "The whole car has a feeling that it is indestructible [and this is] coupled with suspension, ride, road-holding, steering, braking and general good manners that are truly modern, and the nearest

to perfection that production cars have yet reached...Why don't all manufacturers make cars like this? It can't be so difficult."

Porsche's biggest problem with the 911 was adequate supply, because demand for it was strong from the outset. In mid-1963 the company bought Reutter, which assured better quality control but did nothing to increase production capacity. In the end, Porsche contracted with Karmann to supply 911 bodies, a move that effectively forced the 356C to be phased out. (356 production ended in September 1965, by which time the model was being built only for the American market.)

But there would still be a four-cylinder car in the lineup. This new model was designated Type 912 although, as with the 911 on which it was based, the number was originally ten digits below that in actual order. Porsche "officially" introduced both cars at the same time, in late 1964, one works representative stating that he was afraid new car announcements were becoming a habit at Zuffenhausen—"We only had one 15 years before." U.S. 911 deliveries began in early 1965, but the first 912s weren't delivered until June of that year.

The four-cylinder 912 (1968 coupe opposite page, 1969 Targa below) initially outsold the pricier, faster 911. Painted dash (left) was discarded after the first 150 or so 912s built.

The 912 engine was a detuned version of the 1600SC unit from the last of the 356 series, developing 102 bhp (DIN) at 5800 rpm. On paper the 912's performance shouldn't have been as exhilarating as the SC's, because the new bodyshell was heavier and curb weight was about 100 pounds higher. But the 912 was offered with the 911's five-speed gearbox as a $75 option, and it had better aerodynamics than the 356C. Thus, the 912 actually had a higher top speed than the old Super 90. Its typical 0-60 mph acceleration time was 11.5 to 12 seconds, and it could run the quarter-mile in a shade over 18 seconds at about 77 mph from a standing start. Top speed was approximately 120 mph, though the factory's official quote was a conservative, as usual, 116 mph. Predictably, the 912 was much

thriftier than the 911: 25 mpg was the overall average.

"This isn't a car in which one can amble around town in high gear with abandon," *Road & Track* reported. "It's necessary to make full use of the five speeds, and there seem to always be more wrong gears than right ones." They were objecting partly to the five-speed's shift pattern, which put second *above* third in the central plane and first on the dogleg down and to the left, race-car style, instead of in the normal H-pattern arrangement. It was possible, *Autocar* found, to go from first to fourth (instead of second) on the upshift. But once one got used to it, the process became "subconscious." On the other hand, as *Road & Track* said, the 912 engine "runs without fuss at low speeds and idles smoothly at 1000 rpm, but it's anything but quiet. It never sounds overworked, mind you, but it seems that all the clatter comes right through the bulkhead." Neither the 912 nor the 911 were particularly quiet inside.

Aside from its lower acceleration and top speed, the 912 was quite similar to the 911 in most other areas of performance. In both, brakes were strong and well-nigh fade-free; the new steering was light and transmitted little road shock; the German Dunlop SP radials worked perfectly with the suspension to provide strong cornering power. There were some specification changes for the 912 in keeping with its lower price (under $4700 POE). For example, the 911's teakwood lower dash appliqué was eliminated, as were the clock and oil temp/pressure dial. The 912's rev counter was front and center, as in the 911, but it was accompanied only by a speedometer and the combination temperature and fuel level gauge. Warning lights monitored

A trio of early Targa convertibles. Car on opposite page is a U.S. model despite its German markings. Removable rear window gave way to a fixed glass backlight on U.S. Targa after 1968.

everything else.

At the 1965 Frankfurt exhibition Porsche showed a prototype for a second 901-series body style with built-in rollbar, which became the well-loved Targa cabriolet. Available in both 911 and 912 versions, it was introduced for export markets in 1967. Butzi Porsche had objected to retaining the coupe's rear sheetmetal on this model, saying that a conventional "trunked" style was the only proper one for a cabriolet. But the company envisioned much lower sales for the Targa, which made shared rear bodywork mandatory. The good side to this economy measure was that it inspired Butzi to design in the strong, functional rollbar. Initially, the Targa had a zip-out plastic rear window and a removable folding roof panel made of rubberized fabric. The rollbar itself was finished in brushed stainless steel, sort of a throwback to the GM exercises of Harley Earl in the '50s. Butzi said he chose this material to emphasize the functionality of the rollbar.

As things turned out, the public wanted Targas in far greater numbers than Porsche had anticipated, and their initial share of only 12.7 percent of production proved inadequate. It was also found that the 912 models, perhaps not surprisingly in view of the 911's price, sold much better. Of nearly 13,000 cars built in 1966, over 9000 were the four-cylinder sort. But these were problems of success, which everyone at Porsche was happy to endure. The 911 and 912 were solid hits. It hadn't been easy following a legend, but Porsche succeeded.

TYPE 911 1967-73: ALPHABET SOUP

The 1969 Type 911S (left) and T (right) in home-market form

With the advent of three 911s for the 1968 model year, changes in Porsche model designations became increasingly difficult to follow—if not for the Porschephile then surely for the layman. Actually, the year-to-year revisions weren't all that complicated and, being Porsche, were made in a perfectly logical fashion. A chronological unraveling is the best way to examine these developments of Butzi Porsche's T-7 body through 1973.

The first offshoot of the original 911 was the 911S, announced for the 1967 model year with a base price of just over $7000. That made it the most expensive Porsche in history, though far more astronomical prices were coming. With the 911S, Porsche effectively reestablished the three-tier lineup of earlier years. The logical building blocks of 356 Normal, Super, and Super 90 were now the 912, the 911, and the 911S. To make room for the S, Porsche detrimmed the normal 911 to 912 standards (except for instrumentation, carpeting, and insulation) and cut base price by about $320, thus neatly splitting the difference between the $4700 912 and the $7074 911S.

The 911S was a hot car, thanks to changes in carburetion, compression ratio, and valve timing. The CR was raised from 9.0 to 9.8:1 and the Weber carbs, while essentially no different from those adopted for the normal 911 in early 1966, had larger jets. Although the S packed more horsepower (160 DIN compared to 130 on the 911), the big change was in torque, which peaked much higher (5200 vs. 4300 rpm). As on other models, there was no choke, but pumping the accelerator was usually sufficient for starting—and also helped cause chronic plug fouling, which proved a problem.

Make no mistake, the 911S was a free-revving, tremendously potent car. The slightest blip of the throttle was enough to send the tacho needle scurrying to its 7300-rpm redline. Recognizing this propensity, Porsche installed an ignition cutout on the rotor arm, which effectively shut everything down if you approached the limit, this protecting the valve gear from the overly enthusiastic.

The only other mechanical change of importance for the S involved the brakes, which had

Top: The 1969 U.S. 911S storms down a back-country road. Above: The fully instrumented 911S facia. Basic layout remains on the current 911SC.

ventilated rather than solid rotors for better fade resistance. *Road & Track* magazine reported that pedal effort rose only 20 percent, from 35 to 42 pounds, in a six-stop fade test.

Two definite steps in the torque curve were apparent. "The catalogue peak comes at 5200 rpm," noted Britain's *Autocar* magazine, "but before that, at about 3000, the engine takes a deep breath and literally surges up to the next step, where the extra punch feels like an additional pair of cylinders being switched in. This kick in the back leaves passengers unaccustomed to it slightly winded, and it is sudden enough to cause momentary wheelspin on wet surfaces, even in third." Ratios were evenly spaced except for the overdrive fifth, which was purposely very high. In that gear you got a 100-mph lope for only 4500 rpm—hardly a strain for the highly tuned 2.0-liter six. Pulling max revs in the lower gears produced 0-60 mph in eight seconds and quarter-mile times under 16 seconds at close to 90 mph — real drag racer stuff. The top speed was about 140 mph. This power was coupled to fine handling, for which the 911 was already well known, and that feeling, found in only a few cars, that you could easily drive right up the side of a mountain.

The most impressive part of the 911S had to be its beautifully smooth, fantastically willing engine. But *Autocar* approved "the superb lightness of all the controls which, together with excellent seating, immediately put the driver at one with the car and enabled him to go out and enjoy its character to the full. The Porsche 911S is a car one never likes to leave parked when one could be driving it somewhere."

Across the Atlantic, the staff at *Road & Track* was more critical—or perhaps more practical—when it warned that for American conditions, the 911S "offers no real gain over the 911 and perhaps even a slight loss. It is a bit less flexible at ordinary speeds; deceleration below about 1800 rpm brings on bucking and considerable clatter from the drivetrain, demanding an immediate downshift."

Came 1968 and the 911S, so recently introduced, vanished from the States as suddenly as it had appeared. Ostensibly, the reason was U.S. emission controls, but some sources say it was the plug fouling, which had proven a tremendous service problem. The 911S would return to the U.S. a year later (it continued in Europe). Meantime, its place was left open, while the 911L replaced the standard 911 just after the model year began. The L (for *Luxus*, luxury) was essentially the same car as the S except that it used the normal-tune engine. It was an upmarket move for Porsche, because it sold for $600 more than the previous year's base 911. Some of this had gone into modifications for meeting new federal safety and emissions

continued on page 113

1973 Type 911T Targa (with S equipment option)

Above: This 1970 Type 911T coupe wears S-style alloy wheels. Opposite page, top: The 1970 911S. Bottom: It may look odd, but 911 police cars like this actually patrol Germany's autobahnen.

107
POLIZEI
POLIZEI

CALIFORNIA
1AYX821

PORSCHE
CALIFORNIA
ELO BIRD
WGH 140

The timeless 911, represented here by three examples spanning nearly a decade. The red car is a '68 American-market Targa with L specification. It's flanked by a brown '71 911T coupe and a '76 S Targa (with non-standard antenna).

CALIFORNIA
1AYX821

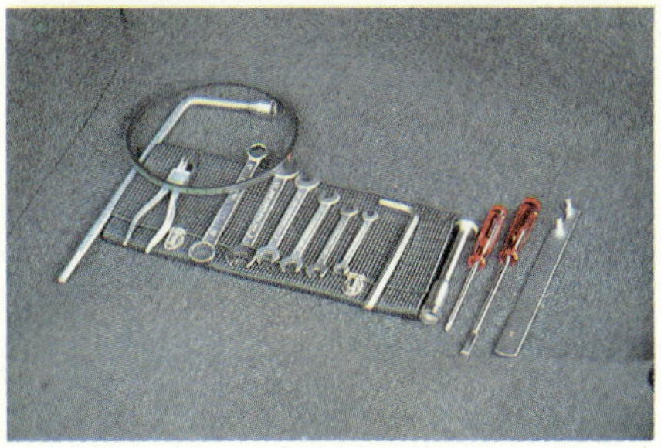

Few outward changes were made to the 911 in its early years. Perhaps the biggest difference between the 1968 L Targa (top both pages) and the '71 T coupe is the latter's longer wheelbase, though even this isn't immediately discernible. Early Targas had a zip-out fabric rear window, later supplanted by fixed glass with a standard electric defroster.

Even if you couldn't afford a 911S, you could still get its basic appearance by specifying the optional "S" equipment package on the T or E models in the early '70s. This 1973 T-type Targa has it, as shown by the foglamps, S-style wheels, and front spoiler. A stroke increase for '72 brought displacement from 2195 cc (1970-71) to 2341cc, though Porsche generously rounded that off to 2.4 liters for the engine lid insignia.

targa

The fabled Carrera name returned to the Porsche lineup on this 1973 competition-only version of the 911. Powered by a 2.7-liter extension of the 911's flat six, this 200-bhp rocket could top 150 mph with ease. Officially named Carrera RS, it sported lightweight body panels, fiberglass bumpers, front and rear spoilers, and broader (7-inch-wide) rear wheels and tires. Note the molded front housing for the oil cooler. A roadgoing model without the RS designation was offered to U.S. buyers for the 1974 model year, and looked superficially similar to this hairy racer.

Carrera

Carrera
Carrera
RMS 132
South Carolina

The latest in the long line of "cooking" 911s, now designated the SC, appeared for 1978. Shown is that year's Targa. Like its coupe companion, it had an enlarged, 3.0-liter engine producing 172 bhp (SAE net), which was good for a top speed in excess of 136 mph. Despite this and a full load of standard luxury features, the SC was remarkably frugal, rated at no less than 27 mpg highway in U.S. government tests. Most exterior brightwork was changed to black finish for the SC, including the Targa model's functional rollbar. Standard equipment included larger, power-assisted brakes and more efficient CIS fuel injection.

CALIFORNIA
CAL BAND

BAND CAL

BAND CAL

Though it sold reasonably well, the original four-cylinder Type 914 was criticized for not being a true Porsche. To give its mid-engine two-seater more appeal, Porsche replaced the basic Volkswagen engine with the 911T's six-cylinder unit to create the 914/6. Shown is the initial 1970 version, which also had wider wheels and tires, larger brakes, and more standard equipment than lesser 914s. Unhappily, the 914/6 wasn't quite as fast as the 911T and cost only about $400 less, so it didn't generate many sales.

The 1980 edition of the 911SC Targa offers proof that great automotive design never grows old.

Above: an aristocratic setting for two Porsche thoroughbreds, the 1969 911T (left) and 911S. Right: The 1969 911T Targa with new fixed glass rear window.

continued from page 96

regulations — and more of the same would be seen in future years.

The fact is that all three models sold in the U.S. through 1968 had a few flaws. There was the plug fouling, which occurred even on the base 911, though with lesser severity. Also, the 911's original Solex carburetors had adjustment problems; Webers helped eliminate this, and Bosch cooperated by developing the WG 265 T2SP spark plug for the 911 six. And, fit and finish had not been up to 356 standards. Perhaps this was inevitable with a newly designed car, even a Porsche. After all, the 356 had been in production so long that its quality control had reached near perfection, and it was a difficult act to follow. Compared to rank and file sports cars, however, the 911 ranked very high for assembly quality. Finally, the 911L was given to rough running and backfiring on deceleration, mainly because its emission control was handled by pumping low-pressure air to the exhaust manifolds. This was a very makeshift method, especially for Porsche, and it wouldn't last.

On the outside all American-market '68 Porsches could be identified at a glance by their new side marker lights, again courtesy federal regulations. Why the factory didn't simply wrap the handsome parking/sidelights back around a little farther isn't known, unless perhaps it wouldn't have satisfied some minimum height requirement. In later years, this treatment was used.

Of special interest for 1968 was a most unexpected development, designated Project Type 905 by the factory. It was an automatic transmission called Sportomatic by Zuffenhausen. More precisely, it was a semi-automatic, with a torque converter, automatic clutch, and manually shifted four-speed gear selector. The torque converter and clutch were supplied by Fichtel and Sachs, while the selector was Porsche's own creation. As *Road & Track* described it, "the converter is a 'loose' one with a stall speed of

2600 rpm and stall torque ratio 2.15:1; its oil supply is in common with the engine's, adding 2.5 qt to that reservoir. The clutch is disengaged by a vacuum servo unit that gets its signal from a microswitch on the shift linkage; thus a touch on the shift lever disengages the clutch. The gearbox is the usual all-synchro 4-speed unit but with a parking pawl added." Gear ratios for Sportomatic differed considerably from those of Porsche's fully manual four-speed:

	Manual	**Sportomatic**
1st	3.09	2.40
2nd	1.68	1.63
3rd	1.12	1.22
4th	0.86	0.96
final drive	4.43	3.86

This meant that the Sportomatic-equipped 911L was commensurately slower in standing-start acceleration but almost as fast at the upper end, maximum converter efficiency being a very high 96.5 percent.

Learning to drive with this novel transmission, however, took a little practice. "For all normal acceleration from rest, D (2nd gear) is used," commented *Road & Track*. "The converter lets the engine run up to 2600 rpm immediately and... gets the car moving briskly, but noisily, if need be. A direct shift to 4th at some casual speed will be the usual upshift. For... vigorous driving the Sportomatic is just like the manual 4-speed except that one shifts without the clutch ...We found that the best technique was to engage 1st gear, let the clutch in (by taking the hand off the stick), 'jack up' the engine against the converter while holding the brakes, and release the brakes to start." Hardly the sort of treatment that promotes long transmission life, but *R&T* got 0-60 mph in 10.3 seconds by this method, and the quarter-mile time was a very good 17.3 seconds at 80 mph.

In effect, Sportomatic was a compromise solution to the perennial problem of Americans lugging their cars in high gear at low speeds, fouling the plugs and otherwise loading up the engines, all because drivers were loathe to use the gearbox. The 4200-rpm torque peak meant lots of shifting on a manual car, but with Sportomatic "it's possible to stay in 4th gear down to ridiculous speeds like 20 mph and still accelerate smartly away with traffic. The 911 engine likes revs, and the converter lets it rev." At the same time the converter made for extra engine noise in the lower rpm range compared with the standard transmission; *R&T* said it sounded "very much like a GM city bus." Yet, Sportomatic was a typically well-thought-out Porsche response to a perceived problem, and in practice it worked better than most journalists expected. It didn't hurt fuel mileage much, and its effect on performance was slight. Being able to disengage the clutch by the merest touch of the hand on the shift lever *was* disconcerting (one driver suggested Porsche put burrs on the lever, to be removed after 500 miles), but you got used to this after brief experience. All in all, it was a novel idea, if not the kind of thing that would appeal to Porsche drivers.

The apparent confusion in Porsche's passenger car line soon ended. By 1969, it was all sorted out, and a three-model 911 lineup returned. (The 912, to be replaced in 1970 by the "Volks-Porsche" Type 914, was carried on unchanged.) This new trio, which continued for the next five model years, was as follows:

911T—110 bhp at 5800 rpm, 8.6:1 CR, 110 mph official top speed. Base price (coupe): $5995.

911E—140 bhp at 6600 rpm, 9.0:1 CR, 134 mph official top speed. Base price (coupe): $7195.

911S—170 bhp at 6800 rpm, 9.8:1 CR, 140 mph official top speed. Base price (coupe): $7895. Of these three, only the 911T was carbureted; both the 911E and the

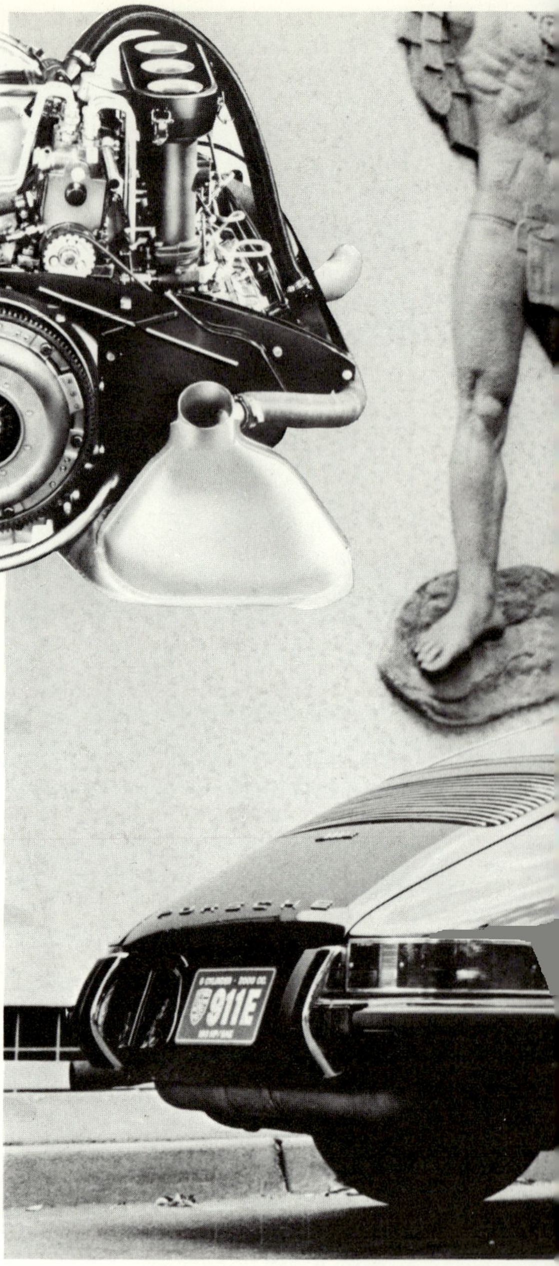

Opposite page: The heart of the 911, its remarkable aircooled flat six, shown here in inital U.S. fuel-injected form. This page: All 1969 U.S. 911s (T above, E left) sported a new 89.3-inch wheelbase, a wider track, and flared rear fenders.

reintroduced 911S utilized fuel injection, the intelligent answer to the emissions-control question.

The injection system, developed by Porsche and Bosch, was a mechanical unit similar to that of Mercedes, with a double-row, six-plunger pump that was belt-driven from the lefthand camshaft. Injection tubes carried mixture to the ports just below; the injection pump was fed by an electric fuel pump, and check valves in the injectors opened at set pressure from the plunger in the injector pump. The use of ram tubes and a rich fuel mixture improved power at higher rpm while reducing dirty exhaust emissions at lower rpm. Capacitive-discharge ignition on both models helped combat the long-running problem of spark plug fouling.

Horsepower was up on both E and S, thanks to tuning changes made possible by the switch to injection. The 911E now had the same cam profile as the original 911, which was thus wilder than on the 911L. The S had no camshaft changes, but did get slightly higher compression and reshaped inlet passages, along with an extra oil cooler to guarantee reliability at the higher power. Crankcases on all 911s were now made of magnesium rather than aluminum. This casting was supplied by Mahle of Stuttgart.

Bodily, the 1969 models could be distinguished by slightly flared wheel openings and, though not immediately detectable, a longer wheelbase: the rear wheels had been moved back about 2.25 inches. This was a key change as it improved weight distribution to 44/56 front to rear. Wheels and tires were wider, putting more rubber on the road and slightly increasing track.

All 911Es through 1971, the first few 911S models, and other models from 1969 as an option had Boge self-adjusting hydropneumatic front suspension struts. These ingenious devices maintained the front end at a specified height regardless of weight distribution and did away with springs, shocks, and sway bars. They required no engine-driven pump, like those of a Citroën, for example; instead they used the up-and-down

This page: Overhead view of 1969 Type 911T Targa (above) reveals well-appointed cockpit. Small "2.2" rear window sticker signalled larger engine for 1970 911s (T model shown right). Opposite page: Accessory mask (upper left) helped prevent stone damage to 911's nose. Appearance remained unaltered for the 1970 911T (above right) and 911S Targa (below).

motion of the suspension itself to keep the pump pressurized. On the 911E, the Boge struts were part of a Comfort Package, which was standard on all U.S. Es. It consisted of 14-inch wheels and tires, ventilated disc brakes with aluminum calipers, a "highway" horn, bumper rub strips, a bright metal trim piece for the rocker panels, gold script on the deck, velour carpeting, leather-covered steering wheel and gauges for oil pressure and oil tank level.

The improvement wrought through fuel injection and CD ignition was tremendous, just what the 911 had needed. It was now possible to do what was impossible before—lug the car down to 35 or 40 mph and accelerate away. Performance was almost equal to 1967 911S standards. The typical E ran to 130 mph and clocked quarter-mile times around 16 seconds, while averaging close to 20 mpg overall—and probably capable of it if driven carefully. Relocating the rear wheels shifted static weight about 1.5 percent toward the front, but this oversteer correction was balanced on strut-equipped cars by the lack of a front sway bar. Oversteer was still the 911's terminal handling trait, but it was never uncontrollable for a good driver. A new three-speed heater fan, flat-black wipers arms, and a heated rear window completed the 1969 refinements for the most tractable and pleasurable touring Porsche since the 356C—the archetypal 911, destined to remain a solid favorite for years to come.

Before we tell you more about the S, let us first explain that all 911s for 1970 were incrementally quicker than the 1969s. A bore increase of 4mm brought displacement to 2195cc (84×66) and commensurate increases in bhp and torque, while compression ratios remained the same:

911T: 125 bhp at 5500 rpm, 128

mph official top speed. Base price (coupe): $6430.

911E: 155 bhp at 6200 rpm, 137 mph official top speed. Base price (coupe): $7895.

911S: 180 bhp at 6800 rpm, 144 mph official top speed. Base price (coupe): $8675.

Porsche took advantage of the extra ccs to detune the 911S a bit. As a result, it ended up with only 4 more DIN horsepower than its 2.0-liter predecessor, but was more tractable and, of course, lower in emissions. "As impressive as the fact that it meets smog laws is the way the 911S runs," said one tester. "It idles smoothly at 800-1000 rpm and runs without any of the common symptoms of mixture leanness found in today's emission control high-output engines at moderate speeds."

Good though it was, the 911S remained too much car for U.S. speed limits and traffic conditions. It displayed "very little torque until about 4500 rpm, and one did not wisely use fifth gear under 50 mph... But going up through the gears to the redline brings out noises that will warm hearts even of those accustomed to exotic V-12s. Glorious noises!" The 911S was now in the same performance class with the big-engine Corvettes and Jaguars, even the Detroit muscle cars. But it was better built than all of them, and its concept was one of finesse rather than brute force. It was becoming frightfully expensive, however; rarely did one leave the showroom for less than $9000. Maybe this didn't matter to the people who bought them. As *Road & Track* quipped, it offered "performance on the order of an American Supercar, but without the stigma of low cost."

By comparison, the bottom-line 911T was still quite moderately priced, running only $6500 in 1970-71, a bargain in an exotic sports car. It did cost more than a Stingray or an E-Type, though it was $1000 below the Mercedes 280SL—and we imagine that the buyer likely to opt for a 911T would be more inclined to consider the Mercedes the main

PORSCHE

alternative rather than the Corvette or Jaguar. In any case, the T beat all three of these competitors in a comparison test conducted by *R&T* in 1969, recording the most "bests" and the least number of "worsts." Wrote the editors, "Perhaps the conclusion is too obvious to need saying," but they said it anyway: "We found the Porsche to have more that was good and less that was bad than the other cars in this comparison."

In the process of compiling this book we found ourselves moved by the same compelling magic that touched John Bentley and Denis Jenkinson before us. By the time we had researched the 356 series we were thinking about adding a Porsche to our stable. After recording the history of the 356C we were sure we should do so. And by the time we got to the 911 our only question was which Porsche it should be. For us, the answer would be the 911T, carburetors and all. They have the advantage of being more easily tinkered with than fuel injection by the home mechanic, and the car's performance is certainly more than adequate. The 911E has certain advantages, the 911S others, but we feel sure we would go to jail within six months of purchasing either of those. Which brings us to our own road test experience with a 1972 S, a tale with a definite lesson.

California, always leading the other 49 states in emission demands, passed a law requiring all new cars sold there for 1972 and beyond to operate on 91-octane gasoline. The answer to this, as far as most manufacturers were concerned, was simply lowering compression—and performance—while the Europeans began employing different pistons, heads and head gaskets for their American-market models. This marked the beginning of a disappointing era when European cars destined for these shores became disparagingly known as "Federal versions" and characterized by an ever-widening performance/fuel economy gap between them and their superior Continental counterparts.

Porsche's answer to the increasing stranglehold of emissions requirements was similar to that of most manufacturers: its 1972 models received both lower compression and higher displacement, 2341cc through an increase in stroke. But there was little if any loss in performance, which was fairly rare that year. The 911E lost its Boge hydropneumatic struts and no-cost five-speed gearbox option, but was 4 mph quicker than its predecessor. The 911S was slower, but only fractionally.

The figures on our flame-red

Opposite page: Another displacement boost brought engine size to 2.4 liters for 1972. Shown is that year's 911T. Below: The three-model U.S. lineup for 1973 (from left), S, T, and E.

This page: Since 1969, U.S. Targas had been equipped with a rigid lift-off roof panel, though a fold-up version continued as an option. Shown is the 1973 911E Targa. Opposite page: The 911 took on a new face for '74 to satisfy U.S. bumper regulations. Engine size was again increased, this time to 2.7 liters. Shown is the standard 911.

test 911S were remarkable for 1972. Our notes show 0-60 mph in 7.5 seconds, the quarter-mile in 15.8 seconds at 95 mph, and a corrected top speed (achieved on an arrow-straight deserted road in the New Jersey pine barrens) of 140 mph. Fuel mileage was as expected: 13.3 mpg. Our 1000-mile experience included a run over the hills and dales of the Pennsylvania back country between Hershey and Philadelphia, and we chose the most deserted secondaries to do unconscionable things with our Porsche.

Halfway between the suggestively named towns of Blue Ball and Intercourse, a winding back road branches off U.S. 322 to connect with the Pennsylvania Turnpike. Frustrated by large, slow-moving animals on 322, we duly aimed the 911S onto this route, hoping to find the way clear. Alas, it wasn't, and not a mile from the turning we were merrily leapfrogging moving obstructions in third and fourth gears.

This joyful romp was pulled up short 20 miles later by a roadblock, extended right across the pavement by the local gendarmes. It seems that one had been tailing us for 10 miles, but could never overhaul the Porsche. Everytime he passed a car to close the gap, the 911S passed two! All great fun in retrospect, but it was no fun being stopped as the herd of trundling behemoths passed by us, the drivers grinning and tooting their horns.

The curious thing is that the local justice of the peace, who also happed to operate the town gas station, was unable to fine us for speeding. The best he could do

was "dangerous passing." We had several times passed the big trucks on double-yellow lines. Although passing on these is not strictly illegal in Pennsylvania, it was enough to frustrate the unmarked fuzzmobile, which lacked the power, handling, or stickability of the 911S, and never got close enough to time us. Of course, we made all the proper noises at the time and escaped with a warning and 15 fewer dollars. But never in the driving did we feel the least bit reckless or dangerous to other motorists, and if that judge is reading this we hereby retract everything we said about regretting our behavior.

If this incident proves anything, it is the often-repeated point of road testers everywhere that the 911S was wasted in the United States, except maybe west of the Rockies. But by 1970—1972 at the latest—the whole 911 line had been carefully improved to a near-perfect state, just as the 356 had before it, by a small group of people in Stuttgart who were just a shade more serious about building automobiles than anybody else. One supposes that the T/E/S of these years were the reasons why there are still 911s you can buy new today. After 1972, Porsche had only to keep doing everything it was doing already. It did—and still is. Thank goodness for the 911—and all of its descendants.

TYPE 914: PRODUCT OF THE JOINT CHIEFS

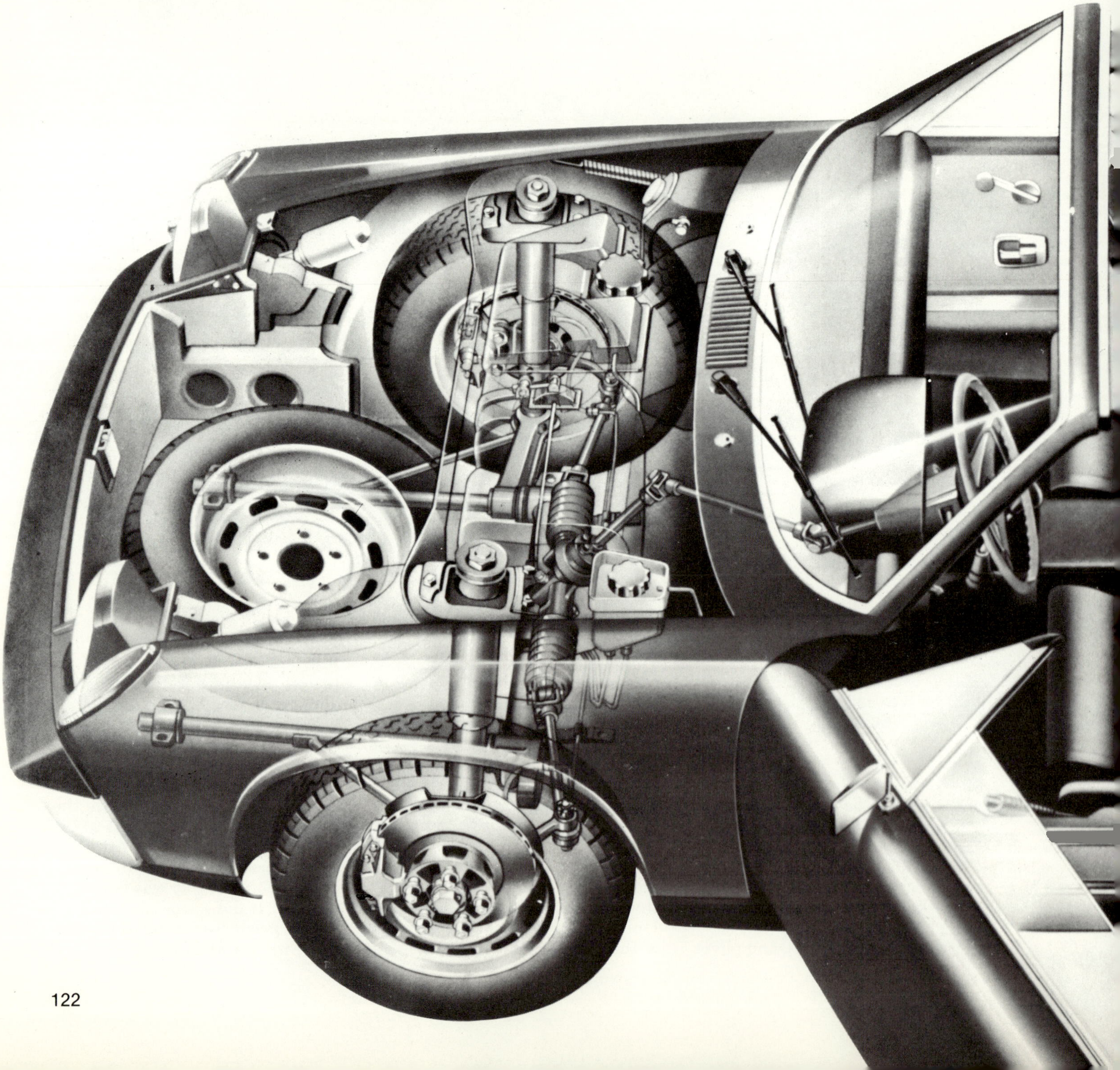

A camel is a horse designed by a committee, goes the saying. And since it vanished in the mid-1970s, the 914 has been written off as Porsche's camel. Everybody makes mistakes, and the pundits say this was Porsche's. A more evenhanded assessment is due the 914 and its derivatives, for they were not unsuccessful. Total production for model years 1970-76 came to 115,596 units, plus 3351 914/6s—an average of close to 17,000 cars per year. This volume was insignificant to Porsche's partner in the exercise, but it was perfectly acceptable to Porsche.

Things don't always work out the way we expect. In 1959, John Bond of *Road & Track* magazine was alerting his readers that the Beetle's days were numbered. In 1969 he was still alerting them. In 1965, it was beginning to look like all cars of the future would be mid-engine and sports cars even sooner. All the buff magazines were telling us so. Yet, it didn't happen.

The mid-engine layout, so perfect for the race track, proves less than acceptable when applied to a road car. Mounting the powerplant behind the passengers means that all its routine noise, vibration, and heat are physically closer to the occupants, requiring more heroic insulation efforts than in a front- or rear-engine car. Most of the mid-engine models we've seen so far have never been entirely free of heat and vibration. It's also difficult, certainly costly, to build a frame around a midships engine, and such installations typically pose horrendous service access problems. The layout does eliminate the need for a

Type 914/6 bares all in factory phantom view. Critics praised 914's roomy cockpit.

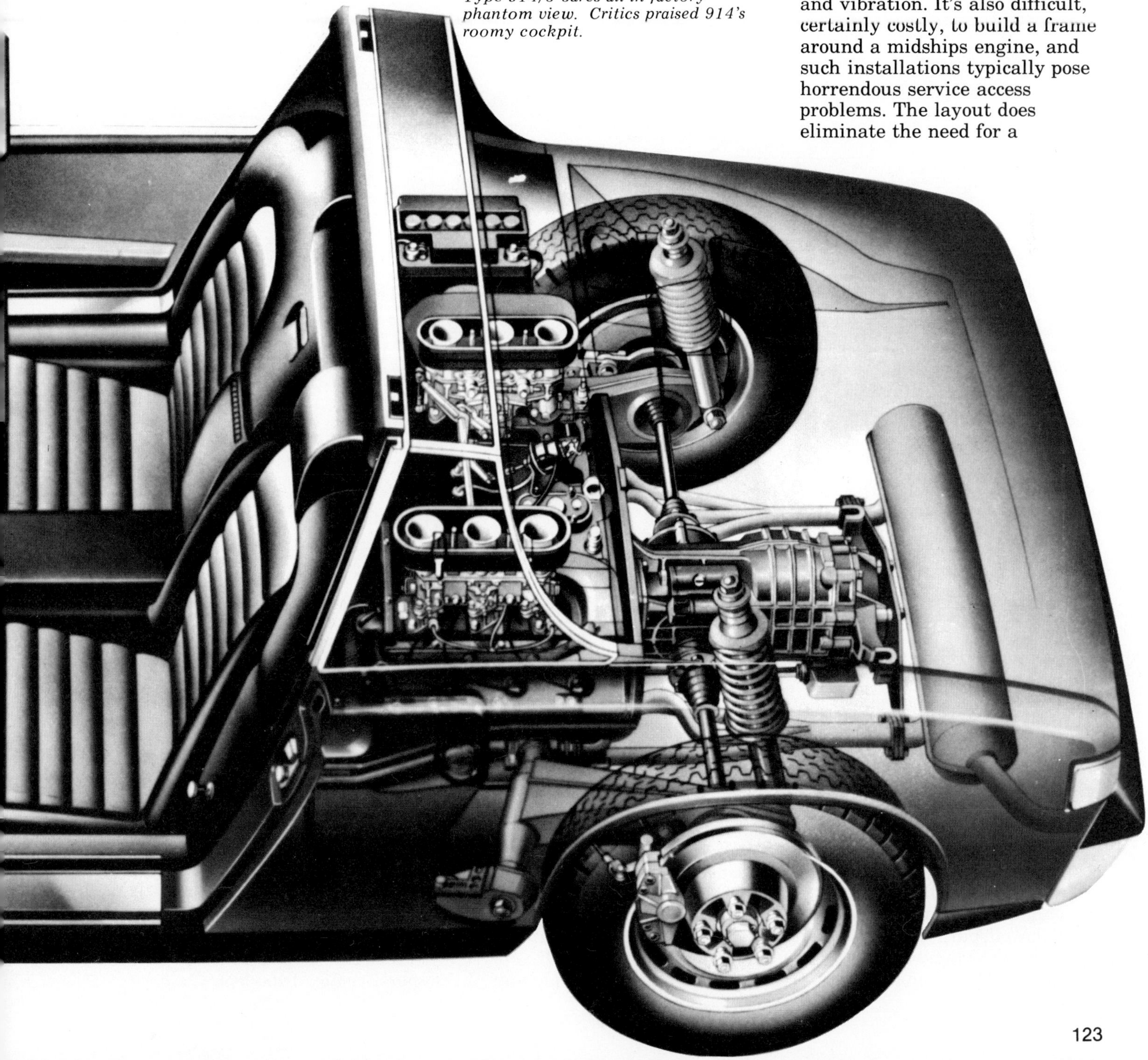

Above: An early European-spec Type 914 displays standard unchromed front bumpers. Also note wider "eyelids" to accommodate European headlamps. Right and opposite page: An early U.S. 914/4. Car was sold here as a Porsche, not a "VW-Porsche."

driveshaft, but it also mandates an expensive, fully independent rear suspension and convoluted gearbox linkages. The only production mid-engine sports car more successful than Porsche's has been Fiat's X1/9, and being number two in this difficult game is hardly something of which Porsche need be ashamed. Besides, for practicality and durability the 914 was miles ahead of the X1/9.

The project was begun, in Ferry Porsche's words, "from the realization that we needed to broaden our program at a less costly level [and] that we couldn't do it alone." The chief of Zuffenhausen thus contracted the chief of Wolfsburg, Heinz Nordhoff, the man who had brought VW to the pinnacle of success and made it the dominant power in the American import car market. It was a natural joint venture. VW and Porsche had worked together for years. The earliest Porsche cars made heavy use of VW components. Both companies were German, with all of the clarity of understanding that implied. VW had expertise in volume production and a desire to broaden its own model line. In fact it had been broadening since 1955 with the Karmann-Ghia, a highly successful two-seater, and the Type 2 Transporter line of Microbus, Kombi, and pickup trucks. More recently, VW had added the 1500 Type 3 in 1962, followed by its 1600 Fastback and Squareback extensions. So why not a mid-engine sports car using VW componentry and designed by their friends at Porsche? It seemed like a great idea.

Porsche was willing. Its dealers were clamoring for a lower-priced model, as 911 and 912 prices had already gone far beyond the level established with the now-superceded 356. And Porsche had had recent experience with the mid-engine concept, in the sports-racing Type 904.

Styling was important, even critical. Nordhoff didn't want the car to look like a VW, and Porsche didn't want it to resemble a 911—for obvious reasons. It was decided to insure this by farming out the styling brief to a third party, Gugelot Design GmbH in Neu-Ulm, about 50 miles from Stuttgart. The result was certainly unorthodox, but then who can be orthodox with a mid-engine layout? To add strength to the roadster body, a Targa-like rollbar (dubbed "basket handle" by many journalists) was designed as an integral part of the package, with a removable fiberglass panel between it and the windshield header. The body was devoid of ornamentation, though the bumpers, designed to meet forthcoming U.S. regulations, were less than beautiful. Because of the car's lowness, Gugelot resorted to pop-up headlamps to meet federal minimum-height requirements.

The latter were, by the way, a typical piece of *Porsche-werk*, with every possible contingency considered. Each unit was raised by an individual electric motor; each also had a manual control in the event of electrical failure. Both methods were engineered so that they could easily break the thickest coating of ice the engineers could encourage in cold-weather tests. To prevent a headlamp's catching an unwary finger on the way down, a safety panel was provided that would give way before one's digit did. It was the only correct engineering approach to a device that was becoming widespread—and fashionable—throughout the industry at the time.

For the two-place cockpit, plenty of room was decreed to suit the largest of American anatomies, although the individual seats were criticized as being too flat. As a cost-cutting measure, only the driver's seat had fore/aft adjustment but, in another piece of clever design, a movable footrest was given to the passenger to provide the proper amount of leg stretch. A large tachometer was centrally located, flanked by a speedometer and a combination dial. The latter contained only one working instrument, a fuel gauge; everything else was monitored by warning lights, another bit of economizing. The bumpers looked better when finished in chrome, and this was available as an option.

The approach to suspension on the 914—MacPherson struts, lower A-arms, and torsion bars up front, semi-trailing arms and coil springs in back, tubular shocks all round was conventional and unspectacular. So little body roll occurred that anti-sway bars were at first considered unnecessary. The ride was quite hard, and many early examples developed rattles and squeaks that had never been heard in a 911 or 356. There was also a lot of wind noise, especially from around the lift-off roof.

VW's Type 411 engine, a fuel-injected ohv flat-four, was lifted intact from Wolfsburg's new upper-range car, though changes would be made to it as time passed. With its standard five-speed manual gearbox, the 914 offered standing-start acceleration comparable to that of an MGB—0-60 mph in about 14 seconds and a 19-second quarter-mile—but its top speed was quite good at about 105-110 mph, doubtless through Gugelot's careful attention to streamlining.

The Type 914/4 was sold as the "VW-Porsche" in Europe but only with the Porsche crest (through Porsche-Audi dealers) in the U.S. It was extremely well built, reliable, and sprightly, with the potential for truly exceptional handling. And it had the magic of the Porsche name. But it was far less than enthusiasts had expected. In price, it was comparable not with the MGB (to which it was clearly superior) but with the Triumph TR6 (more crude but quite a bit faster), the Fiat 124 Spider (fully open bodywork, much prettier) and—worst of all, from Porsche's perspective at least—the Datsun 240Z, a modern if conventional closed GT, bargain-priced at $175 *less*. Exactly what you got in 914 for your money, relative to these rivals, was obscure. Leaving aside the 240Z (in a class by itself and better than the lot), a June 1970 comparison test in *Road & Track* magazine is instructive. The 914 proved slower off the line and marginally faster at the top end. Its braking was equal to the Fiat's and superior to that of the English cars. And it was ahead of all three in fuel economy. Its styling was probably the most controversial of the four. These were somewhat telling points against the 914. The fact that Porsche would eventually sell over 100,000 copies is a tribute to the car's good qualities, which undeniably did exist.

The 1972 version of the 914 looked little different from the 1970 original, but its engine was reworked to accept 91-octane fuel, and delivered approximately 10 percent better gas mileage with no harm to performance. Fresh-air vents were added at both ends of the instrument panel, and the wiper/washer control was relocated to a stalk on the steering column. The passenger seat was now fully adjustable, thus eliminating the need for the footrest. One drastic change was the price, which rose by almost $700. And you could pop for the $311 Appearance Group option. This included vinyl-covered rollbar, chrome bumpers, fog lamps, deep-pile carpeting, 165×15 radial tires on 5.5-inch rims, leather-covered steering wheel rim, and dual tone horn.

For 1973, the 914 was improved again, and this time the tweaks were more energetic. While the 1.7-liter version was retained, with an even more anemic 69-bhp setup for emissions-conscious California, Zuffenhausen added spice to the recipe with a new 2.0-liter model. This engine, rated at 91 net horsepower, was a simple bore and stroke job, and gave performance about midway between that of the 1.7 and the 914/6, of which more in a moment.

The 2.0-liter engine was a definite improvement not only in

This page: 914 cockpit put seats literally on the floor (right). Only driver's seat adjusted on early models. Two roomy trunks (below) were a plus for the mid-engine design. Opposite page: Removable roof stowed in rear trunk (below), gave neat appearance when fitted (above).

performance but in tractability. It started easily and revved quickly up to its 5600-rpm redline. With it, the 914 was now roughly equal to the Triumph TR6 for performance. The five-speed gearbox was particularly useful here, providing good flexibility and allowing the driver to extract the maximum from the fortified engine. Anti-roll bars had now been fitted, and enabled Porsche to soften up the ride through use of lower torsion-bar rates. In fact, the suspension in this form banished the characteristic Porsche oversteer: "The relative stiffnesses of the front and rear anti-roll bars seem to have been chosen to provide understeer, at all times and under all conditions," said *Road & Track*. "When driven around a curve, the front end slides and the back end sticks. Apply full power and the front end pushes toward the outside of the turn. Let up on the throttle and the front end tucks toward the inside of the turn. This is very safe... but the sporting driver may wish sometimes for the freedom of, say, a 911S, in which an occasional 'nasty' trait can be provoked and exploited with skill. Perhaps the not-quite Porsche 914 isn't allowed to provide that sort of test and perhaps that's why the 914/2 [*R&T*'s designation] isn't allowed to be the 914S [the proposed designation, turned down by the factory]."

The Appearance Group previously mentioned was standard on the 2.0-liter 914, as were alloy wheels and a center console mounting oil temperature gauge, voltmeter, and clock. Base price now leaped to $5299, and the 914 remained a difficult package to sell against the opposition.

Porsche had also wanted to field a six-cylinder derivative, to which end the 911 engine and the 914/6 designation were applied. This model sold for about $2500 more than the four-cylinder version. Its engine was the carbureted 911T unit and brought with it much improved go-power, though the rear-engine car was still a hair quicker. The 914/6 was also equipped with larger, internally vented brakes and wider wheels and tires to match the extra go, plus deluxe trim, three-speed windshield wipers with electric washer, a headlamp flasher, dual-tone horn, a 150-mph speedometer, and an 8000-rpm tachometer. Like the 914 it had a five-speed gearbox, though the four needed its flexibility a great deal more than the six.

The extra cylinders made a world of difference between the two cars. It was hard to think of a 914/4 as anything but a VW tweaked by Zuffenhausen; indeed, *Car and Driver* magazine suggested that it would make a fine replacement for the Karmann-Ghia, surely damnation with faint praise. But there was no mistaking the harsh

scream of the 914/6 or that seat-of-the-pants feeling that here was a true Porsche. Yet the 914/6 suffered from the same inherent problems as its four-pot sibling: underwhelming styling and a high price. In fact, it cost only about $400 less than the 911T, and most buyers were inclined to spend the extra bucks for what was obviously a thoroughbred Porsche instead of some weird corporate half-breed.

Porsche hadn't planned it that way: the 914/6 was meant to fill a definite gap, to be priced far less than the 911T. The problem had to do with the financial arrangement with Volkswagen, which was actually making the final product and marketing decisions. Under VW direction, Karmann had to charge more for the 914 body than it did for the 911 body. This completely wiped out the production economies of scale that the 914 had originally been designed to take advantage of. It was not deliberate sabotage, however. As Karl Ludvigsen revealed, quoting Ferry Porsche: "They calculate costs differently in a big firm. They couldn't consider the other advantages of having a sports car in the line, the way it can attract people into the showroom." VW's method was to calculate the cost of body tooling amortization, and against the low volume of the 914 this meant a very high cost-per-body. Porsche, by contrast, never applied the true cost of an individual model to that model alone. According to Ferry, "We put them all together and divide by our total volume." The very nature of the joint operation defeated the cars, too, as Ludvigsen wrote: "The new automotive marque that was

Opposite page: Jazzy Limited Edition 914/4 was issued to boost sales for '74 (above), but that year's more powerful 2.0-liter engine was the big news. This page and left: The little-changed 914 2.0 for 1975. Posing with U.S. Carrera was an attempt at image bolstering.

created, VW-Porsche, had neither image nor tradition. At the same time it was *both* VW and Porsche and neither VW *nor* Porsche."

All this had a predictable outcome: the 914/6 vanished after the 1972 model year and only 3351 examples built. The standard 914 soldiered on three more years, but it wasn't really pushed by either Porsche or VW.

Had the 914 received a better reception—and been treated more seriously by Volkswagen—there's no telling what it might have become. It certainly had genuine development potential. Porsche demonstrated that itself by experimentally fitting a flat eight, the wonderful 3.0-liter Type 908 unit with 310 DIN horsepower, into what they called the 914/8, which had a 0-60 mph time of six seconds flat and a top speed of 155 mph. Then too, several interesting specials were hung around 914 chassis, including a trio of GTs by Louis Heuliez in France, a study by Albrecht Goertz of BMW 507 and Datsun 240Z fame, and one by Frua. And there was the sensational Tapiro gullwing by Giorgetto Giugaro's ItalDesign.

The 914 development that came closest to production was the factory's own Type 916, a swoopy evolution of the basic car powered by a 2.4-liter racing six patterned after an engine developed by Herbert Linge. It would have been the ultimate roadgoing 914, priced between $14,000 and $15,000 and directly competitive with Ferrari's mid-engine Dino 246 GT. Considerably altered in appearance, it sported flared fenders front and rear, plus a fixed roof that provided greater structural rigidity than in the standard car, no doubt necessary with the extra muscle. Fully streetworthy, it had a leather interior, 914/6 instrumentation, even a radio. The suspension incorporated Bilstein heavy-duty shock absorbers, stiff anti-roll bars front and rear, and 911S ventilated disc brakes. Its five-speed gearbox followed the new gate arrangement Porsche was moving to at the time, with the lower four gears in the "H" and fifth forward and to the right. The big attraction naturally was that 2.4-liter 190-bhp 911 engine, which delivered 0-60 mph in under seven seconds.

Unfortunately, the 916 project

was nipped in the bud just after the first press pictures had been distributed. Only 20 prototypes were built. One escaped to America, where it was obtained by Brumos Porsche in Jacksonville, Florida. The problem was, in a word, price. At $15,000, there were grave doubts in Zuffenhausen about the 916's saleability, especially since both the 914 and 914/6 had been criticized in that regard already. It was probably wise to cancel the 916, but it's a shame a few more weren't built.

The last of the 914s quietly disappeared from dealership floors in early 1976. In its place as the budget Porsche, pending release of the front-engine 924 for 1977, was a one-year revival of the Type 912. Designated 912E (E for *einspritzung*, fuel injection), this was a fine car in its own right, and is highly cherished today. Powered by the 2.0-liter VW engine from the 914, it sold for close to $11,000 POE East Coast. While this was a considerable jump over the 914, it had the lovely Butzi Porsche coupe body and cost much less than the 911S. "The 912E will obviously find favor with those who prefer a slightly more practical and tractable Porsche," *Road & Track* commented. "It's a car with almost all the sporting virtues of the more expensive 911S, yet its simpler pushrod 4-cyl. engine should make for better fuel economy and less expensive maintenance than the 911's six."

The forthcoming 924 meant the 912E would be but a stopgap. Porsche knew this, and it was the single instance of "dynamic obsolescence" in the history of the marque. Despite a certain tendency of the fuel injection to misbehave in extreme cold, the 912E was nevertheless popular. It remains one of the more desirable four-cylinder models among enthusiasts today.

And what about the 914? Surely it was hurt by its split personality, neither fish nor fowl, more "Vee-Dub" than Porsche. Had it been a 100-percent Porsche, with a Porsche engine and looks to match, more people would likely have paid the relatively stiff admission price. Remember how Ferry Porsche insisted that the 911 look like an evolution of the 356? He was wise. Though a mid-engine layout has different requirements, the "face" of the car could have been more Porsche-like. As a Volkswagen, on the other hand, it suffered from relatively low production volume that scarcely attracted attention in the Wolfsburg boardroom. Thus the car's considerable potential for further development was never really exploited. Even so, the European designation VW-Porsche was accurate. But as a Porsche, in the U.S., it had to live up to the almost insuperable standards—and image—of the 911 and 356. One cannot help thinking that it would have sold better as a Volkswagen.

In addition to its schizophrenic product planning the 914 suffered greatly from its styling. *Car and Driver* said "it had all the fluidity of line of an Erector set," and *Sports Car Graphic* called it "a pleasant eyesore." *Road & Track*

Stillborn Type 916 would have been the ultimate 914 development, but only 20 prototypes were built. High projected price was Zuffenhausen's chief concern. Note aggressive wheel arches, 911S wheels, fixed roof panel. Opposite page above: The '76 Type 912E, a one-year model, was powered by the 914's 2.0-liter four.

suggested that perhaps we just weren't used to mid-engine sports cars: "...there is not only an unfamiliar relation between the center section and the rear overhang but a difficult problem in getting adequate rear vision combined with decent esthetics. The 'basket handle' roof section of the 914 does indeed look strange, but to make the car more esthetically palatable (i.e. more like the beautiful mid-enginc cars such as the De Tomaso Mangusta) would have meant accepting decreased rear vision or an exceedingly expensive expanse of glass. The truncated roof with its simple flat pane of glass provides good rear vision and, all things considered, is a reasonable solution to the problem."

That was what their heads said. Their hearts said otherwise. A year after that analysis, *R&T* noted that the 1972 model was unchanged, "and that's a disappointment...we were hoping for at least a mild reworking of the uncharming front end." And even in its initial report *R&T* had had to admit that the car was "a great big disappointment... Undoubtedly the mid-engine is the coming thing, but..."

Which only proves one thing: even Porsche isn't perfect.

TYPE 911 AND CARRERA 1973-77: PERFORMANCE PLUS

The rationale that saw the name "Carrera" return to the Porsche lineup in 1973 was mainly competition, a subject Porsche had never ignored. The Carrera RSRs, which blew the wheels off of everything else in sight at races like that year's Daytona 24 Hours, were built to keep the Type 911 in the competition forefront. Dr. Ernst Fuhrmann, who became president of the company in 1972, decided that the second-generation road cars would remain in production well beyond the planned introduction of the front-engine Type 924.

The original Carrera RS concept was a stripped, lightweight 911-based model that could be homologated easily for Group 4 GT racing. The "customer" model had a special 2.7-liter engine (Type 911/93), developed by boring out the 2.4 six to 90mm, the main difference from the standard 911S engine. Both units had the same 8.5:1 compression ratio, Bosch-Porsche fuel injection, valve sizes, and timing. The added displacement gave the RS powerplant 20 more horsepower.

Since it was destined for competition, the Carrera RS 2.7 was lightened drastically and, in some areas, ingeniously. For instance, Porsche used special thin steel and glass and fiberglass rear deck and rear aprons (the latter on racing models only). There was no insulation for the cockpit, which was spartan: rubber mats replaced carpets; the thin, detrimmed door panels had pull-cord door releases; there were thin bucket seats and no clock, passenger sunvisor, or non-functional trim.

The chassis was equipped with gas-pressurized Bilstein shock absorbers, extra stiff anti-sway bars, and aluminum rims, wider than 911S at the rear, with fenders flared to accommodate them. The "ducktail" spoiler had been ordained by wind tunnel experiments. It looked weird but was brilliant in actual use, providing extra downforce to hold the tail firmly to the track at speed as well as increasing air flow through the engine cover's grillework.

Calling this car a Carrera was an obvious move that couldn't be faulted. The name had previously graced the most competitive of Porsches, not only the great four-cam 356s but later the sports

Below: The 1973 European Carrera RS 2.7 with initial duck tail spoiler. Much tamer U.S. version appeared a year later.

racing Carrera 904 GTs and the Type 906 Carrera 6. Stylists made the most of it, with huge bodyside graphics displaying the traditional Carrera script. The hairy one was back!

Porsche was required to build 500 RS Carreras for homologation purposes and, to make sure this quantity sold, the price was held down to about $10,000 in Germany. Actually there was little to fear: production had to be increased to 1000 and later 1800 to meet the demand. This brought with it an important side benefit: it allowed Porsche to homologate the car in Group 3 (series-production GT cars) rather than Group 4, where it required minimal race preparation and stood to dominate the class. With good sales, Porsche happily raised the price by several thousand dollars to more closely approximate the car's true worth.

The Carrera RS was greeted with high enthusiasm, which wasn't hard to muster once you got behind the wheel. Paul Frére in Belgium timed one from a standing start to 100 mph in 13 seconds flat, and registered a true top speed of 150 mph. Although his car was one of the ultra-light RSR variations, the production job was hardly less impressive. None of the road testers could say the RS Carrera was a cushy tourer, but all agreed that it was tractable for street use, where it delivered as much as 15 miles per gallon.

Thus established, the RS converted easily to Peter Gregg's Daytona-winning RSR (entered by Brumos Porsche of Jackonville, Florida), the all-out competition version. The RSR engine had 2806cc and a revised cylinder head with 10.5:1 compression. It produced an astounding 308 DIN horsepower at 6200 rpm, and would leap to 100 mph in 12 seconds flat, according to *Road & Track*. It had a splendid Group 4 career, winning everything in sight in

Opposite page and above: The American 911 Carrera for 1975 displays "whale tail" spoiler adopted that year. Center spread: The European Carrera RS was upped to 3.0 liters for '74.

the IMSA Camel GT series and the Trans Am. In Europe the RSR was GT Champion for 1973, vanquishing the favored DeTomaso Panteras. With some difficulty, the engine was enlarged to 2993cc by a further bore increase (to 95mm) for the Martini Racing team; now it developed 315 horsepower, and beat everything in sight at a four-hour race at Le Mans, blasting down the Mulsanne Straight at up to 179 mph. Later Martini RSRs developed 330 bhp and, in more heavily modified form, entered Group 5, where they continued to excel.

For 1974, Porsche upped the ante all round with the Carrera RS 3.0, needing to build only 100 to homologate it as an "evolution" of the lightweight 1973 model. Incorporated were a wider, horizontal rear spoiler, wider wheels and tires, die-cast aluminum crankcase, and revised inner pivot points for the rear suspension. The 1973 model had required a special permit in Germany owing to the huge spoiler, but the 3.0 had an alternate "street" spoiler, soon nicknamed the "whale tail" with a protective rubber safety surround. Lightening techniques gave the 3.0 a curb weight of only 2400 pounds. Available in a variety of wild colors, it was marked by black exterior trim (window moldings, rearview mirror, door handles, taillight housings). The engine developed 220/230 bhp on premium fuel, and Paul Frére *averaged* 124 mph on 78 miles of Italian *autostrada* with one in mid-year. "This is one of the fastest road cars we have ever timed," Frére said. "60 mph is reached in a staggering 5.2 seconds with the help of superlative rear-wheel grip and the ½-mile mark comes in 14 seconds... The car understeers, though lifting off at the limit of adhesion will swing the tail out rather sharply. On the Casale track, near Torino, I found that fast bends must still be approached with some power on and that getting the car around fast *and* safely still calls for a certain amount of delicacy." Roger Penske helped move out the 109 3.0s built by ordering 15 of them for his International Race of Champions. Another 50 were built with RSR specifications, and this version won the Trans Am and IMSA Camel GT series again, with Peter Gregg up. In 1975, with the racing Type 934 Turbo still a year away, the Carrera RS/RSRs continued to dominate the European Hillclimb Championship, Daytona and Le Mans (where one finished fifth overall).

Meanwhile, Porsche adopted the Carrera name for a new top-of-the-line road car that debuted in America for 1974. Model designations and engine specifications were confusingly juggled once more. Starting at the bottom was a plain 911, equivalent to the previous T, followed by a 911S that was really much like the former E in performance and fuel economy. The U.S. Carrera and both 911s shared the same engine, which had grown to 2.7 liters via a 6mm bore increase. Rated horsepower was 167 bhp (SAE net) for the top two models, 143 bhp for the plain 911. The displacement boost was yet another response to tightening U.S. emissions standards, and was accompanied by a switch to Bosch CIS (continuous) fuel injection, replacing the previous mechanical system, plus minor tuning changes and a lower rev limit (down from 7000 to 6500 rpm).

Another sign of the times was evident outside, as all the 911s acquired redesigned safety bumpers. These were made of aluminum to save weight and were painted to match body color to save the car's looks. Out back was a new full-width taillight lens bearing the Porsche name, along with black-finish engine lid louvers with chrome "2.7" logo. Inside were new high-back bucket seats, redesigned control knobs, tiny air vents at either end of the dash, and new steering wheels. Adoption of a smaller space-saver spare tire left room for a larger gas tank (by 4.7 gallons), and Targa models acquired a one-piece removable top.

Road & Track magazine tested all three versions, and its findings were predictable enough. Performance was down, though not a great deal, as was fuel economy, and driveability was somewhat worse than before. *R&T* also carped about prices, and with good reason: they'd now risen past the $10,000 mark minimum, and the Carrera was quite close to 14 grand. "The Porsche people also have the nerve to charge you extra for opening rear-quarter windows in all but... the Carrera; and the air conditioner costs $1125 [But] they've got you over a barrel: a Porsche is like no other car, and if you want one there's no substitute."

There was little visible change in the Carrera for 1975. The "tea tray" IROC-style engine lid spoiler was the main distinguishing point. The plain 911 disappeared this year, leaving the S as your only other choice. Perhaps responding to *R&T*'s criticism, Porsche expanded standard equipment this year. Now included were those opening rear side windows, plus intermittent wipers and front and rear stabilizer bars. The Carrera also offered standard leather upholstery.

From a performance standpoint the 1974 Carrera was slightly better than the '75. The 0-60 mph time was up to 8.4 seconds (against 7.4), official top speed was down from 142 to 132 mph. Although Porsche continued to avoid the worst maladies of the emission control era, tighter 1975 regs meant that both the S and Carrera (which shared the same engine) had 10 horsepower less than in 1974—15 less on California versions. But the dreaded catalyst had still been avoided: the 49-state cars didn't need it, and California models used twin thermal reactors and exhaust-gas recirculation. In tractability, however, the '75 was superior. It started easily from cold, behaved well in traffic, and offered plenty of low-end torque. And *Road & Track* reported an overall fuel consumption of 17.5 mpg—not bad for this kind of performance!

For the Carrera's $1700 price premium over a 911S the buyer received bodyside graphics with special colors; opening rear quarter windows, electric side windows, RS-type black exterior trim, bulging fenders to accommodate the wider rear wheels, and a tray-like spoiler mounted at an upward angle on the engine lid. Chrome exterior trim could be ordered instead of black if desired. On the inside, the Carrera could be distinguished by a three-spoke steering wheel, but was otherwise much like the 911S. Interiors were funereal in these years, as the Feds banned shiny stuff and matte-black rapidly replaced silver or chromium plate. Outside the U.S. the Carrera had much more power and was a totally different car. But taking it all into account, *Road & Track* said that the '75 was "one of the world's best sports cars, and if an automotive bargain still remains in our inflation ridden world the Carrera, or any 1975 911, is it."

Also in 1975, Porsche offered a special Silver Anniversary 911S, 750 of which were exported to the

U.S. and 750 sold elsewhere. Each was painted diamond silver metallic, had custom interior trim of woven silver-and-black tweed, and bore a plaque with Ferry Porsche's facsimile signature and a sequential serial number.

For 1976, the 911S soldiered on in the American market, while the Turbo Carrera arrived and the unblown Carrera departed, though the latter was still offered to Europeans along with the base 911. In this form it produced 200 bhp at 6000 rpm—still pretty impressive—and sold for DM 44,950 in Germany. Very little was changed on the 1976 S: there were interior-adjustable door mirrors painted body color, and an improved heater blower. The four-cylinder 912E, mentioned in a previous chapter, filled out the lower end of the 1976 lineup.

For 1977, the all-new, water-cooled front-engine Type 924 arrived, while the 911S returned, again with only minor changes: Ate vacuum brake servo and optional tires/shocks for a more comfortable ride. Another evidence of Porsche thoroughness was a governor, plus special speedometer, on U.S. models. The governor interrupted fuel supply to the engine to limit top speed to "only" 130 mph, the speed rating for the tires now specified. The tire/shock package was part of a $495 Comfort Group that also included electric windows. Face-level air vents appeared in the center of the dash for the first time, heater controls were improved, anti-theft door lock buttons were fitted, and floor carpeting was run up the lower door panels.

Prices, of course, skyrocketed in these years, along with the cost of just about everything else. The 911S that had sold for less than $12,000 in 1974 was nudging $15,000 by 1977—and its 1978 successor, the 911SC, would start at over $22,000. But inflation was not confined to Porsche, and in many ways the 911 remained something of a bargain. Throughout one of the most troubled periods for the automotive industry, when engineers and stylists had to bow to the wishes of politicians to sell here, Porsche managed to keep the 911 not only within U.S. law but just as exciting as it had always been. At the 25th anniversary celebration in May 1974, Ferry Porsche confirmed that the old warrior was far from finished: "With all the regulations that are known to us now, we think the 911 can keep going for the next six years." As usual, Ferry was being modest. In the autumn of 1983, the Porsche 911—on balance, one of the all-time automotive greats—had its 20th birthday.

Below: By 1976, inflation and added standard equipment had put the 911S beyond most enthusiasts' reach—which made it all the more desirable. Last year for the 2.7-liter engine size was 1977.

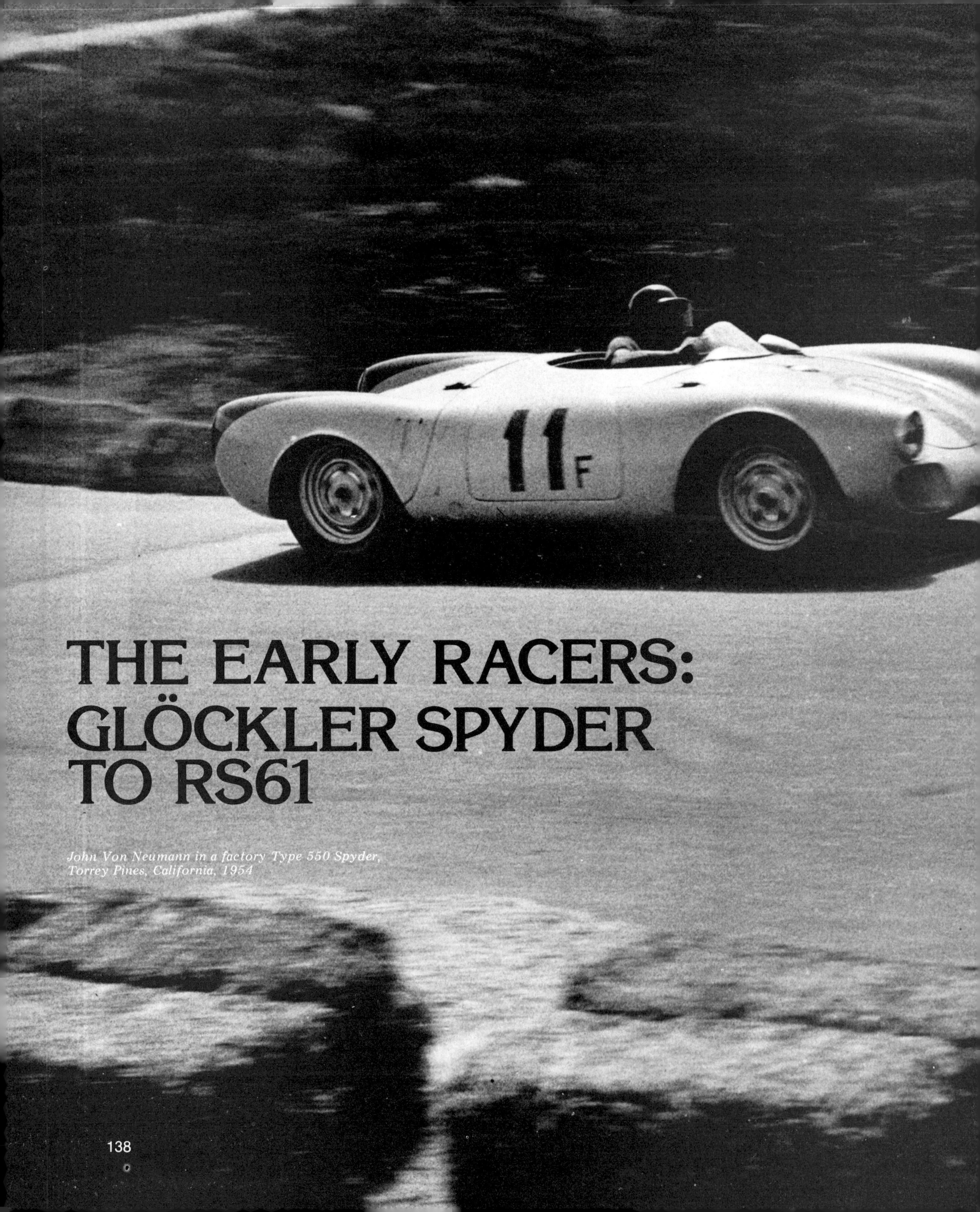

THE EARLY RACERS: GLÖCKLER SPYDER TO RS61

John Von Neumann in a factory Type 550 Spyder, Torrey Pines, California, 1954

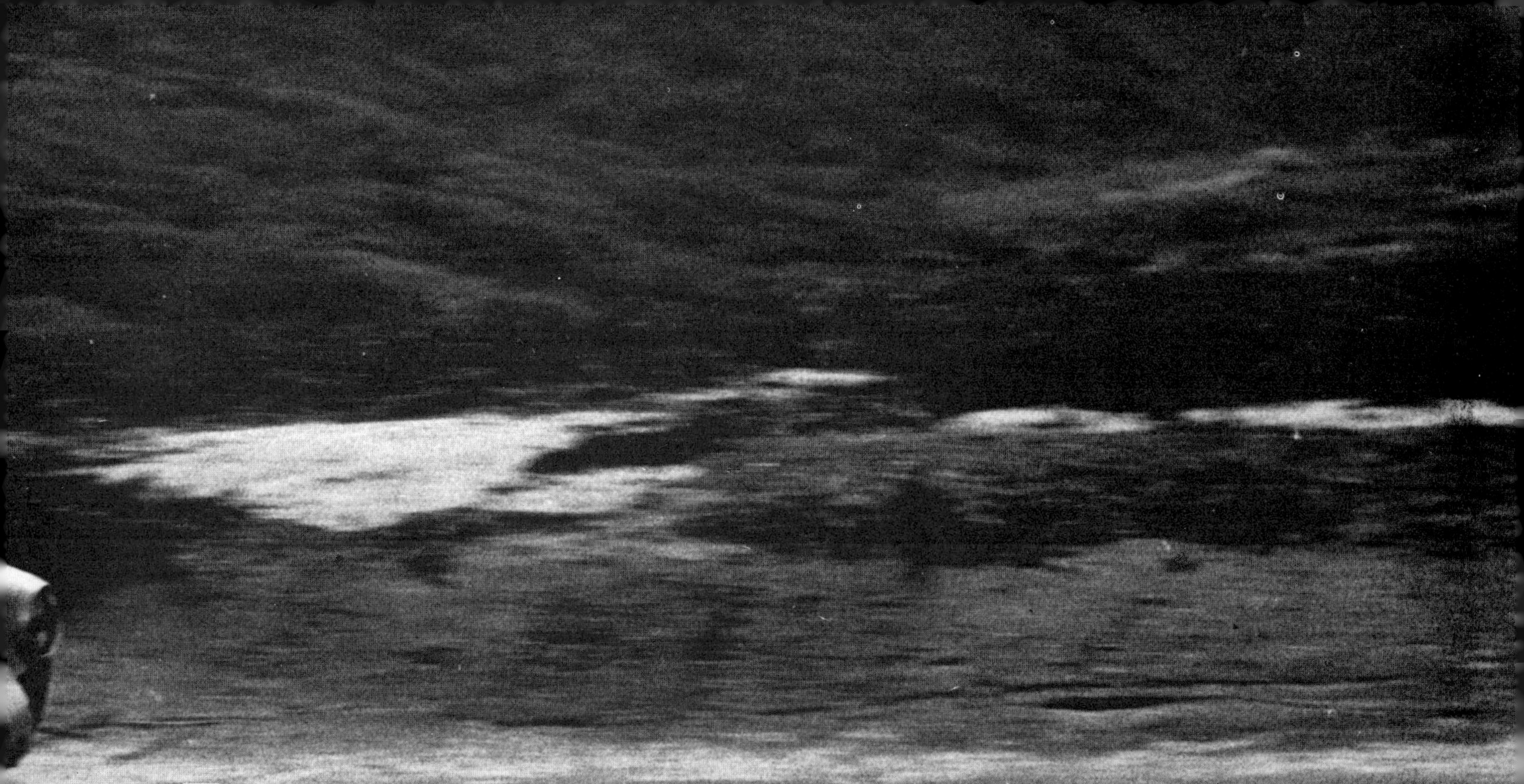

The Porsche Spyders, with their four-cam 1500 and 1600cc engines, were spiritual descendants of the Lohner electrics Ferdinand Porsche had designed over half a century before. In one of these he set a new hillclimb record in Austria on September 23, 1900. Half a century later, the Spyders marked the first attempt by Dr. Porsche's company to enter international competition with a pure track car—and they began not at Zuffenhausen but at Frankfurt, almost 100 miles to the north of Porsche's home base.

Walter Glöckler had been a successful race driver, with motorcycles and 1.5-liter cars, in prewar Germany. Armed with plans to build and race his own design, he began to construct a new racing car at his large VW distributorship in Frankfurt after the war. Completed in 1950, it looked so similar to the later factory models that Glöckler was credited with "fathering" the Porsche Spyder line.

Powered by an 1100cc Porsche engine, mounted ahead of the rear axle for optimum weight distribution and altered to develop 53 bhp (DIN) on alcohol, the Glöckler *Eigenbau* ("homemade") was 78 inches long, a smooth lozenge-shaped roadster on a tubular frame. Like later factory racing models, it proved itself immediately, winning the German 1100cc championship in 1950, 1951 and 1952—different drivers, but the same car. A capable engineer in his own right, Glöckler then went on to a 1500 Porsche engine with 90 bhp in an improved body. This car, the Glöckler-Porsche, captured for Germany the Bugatti class records on France's Monthléry track in 1952. The Glöcklers quickly established Porsche as a manufacturer of respected racing componentry.

After Porsche won its class at the 24 Hours of Le Mans in 1951, Ferry Porsche and Karl Rabe concluded that the pushrod engine, as far as endurance events were concerned, had reached its limit. While the production pushrod powerplants were quickly extended to 1300 and 1500 cc displacements, the factory engaged in a tangential program—a competition engine with four cams placed at the top of the cylinder barrels to serve the four widely spaced sets of valves.

By spring of 1952, a four-cam engine had left the drawing boards and a prototype was being tested on the Zuffenhausen dynamometer. It carried design number 547 and, later, it was placed in the Spyder chassis, designated Type 550. Those numbers were to join "356" as symbols of excitement to Porsche drivers the world over.

Minor development problems kept the four-cam engine out of a yet-to-be-named prototype body, which was a coupe style from Weidenhausen in Frankfurt. In the interim, a souped-up pushrod Type 528 engine was used. In this configuration, the prototype won the *Eifelrennen* on the Nürburgring in 1953 and otherwise distinguished itself on various European circuits. By August 1953, the four-cam engine was ready. Its first test was the Freiburg hillclimb, with former Auto-Union champion Hans Stück at the wheel. The four-cam more than proved itself. In the spring of 1954, Hans Hermann won the 1500cc sports car class in the Mille Miglia, and from this time on the Type 550 Spyder began to mean a great deal in international racing. The name itself was an old-timer, meaning a light, high-performance sports car. The official factory

This page: 1953 Glockler spyder (below). Glockler-Porsche racer at Torrey Pines 1952 (right). Prototype 550RS coupe (bottom) ran at 1953 Mexican Road Race, also seen on opposite page.

154
IV CARRERA PANAMERICANA
"MEXICO"
154

MEXICO
154

nomenclature was 1500RS.

The Spyder had a tubular frame with a slight kick-up front and rear, an open body, a forward-mounted oil radiator, four-speed Porsche gearbox, Ross-type steering, torsion-bar suspension, and three mechanical features unique even to Porsche: a double-admission cooling blower, a large separate oil tank, and dry-sump lubrication. And, of course, it featured the four-cam arrangement, two cams per cylinder bank.

Spyder body production shifted several times. The first batch of but a few cars was built by Karosseriebau Weinsberg. By the time all the engine problems had been sorted out it was late 1954, and private racing drivers had been waiting for months to get their hands on one. What they ultimately received was the Type 550S (Sport), the customer model with a body built by Wendler of Reutlingen and priced at DM25,000 or about $5000 U.S. A factory entry driven by Huschke von Hanstein took eighth place overall in the Sports Car Grand Prix of Caracas, Venezuela, battling a field of Maseratis and Ferraris.

Though intended almost exclusively for racing, the Spyder was regularly catalogued, and was offered with a variety of options. Center-lock wire wheels (modified and laced by Glöckler) were available, along with the necessary axle and hub adapters. The factory also produced chrome-plated center-lock disc wheels that were suited to the post-1954 brake drums. The catalog stated later (for the RS Spyder) that lightweight rims would be made available, saving about 4.5 pounds per wheel. For improved rear wheel adhesion, an aerofoil designed by Swiss engineer and Spyder owner Michael May was offered to Porsche, but management found this forecast of the Chaparral spoiler unacceptable, saying that it greatly obstructed visibility.

By the mid-Fifties, factory-sponsored Spyders were exceeding 120 mph and demonstrating a degree of reliability that few other racing machines could match. "So fantastically durable were these cars that it was only in the most trying races, say the 24-hour Le Mans or Sebring, that they demonstrated their uncanny ability to run flat-out hour after hour, while ordinary attrition strewed the dead-car park with blown-up examples of lesser makes," wrote Ken Purdy. "As the hours passed, spectators at long-distance races came to realize that there were two dominant sounds in the cacophony of passing exhaust howls: the high scream of the Ferraris, and the lower-pitched booming of the Porsches."

Competition was rife in those days, though, and by mid-1956 it had prodded Porsche into building an improvement, the 550A/1500RS. This new Spyder retained much of the earlier body appearance, but its engine now produced 135 DIN horsepower on a higher 9.8:1 compression ratio (vs. the previous 9.5:1). Also, there was a five-speed gearbox, though first was used only to get the car rolling. The swing axle in this version was a two-joint type with a lower fulcrum. A 28.6-gallon total fuel capacity (main plus auxiliary tank) was provided for long-distance races, always a Porsche specialty. Plug

This page: A closeup look at the Type 550/1500RS in its interim 1956 form. Opposite page: Prototype 1953 Spyders at Willow Springs (Von Neumann driving, top) and in 1953 Mexican Road Race (Hans Hermann, lower right). A partly completed 550 (lower left) gets the once-over from Porsche officials.

reach was increased to ¾-inch, and one of Hirth's roller-bearing crankshafts was installed along with lightweight cylinder barrels. This made for a very free-running engine that never seemed to approach its bursting point. Even if 7500 rpm was exceeded, the Spyder kept on going.

In addition to its smooth revving ability on the race track, the Spyder proved to be quite tractable on the street. In fact, of the 100-odd Type 550/1500RS Spyders built for FIA homologation, many are still around today that saw little or no racing activity and can be appreciated for their functional beauty as well as their performance.

Tracing the progressive development of the Spyder is an upward climb in terms of power and design. The 1956 model had a lighter, chest-high steel tube space frame and boasted 135 DIN bhp. In 1957 a works training car, later to be called the RSK Spyder, was being tested. At this point the Type 550 gave way to the Type 718, which was first made available in early 1958 and was known to the factory as the RSK 718/1500.

The RSK took its name from the front suspension, which deviated from Porsche practice by having angled upper members that looked like the letter "K." This layout did not last long, but the RSK name did. The

Above: The improved Type 550A Spyder appeared in 1956, with a more robust steel-tube frame, modified nose and tail, and low-pivot swing axles.

torsion-bar rear suspension on early Spyders was replaced by variable-rate coil springs concentric with the shock absorbers, and a more neutral-handling car resulted. A normal 1500RSK single-seater with 142 bhp (DIN), driven by the famous Jean Behra, triumphed over 14 Coopers, three Lotuses, three OSCAS, and a six-cylinder Ferrari to win the 1958 Formula 2 event at Rheims, France. This car could reach 155 mph at 8000 rpm.

The RSK for 1959 had a 1600cc engine developing 148 bhp (DIN) at 8000 rpm. Porsche introduced the car at a Formula 2 race in Monte Carlo, but driver Wolfgang von Trips crashed it on the first lap. At the end of the year the Spyder's rear suspension underwent a major change. Porsche now adopted wishbones and coil springs, very similar to the layout in its Formula 2 car, and in keeping with its policy of

continued on page 161

A squadron of early Type 356s in a mid-'50s German road race

Even in its earliest form, the Type 356 seemed born to race. As proof, we offer this slick, aluminum-bodied 1949 Gmünd coupe, one of approximately five such cars converted to competition specifications by the Porsche factory. Besides engine tweaks, modifications include full wheel covers, a belly pan, hydraulic brakes, and cut-down racing screen. This car was raced in Europe, and was later sold to Southern California import car magnate John von Neumann, who converted it to roadster form and campaigned it successfully in 1952-53. Note the small circular driver's headrest on the rollover bar.

Left: the rare and highly desirable Abarth-Carrera of 1960, with bodywork by Zagato. Right: Another rarity, the 1959 1600GS Carrera Speedster with competition-oriented GT equipment group.

PORSCHE

This 1959 Speedster is claimed by its owner to be the last factory-built example of that well-liked body type. It certainly represents the ultimate in Speedster performance, built to Carrera 1600GS specifications and equipped with the no-cost GT option. The beautifully made four-cam engine delivered 115 DIN horsepower, and together with the car's lightweight body panels and well-chosen gearing produced a claimed top speed of better than 120 mph. No wonder the Carrera Speedster is so highly prized.

PORSCHE
Carrera

41

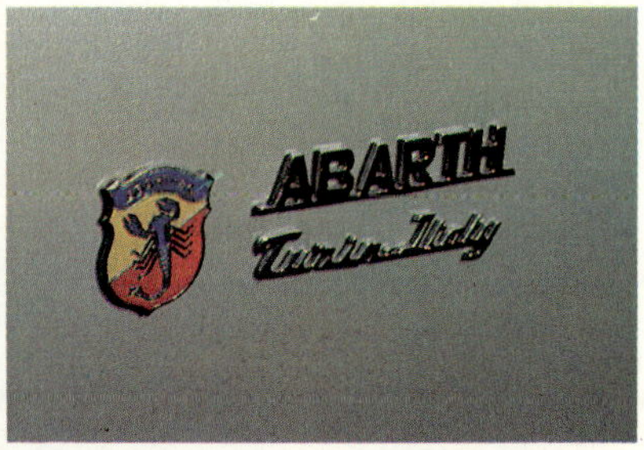

A purposeful-looking machine if ever there was one, this 1960 Abarth-Carrera GTL represented a formidable alliance of German engineering expertise and Italian design artistry. Based on the 356B chassis and running gear, it was ostensibly available with both 1600 and 2000cc four-cam engines. The lightweight bodywork was supplied by Carozzeria Zagato, who was also building bodies for Porsche's GT-class competitors. For this reason, the car was named after tuning wizard Carlo Abarth, even though he had nothing to do with the project. Beautiful as well as aerodynamic, the Abarth-Carrera had a curb weight of just 1800 pounds. Note the simple oval air intake at the front, the mean-looking louvers and scoop on the engine lid, the fully appointed instrument panel, and the fairly spacious engine bay. The GTL's racing career was quite long and successful. Only a handful of these cars was constructed, making them among the rarest of the competition Porsches aside from the various factory prototypes.

The Type 906, also known as the Carrera 6, appeared for the 1966 racing season as Porsche's first, all-out competition car. The smooth body lines were created by Ferdinand Piëch. Power came from a tuned version of the production 911's 1991-cc flat six, but mounted ahead of the rear axle centerline. Output was 200 bhp (DIN) at 8000 rpm on 10.3:1 compression. This was enough to propel the slippery 906 to a top speed of 175 mph. After a slow start, the Carrera 6 went on to score respectably high finishes in Manufacturer's Championship events, the high point coming at Le Mans '66 where it took fourth through seventh.

PORSCHE

One of the most breathtaking beasts ever to roam a race track, Porsche's incomparable 917 competition model burst on an unsuspecting world in 1969. Power was supplied by an ear-shattering flat 12 in 4.5- to 5.0-liter displacements, producing 580-630 horsepower in Group 4 tune. Early 917s were plagued by very skittish handling, mainly due to the aerodynamics of their long-tail bodywork. The car shown here has the K (for kurz, *short) style as seen in 1970-71, which proved to be much more manageable. In this form, the 917 captured the 24 Hours of Le Mans in 1970. The 917 would go on to become the basis for the mighty Group 7 open-body machines that would dominate the Can-Am series in the '70s in the hands of such drivers as George Follmer and Mark Donohue.*

PORSCHE AUDI

Though Porsche never seriously raced its mid-engine 914, many privateers did. This particular car has the full competition treatment, including a 2.8-liter flat six, full roll cage, rear airfoil, flared rear wheel wells, and front air dam.

garretson
enterprises
LSEN BODY WORKS Palo Alto, Ca.
45z
GOODYEAR

garretson
enterprises
CARLSEN BODY WORKS Palo Alto, Ca.
45z
garretsonenterprises

George Follmer, 1972 Can-Am champion, in his 917/10

Right: Two factory Type 550A Spyders head into a turn at a European road race circa 1957. Center: The 1961 mid-engine RS61, a development of the Type 718RSK. Bottom: Porsche team driver Edgar Barth in a Type 718 Bergspyder (hillclimb car) in 1958.

continued from page 144

adapting racing research to "production" vehicles.

By the end of 1959 it could be said that the Spyder had reached its fullest potential. In 1958 and 1959, Porsche took third place in the Sports Car World Championship. This was accomplished with both 1500 and 1600cc cars—against competitors with up to 3.0 liters.

The factory dropped the "K" nomenclature in 1960, when the RS60 emerged. Expected changes in FIA rules for 1962 caused a wait-and-see attitude at Zuffenhausen, so there were few changes in the 1960-61 Spyders. The wheelbase was increased slightly, wheels went from 15 to 16 inches on wider rims, and two engines (1500 and 1600cc) were offered on a limited basis. Twelve cars went to private racing drivers, and four stayed at the factory. With the trend toward more cylinders now underway and Porsche increasingly busy with its eight-cylinder Grand Prix car, Spyder production was halted in early 1962.

The nine-year output of Porsche Spyders did not come from a conventional production line. These were handmade cars, with bodies hammered out of aluminum on wooden forms. They were the work of perhaps a dozen selected craftsmen who, with care and after many years of experience, assembled each car piece by piece. These cars were the epitome of the two most prominent characteristics of early Porsches: air cooling and rear engine mounting. They also proved the worth of simplicity in construction and ironclad reliability in the most severe of racing conditions.

14
E

41

48

Center spread: A trio of Type 718/1500 RSK "customer" Spyders. Opposite page: Al Holbert's father Bob in his RS 61 (top left). The Type 550A Spyder in a recent vintage race (bottom left) and in the '50s (right). This page: Edgar Barth again in the 718 Bergspyder (left). The RS60/61 wooden buck (above) still exists at the Wendler coachworks in Reutlingen.

FORMULA 1: AN UNEXPECTED SETBACK

Initial Porsche Formula 1 car was based on this 1960 F2 design. Above: Dan Gurney in the Type 804 F1 car.

The Ring of Solitude was one of those classic race courses laid out over a system of public roads — the beautiful wooded country around *Schloss Solitude*, outside Stuttgart. It opened in 1922, but saw no official Grand Prix racing before the war. The great Hermann Lang, who drove a demonstration heat there in a GP Mercedes during 1937, described Solitude as "a garden path." But Dan Gurney, who did rather more in 1962, remembers it with fondness: "Solitude was a fantastic circuit. Very fast, very deceptive, very smooth, with drafting and lots of blind downhill turns," Gurney told the German weekly *Auto Motor und Sport* in 1982. "It's one of those tracks where you'd arrive at the turns together, and often it was raining, but it was a majestic circuit. It was a little more than eight miles around, and a lot of it going damn fast through the forest. It took some study to unlock the speed."

Gurney has reason to remember Solitude. For it was here on this narrow, tricky course that he piloted a Porsche Grand Prix racing car in its finest hour.

Formula 1 is the supreme class in automotive competition, outranking the NASCAR Grand National, the TransAm, the IMSA GT Series, and everything else. To build and win with a Formula 1 car is the equivalent of scaling Mount Everest, of setting foot on the moon. As the '50s closed, with the company well established, it was not improbable for competition-minded folk at Zuffenhausen to turn their thoughts toward Grand Prix racing.

Porsche had already carved a great name for itself in the 1500cc Formula 2 category with the 550A Spyders of Edgar Barth, Stirling Moss, and Wolfgang von Trips. An impetus to enter Formula 1 came when the FIA decided to reduce the capacity limit from 2.5 to 1.5 liters for the 1961 season. This was a displacement familiar to the Porsche people, and they felt, along with other manufacturers, that it would open up GP racing to a much broader range of companies.

Porsche's first Grand Prix cars were fours, based on the most recent Formula 2s, the 718s and 718/2s. A Formula 2 Porsche had scored its first win in the German GP of 1957, and its successors would repeat in 1-2 order at the 1960 running. From this grew an F1 variant designated Type 787, built during the winter of 1960-61 for the '61 schedule. Like the 718, it used wishbone suspension and a tubular frame. Power was provided by the well-proven Type 547/3 engine with Kügelfischer fuel injection. Wheelbase was 90.5 inches, track 51.2/50.0 inches front/rear.

Dan Gurney and Joakim Bonnier, two highly competitive and experienced drivers, were assigned 787s for the car's initial outings. The first two races, at Monaco and Zandvoort, were not encouraging. The drivers considered the 787 inferior in handling and performance to the opposition, both British and Italian. After this inauspicious beginning they switched back to 718/2 cars while the 787s were returned to the factory for more study. But the 718s were really outclassed. The hard-driving Gurney did tie for third place in the Driver's Championship with Moss, but no Porsche won an F1

race that year. A privateer, Count Carel Godin de Beaufort, also competed in four-cylinder Porsches even after the appearance of the eight-cylinder cars, but he admittedly raced for the sheer joy of it and never placed high.

Zuffenhausen's experiments with the 787 saw it developing 185 bhp by early 1962. But its last GP outing was anticlimactic. At Zandvoort, where Gurney and Bonnier had been disappointed the year before, Ben Pon of the Dutch importers spun his car on lap four. It was the 787's last appearance as a "factory" entry.

Work on the GP engine designed to take the four's place was begun in 1959 under the direction of a clever young engineer, Hans Mezger. It carried Type number 753, and was fitted in the 787 chassis. Porsche already had an inkling at this time that a derivation of the Spyder/Carrera engine would not be enough. Yet the engine that emerged represented traditional Porsche thinking in that it was a flat-opposed type. This configuration would give the car a low, aerodynamic profile and allow optimum handling through a low center of gravity. It also easily lent itself to air cooling. The difference was that this new powerplant had eight cylinders.

Designing the GP engine was no picnic. According to Karl Ludvigsen, "it was pure hell to work on. It was as hard to adjust the valve timing on the early eight, said Mezger, as it was to do the same job on the 12-cylinder 917. And the assembly...required 220 skilled man-hours, an almost unbelievable 27½ 8-hour days—

Porsche's F2 experience provided the impetus to enter Formula 1 under the 1.5-liter 1961 regulations. The 1960 F2 cars (left and above) were virtually identical with with 718RSK.

which of course do not exist in the world of racing." Porsche calculated that it would need to wring out at least 200 DIN horsepower to have a competitive powerplant, and when the first engines were tested they yielded a mere 120.

The bore/stroke relationship (66.0×54.6 mm) was oversquare, though the reason for such a short stroke was to hold down engine width for aero purposes. The bore could go as far as 78 mm, which it did for the 2.0-liter sports/racing formula. The double overhead cams used a shaft-and-bevel-gear drive system not unlike that of the Formula 2 Spyder engine. Lightness was achieved by cast aluminum cylinder heads and aluminum castings for the valve gear and camshafts. The block and cam covers were made of magnesium. There were two spark plugs per cylinder, governed by twin Bosch distributors, and carburetion was via four 38 mm two-barrel Webers.

By early 1961, engineers had the flat eight up to 160 bhp, but this was still far short of the goal. Rather than field it and lose, Porsche ran four-cylinder cars and experimented with a fuel injection system developed by Kügelfischer in Munich. This provided a single-piston injector pump for each cylinder, and metered the mixture via variations in piston stroke.

Nothing of substance developed in the actual racing that year; Dan Gurney came close at Rheims, but that was with a carburetor model. Porsche tinkered throughout 1961 with suspension and brakes, and its early work with disc brakes (which had begun in 1957) was applied to the Formula racer. Double-wishbone suspension was deemed necessary. Though the engineers found it less worthy than their traditional trailing links, it was needed to allow for constant small camber changes under racing conditions. One heartening point was that engine reliability seemed good: on test, the flat eight ran at maximum rpm for 12 hours before a conrod bearing packed up.

By the start of the '62 season, Porsche felt the flat eight was ready, but meanwhile had developed a better chassis. This was designated Type 804, the only 800-series project number ever assigned by Zuffenhausen. With streamlining very much in mind, this car had a lower, more slippery body and weighed only 15 pounds more than the FIA minimum of 990 pounds. It rode the same 90.5-inch wheelbase used for the four-cylinder racers.

As the season was about to open, Hans Thomalla, who had overseen Mezger for two years, replaced Klaus von Rücker as chief engineer. Determined to get into the GP fray, Thomalla entered the 804 for the lead-off event at Zandvoort, the fast, flat track on the Dutch sands. Bonnier finished seventh, but Gurney had to retire because a bizarre fault: his gearshift lever came adrift on the 48th lap.

Ferry Porsche wondered if he shouldn't give up on the whole idea. Gurney, Thomalla, and racing manager Huschke von Hanstein convinced him to stay with it for the second GP stop, Monte Carlo. Here, Gurney started third on the grid, but a serious pileup on the first lap put his 804 out of commission immediately. Porsche elected to pass up the Belgian Grand Prix at Spa and go back to the drawing boards. The racing team had now grown beards, vowing not to shave until a Porsche triumphed.

Back home, efforts were divided between improving still further both body streamlining and engine power (the flat eight was still not putting out more than 180 bhp). The seat was raked farther back, the rollbar lowered, and the fuel tanks reshaped accordingly; the front suspension was beefed up and a rear sway bar added; Bilstein shocks replaced Konis; horsepower was pushed up to about 185.

After Gurney turned in 15 good test laps at the Nürburgring, von Hanstein was allowed to return to the wars at the French Grand Prix at Rouen. Gurney won this race—the only GP win with championship points ever recorded by Porsche—strictly by attrition. Jim Clark's Lotus and Graham Hill's BRM were both about half a minute ahead when they were successively forced to retire. "If you win a GP, why you take it," Gurney remembered, "but some of the other guys were faster and they had difficulties, so I inherited the darn thing. I was trying my darndest, but it wasn't the same as jumping out and really legitimately blowing them all off." But the team shaved their beards anyway.

Though Solitude's 177-mile marathon would not count toward the championship, it was not conceded by the opposition. Lotus and BRM arrived to do battle. Some 350,000 people gathered at the beautiful circuit, hoping to see the hometown cars repeat the French win of the weekend before. They were not disappointed. Clark was quickest in practice, attaining pole position. But by the end of the first lap Gurney's 804-03 was ahead—and there he stayed. Before long, Bonnier had passed Clark and was holding down second place, gamely pressing on, although short 300 rpm after the loss of one of his four tailpipes. It was Gurney all the way, turning in a record 108.37 mph lap in the process. "Afterward, going around on the victory lap, all those people were throwing their hats in the air as I went by," Gurney said. "I was very proud of that victory."

Alas, Solitude proved the high point of Porsche's Formula 1 fortunes. The team anticipated

Opposite page: The eight-cylinder Type 804 F1 car in its original 1962 form. This page: The 804 as it is today, one of Dan Gurney's mounts from the Porsche Museum.

doing well in the German Grand Prix at the Nürburgring, another home-country circuit known for its twists and turns. Gurney qualified first on the grid, but Hill had his BRM running right, and John Surtees came home second in a Lola. Gurney had to settle for third. All three drove a masterly race on the rain-soaked course, but Gurney termed the event "the most disappointing... We had all worked very hard—all the engineers and mechanics—and then to not win that race was very difficult to swallow. Especially because this car was, even in the wet, capable of winning the race if we could ever have gotten back in front... but it played hell getting around those guys because they could hold me up in the turns and then out-accelerate me."

The next trial for the 804 came at Monza in the Italian Grand Prix, where again the team hoped to have eliminated its problems. Weight was shifted forward by positioning a fuel tank in the nose, and the cooling fan could now be disengaged by the driver for 8-10 seconds when extra power was needed. But Bonnier managed only sixth place due to a slipping clutch, and Gurney's car packed up before the finish with a defective rear axle. Last stop was Watkins Glen, the U.S. Grand Prix, where Gurney finished a disappointing fifth while Bonnier pranged his exhaust system but held on to finish 13th. By the last championship race of the season, at Kyalami in South Africa, Porsche had decided to retire from F1 racing for good.

Though rumors of a fresh onslaught buzzed around during the winter of 1962-63, Ferry Porsche was convinced that in Formula 1 at least, an orderly retreat was necessary. Porsche was one of the few passenger car manufacturers engaged in Grand Prix racing—the largest by far—and its interests were too broad to warrant the colossal expenditure that developing a competitive entry required. Although faithful to racing as an unbeatable testing ground and as a good source of publicity, Ferry saw more fertile fields in Formula 2 and the sports/racing classes where Porsche had already displayed ability. The company released its two GP pilots in December 1962.

One bright spot in the story: one Type 804, the Gurney car, has been preserved by the Porsche Museum. He drove it again for his 1982 retrospective in *Auto Motor und Sport*: "There's a certain time machine aspect to it that's very, very pleasant. You identify with this old faithful horse. You've been through quite a bit together and that's a very special feeling also."

PRODUCTION RACERS 1948-PRESENT: IMPROVING THE BREED

On July 11, 1948, a curious-looking, bathtub-shaped silver roadster driven by Herbert Kaes was entered in an open road race at Innsbrück, Austria. It was not in the least modified for competition, and in fact ran with its standard windshield and road wheels. Its top speed was a mere 84 mph, but it won its class. That inauspicious debut began a victory streak that continues to this day: Porsche has won probably more production-class races than any of its rivals — if indeed there are any.

In the early years of the 356, Porsche was well known for rallying — not rallying in the American style, where precise timing is as important as speed, but in the European form, where speed is almost everything and performance on "special stages" crucial. In 1950 and 1951, for example, Porsches of various displacements from 1.1 to 1.5 liters racked up class wins in the Swedish (twice), Alpine, and Tavemünde rallies, and in the demanding Tour de France. Porsche often handed rally drivers one of the Gmünd coupes, the 356SL. A 1.1 coupe carried the colors on the difficult Liége-Rome-Liége Rally in 1951, when Huschke von Hanstein and Petermax Müller piloted it to second in class, achieving speeds close to 100 mph on only 46 horsepower. In 1952, the 1.5s were ready, and an overall victory fell to Porsche in this famous rally, with Helmut Polensky and Walter Schlüter driving; other Porsches captured third, fourth, ninth, and 10th places overall. Porsche also debuted in style at the 1952 Monte Carlo rally, when a coupe completed the road portion of this always-treacherous event without a single penalty point.

Porsche continued to rally with the later Super 90s and Carreras with increasing success. Its championship wins are too numerous to list here, but they leave no doubt about its cars' ability to stand up to the difficult conditions of these events. In fact, rally experience has been almost as important as track racing in the development of Porsche passenger cars.

America roadster dices with a C-Type Jaguar in 1952.

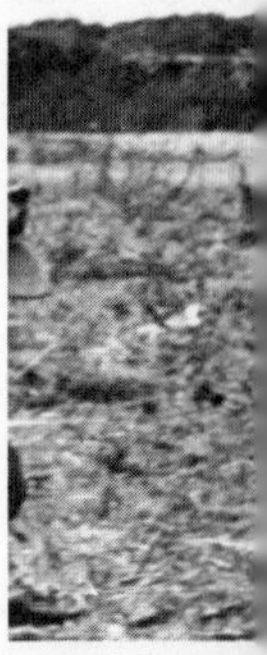

The factory's first Le Mans effort came in 1951, when Porsche planned to enter a quartet of 356SL coupes. Two cars were damaged in practice while a third, made up from the pieces of another, crashed during the race. But Auguste Veuillet, who had originally convinced Porsche to enter the 24 Hours, won his class at 73.5 mph and finished 20th in a field of potent machinery. It may have taken four cars to produce one winner, but Porsche did it. Veuillet returned in 1952, improving his speed to 76.7 mph, and finished 11th with a 1.5-liter car, which again won its class. Last year for the aluminum coupes at Le Mans was 1953, but this event was a disappointment, with mechanical problems interfering.

The man responsible for Porsche's emergence in American competition was Max Hoffman, the energetic Austrian founder of the import car business in the U.S. Hoffman himself drove a 356 cabriolet up Vermont's Mt. Equinox in October 1951 to win his class—Porsche's official competition debut in the States. Later, he brought over three Le Mans-prepped coupes, which didn't distinguish themselves, however. Their best showing was at Torrey Pines, California in July 1952, when John von Neumann (who would set up Porsche's sales operations on the West Coast) drove a 1.5 car to victory in the 1500cc modified class.

In Europe, meanwhile, the 1.5-liter cars were entering and winning more races, the most significant of which was the Mille Miglia, the formidable 1000-mile race up and down the boot of Italy. Driven by Count "Johnny" Lurani and rally ace Konstantin "Tin" Berckheim, a modified 1.5 beat

Clockwise from opposite page top: A '49 356SL converted roadster in restoration. John Von Neumann drove it in 1952 (leading a Glockler-Porsche). Early 356 coupe in action. Jack McAfee's America leads Ken Miles in 1953. A 356 coupe in the '53 Carrera Panamericana. A pair of 356s in an early '50s German road race.

every car in its class, though its overall position was only 46th.

The early 1.5 class victories led Porsche to develop the Type 528 or 1500 Super competition engine. In its initial form it produced 70 DIN horsepower, but it soon had more. It was this engine that would power the first Type 550s (Chapter 12), thus beginning the story of the racing Spyders.

As the cars improved, Zuffenhausen widened its horizons. With the 1953 Type 356, Porsche was able to place eighth overall at the third *Carrera Panamericana* (Mexican Road Race), running in the sports car class at an 83-mph average. This was a much better showing than it appears, because the class at that time was wide open; the higher-placed finishers were all larger, considerably more potent machines—Mercedes 300SLs, Ferraris, and Lancias. (It is also a matter of record that Porsche 550s finished 1-2 in the "Light Sports" class at the last two

Above: A 1954 356 coupe tackles rally mud and muck. Opposite page top: Herbert Linge's Carrera GS/GT 2.0 at the 1963 Nurburgring 1000 Kilometers. Immediate and far right: The lovely and aerodynamic Abarth-Carrera GTL (shown with non-standard wheels) scored numerous wins from 1960 to '63.

Mexican Road Races, 1953 and 1954).

With the mid-Fifties arrival of the 356A, the Speedster, and the 1500GS Carrera, the number of Porsches competing in U.S. production-car races grew into a hoarde. Dr. Richard Thompson, later to win fame with Corvettes, broke the ice in 1954, the first year SCCA ran national championships. Thompson tied with Art Bunker for the F-Production title, both in 1500 Super cabriolets. The light and competitive Speedster allowed Bengt Soderstrom of New Jersey to take the F-Production title the following year, after which F/P became a parade of 1500GS Carreras. It wasn't until 1960, when SCCA no longer classified cars strictly by displacement, that Porsche's stranglehold on Class F ended.

The Speedster was an ideal racing car, almost from the first. John von Neumann teamed with Erich Bücklers in a 1500S Speedster on Thanksgiving weekend 1954, finishing eighth in the Torrey Pines six-hours; they came back the next day to win the 1500cc production class. Speedsters have kept winning through the years, though they are now almost too valuable for such activities. Still, it's not uncommon to see a Speedster rocket up Mt. Equinox (now a venue for the Vintage Sports Car Club of America) in fine time or for a well-driven Speedster to run newer iron off the track in a road race. They'll probably still be doing it years from now.

SCCA classification juggling directly affected the Carrera's competition scorecard. Basically, it was faster than everything in sight in Class C, but not normally quick enough for the small-block Corvettes in Class B. This accounts for a gap in championship crowns after 1960,

when Bruce Jennings won Class C going away and was promptly bumped up to Corvette country. Even then, many were the B/P events where Jennings staged incredible onslaughts against the fiberglass Chevys. Occasionally he'd beat them, especially in the rain. The sight of Bob Grossman's Sting Ray, wearing less and less plastic each lap following a shunt at Connecticut's Thompson Raceway, and with Jennings ever closer at his heels in the Porsche, is not one fans are likely to forget. Of course, the crowd was usually pro-import and would cheer Jennings on, which didn't make the Corvette people any happier. In 1964, when SCCA put the Carreras back into Class C, they took over again. Jennings won the '64 championship; Richard Smith was Pacific champ in the divisionally divided 1965 standings, then national champion in 1966. After that the 911s took over, but the Carreras, like the Speedster, are still seen occasionally. And they're still awesome.

In Europe, the Carrera was in no danger in the displacement-based FIA 1600 GT class during 1959, but a possible challenge from the Lotus Elite and Alfa Giulietta moved Zuffenhausen to commission 20 special lightweight bodies from Zagato. Because Zagato was also building bodies for the competition, Carlo Abarth acted as the ostensible builder. Thus was born the Abarth-Carrera GTL. Clearly designed more for competition than road work, it was nevertheless approved as a production GT by the FIA. The Abarth-Carrera was beautiful as well as aerodynamic, with a light aluminum body helping to keep curb weight down to just 1800 pounds. Its first competition performance was the 1960 Targa Florio, where Paul Strähle and Herbert Linge placed sixth and won their class outright. GTLs took the 1600cc Sports Class 1-2-3 at the Nürburgring, and one won its class at Le Mans, finishing 11th overall. For 1961, the car got a new Type 692/3A engine with plain instead of roller bearings to permit higher revs (up to 7800 rpm), and in this form the highest tuned (Sebring) cars delivered 140 bhp. Class wins and/or high overall finishes were recorded at the Targa, Le Mans, the 1000km of Paris, and Sebring. Even in 1963 the GTL was still competitive, placing fifth and seventh overall at the Daytona Continental in February and finishing at Sebring. Power increases up to 146.5 bhp were planned, but the performance of the prototypes didn't impress.

Gradually, the Porsche most favored for production GT racing became the lightweight, special-bodied Carrera 2. Privateers continued to run the GTL, however; one won the Twin 400 at Bridgehampton, Long Island in 1962. For long-haul events, it was later replaced by the 904 GTS, but the GTL had enjoyed an exceptional career. "Not until the Seventies did [the name Carrera] regain the original sense of a high-performance variant of the normal production Porsche,"

Top left: The Linge/Barth 2000 GS/GT, third overall at the '63 Targa Florio. Above and bottom left: The 911 earned its competition honors in rallying, as in the 1967 and '68 Monte Carlo events.

wrote Karl Ludvigsen. "In its later phase, however, it lacked the incomparably esoteric flavor of the original Carrera, with its race bred engine in a civilized chassis."

The 911 took over where the 356 left off. On introduction, it was classified for D-Production by the SCCA, but encountered little real competition there. In a mildly "prodified" car sponsored by famed dealer and racing enthusiast Vasek Polak, Jerry Titus won the D/P title going away in 1966. Meanwhile, at Le Mans, a 911 that had been driven to the race over public roads finished 14th overall—after which it was nonchalantly driven home again! It was probably one of the best Le Mans finishes for a race-and-ride sports car up to that time.

When the 911 arrived, Porsche offered special competition packages that turned the car into a track star at comparatively low cost. Suspension package #W171, for example, included anti-sway bars, special brake pads, and a driver's footrest. There were also two engine kits, one comprising special carburetor jets and venturis and rudimentary carb filters, the second including blueprinted heads and manifolds. Together, the kits raised output to 175 bhp, and made the 911 formidable in its new C-Production racing class. C/P was dominated by Alan Johnson two years running, 1967-68, and by Milt Minter in 1969, although the class became a Datsun parade after that on the strength of the incredibly fast Z-cars. Johnson also won the GT class at Sebring 1967 and the National Championship at Daytona.

Across the pond, the 911S dominated the GT Hillclimb Championship and numerous rallies. Vic Elford and David Stone, two expert Englishmen with a 911T, won Porsche's first Monte Carlo Rally in 1968, a triumph Zuffenhausen had long sought. The four-cylinder 912 was also competitive, with Polish driver Sobieslaz Zasada winning the 1967 European Rally Championship and outlasting 375 competitors for an outright win in the car-killing Argentine Grand Prix, a 2000-mile open road contest that broke more cars than finished.

Just barely "stock" was the 911R, conceived by Ferdinand Piëch in 1967 to stretch the various rules in rallies and GT racing. The first three Rs used fiberglass bumpers, front fenders, doors, engine cover, and front "hood," and thinner-gauge steel appeared elsewhere wherever possible. Aluminum hinges, Plexiglas side and rear windows, and a lightened, detrimmed cockpit were also featured. Fenders were flared to allow wider tires. The engine (Type 901/22) was quite similar to the Carrera 6 unit, with its dual ignition, valve timing, oversize valves and ports, chrome-plated cylinder bores, and two Type 46 triple-throat Weber carburetors. Compression was 10.3:1. Output was 210 bhp at 8000 rpm with 152 pounds-feet of torque at a towering 6000 rpm. Twin oil coolers and a five-speed gearbox completed the specification. One of the 911R's first achievements was a distance enduro at Monza:

A 911 in SCCA B-Production competition. Car shown was campaigned by the Brumos Porsche dealership and driven by Peter Gregg.

10,000 miles, 15,000 and 20,000km, 72 and 90 hours, all covered at speeds *averaging* over 140 mph. As a result, five world's records in the 2.0-liter class fell to Porsche.

In mid-1967, Porsche assigned the Stuttgart firm of Karl Baur to build 20 more 911Rs, using standard-gauge steel and adding quick-fill fuel tanks plus deep bucket seats. The intention was, eventually, to build 500 copies and homologate the 911R for FIA Grand Touring. But the sales department felt it could not move this many, and the project ended. But had it come off, Porsche would have undoubtedly had a formidable FIA competitor—not to mention what it might do in SCCA B-Production. The 911R did manage an outright win in the 1969 Tour de France, racing in the prototype class, thus proving not only its performance but also its reliability.

The 911's more recent competition outings have included rallying and enduros. A team of 911Es finished 1-2 in the 85-hour *Marathon de la Route*, held on the trying 16-mile Nürburgring in August 1968, just

Below: A special lightweight 911 variant, the 911ST 2.2, was developed for the 1970 racing season.

as that model was making its European debut. A 911S team blitzed the 1970 Monte Carlo rally, finishing first, second, and fourth. The intrepid Sobieslaz Zasada had followed up his overland caper in Argentina with private entries for the East African Safari in 1969-70, so Porsche decided to field a three-car factory team for the 1971 edition of that famous car-killer. The 911 trio used 180-bhp engines, plus extra fuel tanks, raised suspensions, beefy torsion bars, and rally equipment. But the raised suspensions made the shock absorber rods vulnerable, and two cars had to retire. Zasada drove the third S home to fifth place despite an erratic ignition system—proof positive that a 911 could withstand the perils of Kenya, Uganda, and Tanzania: elephant herds, spear-tossing natives, and things that go bump in the night. Zasada tried again in 1973, Björn Waldegaard in 1974, but they failed to nail down the coveted win.

Through the early Seventies, 911s followed up with further racing victories: first in the GT class, sixth overall at Le Mans 1971, the European GT championship and FIA Cup for GT cars, the IMSA Camel GT Challenge, and the Six Hours of Daytona, all in 1972. Zasada came back to place second in the 1972 Safari, while another 911 driven by Gérard Larrouse was second at the 1972 Monte Carlo Rally. After this, the field cleared for the return of the Carrera, the RS and RSR competition models. Details on these brilliant competitors are found in Chapter 11, but their incredible skien of wins may be summarized here:

1973
Targa Florio, 1st (Müller & Van Lennep)
Daytona 24 Hours, 1st (Gregg & Haywood)
Sebring 12 Hours, 1st (Gregg, Haywood & Helmick)
European GT Championship
European Hillclimb Championship
IMSA GT Championship (Gregg)
SCCA Trans-Am GT Championship (Gregg)

1974
European GT Championship (Fitzpatrick)
European Hillclimb Championship (Fischhaber)
IMSA GT Championship (Gregg)

1975
IMSA GT Championship (Gregg)
European GT Championship (Bertrams)
European Hillclimb Championship (Bering)
Daytona 24 Hours, 1st (Gregg & Haywood)

1976
Sebring 12 Hours, 1st (Holbert & Keyser)
European Hillclimb Championship

As for the humble 914, most of the competition effort went into the six-cylinder model. And, though 914/6s were often tested on rally routes or practice sessions, the effort was aimed at track racing, not rallying, which was 911 territory. A lukewarm one-year effort was made in 1970 by Porsche+Audi in SCCA

C-Production, that always hotly contested category then dominated by Datsun 240Zs and Triumph TR6s, both with ample factory backing. The 914/6s did prove competitive, winning four of the seven divisional championships, but they were overpowered by Z-cars in the decisive American Road Race of Champions, and the C-Production title went to Datsun and John Morton. Factory backing melted away, and though several division championships were won in later years the national title eluded the mid-engine Porsche.

For European GT Group 4 competition Porsche readied a special car, the 914/6 GT. It carried wide wheels and tires under bulging fenders, which were created by welded-on extensions. The engine remained at 2.0 liters but was highly modified, with Weber carbs instead of fuel injection, special heads, dual ignition, high-dome pistons, and aluminum cylinders. Horsepower was between 210 and 220 (DIN). Appropriate improvements were made to the suspension and brakes as well. A quartet of GTs performed well at the Nürburgring 1000 Kilometers in 1970, finishing 2-3-4-5 behind the class winner, a 911L. A single GT was entered at that year's Le Mans, where it surprised everybody by finishing first in class and sixth overall in a gale-lashed race of severe attrition. That car, driven by Guy Chasseuil and Claude Ballot-Léna of France, averaged 99.27 mph and 13.56 miles per

Opposite page: A prodified E-Production 914 racer at Road Atlanta. This page: A much-modified, 916-like 914 (left) as seen at a recent vintage race in California. The 911 fared well in early-'70s East African Safaris. The later SC (below) is shown with appropriate equipment.

Above: The winning Elford/Stone 911T in the 1968 Monte Carlo Rally. Below: Tom Brennan took the '81 D-Production crown with his 924.

gallon, placing it second in the Index of Efficiency. Then, a team of 914/6 GTs (two of which ran in Group 6 because of their extra wide tires and wider fender bubbles) knocked off the *Marathon de la Route* at the 'Ring, finishing 1-2-3 with little difficulty. Two more GTs, driven by Prince von Hohenzollern and Günther Steckkönig, landed 1-2 in the Osterreichring endurance race, picking up enough points to clinch the International GT trophy for Porsche. Smiles turned to frowns when a GT onslaught on the 1971 Monte Carlo Rally was stopped cold by the Alpine-Renaults, which gave away 400cc to the 914s yet were faster.

Back in the States, the 914/6 fared better in the IMSA GT Challenge, swept by Peter Gregg and Hurley Haywood in a Brumos Porsche car that managed to win two of the six rounds outright. This gave Porsche the IMSA crown in the under-2.5-liter group. But SCCA stopped the GT cold by shifting it to B-Production the same year, the category that was owned by Allan Barker's Corvettes between 1969 and 1972.

In a competition world dominated by Porsche 935s we tend to lose sight of the long and continuing victory record of the production cars. The 911SC runs on undaunted. At the 24 Hours of Daytona in 1981, for example, the Koll/Kline/McFarlin entry finished third overall, first in the under-2.5-liter class, covering 644 laps.

Though it hasn't been competing nearly as long as the 911, the front-engine 924 has racked up several notable placings. Among these are an astonishing sixth overall (surrounded by Rondeaus, 908s and 935K3s) at Le Mans '80, Manfred Schürti and Jürgen

Opposite page: The turbocharged 924 Carrera GT appeared in 1980 as Porsche's "customer" road racer. Model was never imported to the States, but it inspired the shape of the new Type 944.

Barth driving the 924 Carrera GT for 316 laps. Turbo 924s have been developed for Group 4 competition in Europe, retaining the familiar bodyshell but mounting fiberglass doors and decklid, as well as flared fiberglass fenders to house wide wheels and tires. Their Kügelfischer fuel-injected fours dispense 310 to 320 horsepower. During Le Mans testing in 1980, one of these cars was three to four seconds quicker than the fastest RSR Carrera. And at a "sort-of" Le Mans at Nelson Ledges, Ohio in June 1981, a well-prepared 924 outlasted the field, completing 919 laps and 1839 miles to win outright against a variety of showroom-stock vehicles, including a squad of Ford EXP/Mercury LN7s piloted by staffers from *Road & Track* and *Car and Driver* magazines. In 1982, a new 944 blithely soared home the winner in a repeat performance, the *C/D* and *R&T* boys dicing it up in the backfield with Mustang prototypes.

Showroom Stock is an increasingly popular class in SCCA racing. Only minimal mods are allowed, "just like the good old days," and the 924/944 continues to be a favorite in SS Class A. Ken Williams captured the national title for Porsche in 1980.

Porsche has shown a special interest in the hotly competitive SCCA Production classes, commencing with the 924. The departure of the factory-backed British Leyland Triumphs following the demise of that marque in America makes the D-Production Datsun Z-cars rather obvious targets. Dealers Al Holbert and Joe Herman fielded a pair of experimental 924s for D/P toward the end of the 1979 season, with past champs Tom Robertson and Tom Brennan as drivers. The cars were specially prepared in the competition shops at Porsche's Weissach research center with the object of standardizing a racing kit for amateur drivers. The 1980 D/P kit included a special engine, gearbox, brakes, wheels, suspension, body parts, windows, roll cage, and seats—in other words, anything that didn't come with the road car and that SCCA would allow. The prototypes had aluminum shocks, titanium-alloy coil springs, and lightweight trailing arms; front struts were adjustable for camber and ride height; brakes were ventilated discs taken from the 928; the rear suspension used coil springs instead of torsion bars. The engine, developing 175 bhp in 1980, was fed by a hand-built Kügelfischer mechanical injection system. Fiberglass body panels and plexiglass rear-quarter windows and backlight left the car so light that it required ballast to meet the legal minimum. For the record, "Doc" Bundy and Tom Brennan won the national D/P championship in 1980 and '81, respectively, with 924s. So, an exciting decade is shaping up for the front-engine four-cylinder Porsches.

Lest we forget, the luxurious

Opposite page and above: The Turbo 924 special as seen at Le Mans '80. Left: Rudi Lins and Gerhard Plattner before their New York-Moscow-Paris endurance run in a 928.

928 has won a few laurels of its own. A European version, very similar to the U.S. model, covered over 3700 miles at 155 mph at the Nardo track outside of Brindisi in southern Italy in December 1982. Establishing themselves as "the world's fastest Sunday drivers," the international long-distance team of Gerhard Plattner (Austria), Peter Lovett (Great Britain), and Peter Abinden (Switzerland) experienced virtually no problems during the test; the only maintenance required was replacing one pair of Pirelli tires. With less than half the horsepower, the 928s actually went faster, on the circular track, than the 1982 Le Mans-winning Porsche 956.

With 0-60 mph available in under seven seconds and a top speed of 146 mph, the 1983 American-market 928S is billed as "the fastest 'street legal' production car" sold in this country. Whether or not that's strictly true, such a claim is encouraging, for it shows we've come a long way from the days of the original energy crisis. Then, most builders of high-performance cars dared not let on what they could really do. But Porsche was not really one of them. And that perhaps more than any other fact explains the company, its cars, and why both continue to do so well on the track and on the sales charts.

TYPE 930/934/935: PORSCHE'S MIGHTY TURBOS

The Type 930 Turbo stands a fair chance to become the most sought-after sports car of the late 1970s. Right now, the market is soft. Clean specimens sell for about what they cost new—$26,000 in the beginning—while others, concours examples and low-mileage originals, bring twice that. However, the price these Porsches will command a quarter century from now is something one can only guess at. Collectors might keep in mind that Duesenbergs once sold for as little as $1500 just after World War II, yet today's Turbos, at $30,000 or so, represent just as much relative appreciation potential as the Duesie did back then.

The reason isn't hard to find: the Turbo easily ranks among the great cars of all time. It's a car very much in the tradition of the Mercer Raceabout, the Bugatti Type 35, the Alfa Romeo 8C 2900B, the Mercedes-Benz 300SL Gullwing, and the Ferrari Daytona. It is a jewel of engineering and manufacturing, a machine so superior to just about every other sports car of its time that little else could be fairly—or logically—compared to it. To drive one is to experience the rear-engine concept taken to its

highest form. Lean, mean, devastatingly powerful yet remarkably quiet, it is a masterpiece, a work of art. Leaving aside any technical resemblance to those earlier classics—and there is none—the Turbo was at least conceptually similar in several ways. Like them, it represented an all-out assault on every motoring standard its world had come to accept. Like them, it was restricted both by definition and intent to the fortunate and the wealthy, astronomically expensive and produced only in fairly limited numbers.

The Turbo was yet another creation of the prolific Ernst Fuhrmann, who served as president of the Porsche company from 1972 to 1982. Fuhrmann, it will be remembered, had personally designed the four-cam engine for the 356 Carrera. He also directed design of the later 911-based RS and RSR Carreras. He knew and appreciated good engineers, and he hired many of them himself. He knew without doubt that racing really does improve the breed. And he also knew a good deal about turbochargers from Porsche's work on the tremendous

The 1977-model U.S. Type 930, the Turbo Carrera

12-cylinder blown powerplant for the racing 917. Would a turbo-supercharger work on a Porsche 911? One of the first things Fuhrmann did after becoming president was to set in motion a program to find out.

In 1973, Zuffenhausen displayed a "911 Turbo" at several European auto shows, but remained less than forthright about plans to produce it. In 1974, the Martini & Rossi team raced a turbocharged 2.1-liter 333-bhp Carrera RSR with mixed results (one was doing 189 mph on the Mulsanne Straight at Le Mans when it threw a rod and retired). Based on experience with this racing turbo, Fuhrmann and company began readying a production version—a smooth, quiet, very fast coupe with a 234-bhp version (in U.S. tune) of the 3.0-liter 911 six. This Turbo Carrera debuted in Europe for the 1975 model year, and the American model was ready a year later. Enthusiasts owe a debt of thanks to Fuhrmann and his team, for they pressed on with the "street" Turbo in spite of the Arab Oil Embargo of 1973-74—and all that that seemed to imply at the time for high-performance, high-thirst cars, both European and American. They did defeat the sales department's campaign, Karl Ludvigsen has recorded, to offer the Turbo at an artificially low price. Fuhrmann felt that if they were going to do it at all, they might as well go all-out. They did.

The Type 930, as it was designated (being sufficiently different from the 911 to deserve a separate number), packed almost every luxury and convenience the factory could squeeze in. Air conditioning, automatic heat control, AM/FM stereo (U.S. version), electric antenna and window lifts, leather upholstery, tinted glass all around, headlamp washers, rear window wiper, Bilstein shock absorbers and oil cooler were all included in the 1976 East Coast base price of $25,880. The option list was short: electric sliding sunroof ($675), limited-slip differential ($345), heavy-duty starter ($50), and "Turbo" graphics ($120). The buyer could also specify custom paint for an additional $250. The Turbo came only as a coupe, and was never offered with Sportomatic, although several

Opposite page: The Type 930's blown 3.0-liter flat six (upper left) as used for 1975. It gave the roadgoing European model (upper right) 260 bhp DIN, good for a 150-mph top end. The early version of the Type 934 racing model (lower left) was also called Turbo Carrera RSR, and retained much of the standard 911's body structure. This page: Introduced to America during the 1976 model year (left), the Type 930 was initially sold here as the Turbo Carrera. Its original engine displacement was 3.0 liters. Comparison views of the racing 934 (center spread and below) and production 930 (bottom) for 1976 show close similarities in general shape.

experimental cars were so equipped and worked well.

The turbocharger was placed on a cast-aluminum manifold studded to the heads, with Ultramid plastic tubes for the K-Jetronic fuel injection placed between manifold and inlet ports. Boost pressure was .8 atmospheres or 11.5 psi. The engine was a 2993cc version of the 911 flat-six (95 × 70.4mm bore and stroke), the extra displacement chosen to produce the best possible off-boost torque with the lower compression necessitated by the addition of the turbo. Though this power unit was admittedly less torquey below 3000 rpm than the 911S engine, things started to happen quickly after that.

"There's no sudden surge of power as there is with the cammy S," noted *Road & Track* magazine. "Rather the buildup is ... strong and silent as the turbocharger muffles the usual raucous sounding Porsche exhaust note to a dull roar. It takes the driver a moment or two to realize some awesome unseen force is pushing him back into his seat and thrusting the Carrera forward at an incredible rate. And another brief moment to realize that the engine is starting to stumble because it's reached its 6950 rpm rev limit. Then it's shift into the next gear and prepare for the same heavy loads and fireworks to start all over again."

R&T allowed that its performance figures were on the high side because of a slipping clutch. This may be seen by comparing its results to those of *Car and Driver*, which also tested a Turbo in 1976:

	Car and Driver	**Road & Track**
0-50 mph (sec.)	3.7	5.2
0-60 mph (sec.)	4.9	6.7
0-80 mph (sec.)	7.9	9.9
0-100 mph (sec.)	12.9	15.3
0-¼-mi. (sec.)	13.5	15.2
top speed (mph)	156	156

The 930's handling was basically routine 911, but the Turbo was more stable at higher speeds, in *R&T*'s opinion, because of its larger rear tires and wider track. This view was not always shared. NASCAR driver Bobby Allison, testing a non-turbo Carrera for *Car and Driver* the year before, didn't think the wider rear tires helped at all, and described the handling as "almost squirrely." But *R&T* said the Turbo was "far and away the easiest Porsche to drive near the limit that we have ever tested." Its 62.8 mph through the magazine's slalom test broke a record held by the Ferrari Boxer—by 2.4 mph. And Sam Posey, who happened by while the editors were testing at Lime Rock, hopped in and unofficially broke the track record for production cars!

The Turbo had stiffer shocks and springs in addition to its wider rear wheels, so it didn't ride as well as lesser Porsches. Steering was heavier, and tire noise from its Pirelli Cinturatos was considerable. There were few complaints about its brakes, which exhibited no fade, were impossible to lock, and were capable of bringing the car to a halt from 60 mph in under 160 feet.

Above all, the 930 was a remarkably civilized car, particularly in view of its performance potential. "It can be pottered around town all day in

Opposite page: The American-market 1977 Type 930 Turbo Carrera (top) sold for $26,000 and could hit 60 mph from rest in 5.5 seconds. U.S. 930s got a displacement boost to 3.3 liters for 1978 (middle), good for 253 SAE net horses. Price jumped to $32,500. The 930 bowed out here after the 1979 season (bottom), mostly due to fuel economy mandates, but is still available new in Europe. This page: Contemporary scenes of the 934 in action. That's George Follmer (above) at the Trois-Rivieres Trans-Am in 1976 leading G.W. Dickinson's No. 14 car (below left and right). Hurley Haywood (right) did well with his 934.

This page: The earliest Type 935s (above) had enormous rear wheels and front ends reminiscent of the stock 911/930. A great deal of experimenting was done with nose, tail, and aerodynamic aids from 1976 on until the 935/78 (right) hardly resembled its production relatives. Opposite page: The 935/76 (upper left and bottom) and the 935/77 (upper right).

top gear and a bit of second without any bother," said Britain's *Autocar* magazine. "And when the town limits are past, there is all that ocean of surging performance under your right foot, immediately, with not the slightest need for tiresome plug-clearing first."

Road & Track, anticipating an earlier end for the 911 series and its derivatives than would prove to be the case, said the Turbo's place in history would be assured through its technological achievements: "In one fell swoop Porsche engineers have not only proved that turbocharging and low emissions are totally compatible, but have also silenced the critics who say racing doesn't improve the breed. True, such clever engineering doesn't come cheaply, but then Porsche has never before offered a 911 with the luxury, performance and technical sophistication of the Turbo." This proved to be perfectly true. There would come a day when a great many high-performance cars would meet emission standards through turbocharging as a matter of course. Like many other bold technical breakthroughs, Porsche had pioneered this one.

The Turbo remained on the U.S. market through the 1979 model year, by which time its base price had risen to over $45,000. Racing developments also proceeded apace, and in 1975 another turbo, the Type 934, was introduced for FIA's Group 4 GT category. Its body was basically stock 911, but the fender flares were fiberglass, pop-riveted to the existing sheetmetal, and there was a huge front air dam as well as the

"whale tail" spoiler out back. Some vestiges of the street car remained. In order to meet minimum Group 4 weight requirements, Porsche left in the power window lifts, door map compartments, and other luxury features. Turbo boost could be altered right from the cockpit via a control knob on the dash. In addition to the basic suspension there were coil springs mounted atop gas-filled Bilstein shock absorbers. Hard plastic bushings replaced rubber in the control arms. Adjustable anti-roll bars were provided front and rear, and Goodyear racing tires were fitted. The brakes came from none other than the 917, with drilled discs, finned wheel cylinders, and twin master cylinders. In order to meet the Group 4 requirements for a near-stock engine, the only changes from 930 specifications were in turbo boost pressure and camshaft timing and duration. One fillip of interest was a *water cooling* system — not for the engine, of course, but for the turbo-boosted air on its way to the cylinder head. This was necessary to prevent loss in volumetric efficiency. A water/alcohol mixture was used, and the cooler was mounted in the front air dam. Porsche built 31 of these 934 Turbo RSRs, and sold every one of them for $40,000 apiece.

Then there was the Type 935, yet a further development that barely resembled the 930 and compared to it in performance as a 911 does to a VW Beetle. This car was designed for the Group 5 World Championship. (Both 934 and 935 took the last number of their designation from their GT racing class.) The 930 base was again used, because a ground-up racing car would not qualify: FIA had adopted new "silhouette" regulations, requiring cars to look "approximately" like the street versions—but only approximately.

Two Type 935s were initially built. There was hardly anything on them that resembled the 930: doors, fenders, deck, hood, and spoilers were of fiberglass, windows were of Plexiglas. So much weight was shaved, in fact, that Porsche had to *add* 150 pounds to bring the car back up to minimum. Naturally, all this was laid on the front end. Because the FIA allowed modified fenders, those of later 935s were utterly different from stock: aerodynamically low and smooth, with headlamps mounted in the huge air dam. Inside was a single deep bucket seat surrounded by the regulation rollcage. A big 8000-rpm tach dominated the instrument panel, flanked by boost pressure and other minor gauges. A central lever allowed the driver to adjust rear anti-roll bar stiffness as fuel diminished and weight distribution changed. The front anti-roll bar was also adjustable. The suspension comprised adjustable titanium coil springs up front (instead of the conventional torsion bars) and trailing arms at the rear. The brakes were basically conventional, but with extra cooling ducts, while the tires were an eye-popping 19 inches wide on 14½-inch rims. Front tire width was 16 inches.

Because the engine was turbocharged, the 935's displacement would be multiplied by a factor of 1.4 as a handicap. To keep it under the class limit of 4000cc, the engine was debored to 92mm, giving actual displacement of 2875cc. Bosch mechanical fuel injection replaced the K-Jetronic system of the production 930 Turbo. Also fitted were dual ignition and lightweight engine components such as titanium conrods; boost pressure was higher than stock, 19-22 psi. Result: 590 DIN horsepower at 7900 rpm, with 434

continued on page 209

Below: An American-entered 935/77 for the IMSA GT series. Bottom: The Martini Racing Team won the World Sports Car Championship with this 935/76, shown (bottom) blazing through the night at Daytona.

An example of the Carrera RSR 3.0 racer

PORSCHE

The fabulous Type 930 Turbo was claimed to be the fastest street-legal sports car available in America. Derived from the 911, it was introduced to the U.S. for 1976 (a year behind its European debut) as the Turbo Carrera, and was known simply as Turbo after '77. U.S. imports ceased after the 1979 model year, but production still continues in Germany.

First seen in the U.S. for the 1978 model year, the luxurious Type 928 firmly established Porsche in the luxury GT market. The futuristic body design is the work of American Tony Lapine, and has been little changed since introduction. The 928 was initially offered with a 4.5-liter all-aluminum overhead-cam V-8 with 219 bhp (SAE net). The latest 928S version has a 4.7-liter power unit developing 234 bhp, plus uprated chassis.

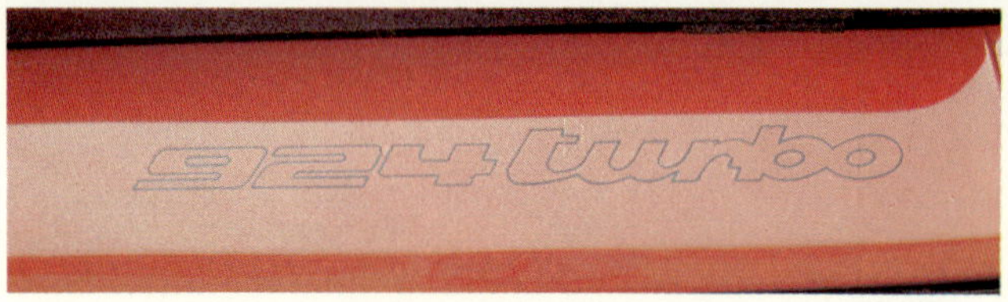

Following demise of the Type 930 Turbo in the U.S., Porsche introduced a turbocharged version of its front-engine 924 for the 1980 model year. Shown is the 1981 edition. Like its normally aspirated counterpart, the 924 Turbo was powered by a 2.0-liter overhead-cam inline four, but the turbo unit boosted output to 143 bhp (SAE net), good for a 0-60 mph time of about 9 seconds and a top-end speed of close to 140 mph. Distinguishing the 924 Turbo externally were a molded-in rubber spoiler at the base of the hatchback window, a functional hood air duct, cooling slots in the nose, and distinctive "spider web" alloy wheels to complement the firmer suspension. Still available in Europe, the model was succeeded in the U.S. by the Type 944.

New to the U.S. for 1977, the sleekly styled Type 924 both maintained Porsche tradition and established a new one. It was the first of the front-engine Porsches, with a rear transaxle resulting in very even weight distribution for near-neutral handling. It was also the first Porsche with a water-cooled engine, which was actually supplied by VW, recalling the origins of the earliest Porsche cars. Unlike the later 924 Turbo, the normally aspirated 924s were assembled by Audi, not Porsche itself. Pictured here is the 1979 American-market model with extra-cost "S" equipment group that included fog lights and the lovely "spider web" alloy wheels. Though criticized initially, the 924 was constantly improved in succeeding years in both performance and refinement. U.S. imports ceased after 1982.

PORSCHE
STUTTGART

The U.S. version of the current four-cylinder Porsche, the 1983 Type 944. Though obviously derived from the Type 924/924 Turbo, the 944 features revised bodywork inspired by the European Carrera GT, though unlike that model's the 944's body is built entirely of steel with no fiberglass add-ons. Under the hood is a new 2.5 liter all aluminum slant four, essentially half the 928's V-8. In American-market form, this Porsche-built engine produces 143 bhp (SAE net), which enables the car to run from 0 to 60 mph in about 8.5 seconds. Top speed is a claimed 130 mph, made possible by the small frontal area and aerodynamic body lines; the drag coefficient is only 0.35. Like all recent Porsches, the 944 has electronic fuel injection, which along with the ignition system is controlled by the Bosch Digital Motor Electronic (DME) system.

The first full convertible in the Porsche line since the days of the beloved 356 series arrived for the 1983 model year. The new 911SC Cabriolet is mechanically identical with other current 911s, and is much the same structurally, too, as the basic bodyshell proved to be rigid enough as not to need a great deal of extra reinforcement. The top is easy to put up or down. When it's up, the Cabriolet takes on the appearance of the familiar Targa. When it's down, there's surprisingly little wind buffeting even at higher speeds. The top mechanism employs a unique three-bow system with self-adjusting spring-loaded steel cables to insure a taut fit at all times, just the sort of engineering thoroughness expected of Porsche. This in part helps the Cabriolet to match the 911SC coupe's 140-mph top speed. The car pictured is a preproduction prototype.

Two recent examples of Porsche's glamorous Type 928. Opposite page, top: The 1982 Weissach Edition model, one of 205 specially equipped cars offered late in the model year. Besides the 928's usual comprehensive equipment, the Weissach Edition was outfitted with two-tone leather interior trim, champagne-gold metallic paint, matching gold alloy wheels, electric sunroof, front and rear spoilers, and a three-piece set of fitted luggage, plus a commemorative dash plaque. Immediate right and below: For 1983, the 928 gained a more powerful, 4.7-liter version of Porsche's advanced V-8, plus front and rear spoilers, forged alloy wheels, and the "S" suffix designation. Previously, the larger powerplant had been available only in Europe.

PORSCHE

The 1982 Type 911SC coupe, the world's most exciting example of the adage, "the more things change, the more they stay the same." Though it's been changed in countless ways over 20 years, the 911 remains contemporary, a tribute to its timeless design.

continued from page 192
pounds-feet of torque peaking at 5400 rpm.

These two steps up from the production 930 had truly unbelievable performance. Here are comparative figures for the two cars as tested by *Road & Track* in 1977:

	934	**935**
0-30 mph (sec.)	3.9	1.6
0-60 mph (sec.)	5.8	3.3
0-80 mph (sec.)	7.7	4.4
0-100 mph (sec.)	10.1	6.1
¼-mile (sec.)	14.2	8.9
¼-mile (mph)	121.0	133.5

Porsche was disappointed when IMSA initially banned turbocharged cars in 1976. This destroyed possibilities for a championship in the Camel GT series, though the ban was lifted at mid-year. Meanwhile, the cars did race in Trans-Am events, and won the championship that year for George Follmer (934), followed by Hurley Haywood, both from the Holbert Racing team. The 935 had similar bad luck with race organizers, this time in Europe. After 935s had won the first two races of the European GT championship, the authorities demanded that the 930's spoiler must be fitted. This required Porsche to adapt the 934's "waterworks" to provide proper cooling. Despite some faltering in mid-season, following these tentative modifications and subsequent difficulties, Porsche pulled out the World Championship for Makes late in the season, outlasting the BMWs at Watkins Glen, New York. The first time the title had been won by a supercharged racing car, it signified a revolution in Group 5 racing: from then on, it took a turbocharger to win. The series became another Porsche parade, with the Cup going to Zuffenhausen again in 1977, 1978, and 1979.

While IMSA rules have more recently permitted far out permutations like the Type 935 GTX, the SCCA's Trans-Am series was restructured in 1980, and returned to cars more similar to production specifications. In the 1980s, Porsche's efforts have increasingly involved front-engine racers like the Bundy team's 924. But it is a pleasant irony that the great rear-engine Turbos have been succeeded only by other Porsches in the winner's circle at tracks all over the world.

Top: The 935/78 driven by Monte Shelton at the '78 St. Jovite Trans-Am. Above: An immaculate 935/79, campaigned by the Interscope team that would later head Porsche's aborted Indy 500 effort. Note unusual dished "lacy-spoked" wheels.

Porsche built a great many more 930 Turbos than it expected. From the initial homologation minimum of 500, production was up to around 1300 by the end of 1976. Current total production of some 5000 guarantees a reasonable supply for collectors. Why then is the demand so high given the number of cars available? Probably because there is nothing quite like the 930. Power, comfort, a great racing heritage—these are the things for which Duesenbergs were renowned half a century ago. Can there by any doubt of the Turbo's standing among the all-time greats?

THE SPORTS/ RACING CARS: BEAUTIES AND BEASTS

The pivotal Carrera GTS, the Type 904, marked Porsche's reorientation to sports car racing after its abortive Formula 1 experience. It was both a harbinger of a new era and a last hurrah for the old one. It was the last competition Porsche that was also usable on the street, yet it laid out the format for an entirely new generation. It broke fresh ground with its fiberglass construction, yet except for that it was familiar technological territory. "It was beautiful, but it wasn't as aerodynamically efficient as it could have been," wrote David Owen. "It was tough ... but it wasn't as light as it should have been. And it used the old four-cam four-cylinder engine, stretched in this case to 1966cc and producing (ultimately) 195 bhp [some sources list 185 DIN] ahead of the rear wheels." The 904's rail chassis, as *Car and Driver* magazine put it, "might be straight out of Frank Kurtis' design book."

All this is true enough, yet it must also be said that the 904 was one of the most beautiful Porsches of all time—low, sleek, exquisitely shaped. And it went like almighty clappers. "Time and again," Owen continued, "in races like the 1964 Rheims 12 Hours, the Porsches would come roaring home just behind the big Ferraris." It was the 904 that returned Porsche to the forefront of international sports car competition.

Certain elements of the 904 design were influenced by the Formula 1 car, notably its double-wishbone front suspension. The rear suspension was a four-link system, and there were telescopic shocks and coil springs at both ends—but no lateral torsion bars. Steering was the new ZF rack-and-pinion mechanism from the recently announced 901/911. Brakes were outboard Dunlop-Ate four-wheel discs, with tiny drums mounted inside the rear discs, 356C-style, for the handbrake.

Fitted out for road work, the 904 greeted its driver with a full complement of instruments, the display dominated by a 9000-rpm rev counter. The windshield was cleared by a huge single wiper blade on a "pantograph" arm that swept side-to-side across the glass for maximum coverage. While the deep bucket seats were fixed, the pedals were adjustable, and different seat sizes were offered to fit a variety of drivers.

"Ze enchine, I was told, ist chust an oldt Carrera mohtorr, vis only 130 horrses. Ist much better vis too litah 180 horrsepowerr rracing enchine," drawled Brock Yates in *Car and Driver*. "Oh sure, only 130 bhp. It didn't seem hardly enough to do any more than pool all our blood along our jellied spine, break our glasses across the bridge of our nose and leave the impression of our belt buckle on our stomach." Huschke von Hanstein, giving Yates his first 904 ride, was doing 100 mph three blocks from the factory. "You're sure President Johnson does this?" Yates asked. "Ja shoor—look!" Huschke removed both hands from the small woodrim wheel. "The 904 tracked along as steadily at 120 mph as a Yankee Clipper." Test results gave 0-60 mph times of between 5.5 and 6.1 seconds and an observed top speed of 160 mph—fast enough for government work.

Whatever else it was—and it was quite a car in most respects—the 904 was as reliable as Big Ben. In its first major race, the 1964 Targa Florio, two of them ran home ahead of a fleet of Ferraris and Shelby Cobras. For 1965, the engine was revalved and the camshaft reprofiled for more horsepower. Output went up again through higher compression in 1966. The 904 was also versatile. It won important rallies as well as track races and enduros like the *Marathon de la Route* at the Nürburgring and the Watkins Glen 500. A few were even fitted with the potent Type 711/1 eight for 2.0-liter racing, in which they were equally impressive.

A remarkable bargain even in 1964 at $7425 at the factory, the 904 saw only 100 copies (50 were required for homologation as a "sports car"). That's far too few today. It was a glorious machine, special even for Porsche. Those fortunate enough to own one, Yates wrote, "won't be dissuaded by the awkwardness of getting in and out, by the expense of setting up and maintaining the four-cam engine, by the harsh ride, nor by the insufficient steering lock. No

Opposite page: Le Mans-style lineup for the 1968 Nürburgring 1000 Kilometers. Note Carrera 6 and Type 910 in foreground. Below: The 904 GTS returned Porsche to international road racing prominence.

Below: A brace of works-prepared 904s (and a 911) ready for the 1965 Monte Carlo Rally. Below right: The 904 in action at the 1964 Targa Florio. Bottom: The 904's monocoque weighed but 320 pounds. Opposite page: The 904 in the esses at Le Mans 1966.

sir, they're utter fools, and we wish we were among them."

The new six-cylinder engine from the 911 went into Porsche's next-generation racer, an all-out competition machine. The 906 or Carrera 6 was the effort of young Ferdinand Piëch, nephew of Ferry Porsche, who had helped to develop the 911 engine. As the 904 was the last and best racing cousin of the 356, so the 906 was the first racing derivative of the 911. It used a very light tubular space frame and an ultra-light, highly streamlined body that gave the car an overall height of only 38.6 inches. The engine was turned 180 degrees from its 911 positioning and mounted ahead of the rear wheels. Though quite similar to the 911 unit in basic design, the Carrera 6 powerplant (Type 901/20) was much lighter, making extensive use of magnesium and aluminum alloys. With dual ignition, 10.3 compression, two triple-throat Weber Type 46IDA carburetors, and specially designed manifolds and exhaust system, it produced 210-220 bhp (DIN) at 8000 rpm and a maximum 145 pounds-feet of torque at 6000 rpm. The clutch and transaxle were 911-based, and a variety of gearsets was offered to suit various tracks and race distances.

The 906 made its debut at the Daytona 24 Hours in 1966, where a dark blue car finished sixth, beaten only by the fleet Ford GTs and a single Ferrari. The lead car at Sebring spun out, but 906s nailed down fourth, sixth, and eighth places. At the Targa Florio they ended up 1-3-4-8. Ford GTs dominated Le Mans, but Carrera 6s were right behind, 4-5-6-7.

The Carrera 6's lineal successor was the 1967 Type 910/6, which used the same engine in a lighter space-frame chassis topped by a more handsome, more slippery fiberglass body. There was also a 2.2-liter flat-eight variation, the 910/8, that triumphed at the Targa Florio, with 910/6s placing second and third. Six-cylinder 910s finished high at Daytona, Sebring, Monza, and Spa, while a trio of these wiped the slates clean at the Nürburgring 1000 Kilometers (a 910/8 might have led them home, but suffered electrical failure on the last lap). Porsche outscored Ferrari in points in the 1967 Manufacturer's Championship, but because only the best five races counted for the

honor, Ferrari narrowly won.

The late Sixties were years of rapid-fire development in racing, one new car after the other. At Porsche, each new competitor was linked with its predecessor. The 904 used the four-cam Carrera four; the 906 used the 904 suspension and brakes; the 910 had a lighter frame derived from that of the 906; the 907 used the 906 engines. The next step was the 908, which had an entirely new powerplant in what was basically a 907 chassis.

Impetus for the 908 was an FIA decision to put a 3.0-liter displacement ceiling on the prototype class, underlining an earlier move by the Le Mans organizers after Ford's GTs swept the 24 Hours for the second time in 1967. Porsche probably did not influence these decisions, but racing manager Von Hanstein was certainly close enough to keep track of them. Work on a new 3.0-liter engine, this time an eight, got underway in July, 1967. With a capacity of 2977cc and developing a formidable 350 horsepower (DIN), it was exactly right for the new formula. More important, Porsche at last had an engine that could compete on equal terms with any rival for overall wins instead of just class victories. As time would prove, the arrival of the 908 and its new powerplant sounded the death knell for the vaunted GT-40s.

In developing the 908's engine, Ferry Porsche gave Piëch and his engineers but one restriction: money. But an expensive, ground-up design wasn't necessary. Instead, Porsche adopted a magnesium-alloy quad-cam version of the 911 six (designated Type 908), added two cylinders and a 5mm bore increase (from 80 to 85mm). Titanium-alloy flywheels and connecting rods were also employed. This power unit was mated to a hefty transaxle with six forward speeds for coupes, five on the later (1969) 908 spyders. Jokingly, it was called the "injected gearbox" by Porsche insiders, because its lubrication was by a jet of oil directed at each pair of gears.

On the outside, the first 908 was difficult to distinguish from the 907—mainly because it *was* a 907—and only minimal chassis modifications were required to accommodate the new engine. Unfortunately, the wind-cheating shape didn't prevail once the 908 was shifted from 13- to 15-inch wheels and tires, which made for higher fenders that reduced aerodynamic efficiency.

High-speed stability was among the problems that plagued the 908 during the 1968 racing season. For the slower tracks a 908K (*Kurzheck*, "short-tail") was developed, and by mid-season this had acquired a strut-mounted rear aerofoil or wing with suspension-controlled flaps—the first appearance for such a device on a Porsche. One of the earlier Ks scored what would be the 908's only victory of the year, at the 1000 Kilometers of the Nürburgring. Continued teething troubles, particularly with the new transaxle, prevented any further wins. Meanwhile, the Fords took Le Mans for a third time.

This underwhelming performance led to some personnel changes back home. Long-time racing manager, the charming Huschke von Hanstein, retired, though he continued as a consultant. His successor, Rico Steinemann, picked up new drivers — Britain's Richard Attwood and Brian Redman, Formula 2 maestro Kurt Ahrens, and rally aces Pauli Toivonen, Björn Waldegaard, and Gérard Larousse — thus forming one of the most formidable factory teams in the business. Steinemann decided to employ the open-body Spyders for shorter courses, long-tail coupes for fast tracks like Monza, and 908Ks for in-between situations. Events lacking championship points were ignored. It was win or nothing, and let privateers worry about non-championship matches.

Not everything went Porsche's way in 1969. The early races at Daytona and Sebring were plagued by breakdowns, and Ford won again at Le Mans in September. In between, though, the plan worked. The 908s finished 1-2 at Monza, 1-2-3-4 at the Targa Florio, 1-2-3-4-5 at the 'Ring — and Waldegaard won the Monte Carlo Rally in a 911S. Porsche won the Manufacturer's Championship going away, trouncing Ford 76 points to 26. And the 908 has continued to score high to this day. In 1981 a 908/80 won the Nürburgring 1000 Kilometers. That's 12 years after the first examples appeared. Not many racing cars can claim as much.

A specialized machine arrived with the 908 in 1968, the short-lived, hill-conquering 909.

Porsche's first all-out competition car of the '60s was the Type 906 Carrera 6, powered by a derivative of the production 911 engine. Car 37 (top) was driven by Vic Elford and Ben Pon to 7th overall at Le Mans '66.

Top: The Type 907 at the 1967 Nürburgring 1000. Middle: The long-tail 907 as used for Le Mans '68. Bottom: An early Type 908 coupe with short-tail bodywork.

It lasted only a year, for Porsche withdrew from hillclimbs to concentrate on Championship events the following season. But while it was around, the 909 was unbeatable.

This *Bergspyder* used a 1981cc eight (Type 771/0) with 275 horsepower (DIN), the highest output among the 2.0-liter eights. On a straightaway, the 909 was capable of 155 mph. Its low, ultra-streamlined body with unusual finned spoilers was wrapped around an aluminum tubular space frame that placed engine and the driver's position very far forward — the driver's legs actually extended over the line of the front sway bar. Titanium alloy was used extensively for the suspension, which employed coil springs at each corner, and for the fuel tank. Weighing only 949 pounds, the 909 had an extra-wide track (57.9/57.6 inches front/rear) and an 89.1-inch wheelbase, slightly less than the 90.6 inches of its racing stablemates.

Designed expressly for running up mountains, the 909 was superb, easily winning the 1968 Hillclimb Championship. The team consisted of Gerhard Mitter, Rolf Stommelin, and Ludovico Scarfiotti, the greatest of the contemporary Italians. Scarfiotti was tragically killed at Rossfeld, when his 909 leaped off the road and plastered itself against a tree. It was the first death at a Porsche racing wheel, a black day for Zuffenhausen. In the wake of "Lulu's" loss, champion Gerhard Mitter declared he had had enough of the hills.

The stage was now set for the biggest, quickest most successful Porsche sports-racer of all time — a car that would recall as no other the screaming silver *Deutschlanders* of prewar fame, also designed by Porsche hands, the supercharged Auto-Unions. This new car would so completely dominate the sport that nothing else could properly be compared to it. Today, only some 15 years since it first came off the drawing board, this Porsche is enshrined with the Grand Prix Mercedes, the Indianapolis Offys, the Alfas and Ferraris. We can only be speaking about the 917.

When the FIA decided in 1967 to restrict prototypes to 3.0 liters, it simultaneously decreed that displacement for Group 4 sports cars would be no more than 5.0 liters. This move was aimed at curbing Ford, but it was an opportunity for Porsche on two levels: the 908 for the prototype class, the 917 for Group 4. However, no one outside the factory knew the 917 was in the works until it was first displayed, at the Geneva Auto Salon in March 1969. And, since Porsche had never before ventured into 4.0/5.0-liter territory, this car sent shock waves throughout the world of racing. Enzo Ferrari at first expressed doubt that anyone could build an aircooled flat-12 racing engine, let alone win with it. He soon learned otherwise—the hard way.

The 917's chassis layout was mainly that of the 908, modified for a larger engine. However, it was not feasible to expand the eight into a twelve simply by adding extra cylinders. That would have produced a long, undesirably "whippy" crankshaft. Nonetheless, Porsche was able to use the 908's reciprocating parts and its 85mm bore and 66mm stroke for the new engine to achieve 4494cc—exactly 150 percent the capacity of the 908. Because of their experience with lightweight chassis and engines, the engineers managed to keep the 917's curb weight very close to the Group 4 minimum of 1763 pounds (800kg). In fact, the car ended up so light that they found it unnecessary to take advantage of the full 5.0 liters they were allowed.

To minimize critical vibration, a two-piece crankshaft was utilized, with the power take-off from a central gear cut into it. A second shaft above the crank drove twin electronic ignition distributors, while the Bosch fuel injection unit was belt-driven from the left intake camshaft. To achieve perfect crankshaft balance Porsche used two connecting rods per crank pin; this also allowed wider flange and bearing widths. With a compression ratio of 10.5:1, the twelve as raced at Le Mans and Spa developed 580 bhp at 8400 rpm and 376 pounds-feet of torque at 6600 rpm. This, plus its extreme light weight, made the 917 potentially the fastest car in Group 4, destined to clean house. And the FIA knew it.

What followed when Porsche presented the 917's homologation papers is another of those stories

fans love to spin about bureaucratic race regulators. Porsche had more than the minimum 25 cars under construction when the FIA's International Sporting Commission (CSI) first visited the factory, but the inspection team demanded that those cars be *ready to roll* before they would approve the model. Following a marathon effort by all hands, 25 completed 917s were lined up in a Le Mans start sort of formation for CSI's second inspection on April 21, 1969. The Porsche folk invited their guests to drive any one at random. The inspectors

Opposite page: This mid-1969 Type 908 hillclimb car (top) was nicknamed "Sole." A later, lighter version (middle) had wider bodywork. The early 917 (bottom) was a tricky handler. This page: The 917 in its two 1970 guises. The Hermann/Attwood Le Mans winner is shown below.

meekly declined.

The 917's highly streamlined fiberglass body was raced in two versions, a long-tail 917L and short-tail 917K. The aft body sections could be exchanged depending on track conditions and distance. The long-tail, intended for high-speed tracks, had a drag coefficient of 0.33, good for 236 mph at Le Mans. Both tails incorporated suspension-controlled air flaps, though these caused intense debate and were banned at some 1969 races. And without them the 917 became a considerable handful to drive quickly.

Like the 908, the 917 required a full race year, 1969, to be completely sorted out. One Le Mans car led the race for 20 hours, but fell out due to a cracked bell housing. The Gulf-Wyer GT-40 won a fourth straight 24 hours for Ford—but only by a scant two seconds over a screaming factory 908. Suitably impressed, Gulf-Wyer agreed to sponsor a team of 917s in 1970. A second sponsor was added, one which old hands highly approved: Porsche-Salzburg, operated by Louise Piëch, sister of Dr. Ferdinand Porsche. The Martini Racing team would also field its first 917 in 1970, at Le Mans—a wildly painted purple and green monster for Larrouse/Kauhsen.

At the 1970 running of the 24 Hours, the big 917s—all three racing teams plus some works entries—dominated the proceedings, sweeping home 1-2-3, led by veteran Hans Hermann, who shared the ride with Richard Attwood in a Porsche-Salzburg car. It was a race marred by crashes and the death of one corner marshal, yet it was also the crowning moment in Hans' career. After Le Mans, Hermann retired, depressed by the tragic race. But his work was complete, his greatest ambition realized. For the Austrian team as well, Le Mans '70 was a milestone. The land where strange, teardrop-shaped coupes had first taken to roads and race courses 22 years before had produced a winner in the world's greatest road race.

As Don Vorderman put it, Porsches were now "the cars to beat." But in 1971, nobody tried. The only apparent challenger was Ferrari's 512M, faster and lighter than Maranello's 512S—but not as light as the 917. To stem any potential threat from this

The current Mitsubishi 2.6 offered in Chrysler's K-cars, he notes, "has a steel timing chain that winds around like a snake and drives two balance shafts parallel to the crankshaft while the two balance shafts turn in opposite directions at *twice* crankshaft speed. It does work... But there is a much simpler way to eliminate almost all vibration. VW did it for 25 years, Porsche still does it with the 911. It is no secret. A 4-cylinder engine with pairs of opposing cylinders is so near to perfect balance that you can forget that two cylinders on one side are less than 1.0 in. forward of the other pair." Bond goes on to recommend a flat-opposed four coupled to *rear* drive.

Perhaps it is the inherent "rightness" of the 911 design, typified by its beautifully designed engine, that has enabled Porsche to successfully update the car over so many years. Today's 911SC is more tractable, more refined, and easier to drive than any of its predecessors, 15 years of safety, emissions, and fuel economy regulations notwithstanding. It is thus the easiest of all 911s to live with. Who cares that it now costs nearly $30,000 minimum? It is unique—and that more than anything explains why there are still plenty of buyers willing to pay the price.

The 911SC debuted for the 1978 model year, and replaced both the 911S and the Carrera in the American market. *Autocar* called it "a Carrera with a broader market appeal," and indeed, interior and exterior changes made the SC closer to the Carrera 3.0 than to the base 911 of old. Its engine progressed to 2994cc via a 95mm bore (stroke remained at 70.4mm) and yielded slightly more horsepower plus a somewhat smoother torque curve than the previous 2.7-liter unit. Also fitted were the Carrera's larger rear wheels, and the SC's rear fenders were similarly flared to accommodate them. A "Sport" derivative was offered, which combined the well-known Carrera spoiler and a front air dam. Other changes included servo-assisted brakes, Bosch breakerless electronic ignition with electronic rpm limiter, and a belt-driven air pump that mixed fresh air with exhaust gases. Quoted power output was 172 bhp net (180 DIN) and 189 pounds-feet torque at 4200 rpm for the U.S. version. The compression ratio of 8.5:1 required a minimum of 91-octane fuel.

As ever, the greatest delight of the 911 engine, the testers said, was its impressive tractability. "The flat-six motor will pull without a murmur of discontent from as low as 20 mph in fifth gear, less than 1000 revs, the needle climbing at first slowly round the tachometer, quickening, and then the car markedly surging forward as the needle passes 3500 rpm," recorded *Autocar*. "...Such is its flexibility that in fourth gear, for example, there is scarcely more than half a second's difference between the times for every increment between 30-50 mph [6.5 seconds in their test] and 80-100 mph [6.3]... Even in fifth gear the same pattern emerges." Across the pond, *Road & Track* added: "...the formerly finicky 911 drives like a big V-8 powered Detroit car. There's lots of torque, so constant downshifting isn't necessary even in slow traffic. No Porsche owner... is going to let the revs fall to 1000 rpm in 5th

Opposite page: The 1978 911SC coupe (above) and 1979 SC Targa (below). This page: The 1980 911SC Weissach Edition(above). Only 400 were built. Detail refinements marked the standard SC coupe for 1980 (left).

gear and then attempt to accelerate. But to prove a point we did this with the SC and the engine accepted the treatment with never a judder of protest...In the early 911s, particularly the 2-liter version, it takes some deft clutching to make a smooth start, but in the SC you just roll your foot off the clutch pedal and glide away. From then on you work your way up through the gears like a proper Porsche driver or cheat and slip into the appropriate cruising cog."

Less experienced road testers have always complained about the notchiness of the Porsche gearbox, but this is something that usually worked itself out after a few thousand miles; the linkage was made purposely stiff in the first place. Curiously, spring loading in the conventionally arranged gate was biased toward the fifth/reverse plane, so the first-time driver had to exert conscious effort to select top gear. This was not a problem for the experienced pilot. Sportomatic was no longer an option. It had never sold well, as good as it was. 911s were for "shifters."

In extremes, all 911s have exhibited inherent oversteer, and the SC is no exception. The difference is that the SC is set up for initial understeer, which it maintains longer than earlier 911s. The larger-size rear wheels and tires were adopted for the SC precisely for this reason. Apply too much power through a hard bend and you risk nothing except stronger understeer and the car's determination to hold its line. But lift off the throttle suddenly in the midst of that turn and the rear end could start catching up to the front. It usually took a professional to reach this point of no return, and long-time Porsche drivers were not bothered or surprised by the final oversteer. Further, the SC's optional Pirelli P7 tires (205/55VR-16 front and 225/50VR-16 rear) worked well with the Bilstein shocks and anti-roll bars, their squat, low-profile design putting four hefty pieces of rubber on the road —what Jackie Stewart would doubtless call "traction management."

In general, the consensus seemed to be that the SC was more manageable and forgiving in its cornering behavior than earlier 911s. "The wide tyres have some demerits in wet weather," *Autocar* noted. "We suffered occasionally from front-end aquaplaning under braking on water covered roads and understeer is also far more noticeable on wet surfaces. In these driving conditions the tail can sometimes be provoked out of line with the throttle and understeer can also be killed by the traditional remedy of easing back on the throttle, being prepared to catch the resulting slide. Such intricacies of handling make the Porsche very much a driver's car; experience with it constantly teaches new skills." There is nothing new in this summation, but it's worth quoting. The 911 had really not changed much; it had merely become progressively better.

Inside the SC, the worst excesses of auto design by decree seemed to have been toned down if not altogether eliminated. The cockpit was still awfully somber, but there was no ticky-tacky trim in sight. Everything confronting the driver was legible, functional, and practical. The steering wheel was still near vertical, the bucket seats "grabby" and comfortable, the five-hole dashboard with its central rev-counter familiar, the steering column stalk controls logical and within fingertip reach. Climbing into the SC was "like putting on a well broken-in pair of shoes," *Road & Track* said. Their testers had only one real quibble —ventilation. There still wasn't enough of it, and neither ventwings nor opening rear quarter windows were available anymore.

It would be less than fair to gloss over the 911's handling, for not everybody admired it—and not just inexperienced types, either. Bobby Allison, for one, was adamant in his condemnation. And Allison had raced IROC Porsches as well as the NASCAR stockers with which he is usually associated. His remarks (to *Car and Driver*) concern the 1974 models, but can be applied to all 911s. His conclusion: "I think they are [$20,000] imported Corvairs.

"The most unnatural thing is, when you see that you are in a little bit of a problem and you lift off the gas, the problem increases," Allison said. "Then you're in trouble. What do you do next? With the race cars we found out you stomp your foot down and start steering like a wild man. But I don't think an inexperienced driver is going to do that. These cars do have a strong reputation...but I don't see why. I'd guess it comes first of all from the racing versions, and then from its quickness at well under its limit...To be fair, the car has unique characteristics and some people may like it. I don't."

Allison thus succinctly stated the one prevailing criticism history will register of the Type 911. Its handling characteristics were, in many ways, just the opposite of what was normally expected of sporting machinery. The answer to this is Allison's emphasis on *inexperienced* drivers. Porsche drivers tend to be experienced. As always, people either approve or disapprove of the basic concept; if they disapprove they will never adapt themselves to the 911's handling. "You pays your money and you takes your choice."

For 1980 the dreaded catalytic converter arrived, but as things happened it was not to be feared. That year's 911SC developed the same horsepower as the 1978-79 models, and lost not a pound-foot of torque. Uncharacteristically, Porsche optimistically pegged its top speed at 139 mph, which was a shade more than most road tests produced. The catalyst had the benefits of eliminating separate specifications for California and the need for the exhaust gas recirculation. It also permitted Porsche to raise compression ratio from 8.5 to 9.3:1. Overall fuel economy was somewhat improved by these changes, as the SC now returned 20 mpg without overly careful driving—fine efficiency in view of the performance.

The SC's price, which had increased by $3500 in 1979, soared by almost $5000 in 1980, due partly to galloping inflation. Some of the increase came from standardizing formerly optional extras: electric window lifts, air conditioning, leather-covered steering wheel, under-dash console. The Targa continued to be priced about $1500 more than the coupe.

It may be worth mentioning some peculiarities of the U.S. models for your general entertainment. Beginning with the 1980 model year, auto manufacturers were required to install speedometers that did not read beyond 85 mph and that emphasized our 55 mph speed limit on the dial. Porsche did this but, as usual, the speedometer was shoveled out of the way and the larger tachometer placed in the central location. Recent waiving of this rule leaves Porsche free to return to an instrument more reflective of the car's true performance. Another odd move was made by Zuffenhausen itself in deference to our "double-nickel" speed limit: the accelerator pedal was placed considerably below the level of the brake, Detroit-fashion, because the factory thought this position would be more comfortable at 55 mph! Pedal travel was unaffected, and happily there was a degree of adjustment in both accelerator and brake pedals so that they could be properly aligned with an hour of minor wrench work. If you asked Ralph Nader to heel and toe he'd probably do a tap dance, but for the more knowledgable the understanding folk in Stuttgart kindly provided relief.

The 911 six, even in its latest 3.0-liter form, was now old enough to be called "venerable" by the road testers. But as ever, there were no peaks, no valleys, no flat spots in the acceleration curve, and the 911SC would lug down to ridiculously low revs in the upper gears without protest. About the only thing anyone could still complain about by 1980 was weak ventilation and the ever-increasing price. The 911 was now next to unattainable by rank-and-file enthusiasts, and this was a shame. Its skyrocketing sticker figures have

Above: As timeless as ever, the 1982 Type 911SC also sported more standard amenities than ever.

been the result of a perceived need to expand standard equipment, not to milk the buyer. In 1978 the factory announced it would continue producing 911s as long as we wanted them and, as there's been no slackening in demand so far, Porsche has nothing to gain by bleeding us. But we *could* wish for a reincarnation of Maxie Hoffman to strip the product a bit to make it more affordable—or to give us another Speedster.

Recently, there have been some 911SC offshoots, but they've all been upmarket variants. Toward the end of the 1981 season appeared the Weissach Edition coupe, named in honor of the Porsche research complex outside Stuttgart. It was offered only in the U.S. and only as long as the supply of 400 cars lasted. The Weissach Edition was perfect for those who felt the basic coupe, then stickered at $27,700, was insufficient for real status. Priced at $32,000, the limited-edition Weissach added stiffer shocks, electric remote-control door mirrors, electric antenna, sealed-beam halogen headlamps, leather interior trim, wider wheels, and special paint. Porsche publicity blurbs said the Weissach actually represented a 15 percent *savings* over the cost of these goodies if ordered individually. But there was no need to press hard: there weren't enough cars to go around.

For 1983, we could again buy a Porsche convertible, the first fully open Porsche in a generation. Unlike the old Speedster, the new 911SC Cabriolet has a civilized top that's completely snug and provides good visibility, thanks to its broadly wrapped backlight. There has been no Max Hoffman at work on this model, which has a list price of $34,450 and usually costs around $40,000. But it will surely one-up those Weissach owners.

Convertibles are making a comeback in the U.S. market these days, though for how long is anybody's guess. The same factors that did them in by the mid-'70s—air pollution, traffic noise and efficient air conditioning—are still present. But, for awhile at least, there's a rear-engine revival recalling the glory days of the original 356 Speedster, cabriolet, and Convertible D.

Cabriolet, Porsche explains, is a term used originally to denote a car with a folding roof. The new SC version employs a manually erected top with a three-bow system and self-adjusting, spring-loaded steel cables to ensure that the fabric remains snug. About 30 pounds lighter than the Targa, the Cabriolet is tight for a convertible. The soft top remains unusually stable at speed, thanks in part to a steel panel beneath the cloth in front. The design also contributes to good sealing, minimal interior temperature loss (in the winter; air conditioning is available for the summer), and low wind noise. With the top down, a boot covers the bits and pieces, and it's a far more streamlined boot than the

Below: The fully open Porsche returned with the '83 SC Cabriolet.

This page: European 911SC Cabriolet (above) and Porsche Design sketch (right). Opposite page: The 911SC Cabriolet (top and center) and 4wd 1981 Frankfurt car.

ones that dangled out back on the 356s. The storage well is so placed that the two vestigial rear seats are retained. A tonneau cover is available as an option.

Porsche says that the "aerodynamic lines of the Cabriolet roof made it possible to match the 140-mph top speed of the 911SC coupe," which is a peculiar claim for Porsche. Obviously it is not as aerodynamic, although only marginally heavier. The Cabriolet's true top speed is closer to 125 mph. Acceleration, while approximately the same as the coupe up to 60 mph, begins to drop off after air drag starts to take its toll—and that's with the top up. But these are minor matters for those attracted to the Cabriolet for its open-air pleasures combined with traditional 911 virtues.

Speaking of virtues, the Cabriolet has several of its own. As mentioned, its very tight for a convertible. Even in the pre-production prototype, sampled by CONSUMER GUIDE® magazine's auto editors, there were hardly any rattles, from the body or the top. Here is

another tribute to the literal integrity of the basic 911 design. In fact, the coupe's bodyshell proved so rigid that very little additional bracing was required to maintain the requisite torsional stiffness. It's also a tribute to Zuffenhausen's high-quality assembly. Porsche offers a detachable rollbar option, but that would add nothing to body stiffness—and, really, nothing extra is needed. Another nice thing about the Cabriolet is that you can drive top down with the side windows rolled up without the annoying and uncomfortable wind buffeting that plagues so many other open cars. We found this true even at speeds modestly above the legal limit on the highway.

There's little doubt that the arrival of the Cabriolet signals Porsche's firm commitment to the 911. It also shows just how much life remains in this well-loved Porsche, which continues to outsell the 928, its ostensible replacement. We understand a few new options may surface for the Cabriolet, such as a power-operated top and zip-in glass rear window (complete with electric defroster elements). Even more intriguing is the possibility of a four-wheel-drive 911. Indeed, the Cabriolet prototype was shown with 4WD at the 1981 Frankfurt Show, and it's quite likely this drivetrain could make it to production in the not too distant future.

What more can we say of today's 911SC? Well, aside from the points already mentioned, there's the curious and old-fashioned over-center action of the clutch and brake pedals, which are not suspended from above but rather from the floor, just like on the VW Beetle. Also, on Pirelli P7s, the low-speed ride is uncomfortably jiggly over the sort of city streets most of us have to contend with, and there's far too much kickback from the steering, which is also heavy for parking. Some people don't particularly like the black-finish alloy wheels. The heater controls are somewhat confusing, some minor switchgear is scattered in an afterthought fashion, and there's not enough space in the front trunk for anything much larger than a lunchbox. But all this only amounts to nit-picking. There's still that immensely strong and high-revving engine, the lightning-quick steering, the powerful brakes, the typically Teutonic build quality, the comfortable seats, and—that tremendous intangible—the Porsche mystique.

We wouldn't be at all surprised to see the 911 survive long past the dawn of the 1990s. It just seems to go on and on—and why not? It's a much different car now than it was in the '60s, yet it hasn't changed so much as to lose its basic appeal or excitement. And for that we can all be grateful.

Left: The initial 1976 version of the European 924. Below: The Euro-spec 924 Turbo. U.S. versions arrived for 1980.

TYPE 924/944: FOUR CYLINDERS UP FRONT

Many an enthusiast must have looked at the Porsche 924 as it was announced in 1976, and agreed with the Second book of Samuel: "How the mighty have fallen and the weapons of battle perished." So it's appropriate to point out right away that the 924 was a successor not to the 911 but the 914, and that it was another product of *VW-Porsche Vertriebsgesellschaft*, the joint marketing organization for Porsche-designed cars using major VW componentry. The Ludwigsburg firm knew within months of its launch that the 914 would be only partly successful in this respect; the only VW component in it was the engine. So, Porsche was immediately given a brief to design a replacement — a task that would take over five years.

The project that led to the 924 got off the ground in a hurry in 1970 when Rudolf Leiding relieved the controversial Kurt Lotz as managing director at VW. Leiding, a sports car advocate and racing-minded, immediately handed a large chunk of VW's developmental engineering work over to Porsche, including a post-914 sports car carrying project code EA425. By this time, VW had acquired Audi-NSU from Daimler-Benz, but VW itself was losing financial ground. This no doubt prompted Leiding to embark on the *Baukastenprinzip* approach to marketing. Basically, this calls for a GM-like plethora of models, sizes, prices, and shapes, and relies on a limited group of components with a high degree of interchangeability to ensure production economies of scale. Accordingly, a number of new models based on previously introduced products were planned: VW Passat/Dasher from Audi 80/Fox, Scirocco from VW Golf/Rabbit.

Project EA425 called for a sports car design with greater passenger/luggage space than the 914 and able to accept a variety of engines in keeping with Leiding's "building block" approach. Initially, a 2.0-liter four already employed in the lowly VW LT Transporter was contemplated, an

This page: "Phantom" drawings highlight 1977 924's front-engine/rear-transaxle chassis and hatchback body (above). Opposite page: 1977 and Championship Edition 924s.

engine also destined for the forthcoming Audi 100 and later, of all things, the AMC Gremlin. The project was well along in 1973 when it ran into snags. Leiding unexpectedly told Porsche he wanted to build the car as a VW. After all, VW had paid the development bill, which then tallied $70 million. This announcement stunned and worried Zuffenhausen — not only because EA425 was *their* design, but also because, as a VW, the new car was potential competition for other Porsches, particularly the 912.

The impasse seemed resolved when Leiding suddenly left VW/Audi in 1974, the company overextended and in trouble following his expensive expansion programs. But then his successor, ex-Ford executive Toni Schmücker, told Porsche there was no need for the EA425 at all. He was reacting to the crippled sports car market in the wake of the Arab oil embargo of 1973-74.

But Porsche had faith in the car, and decided to save it by buying the production rights from VW. The cost at that time: about $60 million, a slight discount on VW's total expenditure. Porsche would spend as much and more before the car was finally ready. A sweetener for VW was an agreement to build EA425 at the Audi-NSU plant in Neckarsulm, a half hour north of Stuttgart. As VW had planned to build it there anyway, this served to occupy what would have been an otherwise idle facility.

From the beginning, Porsche designers had to wrestle with and resolve a conceptual problem. They wanted a car with a family resemblance to the 911, a car with ample room for passengers and luggage. But what kind of car should that be? Front-engine/front-drive machinery had never crossed Zuffenhausen's portals. Rear-engine/rear-drive engineering was a Porsche specialty—but one of *VW-Porsche Vertriebsgesellschaft's* objectives was the eventual use of some larger engine from another VW project. There was little room in a rear-engine car for this sort of flexibility and besides, the rear-engine layout showed every sign of becoming passé. Front engine/rear drive? Maybe, but not if it involved a beam rear axle—

that would be a figurative step back into the Stone Age. What about independent suspension all-round, front engine, and rear-mounted gearbox? A fair solution, all sides agreed. It would provide near even fore/aft weight distribution, thus minimizing the traditional oversteer nemesis of previous Porsches. It would require a very carefully engineered transaxle, of course, but Porsche engineer Jochen Freund thought he could produce one.

Although the car would have used a VW model name under the original agreement, a Porsche type number was definite once Zuffenhausen recovered full rights. Thus, VW project EA425 evolved into Porsche Type 924, a designation chosen to signify a quantum leap from 914. (There were no Type numbers between 917 and 924 save 923, which was merely the 912E four-cylinder engine.)

The front-engine/rear-transmission concept was not new, having been used previously on such diverse machines as the 1961-63 "rope-shaft" Pontiac Tempest and the Ferrari 275 GTB. But Freund's version was cleverly designed with *Baukastenprinzip* in mind. The tiny 20mm-diameter, splined driveshaft, straight and without U-joints, was encased in a tube, where it ran in four bearings strategically placed at points of greatest torsional stress. At its ends were the engine and gearbox, each supported by two rubber mounts. The clutch was located immediately behind the engine. There was a second "clutch housing" at the back end of the tube. Initially empty, it was there to house the torque converter from Audi's forthcoming fully automatic transmission, which would later be a 924 option. The transaxle at first provided only four forward gears (using non-Porsche baulk-ring synchros), but a five-speed came along later. Porsche claimed that this drivetrain arrangement would absorb most of the force from the engine should it be displaced rearward in a front-end crash, thus protecting the car's occupants, and also that exhaust noise would be low because the exhaust system was mounted directly on the drive tube and transaxle.

The inline four with aluminum overhead-cam cylinder head displaced 1984cc, and had oversquare cylinder dimensions at 86.5×84.4mm. Fuel was fed by the reliable Bosch K-Jetronic injection system. The 924 was tuned for 125 bhp (DIN) in European trim but the American version had only 95 bhp (SAE net), the difference being in compression ratio — 9.3:1 versus 8.0:1 — and the U.S. model's smaller valves. Power was the same for all 50 states, the California 924 using a catalyst while 49-state cars relied on an air pump to meet emissions standards.

The borrowed engine was accompanied by chassis pieces also taken from the VW/Audi parts bin. The front suspension consisted of Golf/Rabbit lower A-arms and MacPherson struts from the Super Beetle. Out back were Beetle semi-trailing arms combined with torsion bars and tubular shocks, while the halfshafts came from VW's Type 181, a.k.a. "The Thing." Bilstein shocks, cast-aluminum road wheels, and anti-roll bars would be optional. Steering was the

Rabbit's rack-and-pinion mechanism, with a *slower* (19.2:1) ratio, while brakes were Porsche/Audi discs up front and Beetle drums at the rear. We can clearly see Rudolf Leiding's component-sharing plan at work. Most remarkable is how well all these disparate parts worked together. Certainly the 924 was more of a joint exercise than the 914, more of a "cocktail model." Yet the end result, despite the many delays and difficulties, was a quite affordable car with definite Porsche character. The 924 carried a U.S. base price in 1977 of only $9395, against the contemporary 911 at $15,000.

Styling was all important from the beginning of the 914 project. This was competently handled by a Hollander, Harm Lagaay, supervised by Porsche design chief Anatole Lapine. Lapine admitted that they had been given a directive to retain a familial resemblance with the 911, but the final result was pleasingly different—a classic teardrop-like form that would have appealed to the elder Ferdinand Porsche and Paul Jaray. Lagaay interpreted 911 ideas afresh, with a minimal suggestion of grillework and a strong increase in mass toward the rear. The smooth, low front end swept past a beautifully raked windshield and on back in an unbroken line, terminating in a neat, rounded tail. There was a lift-up "glassback," a large compound-curve rear window, for access to the luggage compartment. European 924s used body-color fiberglass bumpers while American models wore 5-mph aluminum units mounted farther out from the body on hydraulic struts. In appearance, the 924 was, and is, quite unlike almost anything else on the road, though some might argue that its nose is uncomfortably similar to that of Mazda's RX-7, introduced in 1978. One of its most recent compliments comes from Chrysler, which admits that it looked to 924 standards of design and chassis engineering throughout for its 1984 Chrysler Laser/Dodge Daytona sports coupe, previously known by the suggestive code designation G24.

The 924 cockpit embraced the driver with all controls in optimum position, and surrounded the occupants with glass. "At no point," Porsche says, "is more than 63° of the driver's full 360° obscured." There were a few obvious signs of component sharing: a 914-like speedometer flanked by auxiliary gauges from the Rabbit and Scirocco, VW steering column stalks, door handles from the Beetle. Options included leather upholstery, air conditioning, automatic transmission, stereo radio, headlamp washers, rear window wiper, tinted windshield and side

glass (a tinted backlight was standard.) There were also two option packages. Touring Package I ($345) comprised alloy wheels and wider tires, three speakers, antenna, noise suppression kit, and leather-covered steering wheel. Touring Package II ($240) added headlamp washers, righthand outside mirror, and rear wiper.

Early magazine road tests of the 924 showed 0-60 mph times in the 11-12 second range and top speed at around 110 mph, with fuel mileage in the 20-22-mpg area. None of these figures were sensational, but neither were they disappointing for a well-tuned 2.0-liter four in a modern, well-equipped four-seat GT. In a comparison test with the rival Alfa Romeo Alfetta GT and Datsun 280Z, *Road & Track* gave first place to the Porsche—even though the Z-car sold for $3000 less in base form—which was a strong recommendation indeed. They loved the 924 on the track, experiencing beautiful balance, flat cornering response, and light, fast steering—but theirs was a fully suspension-optioned car, and the editors didn't think as highly of the standard setup. The two main problems noted were the rather buzzy engine and a jouncy ride accompanied by lots of thumping over rough surfaces. Porsche ameliorated both these complaints as time passed.

European 924s were considerably quicker and more flexible than American ones, particularly after the five-speed gearbox arrived during 1978 to

Opposite page: Despite running changes that improved refinement and ride, the 924 (1978 models shown) never shed its "VW connection" in enthusiasts' eyes. This page: Another limited-edition 924, the "Sebring '79," marked the model's win at that year's Florida road race (left). The 1979 Type 924 (below).

Top: The 924 Turbo bowed in Europe during 1980. Note neater non-Federal front. Above: Bird's eye view of '81 U.S. Turbo emphasizes 924's huge "glassback" hatch.

supplement the standard four-speeder. By mid-1977, Porsche had partly attended to the lackluster performance of the U.S. version, bumping horsepower up to 110 bhp net at 5750 rpm by means of a higher-lift cam, larger intake valves, modified pistons, advanced timing, and higher 8.5:1 compression ratio. None of this affected the car's ability to run on 91-octane fuel. There was still a terrific amount of engine noise at over 4000 rpm, but *Road & Track* felt sure that the 1978 924 would yet beat the Alfetta and 280Z: "The Porsche's overall design, its interior layout and its handling are better. [It] looks great (especially with the optional alloy wheels), its seating is as comfortable as a well worn Gucci loafer and the car sticks to the road like chewing gum on the bottom of a theater seat." (Somebody had obviously been reading old Tom McCahill road tests to come up with such a colorful assessment.)

In England, where there was a wider choice of like sports cars, *Autocar* magazine compared the hotter UK version with the same two rivals as *Road & Track*, plus three others: the European Ford Capri 3000S, the Lotus Eclat 521, and the V-6-powered Reliant Scimitar GTE. Only the Eclat was more expensive than the British-spec 924 Lux, which cost a cool $22,000 in that heavily taxed market. "The 924 is a very competent car, [yet] there are many similar two-plus-two sports coupes on sale offering the same sort of performance and handling over a wide price range...the Ford Capri 3000S does pretty much the same job for little more than half the price. In between are the others of our comparative group and other less obvious rivals like the Saab Turbo, BMW 323i and Lancia Monte Carlo, all of them currently cheaper than the Porsche. One is, unfortunately, paying a good deal for that prestigious hallmark."

Even *Road & Track* had to admit what it called a paradox in the 924: noise and buzziness that were unacceptable in a $10,000-plus automobile. This was underscored in another, later *R&T* comparison test where the 924 faced more formidable rivals—the Datsun 280ZX, Mazda RX7, and Chevrolet Corvette. It finished third in the standings (ahead of the Corvette) despite winning six "firsts" (braking, handling, visibility, exterior finish, interior and exterior styling). "When it's good it's very good," said the editors, "But when it's bad, watch out." Obviously, fans were getting impatient with the 924's continued lack of power and high noise levels.

Porsche responded. You could now almost hear the Zuffenhausen folk saying, "Very well, we will fix those problems—and we will give you a *Turbo* 924 just for good measure." And they did for the 1980 model year.

The bottom end of the 2.0-liter four was left unaltered for the Turbo, but hardly anything else was. The cylinder head remained cast aluminum, but it was a brand-new design with larger valves, revised combustion chambers, and platinum-electrode spark plugs mounted on the intake rather than exhaust side. Compression, lowered as is usual practice in turbocharging, was 7.5:1 for both American and European models. The turbocharger was mounted low on the starboard side of the severely canted engine. Built by the German firm of KKK, it was fitted with a huge cast pipe that carried a boost of 10.15 psi (7 psi on U.S. models) up and over the head to the intake manifold. From here the charge was routed down and into the ports on the upper left side of the engine. A Bosch K-Jetronic fuel injection system was specially matched to the turbocharged engine, while an oil cooler dealt with anticipated high heat. A wastegate was employed as in the 930 Turbo to prevent boost pressure from exceeding the specified maximum. Porsche also fitted a blow-off valve as a "fail-safe" backup for the wastegate.

The result of all this was 125 DIN horsepower at 5500 rpm and a staggering 181 pounds-feet of torque at 3500 rpm for the European version. The American model's figures were 143 bhp net at 5500 rpm and 147 pounds-feet of torque at 3000 rpm, still a worthy improvement despite the much lower peak torque. Though the 924 Turbo was considerably heavier than manual-shift 924s, the difference in off-the-line acceleration was enormous: compared to the normally aspirated car's 11-12-second 0-60 mph time, the Turbo would leap the gap in 7-8 seconds. Top speed was up by almost 20 mph. Similar improvements were seen in Europe, where the Turbo tested by *Autocar* reached 60 mph from rest in 6.9 seconds and returned a top speed of 144 mph.

In keeping with this sort of urge, Porsche took pains to evolve a competent chassis. The thin tube-encased driveshaft went up from 20 to 25mm, eliminating any chance of whipping. Stronger rear halfshafts for the semi-trailing arms were provided, along with wider wheels and tires. Gear ratios, springs, shocks, and anti-roll bars were all revised and a beefier servo was provided for the brakes, which were ventilated discs all around for Europe, a disc/drum combination for America.

Two problems in turbocharged cars have typically been throttle lag and poor running at low rpm. Neither occurred in the 924 Turbo, where boost began at a low 1600 rpm and peaked at 2800 rpm on the U.S. version. (The larger, slower-revving European turbo unit began producing pressure at 1800 rpm). Transmission gear ratios were altered from those on the standard 924, but were identical on both U.S. and European Turbos except for 5th, which was a somewhat taller 0.60:1 ratio against 0.71:1—more than counterbalanced by the U.S. final drive ratio of 4.71:1 against the European's 3.17:1. Wrote John Dinkel in *Road & Track*: "Even though 5th is an over-overdrive (60 mph is only 2280 rpm), you can let the revs drop to below 2000 in top gear, tromp the go pedal and the engine pulls smoothly, albeit slowly. Try that with a stock 924 and you'll be greeted with a chorus of shakes, shudders, buzzes and groans of protest that won't stop until you downshift at least two gears."

So, the 924's underwhelming powerplant had been transformed competently if not miraculously so. What about the noise that went with it? Much of that was gone too. Porsche had carefully added sound-deadening material

Below: The 1980 American-market 924 Turbo with optional Sport Group that included lovely "spider web" alloy wheels, beefier chassis, rear spoiler.

throughout in both 924 models. The turbo unit itself was audible, but not noisy.

The Turbo was little changed in styling from the regular 924 save for identification, a "NACA" duct on the hood, additional cooling slots in the nose, and a rear spoiler built into the frame for the glass hatch. Porsche said that on the plain-vanilla 924 this spoiler could increase speed beyond the redline: it reduced the coefficient of drag from 0.36 to 0.35 all by itself. Turbo models also came with lovely "spider web" alloy wheels, which were optional on the non-turbo model. On the inside, all was very 924-ish; Turbo speedometer scales read to 160 mph initially, but were later reduced to 85 mph by federal edict. Interestingly, Porsche didn't bother to fit a turbo boost gauge, so it must have had a lot of faith in the installation and the engine's inherent strength.

The 924 Turbo was remarkably frugal, most early tests reporting averages of around 25 mpg. But it wasn't cheap, coming in at just under $21,000 in the 1980 introduction year. Yet it was an improvement the 924 had needed. "Here is another *real* Porsche," *Autocar* said, "A superb high performer which is most emphatically very well worth waiting for."

Another new item for 1980 was the Sport Group option, available for both turbo and non-turbo 924. The "S" package cost $2045 and $1960 POE, respectively, and gave both models ventilated disc brakes all around (as on European Turbos), the five-bolt "spider web" wheels with Pirelli P7 tires (replacing 4-bolt wheels and CN36 Pirellis), stiffer shocks, a thicker front anti-roll bar, and an anti-roll bar at the rear. During the year the Turbo acquired a three-way catalyst for emissions control, certified in all 50 states. Most reviewers found performance somewhat less than the early U.S.-market prototypes tested in Europe. A lot of double talk was offered by Porsche for this, most of it unconvincing. One is inclined to think the prototypes were in fact more potent. Fuel economy stayed about the same. CONSUMER GUIDE® magazine's test of the basically similiar '81 version yielded 23.1 mpg in an equal mix of city driving and suburban commuting. But with a base price $4000 beyond the 924 and most examples actually selling at $4000 higher than that, the 924 Turbo was hardly a bargain.

The three-way catalyst also appeared on the standard 1980 Type 924, which was improved in several ways. The severe judder and hop of the early cars had been attended to via tighter installation tolerances, rubber rear suspension mountings, and hydraulic transmission mounts. Make no mistake, it was still a hard-riding car, but not *quite* as hard. It was also better insulated, "the racket is a bit less objectionable," said *Road & Track*. The 924's five-speed gearbox got a revised, more conventional shift pattern, also adopted for the Turbo. Finally, performance was up moderately through changes in camshaft and ignition timing and a lower final drive ratio for manuals of 5.00:1 (against the previous 4.11:1). Horsepower was now up to 115 net and the 0-60 mph times down to the 10.5-11-second range. Fuel economy had not suffered here either, remaining at around 22-24 miles per gallon.

Just before Porsche introduced its next step forward in the four-cylinder series, rumors broke of a mystery car, the so-called Type 918. This was allegedly an "economy" model bearing 924 styling hallmarks. A Targa-like two-seater, it was reportedly

Opposite page: The standard U.S. 924 for 1980. Power by this time was up to 115 bhp (net). This page: The 924 was little changed for 1981. Shown is the American-marked Turbo. All the blown 924s were marked by nose cooling slots NACA-type hood duct, and molded-in rear spoiler. Car below has optional lift-off sunroof.

based on the VW Scirocco chassis and was to be powered by a 1.8-liter fuel injected VW four planned for the European Golf GTI and the new U.S. Rabbit GTI in 1983. The body was to be of steel and aluminum with polyurethane bumpers. An internal battle had reportedly developed over the "918" at Zuffenhausen, namely whether to move downmarket (to the $12-15,000 level) again, filling a hole left by the mass exodus of British sports cars, or to continue improving the 924 and 928. Whether or not the 918 or something like it will ever appear is an open question (Porsche+Audi isn't talking). Personally, we hope that it will. It's been a long time since there's been a Porsche that the majority of those who would like to own one could actually afford.

Porsche's latest four-cylinder car is the 944, introduced to the U.S. in the spring of 1982. And an important development it is. Packing great performance from its Porsche-built 2.5-liter ohc four, the 944 replaced both the 924 and 924 Turbo in the U.S. market.

Let's vary our analysis and begin with styling. The basis is 924, more precisely the 924 Carrera GT, a turbocharged European variation in the tradition of the "customer" competition cars of the past. Unlike the Carrera GT, which used plastic for its flared fenders and other panels, the 944 body is made entirely of steel. The flexible polyurethane nose cap incorporates a front air dam that directs air up and around the bulging fenders. A low-drag, under-bumper radiator intake is retained from the 924s. The air dam contains flush-mounted fog lights, and an extended rear spoiler is built into the hatchback lid *a la* 924 Turbo. Porsche says these aerodynamic tweaks were developed in extensive wind tunnel work and result in a coefficient of drag of 0.35. But that is no lower than the figure quoted by several sources for the 924 Turbo. Exactly what this means is unclear, but if both figures are accurate then some of the 944's aero mods would appear to be somewhat overrated. Of course, a lot of people like this sort of thing, but those who prefer more understated looks may find the 944 a tad too "racerish."

When it comes to mechanicals, however the 944 shines, superior to the 924 in every way. The noisy, buzzy Audi engine has vanished. In its place is an all-new normally aspirated slant four with cross-flow aluminum head and silicon-aluminum alloy block. It is, in fact, one half of the 928's V-8 with a slightly larger (by 5mm) bore giving 2479cc displacement from very oversquare cylinder dimensions of 100×78.9mm. Output for the U.S. version is 143 bhp net at 5500 rpm, and 137 pounds-feet of torque at only 3000 rpm. Corresponding numbers for the Euro-spec engine are 163 bhp (DIN) at 5800 and 151 lbs/ft. at 3000. The engine incorporates the advanced, no-maintenance Digital Motor Electronic (DME)

System, developed by Bosch, for precise control of fuel injection and ignition functions, as well as internal balance shafts (for which Porsche pays a royalty to Mitsubishi of Japan) to eliminate secondary coupling forces that cause vibration.

Slicing a V-8 in half is scarcely a new idea, but it has benefits, greater interchangeability of components and lower tooling costs being the main ones. Also, the 2.5 offers the balance between performance and economy that Zuffenhausen was looking for in the 924. It was a better choice than the alternatives — the Renault-Volvo-Peugeot V-6 or the Audi five.

The 944 cockpit is familiar to 924 owners, with fully reclining front bucket seats plus two occasional seats with fold-down backrests in the rear. Instrument panel and control layout are also carried over virtually unchanged. A retractable cover is provided to keep cargo out of sight. Optional extras include 16-inch 911-style forged-alloy wheels, leather seat surfaces, stabilizer bars, sport shocks, and wheel locks. Porsche has adopted bright yellow instrument markings for better legibility. Standard upholstery is vinyl, and tweed cloth inserts are available at extra cost. Air conditioning, removable flip-up sunroof, tinted glass, and three-spoke leather-covered steering wheel are all part of the lengthy standard equipment list.

How does it perform? The controls are a bit heavy and the steering wheel still connects with your thighs at times. Aside from that, it goes like a rocket. The 60 mph mark comes in just over eight seconds, and the average driver should see the quarter-mile post in 16.5 seconds from rest. Top gear in the standard five-speed

Opposite page: The 924 Turbo (1982 model shown at top) spawned the Europe-only Carrera GT (middle, bottom) in late '79, intended partly as a customer race car. This page: Carrera GT inspired the shape of the 1983 Type 944, though construction is all-steel. The 944 replaced both 924 models in Porsche's American lineup.

overdrive manual gearbox (three-speed automatic is optional) extends the 944 to a maximum of 130 mph. Fuel economy in mixed driving should average 20-24 miles per gallon, which is borne out by the 22.5 mpg recorded in CONSUMER GUIDE® magazine's test. We also found handling nearly flawless, though wet roads demand caution with the throttle to avoid sudden rear-end breakaway in a tight turn.

The 944 lives up to the badge it bears in a way that the standard 924 didn't, and reassures Porsche partisans that Stuttgart-Zuffenhausen is still on course, as God and Herr Doktor intended. Writer Don Vorderman, a critic not known for liberal praise, calls it "the best small sports car ever made." Is it? Well, for about the same money you can buy a Datsun 280ZX Turbo, the Yokahama rocket, and just outdrag the 944. Bargain hunters may like the rotary rocket, the Mazda RX-7, which costs considerably less than either of these. But the Porsche is better looking, better built, quicker through the esses, and stingier on fuel. What's more, it's a Porsche. And that is one thing they haven't been able to duplicate in Japan.

This page and opposite: Three views of the 928 in its initial 1978 European guise. The futuristic body design, created by American Tony Lapine, caused quite a stir, and still turns heads today. Note optional 16-inch-diameter "egg poacher" wheels, the lay-back headlamps, and smooth body-color nose with vestigal "chin" spoiler. Black "pips" on bumper top are headlamp washer jets.

electrochemically treated so that the silicon acted as the wearing surface. This application was very similar to what GM tried with the Chevy Vega engine, though it worked appreciably better here. The belt-driven cams, one per bank, were angled so that their covers appeared near vertical, giving the V-8 an appearance much like that of the 911's flat-six, which was possibly done on purpose. For lightness, the block was also made of aluminum alloy and contained the traditional forged-steel crankshaft running in five main bearings, plus forged connecting rods paired on common journals. The cylinder heads were also alloy, and 8.5:1 compression was specified. Bosch's reliable K-Jetronic fuel injection system metered the air/fuel mixture. Rated horsepower was 240 bhp (DIN) at 5500 rpm (220 SAE net at 5250 rpm) and torque 257 pounds-feet (254 SAE) at 3600 rpm.

Joe Rusz of *Road & Track* rhetorically asked why Porsche built a simple sohc engine and not an exotic one, then quoted Zuffenhausen press officer Manfred Jantke: "A Porsche is not a toy." Finance director Heinz Branitzki added that the engine was designed "with growth potential." And indeed, as we would learn, there was room for more displacement (as well as a second pair of camshafts).

The front-engine/rear-transmission arrangement was more important to the 928 than it was to the lighter, less powerful 924. It insured a relatively high polar moment of inertia, reducing nose heaviness and the understeer that went with it. Weight distribution was a near-perfect 51 percent front/49 percent rear. The standard gearbox was Porsche's own specially designed five-speed manual, though curiously its gate reverted to the odd racing-style

pattern with first gear below reverse on the far left. Daimler-Benz did provide one major component in the form of a three-speed automatic. Also available for the four-cylinder Porsche, it was a no-cost option for the 928. On manual models, there was a special two-plate clutch of fairly small (7-inch) diameter, designed to accommodate the extra rotary inertia of the thin, rigid driveshaft. A helper-spring release arrangement cut clutch pedal effort to only 33 pounds. Heavy clutch action is fairly common among high-performance GTs, so this sort of careful attention to detail demonstrates just how thoroughly engineered the 928 was.

Nowhere was that more evident than in the suspension. Though the layout looked conventional enough, it really wasn't. Up front were double wishbones acting on coil spring/struts. The rear employed a similar arrangement plus a new feature, actually an effect that Porsche dubbed the "Weissach axle." Here, said *Autocar*, Porsche used "only a bottom wishbone, which takes brake and acceleration torque loads as well as helping the ball-jointed single top link locate the wheel laterally. The bottom wishbone has its inboard pivot axis inclined outwards at the front, like a semi-trailing arm, to provide a measure of anti-squat. And at the front body pivot, it has a sort of double joint. The give of this in a corner under braking and decelerating forces [that ordinarily produce] an oversteer-inducing toe-out [instead] makes the outside rear wheel toe-in slightly. This deliberate understeering self-steer at the rear thus counters the usual accidental oversteering self-steer in the case where the driver who has entered a corner too fast lifts off, or, worse, brakes." The 928's rack-and-pinion steering featured negative offset geometry for better control in a situation where one front wheel might lose traction. Unusually for a Porsche, power assist was standard, with the degree of assist varying with road speed so as to maintain proper effort at higher speeds while providing maximum boost for easy parking. Just 3.1 turns were required lock-to-lock. For an extra $1000 or so you could ride on ultra-low-profile Pirelli P7 tires mounted on special 16-inch-diameter wheels with an unusual "egg poacher" design. The stickability of these tires was uncanny. "They hang on to absurd limits," said *Autocar*, "and combined with the drama-free way the car simply understeers ultimately, it is easy to dismiss the 928 as almost dull in a corner. And then you think about how fast you are going through the corner."

The suspension was so remarkably compliant, absorbing every kind of surface irregularity, that most observers could hardly believe the 928 could cling like a race car when really put to work. The brakes, power-assisted four-wheel ventilated discs, proved equally capable. They could pull up to 1g deceleration, and *Road & Track*'s 60-0 mph panic stop was accomplished in an astoundingly short 139 feet. "One wonders how much the very handsome, wide-eyed wheels help in keeping the fade performance good," added *Autocar*. "Few cars have such nakedly obvious discs ...a piece of functional design that makes the car look all the more what it is—ideally functional."

Performance was nothing less than you'd expect. A five-speed car would run 0-60 mph in 7-8 seconds, the automatic needed perhaps a second more. Ditto the standing quarter-mile, which took about 15-16 seconds with manual, by which time the speedo was reading some 90 mph. Top speed ranged between 135 and 145 mph, more than most owners ever really needed. (In 1983, the trio of Gerhard Plattner, Peter Lovett, and Peter Zbinden needed a bit more, and drove a 928S to a new 24-hour record at Brindisi, Italy. They *averaged* 155 mph.)

Porsche was apparently more than a bit sensitive about the 928's new-wave styling, and went to great pains to explain the advantages of its futuristic new shape to customers and dealers alike. Consider this excerpt (under the heading "Love at Second Sight") from a dealer training booklet called *Porsche 928: The Alternative*, issued in 1978: "Many different factors had to be combined to result in interesting aesthetics. The 928 was designed to have as many Porsche styling points as possible and to be clearly different to other sports cars on the road...Then there was the safety legislation... And, of course, acceptable aerodynamic values had to be reached, e.g., those concerning air penetration and directional stability...The 928 styling with a fastback is an intentional continuation of Porsche tradition in that it is aerodynamically superior, because of the comparatively short front end and a gently tapered and rounded tail, guaranteeing low air turbulence. As well as improving directional stability, the large-surface tail end also means a large passenger compartment and an outstanding amount of headroom for rear seat passengers in a sports car.

"We also believe that rounded forms are more interesting than clean-cut lines, which can be absorbed immediately and do not have anything new to offer the observer. The 928 looks different from each angle, and remains interesting." Porsche also suggested its sales people use the following reply to prospects expressing doubts about the car's looks: "Naturally, every observer will need a certain amount of time to get accustomed to the unusual styling of the 928; but a car which is technically different from other cars has the right to look different than the others, don't you agree?"

The 928 was indeed recognizeable at a glance from its lesser brethren and almost everything else. At the front were exposed pop-up headlamps, which lay flat just below the line of the hood/fender surface when not in use. This was a curious styling device, especially since the lamps on the cheaper 924 were fully concealed (by means of flip-up panels) in an ostensibly more modern, aerodynamic, and expensive style. Porsche claimed the reason for this was to enable the 928 owner to clean the headlamps more easily, not to mention providing a low nose while still meeting minimum headlight height requirements. Fine, but we'll bet the idea was inspired by the Lamborghini Miura. Another note of difference at the front end was the 928's separate fog and driving lights, something not found on the 924, providing for every sort of nighttime condition.

On the inside, the car was exotic, with lots of thoughtful features that just didn't crop up anywhere else. For instance, the long-running complaint about minimum thigh clearance under the wheel of the 924 was answered here with a tilt-adjustable wheel that also

This page and opposite: Aside from the required side marker lamps, the 1978 American-market 928 looked much like its European counterpart. Like the 924, the 928 employed a front-engine/rear-transaxle chassis, but the driveshaft here was rigid. Long intake runners make 928 V-8 look somewhat like the 911's flat six.

moved the whole instrument cluster with it, insuring good gauge visibility at all times. Teutonic thoroughness? What else could it be when you find sunvisors for the *back* seat passengers (they also make perfect blinders, in case the folks back there worry too much at 125 mph). Those seats are, by the way, definitely of the "plus two" variety, yet there's a surprising amount of back seat room considering the 98.4-inch wheelbase and low-slung body. The psychedelic checkerboard velour seat and door trim initially specified was a bit much, but you could substitute leather if you didn't like it.

For a Porsche, the 928 was sinfully luxurious and lavishly equipped. Right from the start, the list of standard amenities ran to air conditioning, central locking system, power windows, rear wiper, headlamp washers, cruise control, an electrically adjustable *heated* door mirror, and four-speaker stereo radio/cassette. Options included the leather interior (progressively expanded as time went on to encompass door panels and headliner as well as the seats), electric sliding sunroof, limited-slip differential, and a factory-fitted burglar alarm. For 1980, leather upholstery became standard on U.S. cars (cloth trim could be specified at no charge) along with a cargo area cover that raised with the hatchback lid. Late that season, Porsche offered a "Competition Package" that comprised most of the "good stuff" from the more powerful European 928S except its engine. Items here were sport shock absorbers, front and rear spoilers (despite Porsche's claims the 928's body benefited from these aerodynamic aids), special sports seats, and 16-inch forged-alloy wheels.

As if all that weren't enough, Porsche gave 205 U.S. buyers a chance to own the special Weissach Edition 928. Offered midway through the '82 model year, it was done up similarly to previous 911 specials. Its main attractions were special Champagne Gold metallic paint, matching gold-colored alloy wheels, sunroof, fore and aft spoilers, and a two-tone leather interior complete with a matched three-piece set of fitted luggage valued at over $1000. Electronic radio with digital tuning and automatic temperature control for the heating/air conditioning were also provided. The Weissach could be had with either manual or automatic transmission. A small plaque was mounted just ahead of the stick as a reminder—if any be needed—that you were in charge of something special.

Then there was the warning light system. Switch on, and bright red and green warning lights appeared as a check that all systems were functioning, fluids topped up, and all exterior lights working. There was also a large warning light to draw your attention to any individual warning light. You could turn off the master warning by pressing a button; it would come on again when you next switched on the ignition. If the fault were serious, the master would not extinguish until the problem was corrected.

Porsche initially made much of the 928's safety construction, even going so far as to compare the function of the car's B-pillars to the rollbar on the 911 Targa. The 928 was indeed robust, for despite the use of weight-saving aluminum for the doors, hood, and the detachable front fenders, the car still tipped the scales at a portly 3300 pounds. No matter, the 928 was designed to go the distance.

Porsche had developed a unique hot-dip zinc galvanizing process that first saw production for 1975 car bodies. This was one result of the firm's research into "long life" technology. Thus, it was no surprise that the 928's unit body/chasis was made of this double-sided, rust-resistant steel,

or that its brake lines were sheathed in copper-nickel iron alloy or its fuel lines treated with chrome and then plastic coated. Beginning with the 1980 model year, Porsche offered a six-year warranty against lower bodyshell rust in addition to its normal new-car warranty on all U.S. models following a program inaugurated in Europe a few years earlier. The only requirement for the owner was that the car be inspected annually at a participating Porsche dealer. The coverage remained in effect even if the car changed hands during the six years. Here was yet another expression of Zuffenhausen's commitment to top-quality craftsmanship.

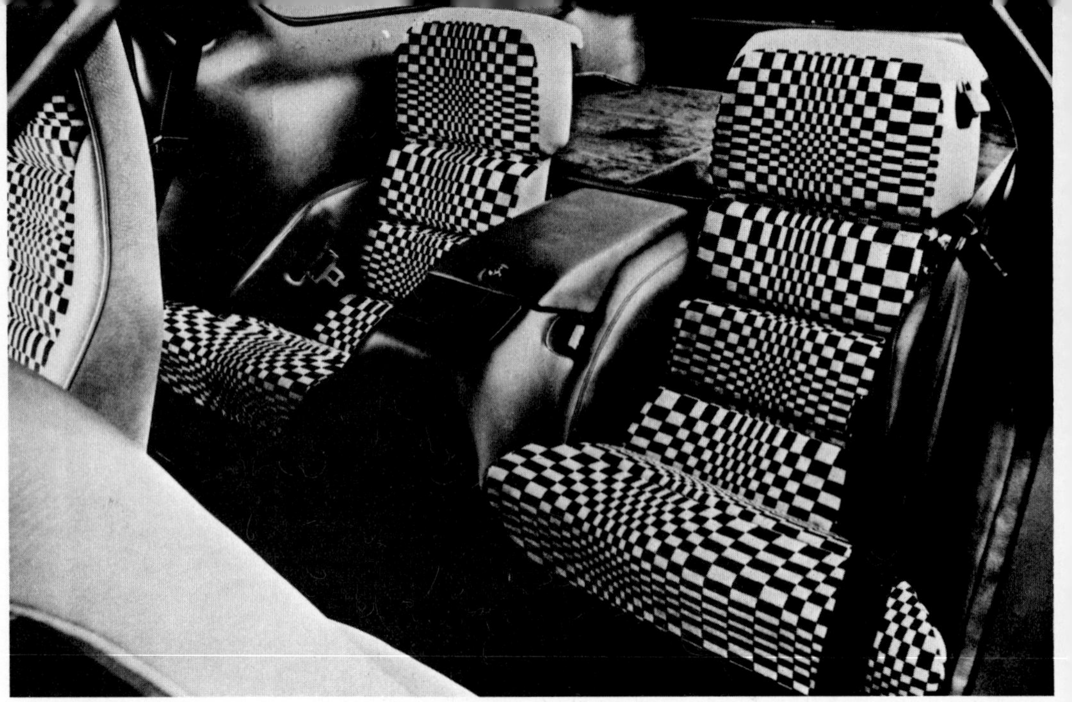

Above: 928's rear quarters are tight. Early op-art upholstery has since been changed on U.S. models. Opposite page: The 1979 Type 928 with Competition Group (top). Porsche's "long-life" vehicle research included an experimental 928 (lower left) and 20-Year Car study, 1973.

The 928 evolved through 1982 with few changes aside from those already mentioned. The central warning light system was relocated from the console to the main instrument cluster, beginning with the '79 models, for easier viewing. For 1980, the mechanical K-Jetronic fuel injection system gave way to an all-electronic system with an oxygen sensor and twin three-way catalysts for better driveability with more precise emissions control. For 1982, a fuel economy gauge was added. This showed instantaneous mpg at highway speeds or fuel use in gallons per hour at idle or in low-speed driving.

For 1983, the 928 became the 928S, gaining the more powerful, 4.7-liter version of the aluminum V-8 previously restricted to Europe. Horsepower on the U.S. version was now up to 234 (net) and torque to 263 pounds-feet. Also new was a 4-speed automatic option, replacing the previous 3-speed, with a better spread of ratios for performance and a numerically lower final drive for economy and more restful highway crusing. On the five-speed gearbox, the lower four ratios were all shortened up, to the benefit of off-the-line punch. As a result, the claimed 0-60 mph time on the manual version was down to about 7.0 seconds, and the official top speed was listed at 146 mph. With automatic, the numbers were 8.5 seconds and 143 mph. Standard equipment now included the functional spoilers front and rear (which reduced the drag coefficient from 0.41 to 0.38), 16-inch forged alloy wheels, and low-profile tires from the previous Competition Package. About the only extra-cost items left were the electric sliding sunroof, fancy digital radio, and limited-slip differential.

Considering its limitations as a specialist car, it's amazing that the 928 has received such high praise from motoring journals. And it's their attitude that tells you more about this car's true worth than anything else. Some say it's not quick enough for the price you pay. The forthcoming 944 Turbo will probably be just as fast, if not faster. Yet heaven knows the 928 can go faster than you probably will ever want to, and it goes around corners like it's painted on the road.

"While the sports car driver is coping with his challenge at every bend, the man in the 928 can go every bit as fast—and often a great deal faster—with cool confidence," wrote English journalist Ray Hutton. "I doubt that even a very aggressive fast driver would find [its] limits on the road. One can play tricks with the 928, lift off mid-corner, wind on too much lock, and it remains unperturbed. It is quite happy to corner at speeds which may be disconcerting for the driver who has set his standards on lesser cars."

Is it a sports car? Hutton thinks not: "It is as a sort of ultra high speed transport capsule that the 928 becomes something, for this writer at least, that other cars are not. It isn't really a sports car in the accepted sense... But it isn't like a coupe version of an expensive saloon [sedan] either...

"The 928 does not have the best performance in the world, but by any standards it has enough. And in terms of A-to-B journey speed, primary safety and the sheer enjoyment of driving a car that corners and handles better than anything on the road, it stands alone. The Best Car in the World?"

Looking back, in a 1979 interview with Jan P. Norbye, chairman of the board Ferry Porsche, who turned 74 on September 19, 1983, is satisfied. To a certain extent the new

front-engine cars were concepts forced on Zuffenhausen by government regulations, he says, but the results have been more than pleasing. "We believe that even our new models get their power onto the road very well, via the rear wheels. The transaxle with its favorable weight distribution sees to that. Front-wheel drive is undoubtedly the more economical solution and one widely used these days. But we tried that too, after all. The 911 powerplant could be put in front just as well. But imagine a Turbo with FWD — it would probably never get its power onto the road."

Was the move to front-engine design a contradiction for Porsche, a renouncing of tradition? "It was never my philosophy to ask where the engine should be placed," Ferry Porsche says, "but rather, which solution would bring the greatest gains. You can see from the Alfasud, for instance, that one could also install a flat-four engine in front."

And what of the future? Here, Dr. Porsche is optimistic, not only for his company but for the automobile in general: "There is no sensible alternative to the automobile as a means of transport...There is nothing new under the sun. Take energy. Conditions were very similar after the first war. The entire world was building economical, small autos. In those days my father built the Sascha. We had great success in hillclimbs and track races with this economy racer... Fuel consumption will be vitally important in the future and consumption has always depended on weight and air resistance. To cut consumption we can apply developments promoted by racing — the turbocharger, for instance. We can also improve the efficiency rating of an engine with it, thus reaching extremely low consumption values... An engineer requires freedom for such developments. I can only hope that this freedom will be insured for us in the future, allowing us to make useful contributions."

Whatever the future holds, Porsche's record has been pretty good so far. For that—and most of all the cars bearing this proud marque — we may thank this gifted man and the talented people he has attracted and encouraged. Of Ferry Porsche we can truly say something that sons around the world are always pleased to hear: "His father would be proud of him."

COLLECTOR PORSCHES: THE CONNOISSEUR'S CHOICE

A premium connoisseur's collectible: The 1958 Type 356A coupe (to European specifications)

The dictionary defines "connoisseur" as one who has "expert knowledge and keen discrimination." However, this definition neglects to say whether the discrimination is objective or subjective. Now a subjective automobile connoisseur might say that any Porsche model is highly collectible. There might be certain superior characteristics in a model group here and there but, in general, any car from Stuttgart-Zuffenhausen is worthy. The objective connoisseur, on the other hand, might overlook Porsche completely. After all, the marque is but 35 years old, very young for Hall of Fame status. How could it possibly compare with the grand marques of the golden age?

Somewhere between these extremes lies the path of knowledge. In Porsche collecting, like most automotive subjects where personal opinion runs high, the "truth" depends very much on the individual. But certain broad facts do stand out, and should be mentioned. That is the purpose of this chapter.

As a small company, Porsche has often built special models in very small quantities, perhaps as few as a dozen or even one. If you find one of these—and if you can afford it—there is only one piece of advice we can offer: buy it now. The America roadster falls into this category. Built in two series by Gläser and Heuer, it is an extremely uncommon collector's piece today. Even the early 356s built at Gmünd numbered only 50, and there are far fewer than that left today (though you might be surprised at how many).

Condition always plays a role, perhaps the deciding role, in determining the worth of a collectible anything, and Porsches are no exception. Like other cars, the Porsches you'll find on collector markets today range from restored or original-condition show winners to "walking wrecks." And restoration doesn't necessarily qualify a car as desirable: a superficial or "quickie" re-do of exterior, interior or engine my result in a Porsche that drives and handles like a Buick. An original, low-mileage specimen is, by and large, your best choice—if its mechanicals are in good order and its body solid and tight.

This doesn't mean you should overlook higher-mileage, well-maintained examples, however. A typical 911, for instance, should be good for 100,000 miles before it needs a major engine overhaul. But remember that, car for car, the higher the mileage the greater the chance you'll run into major problems sooner or later—probably sooner.

With these general guidelines in mind, let's take a look at the must-haves and also-rans among Porsche collectibles. We divide them into two groups, the Type 356 production models and their derivatives, and the "901-series" road cars beginning with the original 911/912.

TYPE 356 PRODUCTION MODELS

In the beginning, there were the Gmünd cars, the first Porsches. About 10 of the 50 built are known to exist in the United States today, and they are predictably expensive even in decrepit condition. Yet they may still be "sleepers," since their value continues to increase. Besides, there will never be more than 50 to be found. That may be just as well, because it takes know-how as well as money to own a Gmünd car. The main problem is that they were all hand-made one at a time. Not only are there not many spare parts left now, but car number 7 may have completely different trim than car number 42. So, restoring any particular one to *original* condition shapes up as an exercise in frustration.

One of the early Swiss-built, Beutler-bodied Gmünd cabriolets is on display at the Swiss Museum of Transportation in Lucerne, but where are the others? One was reportedly seen in California several years ago. For many reasons, it would be difficult to put a value on these cars.

The first Stuttgart-built 356s date from 1950 to 1955, and can be identified by 16-inch wheels and a split windshield on very early examples, a creased windshield on 1954s, one-piece curved on the '55. The coupe was the most numerous body style, and if there is a Porsche sleeper anywhere it's this one. There are still some around begging for homes, and they're priced surprisingly low. The original Type 356 Cabriolet, on the other hand, is a high-ticket item. The cabriolet is a German invention, a sort of deluxe convertible, with a padded top and the bows concealed by a headliner. The early 356 Cabriolets are rare and thus extremely expensive today, with values running well above the $20,000 mark. So, too, are the America roadsters—if you can find one for sale.

We should point out here that only 7500 of the first-generation 356s were produced when the series was superseded in 1955 by the 356A. That's not a lot, which makes the coupes' current relatively low prices even more amazing. The lack of a synchromesh gearbox may have something to do with this.

If Porsche makes an engine, sooner or later there will be an "S" version of it. In the early years, before 1955, there were "S" engines in all three displacements, 1.1, 1.3, and 1.5 liter. A warning about the last, the 1500S: it used a Hirth roller-bearing crankshaft, and as that company is no longer in business, the crank will be all but impossible to replace. Most of these cars have already had standard plain-bearing crankshafts substituted, an invisible change that does, however, effect their authenticity and hence price.

Turning to the "non-sleeper" Type 356A, we enter the era of the "classic" Porsche, at least as far as prices and desirability are concerned. A prime example of any model here will run in excess of $20,000 today, and prices are rising.

Thirty years ago, Porsche's U.S. sales were handled mainly by that foreign-car impressario, Max Hoffman. Max called the shots, and Ferry Porsche listened. The Speedster is one model attributed directly to the "wizard of Park Avenue." In its day it was a price leader and definitely *not* a strong seller. Only 5000 Speedsters were made, yet they are tremendously coveted today—it's the model many people think of when you say "Porsche." Why this 180-degree shift? Perhaps it has to do with the Speedster's innate honesty: it was a no-frills car, yet it provided everything in the way of performance the more expensive models did, reliably and well. And with its minimal canvas top stowed away out of sight it looked racy, interesting, and different.

The Cabriolet was the luxury liner in those days, although a coupe owner could enjoy part of its open-air fun by ordering the sunroof option. Both the Speedster and Cabriolet were available with a detachable fiberglass hardtop, and this, of course, is desirable, adding to the value of a car so equipped. Make sure, though, that it's a factory-issue top and not one of those from a contemporary aftermarket source. By 1958 the Speedster was being phased out, except for a handful of Carrera versions built through 1959. In its place came the more civilized Convertible "D," really the Speedster concept with a higher windshield, roll-up windows and a more practical, built-in folding top. All the open cars are desirable and the Convertible "D" is more desirable than most, but the Speedster maintains a lead on it in collector values today.

The most costly 356A models are, of course, the four-cam Carreras, with their potent Spyder engine offering wickedly fast street performance and championship racing potential. But there weren't many built, and that means high prices today. The least common variation is the special-bodied GS/GT, which had sleeker, un-Porsche-like lines and lightweight aluminum body panels.

Any 356A is a solid collector choice. The House of Porsche was on the rise, and there wasn't a bad model from 1956 to 1959. But there just aren't any bargains left now, and the least expensive version you can buy is the Normal coupe.

The Type 356B ran from model year 1960 to 1963. A body change was instituted for the 356B in mid-1962. This can be identified by the fuel filler, relocated from inside the trunk to the right front fender and capped by a lid with a remote cable release operable from the cockpit. Also, the front hood's lower edges took on a square look, and twin grilles appeared on the engine cover. This was referred to as the T-6 body, replacement for the previous T-5. A notchback coupe was added to the line about the same time that the Roadster was dropped, also in 1962. Built by Karmann, it looked very much like the cabriolet with the removable hardtop in place except that the roof was fixed. This was a low-volume item, yet it commands no exceptional price premium now compared to other contemporary models. Rarity alone does not establish high prices; it takes demand to do that.

A major development accompanying the B was the Super 90 engine, which replaced the Carrera unit. A small and now very desirable series of Super 90 GT coupes were built, with lighter aluminum hood, trunk, and door panels and pop-out plastic side windows. The regular Super 90 featured standard steel-belted radial tires and rear camber compensator, and had accordingly better handling than previous models. Also, in 1962, the Carrera 2 option appeared with a revived four-cam engine punched out to 2.0 liters. It is very desirable Porsche today.

Right-hand-drive Porsches have been produced since the Gmünd days, destined for England or Commonwealth countries. They are generally less valuable, car for car, for obvious reasons. And, curiously, they seem more prone to rust.

But rust in any Porsche is serious and difficult to eradicate. Look at it as the tip of an iceberg: what you see is probably 10 percent of the real damage. The floorpan is the most common and critical rust area, and a proper replacement costs about $3000. A simple precaution is to ask the seller to jack up one side of the car. If he "misplaced" the jack or if it suddenly "doesn't work," look elsewhere. Remember that the floorpan is, in effect, the frame of any monocoque car, and if solid it should easily support the car's weight on the jack. If not, structural rigidity of the whole car has been compromised.

As with the 356A, there are no bargains among the Bs, although they are more numerous. The very best examples are already running above $20,000, because demand continues to grow while the supply doesn't. It's an axiom among collectors that good cars will always be good, while bad ones will never be good. And a Porsche definitely is one of the good ones.

The final 356 series, the C model, was offered for 1964-65, and was produced right alongside the first 911s. With other marques, this sort of obsolescence would reduce the collector value of an interim model, but with Porsche the opposite is true. The highly developed 356C was the most perfect of its generation, and as such commands a premium on the collector market today.

Again, it's significant to consider that we're talking about only 78,000 cars built during the 356's entire design life, 1948-65. That's hardly more than a handful by Detroit's yardstick. The "classic Porsche" is, therefore, a rare breed both in numbers and in character. Diehards say these are the only "true" Porsches, but however you view them they were very good sports cars. None can be had for little money now and sold for a lot a year or two. Investments are what they are, like money in the bank. A pity all investments aren't this much fun or provide so much satisfaction.

TYPE 901-SERIES PRODUCTION MODELS

The early 911s and 912s are now somewhat rare, mainly due to attrition. The first 145 Type 912s with painted dashboards and three-dial instrumentation are the least common. The 912 was not fast compared to the 911, but its handling was better thanks to its lighter engine.

Most 912 bodies were supplied by Karmann, whereas most early 911 bodies were built at Porsche. The Type 901 bodyshell was generally not as rust-prone as the Type 356, which is all to the good, but this is not to say you shouldn't be equally wary with these cars. It's a good idea to follow the same checking procedure as that noted for the 356.

The 912 is a desirable collector's car since it shares the 911's attractive body styling, is more sparing with fuel, and is far less costly to repair. Most 911 equipment was offered for it at extra cost, including the lovely Fuchs alloy wheels and the five-speed transmission. The best 912 vintage is likely 1967, since the 1968 and later U.S. models were detuned to meet emissions regulations and acquired safety equipment that doesn't appeal to the purist. Most of the early cars should have been repaired or restored by now, but beware of cracked heads, which were commonplace. The 1969 model shared the small wheelbase increase with the 911. This would be the last U.S. 912 until 1976, when the 912E powered by the VW 411/412 engine appeared.

Views on the relative merits of the four- and five-speed transmission are mixed. While the five-speed allowed one to get the most out of either a 911 or 912, it had a peculiar shift pattern up through 1971, with first gear hung out racing-style to the lower left, under reverse, an arrangement some drivers find annoying. The four-speed box used slightly wider gear spacings but was otherwise adequate for most driving situations.

Among 911 models, the 1967 S, despite its plug-fouling tendency, should rank high on anyone's collectible list because it was the first and last S available to American buyers before serious emission controls set in. The 911L of 1968 did not replace the S which, as we've seen, was only withdrawn from the U.S. market temporarily. In addition to the roadgoing trio of 911T, 911E, and 911S that appeared for 1969, there was the limited-production 911R (racing) version with lightweight body panels and plastic, vented rear quarter windows. Though certified and sold only for competition use when new, this is a highly desirable and fast-appreciating car, one of those models that hardcore Porsche addicts will want regardless of whether or not they've thought about where they're going to get the money. The Sportomatic option of the late Sixties can be safely ignored by the collector despite its relative rarity.

In mid-1973, the 911T was switched from mechanical to CIS fuel injection, and all 911 models had it for 1974 and beyond. This system brought about increased power and gas mileage — no mean feat — and allowed use of low-octane unleaded gasoline. A mostly trouble-free component, it is a plus for collectors. The 1972 and newer models may be found with the Type 915 five-speed transmission, which relocated first and fifth gears in the arrangement now commonly used in passenger cars. Roger Penske said this gearbox was difficult to shift in the corners, but he couldn't have understood: a Porsche driver does not shift in corners. In the 1974-77 models years, the 911 was plagued by emission control problems that hampered driveability and performance. Though officially aircooled, the engine should really be labeled "oil-cooled." Running temperatures began to rise, which bode ill for longevity. For 1974, the 911S yielded its top-line status to the U.S. version of the Carrera. Though a true high-performance car in its European specification, the Carrera we got was merely a trim option with fancy graphics and few mechanical differences from the 911S. To date, this model has shown no sign of outstripping other mid-'70s 911s in value, though this could change in a few years should Carreras suddenly become scarce.

If there is a sleeper among Porsches of the Seventies it has to be the 914. You can still buy one of the four-cylinder versions for under $5000, and many are available, something you can't say about most other Porsche models. It was a neat car, too. The 911-powered 914/6 is, of course, a more serious automobile, but there are far fewer around. This means it's a good investment with high appreciation potential, but finding one in good condition won't be that easy.

We have attempted here to outline both the good buys and not-so-good buys among Porsche cars today, purposely avoiding hard and fast statements in an area where few rules exist. To summarize: the established blue chips are all the Type 356s, especially 356Cs and Speedsters, the 1967 911S, the 1973 911T with CIS injection and the 930 Turbo/Turbo Carrera. Ranked just below these on the desirability ladder are the post-1967 911S, the 914/6, and the 912. Long shots are the current 911SC, 928, and 944. Like their predecessors, they will undoubtedly become collector's items. Meanwhile, they are worthy investments you can drive and enjoy now and for years to come. Sportomatic cars, the 1969 911E with other than MacPherson struts, the heavily detoxed 1974-77 911s, and 924s (except the European Carrera GT are not collectible and may never be, but as Porsches they're hardly not worth having. The "sleepers?" Only 914s, really. The 2.0-liter models should be your choice, with the smaller-displacement (1.7/1.8-liter) versions just behind.

MAJOR SPECIFICATIONS: U.S. PRODUCTION MODELS FROM 1948

1948 Type 356 Prototype
Engine: Four-cylinder horizontally opposed with Porsche-modified cylinder heads. Bore and Stroke: 75 × 64mm (2.853 × 2.52 in.), 1131cc (169.0 cid). Bhp: 40 (DIN), 46 (SAE) at 4000 rpm. Compression ratio: 6.5:1. Overhead valves, four plain bearings, single Solex Type 26VFJ carburetor.
Chassis: Trailing-arm front suspension, swing-axle rear suspension, VW brakes and worm gear steering, VW 9-inch drum brakes (cable actuated), single dry-disc clutch, VW non-synchromesh gearbox. Final drive ratio: 4.43:1.
Measurements: Weight: 1324 pounds (unladen). Tire size: 5.00×16. Track: 53.4″ front, 53.5″ rear. Wheelbase: 84.6″. Overall length: 152.4″. Overall width: 65.7″. Overall height: 49.8″. Maximum speed: 90 mph. Fuel consumption: 35 mpg.

1949 Early Production Type 356 1100
Engine: As per 1948 prototype, except twin carburetors.
Chassis: As per 1948 prototype.
Measurements: Weight: 1332 pounds (unladen). Tire size: 5.00×16. Track: 50.8″ front, 49.2″ rear. Wheelbase: 82.7″. Overall length: 152.3″, Overall width: 65.5″. Overall height: 51.2″. Maximum speed: 90 mph. Fuel consumption: 33.6 mpg.

1950-54 Type 356 1100
Engine: Porsche Type 369, four-cylinder flat-opposed. Bore and Stroke: 73.5 × 64mm (2.89 × 2.52 in.), 1086 cc (66.3 cid). Bhp: 40 (DIN), 46 (SAE) at 4000 rpm. Compression ratio 6.5:1. Overhead valves, four plain bearings, twin Solex Type 32PBJ carburetors.
Chassis: Trailing-arm front suspension, swing-axle rear suspension, torsion bars front and rear, VW worm-gear steering, Ate hydraulic brakes, single dry-disc clutch, VW non-synchromesh transmission (through Autumn 1952) or Porsche Type 519 all-synchro transmission. Final drive ratio: 4.43:1.
Measurements: Permissible total weight: 2425 pounds. Tire size: 5.00×16. Track: 50.8″ front, 49.2″ rear. Wheelbase: 82.7″. Overall length: 151.6″. Overall width: 65.4″. Overall height: 51.2″. Maximum speed: 90 mph. Fuel consumption: 35 mpg.

1951-54 Type 356 1300
Engine: Porsche Type 506, four-cylinder flat-opposed. Bore and Stroke: 80 × 64mm (3.14 × 2.52 in.), 1286 cc (78.5 cid). Bhp: 44 (DIN), 50 (SAE) at 4200 rpm. Compression ratio: 6.5:1. Overhead valves, four plain bearings, twin Solex Type 32PBI carburetors.
Chassis: As per 1950-54 1100.
Measurements: As per 1950-54 1100, except Overall length: 152.4″. Overall width: 65.5″. Maximum speed: 92 mph. Fuel consumption: 32 mpg.

1953-55 Type 356 1300S
Engine: Porsche Type 589, four-cylinder flat-opposed. Bore and Stroke: 74.5 × 74.0mm (2.93 × 2.91 in.), 1290 cc (78.8 cid). Bhp: 60 (DIN), 71 (SAE) at 5500 rpm. Compression ratio: 8.2:1. Overhead valves, four roller-type bearings, twin Solex Type 32PBI carburetors.
Chassis: As per 1950-54 1100, except Porsche Type 519 all-synchromesh gearbox all years. Final drive ratio: 4.375:1.
Measurements: As per 1950-54 1100, except Overall length: 155.5″. Maximum

speed: 100 mph. Fuel consumption: 32 mpg.

1951-52 Type 356 1500
Engine: Porsche Type 527, four-cylinder flat-opposed. Bore and Stroke: 80 × 74mm (3.14 × 2.91 in.), 1488 cc (80.8 cid). Bhp: 60 (DIN), 71 (SAE) at 4800 rpm. Compression ratio: 7:1. Overhead valves, four roller-type bearings, twin Solex Type 40PBI carburetors.
Chassis: As per 1950-54 1100.
Measurements: As per 1953-55 1300S, except Maximum speed: 96 mph. Fuel consumption: 29 mpg.

1952-55 Type 356 1500
Engine: Porsche Type 546, four-cylinder flat-opposed. Bore and Stroke: 80 × 74mm (3.14 × 2.91 in.), 1488cc (90.8 cid). Bhp: 55 (DIN), 64 (SAE) at 4400 rpm. Compression ratio: 6.5:1. Overhead valves, four plain bearings, twin Solex Type 32PBI carburetors.
Chassis: As per 1953-55 1300S.
Measurements: As per 1951-52 1500.

1952-55 Type 356 1500S
Engine: Porsche Type 528 (528/2 from November 1954), four-cylinder flat-opposed. Bore and Stroke: 80 × 74mm (3.14 × 2.91 in.), 1488cc (90.8 cid). Bhp: 70 (DIN), 82 (SAE) at 5000 rpm. Compression ratio: 8.2:1. Overhead valves, four roller-type bearings, twin Solex Type 40PBI carburetors (Type 40PBIC from May 1954).
Chassis: As per 1953-55 1300S.
Measurements: As per 1953-55 1300S, except Maximum speed: 105 mph. Fuel consumption: 21 mpg.

1954-55 Type 356 1300A
Engine: Porsche Type 506/2, four-cylinder flat opposed. Bore and Stroke: 74.5 × 74mm (2.93 × 2.91 in.), 1290cc (78.7 cid). Bhp: 44 (DIN), 50 (SAE) at 4200 rpm. Compression ratio: 6.5:1. Overhead valves, four plain bearings, twin Solex Type 32PBI carburetors.
Chassis: Trailing-arm front suspension, swing-axle rear suspension, torsion bars front and rear, VW type worm gear steering, Ate Hydraulic brakes, single dry-disc clutch, Porsche Type 519 transmission. Final drive ratio: 4.375:1.
Measurements: Permissible total weight: 2425 pounds. Tire size: 5.00×16. Track: 50.8″ front, 49.2″ rear. Wheelbase: 82.7″. Overall length: 151.6″. Overall width: 65.4″. Overall height: 51.2″. Maximum speed: 87 mph. Fuel consumption: 35 mpg.

1954-55 Type 356 1300S/A
Engine: Porsche Type 589/2, four-cylinder flat-opposed. Bore and Stroke: 74.5 × 74mm (2.93 × 2.91 in.), 1290cc (78.7 cid). Bhp 60 (DIN), 71 (SAE) at 5500 rpm. Compression ratio: 8.2:1. Overhead valves, four roller-type bearings, twin Solex Type 32PBI carburetors.
Chassis: As per 1954-55 1300A.
Measurements: As per 1954-55 1300A, except Maximum speed: 100 mph. Fuel consumption: 31.5 mpg.

1954-55 Type 356 1500A
Engine: Porsche Type 546/2, four-cylinder flat-opposed. Bore and Stroke: 80 × 74mm, 1488 cc. Bhp: 55 (DIN), 64 (SAE) at 4400 rpm. Compression ratio: 6.5:1. Overhead valves, four plain bearings, twin Solex Type 32PBI carburetors.
Chassis: As per 1954-55 1300A.
Measurements: As per 1954-55 1300A, except Maximum speed: 96 mph. Fuel consumption: 29 mpg.

1954-55 Type 356 1500S/A
Engine: Porsche Type 528/2, four-cylinder flat opposed. Bore and Stroke: 80 × 74mm (3.14 × 2.91 in.), 1488cc (90.8 cid). Bhp: 70 (DIN), 82 (SAE) at 4400 rpm. Compression ratio: 6.5:1. Overhead valves, four roller-type bearings, twin Solex Type 40PBIC carburetors.
Chassis: As per 1954-55 1300A.
Measurements: As per 1954-55 1300A, except Maximum speed: 105 mph. Fuel consumption: 21 mpg.

1955-57 Type 356A 1300
Engine: Porsche Type 506/2, four-cylinder flat-opposed. Bore and Stroke: 74.5 × 74mm (2.93 × 2.91 in.), 1290cc (78.7 cid). Bhp: 44 (DIN), 50 (SAE) at 4200 rpm. Compression ratio: 6.5:1. Overhead valves, four plain bearings, twin Solex Type 32PBIC carburetors.
Chassis: Trailing-arm front suspension, swing-axle rear suspension, torsion bars front and rear, VW-type worm-gear steering, Ate hydraulic brakes, single dry disc clutch, Porsche Type 519 transmission (Type 644 from 1956). Final drive ratio: 4.375:1.
Measurements: Permissible total weight 2425 pounds. Tire size: 5.60 × 15. Track: 51.4″ front, 50.1″ rear. Wheelbase: 82.7″. Overall length: 155.5″. Overall width: 65.7″. Overall height: 51.6″. Maximum speed: 90 mph. Fuel consumption: 35 mpg.

1955-57 Type 356A 1300S
Engine: Porsche Type 589/2, four-cylinder flat-opposed. Bore and Stroke: 74.5 × 74mm (2.93 × 2.91 in.), 1290cc (78.7 cid). Bhp: 60 (DIN), 71 (SAE) at 5500 rpm. Compression ratio: 8.2:1. Overhead valves, four roller-type bearings, twin Solex Type 32PBI carburetors (Type 40PICB from 1956).
Chassis: As per 1955-57 1300.
Measurements: As per 1955-57 1300, except Maximum speed: 100 mph. Fuel consumption: 31.5 mpg.

1955-59 Type 356A 1600
Engine: Porsche Type 616/1, four-cylinder flat-opposed. Bore and Stroke: 82.5 × 74mm (3.24 × 2.91 in.), 1582cc (96.5 cid). Bhp: 50 (DIN), 70 (SAE) at 4500 rpm. Compression ratio: 7.5:1. Overhead valves, four plain bearings, twin Solex 32PBIC carburetors (Zenith Type 32NDIX from engine number 67001).
Chassis: As per 1955-57 1300, except ZF Type 7155 steering (from September 1957). Final drive ratio: 4.43:1.
Measurements: As per 1955-57 1300, except Permissible total weight: 2425 pounds, 2750 pounds from 1958. Maximum speed: 100 mph. Fuel consumption: 31.5 mpg.

1955-59 Type 356A 1600S
Engine: Porsche Type 616/2, four-cylinder flat-opposed. Bore and Stroke: 82.5 × 74mm (3.24 × 2.91 in.), 1582cc (96.5 cid). Bhp: 75 (DIN), 88 (SAE) at 5000 rpm. Compression ratio: 8.5:1. Overhead valves, four roller bearings (Alfing crankshaft from September 1957), twin Solex Type 40PBIC carburetors (Zenith Type 32NDIX from engine number 81201).
Chassis: As per 1955-59 1600.
Measurements: As per 1955-59 1600, except Maximum speed: 110 mph. Fuel consumption: 29.5 mpg.

1959-63 Type 356B
Engines: Porsche four-cylinder flat-opposed. Bore and Stroke: 82.5 × 74mm (3.24 × 2.91 in.), 1582 cc (96.5 cid). 1600: 60 Bhp (DIN) at 4500 rpm, compression ratio 7.5:1. 1600S: 75 bhp (DIN) at 5000 rpm, compression ratio 8.5:1. 1600 Super 90: 90 bhp (DIN) at 5500 rpm, compression ratio 8.7:1, later 9.1:1.
Chassis: As per 1955-59 Type 356A 1600, except Al-Fin aluminum brakes.
Measurements: As per 1955-59 356A/1600, except Curb weight: 1980 pounds. Permissible total weight 2750 pounds. Tire size: 5.60 × 15. Factory official maximum speeds (mph): 100 (1600), 110 (1600S), 116 (Super 90).

1963-65 Type 356C
Engines: Porsche four-cylinder flat-opposed. Bore and Stroke: 82.5 × 74mm (3.24 × 2.91 in.), 1582cc (96.5 cid). 1600C: 75 bhp (DIN) at 5200 rpm, compression ratio 8.5:1. 1600SC: 95 bhp (DIN) at 5800 rpm, compression ratio 9.5:1.

Porsche Spyder Specifications

year	model	bore × stroke	cc	CR (:1)	bhp @ rpm	gears	WB (in.)	length (in.)	width (in.)	height (in.)	weight (lbs)
1953	550/528	74.0×80.0	1488	9.0	79 @ 5200	4	82.8	141.8	61.0	40.0	1512
1953	550/547	66.0×85.0	1498	9.0	110 @ 7000	4	82.8	141.8	61.0	40.0	1500
1954	550/547	66.0×85.0	1498	9.0	110 @ 7000	4	82.8	140.0	60.0	40.0	1500
1955	550S	66.0×85.0	1498	8.8	110 @ 6200	4	82.8	140.0	60.0	40.0	1440
1956	550/1500RS	66.0×85.0	1498	9.8	135 @ 7200	5	82.8	149.5	63.8	36.0	1301
1957	718/1500RSK	66.0×85.0	1498	9.8	142 @ 7500	5	82.8	149.8	58.3	34.6	1146
1958-59	718/1600RSK	66.0×87.5	1598	9.8	165 @ 8000	5	82.8	149.8	58.3	34.6	1148
1960	718/RS60	66.0×87.5	1598	9.8	165 @ 8000	5	82.8	149.8	57.8	34.9	1058
1961	718/RS61	66.0×85.0	1498	9.8	150 @ 7800	5	82.8	149.8	57.8	34.9	1058
1961	718/RS61	66.0×87.5	1598	9.8	165 @ 8000	5	82.8	149.8	57.8	34.9	1058

BHP is in DIN measurement.

Chassis: As per 1959-63 Type 356B, except four-wheel disc brakes.
Measurements: As per 1959-63 Type 356B, except factory official maximum speeds (mph): 110 (1600C), 116 (1600SC).

1966-69 Type 912
Engine: Four-cylinder, flat-opposed. Bore and Stroke: 82.5 × 74.0mm. Displacement: 1582cc (96.5 cid). Bhp (SAE): 102 at 5800 rpm. Torque (lbs/ft SAE): 90 at 3500 rpm. Compression ratio: 9.3:1. Overhead valves, two twin-choke Solex carburetors.
Chassis: MacPherson-strut front suspension with lower A-arms, coil springs, transverse torsion bars, anti-roll bar; semi-trailing arm rear suspension with transverse torsion bars; rack-and-pinion steering; four-wheel disc brakes with vacuum assist; Porsche four-speed or (optional) five-speed overdrive manual transmissions; single dry-disc diaphragm clutch. Final drive ratio (five-speed): 4.43:1.
Measurements: Curb weight (lbs): 2100. Tire size: 6.95 × 15. Track: 52.6 in. front/51.8 in. rear. Wheelbase: 87.0 in. Overall length: 163.9 in. Overall width: 63.4 in. Overall height: 52.0 in.

1965-68 Type 911/911L
Engine: Six-cylinder, flat-opposed. Bore and Stroke: 80.0 × 66.0mm. Displacement: 1991cc (121.4 cid). Bhp (DIN): 130 at 6100 rpm. Torque (lbs/ft SAE): 143 at 4300 rpm. Compression ratio: 9.0:1. Single overhead camshaft per cylinder bank, eight main (forged-steel) bearings, light-alloy crankcase and cylinder block, aluminum-alloy cylinder head, six Type 40PJ Solex carburetors (Weber 40IDA 3C from February 1966).
Chassis: As per 1966-69 Type 912 except, Porsche five-speed manual transmission standard. Sportomatic four-speed semi-automatic transmission optional Type 911.
Measurements: As per 1966-69 Type 912 except, Curb weight (lbs): approx 2270. Tire size: 165HR-15.

1966-67 Type 911S
Engine: As per 1965-68 Type 911/911L except, Bhp (DIN): 160 at 6600 rpm (180 SAE). Torque (lbs/ft SAE): 144 at 5200 rpm. Compression ratio: 9.8:1.
Chassis: As per 1965-68 Type 911/911L except, rear anti-roll bar standard. Final drive ratio (five-speed): 4.43:1.
Measurements: As per 1965-68 Type 911/911L except, Curb weight (lbs): approx 2280. Rear track: 52.2 in.

1969 Type 911 T/E/S
Engine: As per 1965-68 Type 911 except, Bhp (DIN): 110 at 5800 rpm (T), 140 at 6600 rpm (E), 170 at 6800 rpm (S). Compression ratio: 8.6:1 (T), 9.1:1 (E), 9.8:1 (S). Carburetors on T, Bosch mechanical fuel injection on E and S.
Chassis: As per 1965-68 Type 911/911L except, Boge self-adjusting hydropneumatic front struts standard on E, optional T and S.
Measurements: As per 1965-68 Type 911 except, Tire size: 185-14 standard T and E, 185/70HR-14 optional E, 185/70HR-15 optional S. Wheelbase: 89.3 in.

1970-71 Type 911 T/E/S
Engine: As per 1965-68 Type 911/911L except, Bore and Stroke: 84 × 66mm. Displacement: 2195cc (133.9 cid). Bhp (DIN): 125 at 5800 rpm (T), 155 at 6200 rpm (E), 180 at 6500 rpm (S). Zenith Type 40TIN carburetors on T.
Chassis: As per 1969 Type 911 models except, Porsche four-speed manual transmission standard T; five-speed standard E and S.
Measurements: As per 1969 Type 911 models.

1972-73 Type 911 T/E/S
Engine: As per 1965-68 Type 911/911L except, Bore and Stroke: 84 × 70.4mm. Displacement: 2341cc (142.9 cid). Bhp (DIN): 140 at 5600 rpm (T), 165 at 6200 rpm (E), 190 at 6500 rpm (S). Compression ratio: 7.5:1 (T), 8.0:1 (E), 8.5:1 (S). Bosch mechanical fuel injection all models; Bosch K-Jetronic fuel injection on T from mid-1973.
Chassis: As per 1965-68 Type 911/911L except, softer shock absorber valving and adoption of Type 915 five-speed manual transmission with conventional shift pattern.
Measurements: As per 1969 Type 911 models except, Curb weight (lbs): approx. 2480-2550. Tire size: 165HR-15 (T), 185/70VR-15 (E and S). Overall length: 168.4 in. (1973 models).

1974-77 Type 911/911S/Carrera
Engine: As per 1965-68 Type 911/911L except, Bore and Stroke: 90.0 × 70.4mm. Displacement: 2687cc (164 cid). Bhp (DIN): 150 at 5700 rpm (911), 175 at 5800 rpm (1974 S and Carrera), 165 at 5800 rpm (1975-77 S and Carrera). CIS electronic fuel injection. Air pump or twin thermal reactors and exhaust-gas recirculation from 1975.
Chassis: As per 1972-73 Type 911 T/E/S except, rear anti-roll bar optional 911 and 911S, standard Carrera.
Measurements: As per 1972-73 Type 911 T/E/S except, Overall length: 168.9 in.

1976 Type 912E
Engine: Volkswagen four-cylinder, flat-opposed. Bore and Stroke: 94.0 × 71.0mm. Displacement: 1971cc (120.3 cid). Bhp (SAE net): 86 at 4900 rpm. Torque (lbs/ft SAE): 93 at 4000 rpm. Compression ratio: 7.6:1. Overhead valves, light-alloy cylinder head, cast-iron block, forged crankshaft with four plain bearings, Bosch L-Jetronic fuel injection, air pump, thermal reactors, exhaust-gas recirculation.
Chassis: As per 1974-77 Type 911 except, non-ventilated disc brakes, different five-speed manual transmission.
Measurements: As per 1974-77 Type 911 except, Curb weight (lbs): 2560. Tire size: 165HR-15.

1978-date Type 911SC
Engine: As per 1965-68 Type 911/911L except, Bore and Stroke: 95.0 × 70.4mm. Displacement: 2994cc (183.0 cid). Bhp (SAE net): 172 at 5500 rpm. Torque (lbs/ft SAE): 175 at 4200 rpm. Compression ratio: 9.3:1. CIS fuel injection with oxygen sensor.
Chassis: As per 1974-77 Type 911 models except, front and rear anti-roll bars standard, Sportomatic transmission no longer available. Final drive ratio: 3.875:1.
Measurements: Curb weight (lbs): 2756. Tire size: 185/70VR-15 front, 215/60VR-15 rear (205/55VR-16 front and 225/50VR-16 rear optional). Track: 53.9 in. front, 54.3 in. rear. Wheelbase: 89.5 in. Overall length: 168.9 in. Overall width: 65.0 in. Overall height (unladen): 51.6 in.

1970-73 Type 914/4
Engine: Volkswagen four-cylinder, flat-opposed, mid-mounted. Bore and Stroke: 90.0 × 66mm. Displacement: 1679cc (102.5 cid). Bhp (DIN): 80 at 4900 rpm. Torque (lbs/ft SAE): 103 at 2800 rpm. Compression ratio: 8.2:1. Overhead valves, light-alloy cylinder head, cast-iron block, forged crankshaft with four plain bearings, electronic fuel injection.
Chassis: MacPherson-strut front suspension with coil springs, transverse torsion bars, lower A-arms; semi-trailing-arm-rear suspension with coil springs; front-disc/rear-drum brake system with vacuum assist; rack-and-pinion steering; five-speed overdrive manual transmission. Final drive ratio: 4.43:1.
Measurements: Curb weight (lbs): Approx. 2100. Tire size: 155-15 (165-15 optional). Track: 52.6 in. front, 54.1 in. rear. Wheelbase: 96.4 in. Overall length: 156.9 in. (159.4 in. 1973 models). Overall width: 65.0. Overall height: 48.0 in.

1970-71 Type 914/6
Engine: As per 1965-68 Type 911 except, mid-mounted. Two Weber Type 40JDT3C carburetors.
Chassis: As per 1970-73 Type 914/4 except, ventilated front disc brakes and solid-rotor rear disc brakes.
Measurements: As per 1970-73 Type 914/4 except, Curb weight (lbs): 2195. Tire size: 185HR-14 (on light-alloy wheels). Track: 53.6 in. front, 54.4 in. rear.

1974-75 Type 914/4
Engine: As per 1970-73 Type 914/4 except, Bore and Stroke: 93.0 × 66.0mm. Displacement: 1795cc (110 cid). Bhp (SAE net): 73 at 4800 rpm. Torque (lbs/ft SAE): 89 at 4000 rpm. Compression ratio: 7.3:1.
Chassis: As per 1970-73 Type 914/4.
Measurements: As per 1970-73 Type 914/4 except, Curb weight (lbs): approx. 2160. Tire size: 165SR-15. Overall length: 161.2 in.

1973-76 Type 914 2.0 Liter
Engine: As per 1970-73 Type 914/4 except, Bore and Stroke: 94.0 × 71.0mm. Displacement: 1971cc (120 cid). Bhp (SAE net): 91 at 4900 rpm (84 bhp after 1973). Torque (lbs/ft SAE): 109 at 3000 rpm (108 at 3500 rpm after 1973). Compression ratio: 7.6:1.
Chassis: As per 1970-73 Type 914/4 except, solid-rotor four-wheel disc brakes with vacuum assist.
Measurements: As per 1970-73 Type 914/4 except, Curb weight (lbs): approx. 2150. Tire size: 165HR-15. Overall length: 161.2 in. (159.4 on 1973 models).

1976-77 Type 930 Turbo Carrera
Engine: Six-cylinder, flat-opposed, turbocharged. Bore and Stroke: 95.0 × 70.4mm. Displacement: 2993cc (183 cid). Bhp (DIN): 245 at 5500 rpm (234 SAE net). Torque (lbs/ft SAE): 246 at 4500 rpm. Compression ratio: 6.5:1. Single overhead camshaft per cylinder bank, eight main (forged-steel) bearings, light-alloy crankcase and cylinder block, aluminum-alloy cylinder head, Bosch CIS electronic fuel injection.
Chassis: As per 1965-68 Type 911 except, front and rear anti-roll bars standard, Porsche four-speed manual transmission. Final drive ratio: 4.22:1.
Measurements: As per 1974-77 Type 911 models except, Curb weight (lbs): approx.

2800. Tire size: 185/70VR-15 front, 215/60VR-15 rear. Track: 56.4 in. front, 59.1 in. rear. Overall width: 69.9 in.

1978-79 Type 930 Turbo
Engine: As per 1976-77 Type 930 except, Bore and Stroke: 97 × 74.4mm. Displacement: 3299cc (201.3 cid). Bhp (DIN): 265 at 5500 rpm (253 SAE net). Torque (lbs/ft SAE): 282 at 4000 rpm. Compression ratio: 7.0:1.
Chassis: As per 1976-77 Type 930.
Measurements: As per 1976-77 Type 930 except, Curb weight (lbs): approx. 2860. Tire size: 205/55VR-16 front, 255/50VR-16 rear.

1977-82 Type 924
Engine: Four-cylinder, inline, water-cooled. Bore and Stroke: 86.5 × 84.4 mm. Displacement: 1984cc (121 cid). Bhp (SAE net): 95-115 at 5500-5750 rpm. Torque (lbs/ft SAE net): 109-111.3 at 3500 rpm. Compression ratio: 8.0:1-9.0:1. Single overhead camshaft, five main (forged-steel) bearings, cast-iron cylinder block, cast-aluminum alloy cylinder head, CIS electronic fuel injection (with oxygen sensor from 1980).
Chassis: MacPherson strut front suspension with coil springs and negative roll radius geometry (anti-roll bar optional), independent rear suspension with integral transaxle, diagonal control arms, transverse torsion bars anti-roll bar (optional), rack-and-pinion steering; front disc/rear drum brakes with vacuum assist; Porsche five-speed overdrive manual or Audi three-speed automatic transmission; single dry-disc clutch. Final drive ratio: 3.44 to 5.00:1 (manual transmission), 3.73:1 (automatic transmission).
Measurements: Curb weight: 2625-2675 lbs. Tire size: 165HR-14, 185/70HR-14 from 1979 (205/60HR-15 optional from 1980). Track: 55.9 in. front, 54.0 in. rear. Wheelbase: 94.5 in. Overall length: 170.0 in. Overall width: 66.3 in. Overall height (unladen): 50.0 in.

1980-82 Type 924 Turbo
Engine: As per 924 except for, Bhp (SAE net): 143 at 5500 rpm. Torque (lbs/ft SAE net): 147 at 3000 rpm. Compression ratio: 7.5:1.
Chassis: As per 924 except for, standard 23mm-diameter front anti-roll bar; 14mm-diameter rear anti-roll bar optional with Sport (S) Group. No. automatic transmission option. Final drive ratio: 4.71:1.
Measurements: As for 924 except for, Curb weight: approx. 2825 lbs. Tire size: 185/70VR-15 (205/55VR-16 optional with Sport Group). Overall length: 168.9 in.

1983 Type 944
Engine: Porsche four-cylinder, inline, water-cooled. Bore and Stroke: 100 × 78.9 mm. Displacement: 2479cc (151 cid). Bhp (SAE net): 143 at 5500 rpm. Torque (lbs/ft SAE net): 137 at 3000 rpm. Single overhead camshaft, five main (forged-steel) bearings, silicon/aluminum-alloy cylinder block, aluminum-alloy crossflow cylinder head, electronic fuel injection with oxygen sensor, Bosch Digital Motor Electronics injection/ignition control.
Chassis: As per 924 except for, standard 20mm-diameter front anti-roll bar (21.5mm diameter optional) and 14mm-diameter rear anti-roll bar, four-wheel ventilated disc brakes. Final drive ratio: 3.89:1 (manual transmission), 3.45:1 (automatic transmission).
Measurements: As per 924 except for Curb weight: 2778 lbs. Tire size: 215/60VR-15. Track: 58.2 in. front, 57.1 in. rear. Overall width: 68.3 in. Overall length (unladen): 50.2 in.

1978-79 Type 928
Engine: Eight-cylinder in 90-degree "V," water-cooled. Bore and Stroke: 95.0 × 78.9mm. Displacement: 4474cc (273 cid). Bhp (SAE net): 218 at 5250 rpm. Torque (lbs/ft SAE): 254 at 3600 rpm. Compression ratio: 8.5:1. Single overhead camshaft per cylinder bank, five main (forged-steel) bearings, silicon/aluminum-alloy cylinder head and block, iron-coated aluminum pistons, CIS electronic fuel injection.
Chassis: Coil spring/strut front suspension with twin control arms, anti-roll bar, negative offset steering geometry; coil spring/strut rear suspension with integral transaxle, "Weissach axle" lower control arms, anti-roll bar; rack-and-pinion steering with speed-variable power assist; ventilated four-wheel disc brakes with hydraulic assist; Porsche five-speed overdrive manual or Daimler-Benz three-speed automatic transmission; double dry-plate clutch with hydraulic actuation. Final drive ratio: 2.75:1 (manual), 2.00:1 (automatic).
Measurements: Curb weight (lbs): 3300. Tire size: 225/50VR-16. Track: 61.1 in. front, 60.2 in. rear. Wheelbase: 98.4 in. Overall length: 175.7 in. Overall width: 72.3 in. Overall height: 50.5 in.

1980-82 Type 928
Engine: As per 1978-79 Type 928 except, Bhp (SAE net): 220 at 5500 rpm. Torque (lbs/ft SAE): 265 at 4000 rpm. Compression ratio: 9.0:1. AFC (air flow control) electronic fuel injection with oxygen sensor and three-way catalyst.
Chassis: As per 1978-79 Type 928 except, 2.12:1 final drive ratio with automatic transmission on 1981-82 models.
Measurements: As per 1978-79 Type 928 except, Tire size: 215/60VR-15 (225/50VR-16 with optional Competition Group). Curb weight (lbs.): 3351 (manual), 3385 (automatic).

1983 Type 928S
Engine: As per 1978-79 Type 928 except, Bore and Stroke: 97.0 × 78.9mm. Displacement: 4644cc (285 cid). Bhp (SAE net): 234 at 5500 rpm. Torque (lbs/ft SAE): 263 at 4000 rpm. Compression ratio: 9.3:1.
Chassis: As per 1978-79 Type 928 except, optional four-speed automatic transmission from late-1983. Final drive ratio: 2.27:1 (manual), 2.20:1 (automatic).
Measurements: As per 1978-79 Type 928 except, Tire size: 225/50VR-16.

Condensed Specifications: Porsche Sports/Racing Cars 1964-date

years built	type	body type	no. cyls.	cc	bore × stroke	CR (:1)	bhp @ rpm	top speed (mph)
1964-66	904	coupe	4	1966	92.0×74.0	9.8	180-195 @ 7000	160
1966-67	906	coupe	6	1991	80.0×66.0	10.3	210-220 @ 8000	165
1966-68	907	coupe	6	1991	80.0×66.0	10.3	220 @ 8000	165 (907L: 186)
1968	908	coupe	8	2997	85.0×66.0	10.4	310-350 @ 8400	180 (K/L: 190)
1968	909	spyder	8	1981	76.0×54.6	10.4	275 @ 9000	155
1967	910/6	coupe	6	1991	80.0×66.0	10.3	220 @ 8000	165
1967	910/8	coupe	8	2195	80.0×54.6	10.2	270 @ 8600	175
1969-70	917	coupe	12	4494	85.0×66.0	10.5	560-580 @ 8400	210+
1970-71	917	coupe	12	4907	86.0×70.4	10.5	600-615 @ 8400	240
1970	917	coupe	12	4999	86.8×70.4	10.5	630 @ 8300	200
1970	917	coupe	12	5374	90.0×70.4	10.5	660 @ 8300	240
1972	917/10	spyder	12*	4494	85.0×66.0	8.5	850 @ 8000	220+
1972	917/10	spyder	12*	4999	86.8×70.4	8.5	950-1000 @ 7800	230+
1973	917/30	spyder	12*	5374	90.0×70.4	8.5	1100 @ 7800	245
1976-date	936	coupe	6*	2142	83.0×66.0	6.5	520-540 @ 8000	200+
1981-date	956	coupe	6*	2649	92.3×66.0	7.0-7.6	600-700 @ 8200	205+

*turbocharged

EHPAD,
UNE HONTE FRANÇAISE

ANNE-SOPHIE PELLETIER

EHPAD, UNE HONTE FRANÇAISE

PLON

ISBN : 978-2-266-29969-5
Dépôt légal : janvier 2020

À ma grand-mère
1928-2016

Prologue

Elles étaient toutes là, assises dans le Saugeois, ce joli parc derrière chez Mémé. C'était le rendez-vous quotidien des anciens du village de Conliège, dans le Jura. Sous les grands tilleuls, elles discutaient de tout, de rien ; parfois, même, les conversations n'avaient aucun sens, tant leur audition défaillait. Je n'étais qu'une enfant, pourtant ces souvenirs sont gravés dans ma mémoire. Et puis, j'étais avec Mémé. Mon havre de paix, mon exemple, cette femme qui me transmettait, de sa voix douce, sans en avoir l'air, les valeurs de nos anciens et ses connaissances sur la vie.

À la retraite depuis quelques années, elle avait été directrice d'école primaire ; de la trempe des instituteurs qui valorisaient la morale et qui exigeaient des cahiers d'élève bien tenus, où pleins et déliés, exécutés avec soin, ressemblaient à des tableaux de calligraphie. Mémé a toujours été très attachée à la morale, et je bénéficiais de ses recommandations. Elle tolérait les résultats scolaires moyens mais ne pouvait accepter le manque de respect.

C'est elle qui m'a élevée, véritable mère de substitution. Elle m'a aimée, avec tendresse mais sans effusion – comme elle me le dirait aujourd'hui, caresses de chien donnent des puces. L'expression peut sembler sévère, mais la génération de ma grand-mère, qui a connu la guerre, n'était pas démonstrative ; cela ne l'empêchait pas d'avoir un amour débordant pour ses petites-filles.

Mémé ne m'en voudra pas si j'ose dire d'elle qu'elle était un peu bourgeoise, au sens où elle ne se mélangeait pas avec ceux qu'elle estimait ne pas être à la hauteur de son intellect.

Avec l'âge, elle était moins intransigeante. De même, elle se rendait compte qu'elle radotait, parfois, et que tout ce qu'elle savait, au fur et à mesure, s'effaçait de sa mémoire comme la neige fond au soleil. Finalement, elle devenait comme les autres anciens, une dame âgée, qui avait vécu, qui continuait de transmettre, mais qui oubliait.

Elle oubliait son repas de la veille, mais pas les poésies enfantines, ni une certaine d'Arthur Rimbaud.

Avec l'âge, son A était bel et bien devenu noir, et signifiait désormais arthrose, qui lui déformait les doigts et l'empêchait, peu à peu, de poursuivre ses ouvrages. Son E était blanc, aussi, couleur de ses cheveux. Son I, elle aurait aimé ne pas le connaître, ce poison d'incontinence qui l'obligeait à se promener avec des changes. Son O, lui, demeurait d'un bleu éternel, celui de ses yeux. Quant à son U, il resterait vert tant que la dépendance se tiendrait à distance.

Malgré sa vue défaillante et ses doigts malhabiles, Mémé était du genre tenace : elle continuait de lire chaque jour quelques pages du vieux *Quid* rafistolé au

Scotch marron ou du dictionnaire. Et elle s'offusquait toujours avec autant de véhémence des fautes qu'elle trouvait dans le journal chaque matin, réflexe de ses nombreuses années d'enseignement de l'orthographe.

*

Ma grand-mère était mon fondamental, à la fois ma mère et ma maîtresse, cette jolie femme aux cheveux d'argent et aux yeux bleus comme l'océan qui m'apprit avec patience à nager, à réfléchir et à ne jamais porter de jugements trop hâtifs sur les choses et les gens. Cet ange m'a construite et a fait de moi la femme que je suis aujourd'hui, avec des valeurs morales, des valeurs de lutte, des valeurs d'entraide.

Elle fut surtout celle qui me donna confiance en moi, et qui réussit à me convaincre que je n'étais pas cette jeune fille bête qui, malgré des études tout à fait honorables, ne ferait rien de sa vie.

Aujourd'hui, Mémé est partie ; comme le diraient certains textes, elle est dans la pièce d'à côté. Pas pour moi : Mémé est toujours là, telle une étoile qui veille, un trésor précieusement gardé tout contre mon cœur qui pleure son absence. Encore aujourd'hui, avant toute décision, je me pose la question : qu'en penserait Mémé ? Que me dirait-elle ? M'encouragerait-elle : « Vas-y, ma Sophie – c'est toujours ainsi qu'elle m'appelait –, je suis très fière de toi » ? Ou bien : « Réfléchis avant d'agir, pèse le pour et le contre, ma Sophie, ne pars pas tête baissée sans avoir imaginé tous les tenants et les aboutissants » ?…

Je pense que, sans ma grand-mère, je ne serais pas devenue aide médico-psychologique dans une maison de retraite. C'est mon amour des personnes âgées qui guide mon besoin de les protéger et de lutter pour que nos sages soient pris en charge dans toute la dignité qui leur est due dans les maisons de retraite, et pour qu'ils continuent de nous transmettre leurs expériences de vie.

Ils sont notre patrimoine commun, ils sont nos mémoires vivantes.

1

« Le numéro que vous avez demandé n’est plus attribué… »

Mercredi 13 avril, mon téléphone sonne. C’est ma sœur aînée, Cécile. Mémé a été hospitalisée, suite à une chute, chez elle, où elle ne fut retrouvée par terre que le lendemain. Ma famille et moi habitons à l’époque dans les Bouches-du-Rhône, et Mémé est à l’hôpital dans le Jura.

— Allô, Sophie, Mémé est dans le coma…

Je crie, non, pas Mémé, s’il vous plaît, pas Mémé ! S’il vous plaît, laissez-la-moi encore, je n’ai pas terminé mon apprentissage ! Prenez-moi, moi, mais pas elle, pas ma grand-mère, ce n’est pas juste ! Je veux mourir à sa place, s’il vous plaît ! Je pleure, lance mon téléphone à travers la pièce, non, je ne veux pas qu’elle parte, non ! Mon époux essaie de me calmer comme il le peut, mais la douleur est si grande qu’il n’y parvient pas. La tête enfoncée dans les coussins du canapé, je ne peux m’arrêter de hurler que ce n’est pas juste : pourquoi m’enlève-t-on ma grand-mère, pourquoi ? Certes, elle a quatre-vingt-huit ans, et certains diront que c’est déjà bien d'être arrivé à cet âge, mais non, ma grand-mère ne peut pas mourir, non ! Je supplie – je ne sais pas qui d'ailleurs – que la mort me prenne et laisse vivre ma grand-mère. À cette heure, je n'ai plus de mari, plus d'enfants, je veux partir à sa place.

Ma sœur tente de m'apaiser, rien n'y fait ; ce ne sont plus des larmes qui coulent de mes yeux, mais une véritable rivière en crue.

Je deviens orpheline.

Mon époux a récupéré le téléphone ; je dois parler à ma sœur, me dit-il. Je ne veux pas, ma grand-mère s'en va, foutez-moi la paix, vous ne pouvez pas comprendre.

Finalement, j'accepte de prendre le combiné. Ma sœur est toujours au bout du fil.

— Ma Sophie, si tu veux parler à Mémé une dernière fois, c'est le moment, je suis près d'elle, si tu veux je mets le haut-parleur…

— Oui, vas-y…

— C'est fait, elle t'entend.

Il fallait que je trouve la force de lui parler. Même si je m'en sentais incapable, ce serait ma dernière chance de m'adresser à elle. Je suis soignante, je sais ce que signifie, pour nos aînés, de se laisser partir. Mais que c'était dur ! Je refusais qu'elle entende mes pleurs, que ce soient des sanglots qu'elle perçoive de moi lors de notre ultime échange. Je devais prendre ce téléphone, je n'avais pas le choix. Je m'en serais voulu toute ma vie si je n'avais pas pu lui dire à ce moment-là tout l'amour que j'éprouvais pour elle. Cette fois, je pourrais le lui dire sans qu'elle me taxe de sensiblerie ; cette fois, elle m'écouterait.

— Allô, Mémé, c'est ta Sophie, s'il te plaît, Mémé, ne pars pas, j'ai encore besoin de toi. J'ai besoin de nos promenades, j'ai besoin de t'entendre, Mémé, ne me quitte pas. Je t'aime, Mémé, merci, Mémé, mille mercis pour ce que tu as fait pour moi, mais s'il te plaît, ne pars pas. S'il te plaît… Je t'aime.

Ma sœur et moi décidons que vendredi nous nous retrouverons à l'hôpital – c'est notre seule disponibilité, eu égard à nos emplois du temps respectifs et à nos lieux d'habitation –, en espérant que Mémé tienne jusque-là.

Quand je raccroche, tout remonte : quand avons-nous vu Mémé pour la dernière fois ? En 2010, et nous sommes en 2016… Quand l'ai-je appelée pour la dernière fois ? Il y a une semaine, pour son anniversaire. Quand…

« Arrête d'y penser, me sermonné-je. Tu n'as pas su profiter d'elle quand elle était là, maintenant c'est peut-être trop tard, tu ne peux t'en prendre qu'à toi. » Mémé disait toujours : on ne se souvient de nos absents que pour la Toussaint ; elle avait raison. Je m'en veux, j'aurais dû aller la voir plus souvent, le travail n'est pas une excuse valable, la distance non plus…

*

5 heures du matin, vendredi 15 avril 2016. Mon époux et moi partons à moto vers le Jura. La route est longue et le froid mordant, mais qu'importe. Malgré plusieurs arrêts pour faire le plein d'essence – une moto a besoin d'être ravitaillée plus souvent qu'une voiture –, nous avons privilégié ce mode de locomotion pour éviter les embouteillages en arrivant à Lyon et ainsi gagner du temps.

Après plusieurs heures de route, nous entrons dans la ville vers 13 heures. Nous sommes dans les temps pour retrouver Cécile. Quand, soudain, mon portable sonne. Ma sœur…

— Où êtes-vous ?

— Nous venons d'arriver à l'hôpital, pourquoi ?

— Sophie… Mémé vient de partir, on vient de me prévenir… Elle est chambre 217.

— Quoi ? Mais non ! Nous sommes là… Non.

La moto vite garée sur le parking de l'hôpital, nous pénétrons dans le bâtiment sans attendre Cécile, des larmes dans les yeux. Nous sommes accueillis par une infirmière peu plaisante.

— Bonjour, madame, je suis la petite-fille de Mme Desanti, je…

— Vous êtes au courant ? Elle est décédée…

— Oui, mais je voudrais aller la voir.

— Je vous emmène. Vous nous excuserez, nous ne l'avons pas préparée…

Tandis que nous suivons le cerbère, mille questions se bousculent dans ma tête : que signifie « nous ne l'avons pas préparée » ? Dans quel état vais-je retrouver ma grand-mère ? Et puis, vais-je réussir à entrer dans la chambre ?

— Voilà, c'est ici, annonce l'infirmière en pointant du doigt une porte close.

— Merci, réponds-je mécaniquement.

L'infirmière nous abandonne devant la porte. Mémé est de l'autre côté. Après quelques secondes, nous trouvons la force d'entrer. Mémé est allongée sur son lit, elle dort paisiblement. Elle est belle.

Je ne me souviens même plus de ce que j'ai dit, je ne me souviens plus de ce que j'ai fait ; Mémé était là, c'était le principal. Je me suis mise à penser qu'elle avait préféré mourir seule, ne pas honorer ce dernier rendez-vous avec Cécile et moi. Elle n'avait pas souhaité que nous soyons là quand elle partirait. Encore cette forme de pudeur, cette indépendance… Même dans la mort, Mémé a gardé sa dignité ; comme elle le disait souvent, nos physiques ne supportent pas la négligence.

Je ne sais depuis combien de temps nous étions dans sa chambre quand ma sœur est arrivée avec mes nièces. Les filles pleuraient, ma sœur n'était pas dans un meilleur état que moi. Que faire ? Rester dignes, comme l'aurait voulu Mémé, ou se laisser aller à nos émotions ? Mémé nous répétait que nous devions montrer que nous étions fortes ; mais comment être forte dans un moment pareil ?

Malgré tout, ensemble, nous lui avons dit au revoir, chacun à notre manière. Ses petites-filles, arrière-petites-filles qu'elle aimait tant étaient près d'elle, elle devait être contente.

La pluie avait cessé, et une éclaircie avait duré tout le temps de notre recueillement. Probablement un signe, enfin, nous l'imaginions. On se raccroche à de petits riens quand la perte est trop grande.

Quant à ma sœur et moi, nous étions orphelines… Il allait falloir s'adapter à ce nouveau statut, et il serait long à accepter, nous le savions.

Puis ce fut le moment de repartir, nous avions de la route. La pluie s'est remise à tomber, le voyage de retour à moto serait long et fatigant.

Une conversation avec Mémé me revint alors en mémoire :

— Quand je serai morte, l'important, ce n'est pas ma personne, c'est le souvenir que je vous laisserai, c'est ça, le plus important, ne l'oublie pas, ma Sophie.

— Oui, Mémé, promis…

Quelques semaines plus tard, machinalement, je pris mon téléphone et composai ce numéro que je connais par cœur…

« Le numéro que vous avez demandé n'est plus attribué, nous ne pouvons donner suite à votre appel… »

J'avais appelé Mémé.

2

Comme une évidence

Cela faisait des années que j'arpentais les couloirs des établissements hôteliers. J'y avais occupé des postes de direction, j'avais des émoluments plus qu'honorables, mais je croupissais à une place où finalement je ne m'épanouissais plus. Toujours les mêmes bilans à faire, les mêmes clients à recevoir, les mêmes résultats à augmenter régulièrement pour obtenir une prime de chiffon… Je m'engluais dans une routine qui m'ennuyait. Et puis, je n'avais pas vu grandir mes enfants, palliant mes absences en leur offrant toujours plus de cadeaux, histoire de me rabibocher avec ma conscience de mère. Mais les cadeaux ne remplacent pas un « bonne nuit, mon ange », un câlin, un « comment s'est passée l'école aujourd'hui ? ».

Il était temps de changer. De se sentir utile… mais que faire ?

La décision s'imposa comme une évidence un soir durant le dîner : j'irais dorénavant m'occuper de nos anciens à leur domicile.

Lorsque je l'annonçai, ma famille en fut abasourdie : j'allais quitter un bon salaire, une situation stable, un statut établi pour recommencer ma vie professionnelle de zéro et devenir aide à domicile… femme de ménage !

Mais qu'importait l'avis des uns et des autres, j'allais avoir une relation différente aux gens, j'allais aider nos aînés en perte d'autonomie à entretenir leur intérieur et donc à rester chez eux. Ne dit-on pas que, pour être bien, il faut que l'on se sente bien chez soi ? Alors, si en faisant le ménage je contribuais à leur bien-être, je partageais avec eux un moment où ils ne seraient pas seuls, un moment d'échanges, qui sait, mon pari serait gagné.

*

Armée de mon CV qui détonnait un peu dans l'assistance, je me présentai à une réunion à laquelle j'avais été invitée par la mairie de mon village. Là, je rencontrai une dizaine de filles. Je les écoutais parler de leur métier, qui ne me parut pas si rose que je me l'étais imaginé. Mais qu'importe, j'allais changer les choses, rendre le sourire aux anciens du village. Les rendre heureux était mon leitmotiv, quelle que soit la manière.

Je n'allais *a priori* pas au-devant de grandes difficultés : pas besoin de reprendre mes études, il n'y a pas de formation pour être femme de ménage ; d'autre part, il est assez rare d'être agressée verbalement par un torchon ou un seau d'eau, et la poussière ne vous insulte pas quand vous la déplacez. Je n'aurais plus à m'accommoder de la colère ni de la vulgarité de clients mécontents, de l'absence des employés et de leur remplacement. Cette nouvelle vie allait être beaucoup plus simple et moins stressante. Et puis, je verrais enfin mes enfants. Je ne rattraperais pas le temps perdu, mais je serais plus présente à la maison, et je ne rapporterais pas de travail le soir.

À la fin de la réunion, mon tour vint de prendre la parole. J'avais bien entendu toutes les discussions croisées sur les difficultés de mes futures collègues, notamment lorsqu'elles réclamaient avec véhémence une augmentation du temps d'intervention chez certains, tant les tâches s'alourdissaient chaque jour, du fait de la dépendance toujours plus importante des bénéficiaires, arguant qu'elles ne pouvaient plus fournir un travail de qualité dans ces conditions. La culpabilité les rongeait ; leur physique éprouvé, fatigué, leurs yeux cernés en étaient la preuve flagrante.

J'avais entendu tout cela, mais, à ce moment précis, je n'avais pas pris conscience de ce qu'allait être mon futur métier. J'étais dans l'euphorie d'apporter un peu d'aide et d'humanité à des personnes âgées dépendantes. Ces futures collègues n'avaient pas réussi à écorner ma détermination.

Mon entretien fut succinct et dura à peine quelques minutes. J'avais évidemment dû répondre aux interrogations de cette responsable de secteur quant à mon choix de réorientation professionnelle. Ce n'était pas la première fois : j'avais eu à me justifier quelques années plus tôt lorsque, après un bac scientifique, j'avais décidé d'intégrer une école d'arts décoratifs pour devenir licière, puis pris la décision de faire fi de tous mes diplômes pour me retrouver en bas de l'échelle. À l'époque, les valeurs que nous inculquait

Mémé étaient déjà ancrées en moi, et j'avais besoin de me sentir utile. Tout simplement.

Après des années à travailler pour nourrir ma famille, j'avais besoin de travailler autrement pour m'épanouir.

La responsable en face de moi me répétait que d'un bon salaire je passerais à un SMIC. J'en avais conscience, mais l'argent n'avait jamais conditionné mes choix professionnels. On aurait pu me faire des ponts d'or, s'ils n'avaient pas été en accord avec mon savoir-être, je les aurais refusés sans hésitation.

Je voyais ses yeux s'écarquiller au fur et à mesure de mes réponses. Pourtant, elle apposa un TB sur ma lettre de motivation, comme on met une bonne note sur une copie d'élève. J'avais réussi l'examen d'entrée. Je n'avais pourtant raconté que ma vie, mes études et mes expériences professionnelles, pas mon besoin viscéral d'apporter ce que je suis à nos aînés souvent bien seuls à leur domicile.

C'était gagné : on me signerait dans les jours à venir un contrat à durée déterminée. J'étais persuadée que je révolutionnerais le monde de l'aide à domicile, que j'apporterais tellement plus que du ménage aux bénéficiaires et que eux deviendraient rapidement autre chose que mes patrons…

Optimiste, utopique, je ne savais pas à cet instant que la tâche serait si ardue et parfois si ingrate. Je me doutais que tout ne serait pas rose, que je serais confrontée à la maladie, la démence, la mort. Mais ce serait le temps qui me montrerait les limites de l'aide à domicile.

Pour l'instant, je partais la fleur au fusil, et *carpe diem* ! J'étais forte, j'en avais vu d'autres !

Cette intime conviction de pouvoir y arriver sans l'avoir vécu nous rassure. On se persuade que ce sera plus facile parce qu'ils ou elles ne sont pas de notre famille, que l'affect n'entrera pas en ligne de compte, du moins de loin. Parce que j'ai ce recul dont m'a parlé la responsable de secteur, qui m'aidera à ne pas m'attacher à mes allocataires. Je suis une professionnelle de la serpillière et du torchon à poussière, qui apporterait son sourire, sa bonne humeur et ses connaissances. Rien de plus, rien de moins.

J'étais convaincue que je serais différente des collègues que j'avais croisées lors de la réunion. Elles semblaient blasées, fatiguées ; j'étais toute neuve, pleine d'entrain, d'enthousiasme et d'envie d'égayer un peu la vie des bénéficiaires. J'allais mettre à profit tout ce que Mémé m'avait transmis.

Ma nouvelle vie pouvait enfin commencer.

3

Georgette[1]

J'ai reçu mon planning par mail quelques jours après la réunion. Mon premier contrat, à plein temps, me mènerait chez Georgette : trois heures le matin et deux heures le soir. Sur la fiche de poste, il était stipulé « entretien de la maison », « courses », « repas ».

J'étais impatiente d'effectuer ma première intervention. J'avais hâte de passer du temps avec Georgette, d'en apprendre plus sur sa vie.

Une fois devant la porte, je sonnai. J'entendis un « Entrez… » fébrile qui m'invitait à franchir le seuil.

— Je suis dans la chambre, poursuivit la vieille dame.

Comme je ne connaissais pas la maison, je me suis mise en quête de la chambre. Je la trouvai rapidement : une partie du salon avait été transformée pour accueillir un lit médicalisé. La pièce était grande, ornée d'une jolie cheminée en pierre. Le décor était succinct : une

1. Tous les noms et prénoms cités dans ce livre ont été modifiés.

table de chevet, une télé, une commode où gisaient le pilulier et une montagne de médicaments. Les cadres au mur avaient visiblement été enlevés, seules quelques cartes postales épinglées sur une corde subsistaient.

J'avais la sensation étrange de me trouver dans une chambre d'hôpital alors que j'étais au domicile d'un particulier. Pas de fioritures, pas de gaieté, rien…

*

Je trouvai Georgette, une dame de quatre-vingt-quatorze ans, couchée dans son lit. Je me suis d'abord présentée, puis elle prit la parole pour m'expliquer d'une voix frêle sa pathologie et ce que j'avais à faire. Je ne ferais pas que du ménage : j'aiderais aussi les infirmières libérales à la toilette, qui se faisait alitée. Georgette, après une chute et un col du fémur qui avait décidé de la lâcher, ne pouvait plus ni se lever ni marcher. Elle me montra ensuite du doigt un engin de torture appelé lève-malade repoussé dans le coin de la pièce ; c'est grâce à cet appareil que nous allions la transférer de son lit à son fauteuil roulant.

D'un coup, je me suis mise à douter : je n'avais aucune expérience avec cet engin, et je n'avais reçu aucune formation. Et si je n'y arrivais pas ? Je devais être la reine de la serpillière, pas grutier avec la lourde responsabilité de ne pas laisser échapper une vieille dame !

Georgette m'expliqua que je devais préparer sur la table le matériel nécessaire aux infirmières afin qu'elles aient tout à portée de main sans avoir à se déplacer. Je m'exécutai et suivis à la lettre les instructions qu'elle me donna. Évidemment, j'avais attendu avant de mettre l'eau chaude dans la bassine qui servirait pour la toilette, car Georgette me raconta que les infirmières n'avaient pas d'horaires fixes, et que nous allions probablement les attendre longtemps. Elle s'énerva contre cet état de fait : elle était couchée dans son lit depuis la veille, avec la même protection urinaire ; elle avait besoin de se sentir propre, au sec, c'était sa dignité qui était malmenée !

Elle ne supportait plus de se sentir ainsi, à la merci du planning de ces dames qui arrivaient quand elles arrivaient. Elle n'osait pas, malgré tout, hausser le ton en leur présence, de peur de les blesser d'abord, mais aussi par crainte de représailles.

Le mot « représailles » me sauta au visage. Georgette aurait donc pu subir des brimades si elle avait exigé d'être prise en charge plus tôt dans la matinée ? Je commençai à apercevoir des réalités que je n'avais même pas osé imaginer…

J'étais abasourdie par notre discussion, tout en tentant de me rassurer : Georgette était peut-être un cas isolé… Je continuais de croire avec force que ce n'était pas possible, et que ce n'était pas ainsi que l'on prenait en charge nos aînés à domicile.

Au fur et à mesure que nous échangions, avec Georgette, en cette première matinée, je pris conscience de ce que la perte de dignité signifiait dans les paroles de cette dame âgée.

Très vite, je fus confrontée à un premier dilemme : comment dénoncer cet état de fait, si odieux soit-il, le jour de ma prise de poste ? Alors je me suis offusquée intérieurement, mais je me suis tue. J'étais déjà insidieusement complice de cette prise en charge des personnes âgées sans aucun sens de l'humain.

Georgette me raconta sa vie avant cet accident domestique. Elle aimait être propre – elle ne comptait pas les douches qu'elle prenait dans une journée –, que sa maison soit bien tenue, se promener le long de la plage avec ses amies. Aujourd'hui, que lui restait-il ? Elle ne se promenait plus, elle n'entretenait plus sa maison, elle se voyait comme une charge pour tout le monde. Elle m'avoua même avoir oublié la sensation de l'eau chaude qui ruisselle sur le corps lors d'une douche. Désormais, Georgette n'aspirait qu'à rejoindre son mari décédé ; sa vie n'était que souvenirs, regrets. Ses enfants, qui habitaient loin, lui rappelaient par un coup de fil hebdomadaire de quelques minutes qu'elle avait été une femme et une maman.

Une heure déjà que nous discutions de sa vie en attendant les infirmières qui n'arrivaient toujours pas ; une heure de plus dans un change souillé. Georgette vivait dans cette cité depuis plus de soixante-dix ans. Elle avait été vendeuse d'une boutique de tissus, sa passion était la couture et la dentelle qu'elle avait apprise enfant avec sa mère sur les marchés. Elle me dit :

— J'ai appris parce qu'il fallait bien que je m'occupe toute la matinée sur le marché, ma petite, vous comprenez ?

Bien sûr, que je comprenais. Son « ma petite » me fit sourire ; cette marque d'affection qu'elle me témoignait sans me connaître me toucha au cœur. J'écoutais Georgette me conter l'histoire de sa vie comme si je lisais un roman. Sa façon si naturelle de me la raconter m'émeut encore aujourd'hui. L'espace d'un instant, elle oubliait cette protection souillée qui avait débordé et qui avait gagné la majeure partie des draps. Je tentai alors de les changer seule, mais l'alèse refusa d'obtempérer, laissant Georgette baigner dans son urine et ses selles. La colère montait en moi : quand allaient-elles arriver, ces infirmières ? Combien de temps encore Georgette allait-elle devoir subir ce traitement ?

Pourtant, elle continuait de me raconter sa vie, ponctuant son récit de réflexions sur l'ancien monde, notamment comment, à son époque, on ne perdait pas son temps, on l'utilisait à bon escient.

Il m'arrivait quelquefois de voir Mémé sous les traits de Georgette. Mais, très vite, je chassais cette idée de mon esprit. Ma responsable de secteur me l'avait assez répété : « Ne vous attachez pas à vos allocataires ! »

Plus facile à dire qu'à faire…

*

Une heure et demie s'était écoulée, et toujours aucune infirmière en vue. Que dire ? Que faire ? Je n'avais pas l'autorisation de commencer la toilette, n'étant pas diplômée, et mon inutilité me tuait.

Je n'avais encore pris ni seau ni serpillière, j'étais restée au chevet de Georgette ; elle avait besoin de discuter, le sol attendrait bien encore quelques heures. Il ne m'en voudrait pas, et ce n'était pas le peu de personnes qui venaient visiter Georgette qui salissaient son intérieur.

Finalement, l'infirmière arriva. Elle n'enleva même pas son manteau, dit à peine bonjour, remplit la bassine et débuta la toilette. Elle d'un côté du lit, moi de l'autre. Elle déshabilla Georgette, à vrai dire sans grande délicatesse. Elle commença par lui laver le torse ; Georgette était seins nus, j'étais gênée. Son regard dans le mien, je n'osais imaginer ce qu'elle vivait. Sa pudeur était sacrifiée sur l'autel de l'efficacité, du temps à ne pas perdre. Une fois que l'infirmière eut terminé la toilette du haut du corps, je remis sur les seins de Georgette une serviette ; non pas que la vue de sa poitrine me gênât, mais j'essayais de préserver à cette vieille dame le peu d'intimité qui lui restait. Elle me regardait en souriant et continuait de se laisser faire sans broncher. Et que je te tourne d'un côté, et que je te tourne de l'autre…

Puis arriva le moment fatidique du changement de la protection, qui avait largement débordé. J'entrai alors encore un peu plus dans l'intimité de Georgette. Je pensais en moi-même : « Et dire que je ne devais qu'être femme de ménage… » J'agissais comme une marionnette, l'infirmière tirait sur mes fils, et j'exécutais, sans regarder, sans réfléchir. Là aussi, peu de délicatesse dans les gestes. Je voyais Georgette grimacer ; elle lui faisait mal… Mais pas le temps d'écouter les jérémiades, l'infirmière avait encore tant de patients à voir… Alors Georgette s'est tue et a fermé les yeux en attendant la fin de son calvaire.

Dix minutes avaient dû s'écouler, pas plus, et nous sommes passées à l'habillage. Même procédé : je te tourne, je te retourne… L'infirmière râlait parce que les robes n'étaient plus assez larges. Si Georgette n'a pas eu de nausées après ce tour de manège improvisé, c'est que son estomac était bien accroché !

J'étais abasourdie par le spectacle que je venais de voir et auquel j'avais participé. C'était donc cela, mon métier ?

Avant de partir, l'infirmière devait installer Georgette dans son fauteuil roulant en utilisant l'élévateur. Il fallut d'abord passer la sangle sous elle et la croiser entre ses jambes, puis prendre l'engin, l'y accrocher et effectuer le transfert.

Malgré mes inquiétudes, la manœuvre s'acheva sans accroc. La manipulation était finalement moins compliquée que je ne me l'étais imaginée, et Georgette était enfin au propre, habillée et levée.

Je passai la brosse sur ses cheveux très courts et la parfumai. Elle avait retrouvé le sourire ; moi, j'avais perdu celui que j'avais en entrant dans sa maison. Je n'avais pas imaginé que nos anciens puissent être pris en charge de cette façon à leur domicile. Je ruminais, je fulminais. Il était presque midi ; après avoir installé Georgette dans le salon où elle passerait l'après-midi, seule avec elle-même et la télévision, je m'attelai au lit ; laver les draps (Georgette avait un lave-linge), nettoyer ce que l'infirmière avait laissé en plan en partant précipitamment… J'étais bien la femme de ménage, mais pas seulement de Georgette. Il fallait aérer la pièce qui empestait le renfermé et les excréments ; personne n'aurait supporté de dormir avec une telle odeur. J'ouvris donc les grandes baies vitrées de la véranda en espérant qu'un courant d'air évacuerait cette odeur nauséabonde.

Revenant vers Georgette dont j'avais installé le fauteuil dans un coin de la véranda où le soleil se faufilait, je lui demandai ce qu'elle souhaitait manger. Elle me répondit qu'elle n'avait pas très faim, qu'elle aimerait quelque chose de frais, une salade composée par exemple. J'entrepris d'analyser le contenu du frigo : une tomate, un reste de salade verte, une pomme et un filet de poulet. Dans les placards je trouvai une conserve de pointes d'asperges. J'arriverais bien à composer une salade avec tout ça. La serpillière m'attendait toujours ; son appel était cependant si discret que je l'entendis à peine.

Je m'amusais donc à préparer une jolie assiette, réminiscence de mes années hôtelières. Je jouais la comédie jusqu'au moment où je servis Georgette :

— Petite assiette fraîcheur au poulet juste grillé ! annonçai-je avec emphase, tel un serveur de restaurant gastronomique.

Elle sourit. Ne dit-on pas que la vue des aliments que vous allez manger est déterminante sur votre appétit ?

— Mais c'est la première fois que l'on me sert une si belle assiette… Comment avez-vous fait ?

— Un peu d'ingrédients, un peu d'envie, un peu de magie, et le tour est joué.

Georgette avait un sourire que je n'oublierai jamais. Elle mangea avec appétit et finit son repas avec un yaourt nature.

Bientôt 12 h 30, j'allais devoir la quitter, à regret. Vaisselle terminée, goûter installé, eau placée à portée de main, télécommande, téléphone et lunettes sur le guéridon près du fauteuil, elle était armée pour son après-midi. Je pris congé en lui indiquant que je revenais à 17 heures, elle acquiesça. Son sourire avait disparu, plus un mot ne sortait de sa bouche, elle venait de comprendre que, depuis cette minute, et jusqu'à ce soir 17 heures, elle serait seule.

*

Je quittai la maison en courant. Besoin de hurler, besoin de pleurer. Je ne rapportais pas de travail chez moi, ça non, je rapportais des larmes, de la colère. Et c'était pire.

En arrivant, je m'écroulai. Ce que j'avais vécu en cette première matinée m'avait fait si mal, m'avait tant choquée… Le constat était sans équivoque : on m'avait prévenue, du moins on avait tenté, et je n'avais pas voulu entendre. Je ne m'y étais donc pas préparée, et je m'en voulais. J'en voulais aussi au système, à la situation : qui supporterait d'être traité ainsi ? De n'être changé que deux fois dans la journée ? Un bébé est changé plus souvent ! J'ai compris ce matin-là que la société refusait de prendre ses anciens en compte, elle préférait les cacher, faire comme s'ils n'existaient plus.

J'ai aussi compris ce matin-là que j'avais un combat à mener.

J'ai pleuré longtemps. Je me suis demandé si je devais continuer. Et j'ai continué parce que, depuis ce jour-là, je me suis juré que plus jamais je n'accepterais que toutes ces Georgette soient si indignement traitées.

4

Juan

Je repris dès le lendemain le chemin du travail. J'enchaînais les heures, remplaçant même une collègue absente. Mes journées débutaient à 7 h 30 et se terminaient vers 20 heures. Mais peu importait : quelqu'un manquait, j'étais la première à me porter volontaire. Je ne supportais pas l'idée qu'une dame ou un monsieur reste seul, abandonné, sans personne pour l'aider. Ma fatigue était fantomatique ; il m'arrivait de travailler trois semaines sans congé, mais j'avais déjà connu cela. Dans l'hôtellerie, il est rare de pouvoir prendre de véritables jours de repos. En revanche, ma copie était largement à revoir quant à ma présence plus fréquente à la maison ; j'avais visiblement mal évalué mon engagement, et mes enfants ne voyaient finalement aucun changement.

*

J'avais récupéré un nouvel allocataire dans mon emploi du temps : Juan. Je devais intervenir chez lui de 7 h 30 à 8 h 30, après j'enchaînais chez Georgette. La fiche de poste stipulait : « aider au lever, préparation du petit déjeuner et ménage ». Je n'avais eu jusqu'à maintenant que des femmes à charge. M'occuper d'un homme changerait mes habitudes.

Quand j'arrivai dans le minuscule appartement de Juan, je fus frappée par son état d'insalubrité. Les murs étaient rongés par l'humidité et tenaient encore debout par miracle. Cette vision me glaça : ce vieil homme vivait dans un taudis.

Des questions envahirent mon esprit : comment laisser un homme âgé vivre ici ? N'avait-il donc pas de famille pour s'occuper de lui ? Cet homme n'avait-il pas travaillé de sa vie ? Ou bien sa maigre retraite ne lui permettait-elle pas de vivre décemment ?

Je fus vite stoppée dans mes interrogations car Juan m'appelait. J'entrai dans sa chambre et je découvris un homme grand, beau, le visage buriné par le soleil. Ses mains étaient celles d'un travailleur manuel, abîmées, particulièrement grandes. J'imaginais qu'il avait dû exercer un métier du bâtiment. Mais ma rêverie fut de courte durée, c'était le moment d'être efficace.

— Bonjour madame, pouvez-vous m'aider à me lever, s'il vous plaît ? Je dois aller aux toilettes.

— Bien sûr. Je m'appelle Anne-Sophie, votre nouvelle aide à domicile, me présentai-je en lui tendant la main.

— Ah ! Sophia, *muchas gracias*, me répondit-il.

Je dus le prendre dans mes bras, l'asseoir dans son lit et le faire pivoter vers le bord du matelas. Il était si lourd… Or, dans l'urgence, nos forces sont décuplées. Chaussons enfilés, déambulateur à proximité, il fallait maintenant passer de la position assise à la position debout. Cela ne s'annonçait pas sous les meilleurs auspices : les jambes de Juan le tenaient à peine. J'allais devoir créer une impulsion assez forte pour lui donner l'élan nécessaire à sa levée. L'envie était pressante, il fallait faire vite.

Je me positionnai face à lui, et je l'attrapai de telle sorte que ce ne soient pas mes bras qui le soulèvent mais bien mes jambes. Gagné ! Quelques pas vers la cuisine, et Juan me demandait un seau. Un seau ? Oui, un seau, le vieil homme n'avait plus la force de se rendre jusqu'aux toilettes. Papier hygiénique arraché à la hâte, voilà que je lui présentais le seau. Je dus le tenir pendant qu'il éliminait ce liquide jaunâtre et fort odorant ayant trop attendu avant d'être expulsé.

— *Gracias*, Sophia…

Visiblement, Juan parlait plus espagnol que français, et l'espagnol n'était pas une langue que j'avais apprise à l'école. Mais mes restes de vocabulaire hôtelier acquis en autodidacte allaient me servir. J'avais vidé et désinfecté ce seau quand je revins et trouvai Juan à la place où je l'avais laissé pendant cet intermède ménager. Il m'attendait, accroché à son déambulateur. Il avait besoin d'aide pour rejoindre la table de la salle à manger. Il n'avait pourtant que cinq pas à faire… Une fois assis, il me parla espagnol et me donna des directives que je ne compris pas toutes. Je commençais à regretter d'avoir choisi le latin et non l'espagnol en troisième langue…

Après avoir mis le couvert, je coupai en deux des petits pains au lait, que Juan tartina seul ensuite. *Idem* pour le café : je le préparai, mais ce fut lui qui servit. Notre organisation était finalement quasi militaire, et je me réjouissais de voir cet homme si participatif. Je m'apprêtais à faire son lit quand il m'interpella :

— Sophia, as-tu déjeuné ?

— Oui, bien sûr, pourquoi ?

— *No, no*, pas possible, trop tôt, et tu es maigre…

Nous n'avions pas la même notion de la maigreur, mais je pris le compliment avec plaisir.

— Viens à côté de moi, je t'ai préparé ton petit déjeuner.

— Mais il faut que je fasse votre lit et votre ménage…

— Viens, je te dis !

Le contredire l'aurait mis en colère, et tout compte fait j'avais un peu faim : je lui avais menti, je n'avais pas déjeuné, car j'étais intervenue chez une dame avant d'aller chez lui…

Je m'approchai donc de la table, où deux pains au lait et une chaise m'attendaient. Finalement, nous avons déjeuné ensemble. Son lit et le ménage attendraient bien quelques minutes, Juan avait avant toute chose besoin de ne pas être seul. Il me raconta sa vie, à moitié en espagnol et à moitié en français. Je compris que Juan avait fui l'Espagne et la dictature de Franco, qu'il avait été mécanicien et avait travaillé tout le temps. Veuf depuis de nombreuses années, il évoqua longuement son épouse décédée.

Le temps avançait, je n'avais toujours fait ni son lit ni le ménage. Je me dis alors que je resterais quelques minutes de plus que ce que mon intervention prévoyait pour terminer mon travail ; pas question de laisser un champ de bataille dans cet appartement en ruine.

L'État, dans sa grande générosité, avait attribué à Juan une heure d'intervention le matin. Je me demandai soudain comment il vivait le reste de la journée. Vu qu'il n'était pas en mesure de préparer son petit déjeuner, comment faisait-il pour se préparer son déjeuner et son dîner ? Allait-il manger ? Serait-il capable d'aller aux toilettes ? Toutes ces questions m'agressaient l'esprit.

Il allait passer sa journée seul, immobile, dans son gros fauteuil, devant sa télévision.

Les infirmières viendraient procéder à sa toilette à un moment ou à un autre, mais, d'après ce que j'avais constaté, elles ne resteraient pas plus de dix minutes. Dix minutes de présence contre plusieurs heures de solitude… En résumé, sur vingt-quatre heures, Juan n'était pas seul une heure et dix minutes en moyenne.

J'aurais tant aimé rester plus longtemps avec lui. Mais d'autres personnes m'attendaient, et je partis, le cœur gros.

*

J'ai accompagné Juan pendant quelques mois, durant lesquels j'ai vu son état se dégrader. Le lever en arrivant le matin devenait de plus en plus compliqué. Notre organisation militaire pour préparer le petit déjeuner n'était plus aussi fluide, et Juan perdait un peu chaque jour en autonomie. Il insistait toujours pour que je déjeune avec lui, mais il était moins alerte, et désormais même quelques pas le fatiguaient.

Il était grand temps de réclamer un certificat d'aggravation. Ce certificat est en général demandé par la famille, mais je n'avais pas le choix, l'état de Juan empirait. Il fallait appeler les conseils départementaux, qui envoyaient le document dans la foulée, document à faire remplir par le médecin traitant. Si le conseil départemental jugeait que l'état du patient s'était en effet aggravé, il accorderait plus d'heures de présence, et je pourrais ainsi mieux m'occuper de Juan.

Je savais par mes collègues que, si la demande émanait de mes supérieurs, la procédure prendrait plus de temps ; j'avais donc pris l'initiative. Le certificat arriva rapidement, par courrier, et, un jour où son médecin traitant était là, il me rédigea une ordonnance pour un lit médicalisé, qui aiderait Juan à se lever.

Tous ces documents en poche, je pris la direction de la poste la plus proche, et j'envoyai le dossier en espérant que le conseil général soit réactif, ce certificat d'aggravation permettant d'augmenter le nombre d'heures d'intervention au niveau du conseil départemental, et ainsi à Juan d'être moins seul…

*

Au fil des jours, Juan occupait mes pensées : que faisait-il ? Comment allait-il ?

J'étais si inquiète que, chaque soir, quand je ramenais ma fille de l'école, nous passions devant chez lui et, à travers le carreau de la grande baie vitrée, je le voyais à la même place où je l'avais laissé le matin. Dans son grand fauteuil devant la télévision.

Un matin, lorsque je franchis le seuil de chez Juan, je compris tout de suite qu'il n'allait pas bien, pas bien du tout. Sans attendre, j'appelai les urgences et je décrivis les symptômes au téléphone. Les pompiers arrivèrent rapidement et le transférèrent immédiatement à l'hôpital. Pas de petit déjeuner ce jour-là.

Ce fut ma première situation d'urgence. Je me suis rendu compte que, une fois dans le feu de l'action, j'étais allée à l'essentiel. Mais lorsque j'ai fermé la porte à clef après son départ, les larmes ont coulé sur mes joues. Ce fameux recul professionnel que l'on me demandait d'avoir s'effritait miette après miette. J'avais mal, et j'avais peur.

La colère prit alors le pas : s'il n'avait pas été si seul, la situation aurait-elle été différente ? Aurait-on pu éviter ce qui venait de se produire ? Déjà quinze jours que j'avais envoyé le certificat d'aggravation, et toujours aucune nouvelle. Qu'attendaient-ils, dans les hautes sphères ? N'avaient-ils donc à ce point aucune idée de l'urgence ? J'avais eu beau les relancer, la réponse était toujours aussi laconique : « Le dossier est en cours de traitement. »

Et la vie de Juan ? Cette façon qu'a l'Administration d'être déconnectée de la réalité me montrait sans fard les limites de mon action et la difficulté à faire évoluer les choses. Combien de fois me suis-je disputée avec ces bureaucrates en bonne santé !

Les espérances qui étaient les miennes en commençant l'aide à domicile se heurtaient à la dureté du quotidien : Juan était mon urgence, ce n'était qu'un numéro de dossier pour l'Administration.

Une sourde colère monta en moi : s'il fallait que je me rende à Marseille pour plaider la cause de Juan et obtenir ce à quoi il avait droit, j'irais ; c'était de la vie d'un homme qu'il était question…

Je perdais tout recul, et donc toute la distance nécessaire pour effectuer correctement mon travail, mais quand le cœur parle, quand vous faites ce métier avec la conviction chevillée au corps, que votre vocation est d'apporter du bonheur à l'autre, au diable le recul.

*

Juan est resté trois semaines à l'hôpital avant de rentrer chez lui, et toujours aucune nouvelle d'une potentielle augmentation des heures d'intervention.

L'homme que j'avais laissé trois semaines plus tôt n'existait plus : il était si amaigri… Dorénavant, les petits déjeuners se prenaient dans le lit, il ne pouvait plus marcher.

Je restai à côté de lui, le ménage attendrait encore. Je l'observais. Les maux remplaçaient les mots, sa douleur se lisait sur ses expressions fatiguées. Et aucune nouvelle du conseil départemental malgré mes relances incessantes.

Il passait ses journées dans son lit, ce qui signifiait port de changes obligatoire. Il était abonné au même traitement que les autres bénéficiaires invalides : changement de protection le matin et le soir, et, entre les deux, il baignait dans ses excréments en attendant que les infirmières passent…

Même la télé s'était tue.

Souvent sa main venait chercher la mienne. Ne pas pleurer, ne surtout pas pleurer, même s'il fallait bien se rendre à l'évidence : Juan était en fin de vie. L'hôpital l'avait renvoyé chez lui car il n'y avait plus rien à faire.

*

La situation dura ainsi quelques semaines. Chaque matin, en arrivant, je craignais de le retrouver endormi à jamais dans son lit.

Quand, un soir, alors que je passais devant chez lui en rentrant de l'école avec ma fille, j'ai vu que les pompiers étaient là… Juan est parti seul, dans son lit non médicalisé, celui qui avait été commandé, ironie du sort, devait arriver quelques jours plus tard. Et son dossier était toujours en attente.

Ne pas pleurer, ne pas pleurer… Et puis si ! Qu'en ai-je à faire, de ce recul professionnel ? J'ai pleuré, beaucoup pleuré, et je pleure encore en pensant à Juan qui me tartinait chaque matin deux petits pains au lait.

Cher État français, soyez rassuré, Juan ne vous coûtera plus rien. Il n'était pour vous qu'un numéro de dossier ; il était pour moi un être humain en souffrance, si seul, qui avait avant tout besoin qu'on prenne soin de lui. Et vous l'avez abandonné.

5

Je vais changer les choses

Cela faisait maintenant un an que j'arpentais les rues de mon village, allant de bénéficiaire en bénéficiaire. J'avais accepté de nouveaux « dossiers », comme les appelle l'Administration. Je n'aime pas ce mot. Nos aînés ne sont pas des dossiers, mais des personnes. Le terme annonçait la financiarisation de la vieillesse que j'entrevoyais. Même si j'étais salariée d'une association loi 1901, on nous parlait chiffres, on nous parlait rentabilité, on nous parlait rendement. En plus de nos métiers, nous devions être les commerciaux de l'association.

Mais je n'étais pas marchande de tapis, ma tâche était d'accompagner au quotidien des aînés en perte d'autonomie, pas de réaliser un chiffre d'affaires !

Souvent, les factures que recevaient les bénéficiaires traînaient sur les tables et les guéridons. J'en connaissais le montant : l'heure normale était facturée 20 euros, l'heure du week-end 33. Certes, ils restaient chez eux, mais le prix à payer était si élevé que leurs économies fondaient comme neige au soleil. Je voyais donc passer des factures avoisinant les 2 000 euros par mois, que les retraites suffisaient rarement à payer. Peu à peu, les bénéficiaires se ruinaient.

C'est à ce moment-là que j'ai commencé à prendre conscience de l'immoralité du système. Le conseil départemental accordait un minimum d'heures, histoire de ne pas coûter trop cher à l'État, et derrière l'association y allait à grands coups d'euros…

Quant à moi, aide à domicile, je travaillais certains mois plus de cent quatre-vingts heures et mon salaire atteignait à peine les 1 100 euros. Comment était-ce possible ?

J'avais un contrat à durée indéterminée, mais auquel il était apposé le terme « modulé ». Or un contrat à durée déterminée modulé signifie que vous êtes payé le même salaire tous les mois, donc que les heures supplémentaires ne vous sont pas rémunérées mais placées sur un compte, et vous permettent d'être payé en cas d'hospitalisation d'un de vos allocataires, ou qui vous seront payées au « une pour une ». Inexistantes, les majorations, ignoré, le code du travail… En toute légalité.

Je commençais aussi à comprendre les logiques comptables de mes employeurs. En tant qu'aide à domicile, nous utilisons notre véhicule personnel, et les kilomètres nous sont remboursés sur la base très généreuse de 0,35 euro du kilomètre. Nous avons l'obligation de contracter une assurance particulière, car on ne peut promener nos aînés sans être assurés, quand cela nous est demandé. Mais il y a un mais…

J'effectuais des interventions à douze kilomètres de mon domicile ; je devais donc prendre mon véhicule pour m'y rendre. En Camargue, j'aurais pu y aller à cheval, mais le tarif de remboursement des frais kilométriques de ce mode de déplacement n'étant pas stipulé dans la convention collective, j'avais peur que le pauvre animal fasse du bénévolat… Toute plaisanterie mise à part, les frais kilométriques ne m'étaient remboursés que si et seulement si je n'avais qu'une demi-heure pour me rendre à l'intervention suivante. Au-delà de cette demi-heure, aucuns frais kilométriques n'étaient pris en charge.

Ainsi, l'association m'envoyait à douze kilomètres à 9 heures, où je restais trois heures. Je repartais donc à midi, et mon intervention suivante ne commençait qu'à 14 heures… Malin. Le cas se présenta deux fois par semaine, et ce pendant un an.

C'est par ce genre de procédé que certains arrivent à économiser de l'argent sur le dos des salariés. Quand on a plein d'employés, imaginez le montant que ce petit stratagème peut générer…

Déjà, sans en avoir véritablement conscience, je constatais que certains de ces employeurs jouaient sur la précarité. En effet, nous sommes majoritairement des femmes dans ce milieu professionnel, des femmes souvent seules avec enfants, qui ont besoin de travailler, et qui deviennent taillables et corvéables à merci. Sans aucune formation, sans aucune aide psychologique, nous sommes envoyées dans le grand bain. Comme nous sommes des femmes, il est *de facto* inscrit dans nos gènes que nous savons nous occuper des autres…

Et puis, certaines collègues ne savent ni lire ni écrire, c'est du pain bénit pour ces employeurs. Elles ne risquent pas d'aller fouiner dans la convention collective pour vérifier si leurs droits sont respectés. De même, pas de formation proposée, ce serait la porte ouverte à une possible rébellion.

Je continuais malgré tout mon petit bonhomme de chemin, tout en développant mes connaissances sur les véritables fiches de poste d'une aide à domicile, d'une auxiliaire de vie sociale… jusqu'au jour où il me prit l'idée saugrenue de demander à mon employeur de passer le diplôme d'auxiliaire de vie sociale par le biais de la validation des acquis de l'expérience (VAE). J'avais emmagasiné en un an et demi autant d'heures que si j'avais travaillé trois ans de temps plein. Et comme un pôle de formation était hébergé dans les locaux de l'association, c'est confiante que je me suis rendue le 28 août à 18 heures au rendez-vous que m'avait fixé ma chef de service.

— Bonsoir, je voudrais bénéficier de mes heures DIF pour un accompagnement afin de passer le diplôme d'État d'auxiliaire de vie sociale, est-ce possible ?

— Oui, quand ?

— Là, dans les mois qui viennent, si c'est possible.

— Ah non, ça ne va pas être possible tout de suite, notre formatrice est en congé maternité, elle revient dans six mois, patientez…

— Patientez ?

— Oui ! C'est quoi, six mois. Pas grand-chose.

— Donc, si je comprends bien, votre formatrice étant absente, aucune formation n'est dispensée.

— Oui, c'est ça.

— Et si je ne veux pas attendre, quelles sont mes possibilités ?

— Aucune.

— Je peux tout de même essayer de passer le diplôme seule, si je le souhaite ? Sans accompagnement ?

— Oui, mais vous savez, c'est difficile, moi, il m'a fallu presque un an pour monter mon livret…

— Très bien, mais sachez que tout le monde n'est pas comme vous, peut-être pourrons-nous en discuter de nouveau lorsque j'aurai eu mon diplôme…

— Bon, je dois vous laisser, j'ai encore du travail, moi.

— Moi aussi, il est 18 h 15, et j'ai encore trois interventions à effectuer chez nos aînés, alors bonne soirée.

En clair : si je voulais passer mon diplôme, il faudrait que je me débrouille sans eux… Pourtant, ils ont, comme tous les employeurs, des budgets alloués pour la formation, un pourcentage de la masse salariale, et la convention collective stipule clairement que la priorité doit être donnée aux employés non qualifiés.

Il en fallait plus pour me décourager. Je demandai donc le fameux livret si difficile à remplir. Il arriva assez vite. Il s'agissait de raconter ses expériences suivant les attentes du jury. La difficulté était donc de ne pas faire de hors sujet. Ensuite, il fallait respecter un calendrier strict : pour passer devant le jury au mois de mars de l'année suivante, il fallait que mon livret soit reçu avant le 31 octobre. Nous étions début septembre ; si je commençais dès à présent, ça devait être jouable.

Après quelques nuits blanches, j'avais rempli les pages de mon livret dans les temps, relatant mes rencontres avec Georgette, Juan et tous les autres.

Je suis passée devant le jury le 20 mars, et j'ai obtenu mon diplôme d'État d'auxiliaire de vie sociale, au grand dam de ma chef de service.

Quel bilan tirer de cette aventure, qui se terminait finalement bien pour moi ? Que les employeurs ne souhaitent pas vraiment former leurs employées – des femmes, pour la plupart, on l'a dit –, parce que cela leur coûterait trop cher et que cela leur permet de les maintenir dans la conviction qu'évoluer leur est impossible. Certaines ignorent même qu'elles y ont droit. Mensonge par omission.

La dévalorisation du personnel est une discipline olympique dans laquelle certains employeurs obtiendraient la médaille d'or. Après tout, ce ne sont que des femmes de ménage, pas besoin de formation pour être la reine du torchon à vaisselle !

Le cynisme de certains patrons va plus loin : comme dans tous ces métiers on abuse toujours plus des glissements de tâche – j'entends par là que ces « aides ménagères », dont la définition de poste stipule qu'elles ne doivent exécuter que des tâches « ménagères », commencent à faire des toilettes sans formation, utilisent des lève-malades, sans formation, déplacent des personnes âgées, sans formation... –, on les envoie volontairement au casse-pipe, et les accidents de travail s'enchaînent. Mais cela importe peu aux employeurs : il y a tant de chômage que, si ce n'est pas cette femme de ménage-là, c'en sera une autre. La liste d'attente de non diplômées prêtes à enfiler la blouse pour gagner quatre sous et nourrir leur famille est sans fin.

Mais la réalité est bien celle-ci : combien de femmes ont-elles été licenciées suite à des incapacités au poste ? Combien ont souffert de troubles musculo-squelettiques, de mal-être voire de dépression ? Combien ont succombé à des burn-out ?

Et les conséquences pour nos aînés sont désastreuses : comment assurer une prise en charge efficace et de qualité si l'intervenante change constamment, ignorant tout de la pathologie, de l'histoire et des besoins du bénéficiaire ?

Quand nous intervenons au domicile d'une personne, nous pénétrons dans son intimité, ses souvenirs, sa vie, et d'étrangères, avec le temps et la confiance qui s'installe, nous devenons confidentes, réconfort, cette indispensable présence qu'elle attend chaque jour, parce que c'est la seule qu'elle aura.

Mais pour parvenir à ce résultat, encore faut-il qu'on nous en laisse le temps et les moyens. Trop d'employeurs abusent de leur autorité pour retirer des dossiers de peur que l'intervenante ne « s'attache trop » au bénéficiaire. Or c'est à ce prix que le travail est bien fait !

Au diable le recul professionnel, bonjour l'empathie.

6

Dérive

Nouvellement diplômée, j'avais atteint le Graal ; je n'étais plus seulement une femme de ménage, je devenais un acteur social dans toute la grandeur du terme. J'allais *faire du social.* En réalité, j'en faisais déjà, outrepassant largement mes fiches de poste, mais cette fois c'était officiel. Et puis j'avais gardé dans un coin de ma tête la réaction de ma responsable ; je l'avais bien mouchée, et elle avait même été obligée de me féliciter. Je n'avais pas remué le couteau dans la plaie – je n'en voyais pas l'utilité. D'autant que mon succès suffisait à la mettre mal à l'aise ; pas besoin de vider mon chargeur, elle était déjà à terre.

Tout auréolée de ce titre prestigieux de niveau cinq (l'équivalent d'un CAP ou d'un BEP), voilà que l'on me proposait un nouveau dossier : une dame âgée qui vivait avec ses enfants.

Il était stipulé : « entretien de la maison », mais j'allais bien trouver un moyen de faire de l'humain. C'est du moins ce que je croyais…

En bas de l'immeuble, je sonnai ; on m'ouvrit, et je montai au dernier étage, où se trouvait l'appartement. Je fus accueillie par un chihuahua braillard qui n'aspirait pour l'heure qu'à une chose, me croquer un bout de mollet. L'appartement était immense et couvrait toute la superficie de l'étage. Table en cristal de Baccarat, sièges en cuir, tapis d'Orient, vase magistral d'inspiration chinoise… un véritable musée. Des ivoires en guise de bibelots, des photophores en biscuit de Limoges, des tables cabaret en marqueterie, cet environnement m'était familier : j'avais le sentiment de me retrouver chez mes parents…

Une femme toute menue d'une soixantaine d'années m'accueillit et me fit visiter l'appartement : un coin bureau, immense, la chambre de la dame dont je devais avoir la charge, la chambre du couple, la salle de bains du couple, etc.

Je n'avais pas encore eu le temps d'aller saluer Angèle, la bénéficiaire de la prestation, qui était endormie dans un grand fauteuil en robe de chambre. J'essayais pourtant, mais sa fille préféra d'abord me montrer où se trouvait l'aspirateur, la serpillière, le seau et le chiffon à poussière. J'avais du matériel haut de gamme : j'aspirerais avec un Dyson, j'époussetterais avec des Swiffer, je récurerais avec des produits vendus uniquement lors de présentations à domicile.

Moi qui voulais changer de statut, j'étais servie : j'étais devenue une femme de ménage de luxe ! J'étais une privilégiée !

Oui, oui, une privilégiée ! Mon employeur avait bien pris conscience que j'avais changé de statut, maintenant on m'envoyait chez les riches…

Une fois la visite terminée et les multiples démonstrations sur l'utilisation de l'aspirateur faites, je dus me mettre à l'œuvre. Je devais commencer par la chambre d'Angèle, j'étais là pour elle. Quelle ne fut donc pas ma surprise lorsque je m'aperçus que la pièce était ridiculement petite : un lit, un chevet, une douche et un lavabo dans une pièce qui devait avoisiner les neuf mètres carrés. Deux heures pour nettoyer neuf mètres carrés, j'avais le temps de faire les plinthes à la brosse à dents ! Et même en déménageant tous les meubles, en une demi-heure grand maximum, j'aurais terminé… Je me demandais ce que j'allais bien pouvoir faire pendant l'heure et demie qui me resterait. J'eus rapidement la réponse à ma question.

Une fois le ménage dédié à Angèle achevé, sa fille vint vers moi et me dit :

— Vous avez terminé, très bien, maintenant il y a notre chambre à faire, notre salle de bains, notre bureau et évidemment le coin salon, en une heure et demie, vous avez largement le temps. D'ailleurs, nous allons mettre un programme de tâches à faire, si cela ne vous dérange pas ; le lundi, ce sera la chambre de ma mère, notre chambre à nous, le salon, et la cuisine. Le jeudi, vous devrez nettoyer le coin bureau et la véranda, la terrasse, l'escalier qui descend au rez-de-chaussée, et bien sûr un petit coup dans notre chambre et dans la salle de bains.

— Très bien, répondis-je sans me démonter, mais savez-vous que l'argent que vous touchez du conseil général est exclusivement alloué pour votre maman ? Je veux bien exécuter ces tâches, mais si elles entrent dans le cadre des besoins de votre maman.

— Elles entrent, elles entrent, j'ai vu avec vos supérieurs, voilà ce quc nous avons mis en place.

— Si c'est ce que vous avez mis en place avec mes supérieurs, alors je vais m'en tenir à cela.

Je commençais à fulminer, mais j'exécutai bêtement les ordres. Je ne vis pas beaucoup Angèle, mais plus qu'il ne m'en fallait le chihuahua collant, gueulard et méchant dont j'essayais d'éviter les crocs. Jour après jour, j'exécutais les ordres et effectuais le ménage de l'appartement entier. J'aimais bien nettoyer le bureau ; je m'attardais quelquefois sur les titres des livres, jusqu'au jour où j'y vis *Mein Kampf*. Chacun est libre de lire ce qu'il veut, mais cette rencontre inattendue m'avait un peu perturbée.

Je les entendais régulièrement parler d'argent, de ce que leur coûterait la réfection de la cuisine, 10 000 euros par-ci, 20 000 euros par-là. Je souriais dans mon coin en les écoutant. Ils parlaient suffisamment fort pour impressionner la simple femme de ménage que j'étais censée être. Mais je n'étais ni impressionnée par le Baccarat, ni par le cristal de Daum, ni par ces vases, ni par tout ce luxe dont j'avais eu horreur pendant mon enfance.

Une seule chose me dérangeait : que l'argent public destiné à Angèle serve à ces deux nantis.

*

Un jour, j'ai atteint les limites de ce que je pouvais supporter. Ce jour-là précisément, je n'avais même pas pu nettoyer la chambre d'Angèle, car le couple recevait et avait préféré que je me charge d'astiquer l'argenterie pendant deux heures – et tant que j'y étais, j'avais aussi nettoyé les belles casseroles en cuivre suspendues dans l'ordre décroissant au-dessus de la hotte… Je n'avais pas bronché, même lorsque mon inspecteur des travaux finis avait exigé que je recommence les porte-couteaux, tant les dessins étaient fins et tant il fallait passer absolument dans tous les recoins.

Cependant, combien de fois j'ai eu envie d'envoyer valser ce chihuahua de malheur qui me suivait partout, prêt à dégainer les crocs au moindre mouvement, et qui était mieux traité que bien des humains : il avait sa propre garde-robe, avait droit au toiletteur, était porté dès qu'il se sentait fatigué, avait sa chambre, ses joujoux, et droit à toutes les attentions.

Pour Angèle, pas de vêtements neufs, pas de coiffeur ni de précautions dues à son âge, encore moins d'attention ni de mots gentils. Elle restait dans son fauteuil stoïque et seule.

C'en était trop ! J'appelai ma responsable, celle-là même qui pensait que je n'aurais pas mon diplôme.

— Bonjour, c'est Anne-Sophie, je sors de mon intervention de deux heures chez Angèle, il y a quelque chose que je ne saisis pas bien, pouvez-vous m'éclairer ?

— Oui, que se passe-t-il ?

— L'argent de son allocation personnalisée d'autonomie doit-il servir à fournir une femme de ménage à ses enfants ?

— Je ne comprends pas…

— Si, si, vous comprenez, il semble même que vous soyez au courant et que vous ayez vu ça avec la famille. Du moins, c'est ce que sa fille m'a dit. Je vous remercie de m'envoyer chez des gens riches, une conséquence de l'obtention de mon diplôme, je suppose, et d'égayer ainsi mon cadre de travail, mais est-il normal que je ne fasse que le ménage des enfants qui habitent la maison d'Angèle ? Et que je passe en gros, en voyant vraiment très, très large, quinze minutes à m'occuper de la bénéficiaire ?

— Anne-Sophie, c'est un dossier, et vous savez que nous avons besoin de nouveaux…

— Pardon ? la coupai-je assez sèchement. Mais ne considérez-vous pas que c'est limite comme attitude ? Et qu'on s'en accomode ?

— Je ne vous permets pas !

— Vous peut-être pas, mais moi, oui, je me permets de signaler que ce cas précis pose un problème de moralité.

— Si vous le dites. C'était le motif de votre appel ?

— Oui.

— Alors, au revoir, et bonne journée…

Et la conversation prit fin, me laissant perplexe. Je pensais à Juan et à quel point ces quatre heures par semaine lui auraient été utiles, à lui. Visiblement, mes employeurs et l'État préféraient privilégier ceux qui avaient tout à fait les moyens de se payer une femme de ménage plutôt que d'aider les gens vraiment dans le besoin.

Surtout, mon appel ne servit à rien. Je savais que l'Administration ne bougerait pas le petit doigt pour changer la situation. Mais je refusais d'être la complice de ce jeu malsain. Après mûre réflexion, je finis par trouver le moyen de ne plus participer à cette mascarade. La solution était simple et je savais qu'elle fonctionnerait.

*

Lors de l'intervention suivante, j'arrivai comme à mon habitude, et je commençai par le nettoyage de la chambre d'Angèle. Je mis un temps infini à terminer la pièce. Une bonne heure et demie à astiquer, déménager tout ce qui pouvait gêner le passage de mon super aspirateur. J'eus même peur d'user le tapis à force de l'aspirer. Le robinet du lavabo était un véritable miroir, la céramique étincelait comme dans un spot de pub, et les meubles, que j'avais cirés, donnaient à la pièce cette odeur si particulière d'encaustique. J'étais fière de mon ménage, Angèle n'allait pas reconnaître sa chambre.

Évidemment, il ne me restait plus qu'une demi-heure pour toutes les autres tâches. J'avais bien calculé mon coup : comme il me fallait environ trente minutes pour la salle de bains, je n'aurais pas le temps de faire la chambre. Au fur et à mesure que le temps s'écoulait, je voyais bien que l'inspectrice des travaux finis, la fille d'Angèle, s'énervait. Quand les deux heures attribuées furent terminées, j'étais fière de mon travail. Mais les choses allaient se corser. Même le chihuahua s'y mettrait, confortant ma confiance toute relative en lui.

La fille d'Angèle avança vers moi tandis que je m'apprêtais à partir et me dit :

— Anne-Sophie, vous avez fait exprès de mettre deux heures pour nettoyer la chambre de ma mère, et donc n'avoir que ça à faire aujourd'hui, n'est-ce pas ?

— Comment ça, « que ça » ?

— Oui, d'habitude vous faites aussi le salon, le coin repas…

— C'est vrai, mais aujourd'hui votre salle de bains était plus sale.

— Ne me prenez pas pour une imbécile, Anne-Sophie.

— Ah, mais madame, loin de moi cette idée, je n'oserais pas, eu égard à votre rang. J'ai quelque éducation, madame.

— Vous êtes là pour faire le ménage, vous devez faire le ménage.

— Effectivement, je suis censée prendre soin de ce qui est utilisé par Angèle, car l'argent que vous touchez du conseil général doit exclusivement servir à accompagner votre maman. Donc, dites-moi, votre maman, elle utilise la baignoire, elle utilise votre chambre, elle utilise l'escalier, elle utilise la terrasse ?

— Non, mais…

— Et, sauf erreur de ma part, vous n'êtes ni malade ni en situation de handicap ?

— Non…

— Donc je m'en tiendrai désormais à la tâche qui m'incombe, et estimez-vous heureuse que j'aie accepté de vous obéir jusqu'à aujourd'hui.

— Ça ne va pas se passer comme ça ! vociféra alors mon cerbère. Je vais appeler votre direction…

— Mais faites, lui répondis-je, ne vous gênez surtout pas. De mon côté, je vais prévenir le conseil général, et on avisera.

C'est alors qu'elle me prit méchamment par le bras et me secoua. Je vis rouge.

— Lâchez-moi, c'est une agression…

— Agression ? Je vais vous mettre deux gifles, ça vous remettra les idées en place, Anne-Sophie.

— Je vous demande de me lâcher immédiatement.

Elle continuait de me serrer le bras, tandis que le chihuahua essayait de me mordre. Son mari apparut sur ces entrefaites et lui demanda de me lâcher ; ce qu'elle fit. Je récupérai mes affaires, saluai Angèle et plantai là le couple.

Je savais en claquant la porte que je n'interviendrais plus jamais chez eux.

Ce fut ma première expérience de l'utilisation de l'argent public à d'autres fins que celles prévues.

7

Louise

Je ne revins jamais chez Angèle ; je savais qu'une collègue prendrait ma place, et c'était bien là l'essentiel. Je décidai par ailleurs de ne pas porter plainte pour agression ni de prévenir le conseil général. Mais l'ambiance au travail se dégradait à vue d'œil : les démissions commençaient à pleuvoir, les réunions à la mairie devenaient de plus en plus houleuses. Nos plannings nous étaient toujours fournis la veille ou l'avant-veille du mois qui allait débuter. Difficile dans ces conditions, pour une mère de famille, d'organiser son emploi du temps. J'avais appris que mes collègues demandaient depuis des mois de recevoir les plannings dans un délai raisonnable, en vain… Une nouvelle fois, la moutarde me monta au nez. De quel droit nous traitait-on de la sorte ? Je pris donc la décision d'étudier avec précision la convention collective, et ainsi de recueillir un maximum d'éléments pour que mes collègues et moi obtenions gain de cause.

*

Dans le même temps, j'héritai d'une nouvelle allocataire : Louise. Elle avait soixante-quatorze ans et vivait dans le village depuis quelques années. Après un divorce houleux, ses moyens financiers avaient largement baissé. Elle avait quitté un mari chef d'entreprise en Suisse et vendu son salon de coiffure pour s'installer en Camargue.

Louise habitait un appartement joliment décoré ; les murs, comme chez Juan, étaient quelque peu rongés par le salpêtre, mais l'endroit était luxueux. Louise était diabétique insulino-dépendante. Sa maladie, elle la gérait seule. Ses piqûres étaient devenues un automatisme. Mais le sort voulut que Louise fût touchée par un cancer. Opération, chimio, elle en avait pour deux ans avant de savoir si elle était ou non en rémission.

Quand je commençai mes interventions à son domicile, Louise avait pris la décision de se raser la tête pour ne pas avoir à subir la vue de ces cheveux qui tombent suite à la chimio. Elle, l'ancienne coiffeuse, qui prenait tant de plaisir à se faire brushing et mises en plis, elle qui considérait les cheveux des femmes comme un de leurs plus beaux atours, elle n'en avait plus. Elle n'était plus une femme dans son esprit, mais une malade. Je m'en rendis compte lors de ma première visite. Je compris alors que je devrais tout mettre en œuvre pour lui redonner la confiance que le cancer lui ôtait peu à peu, sinon elle dépérirait rapidement.

Avant de tomber malade, Louise était très active dans la vie de notre cité, elle allait à la chorale ou se promener, elle avait de nombreux amis et était bien entourée. Aujourd'hui, elle restait enfermée chez elle ; la crainte du regard des autres, les effets secondaires de la chimio et la fatigue qu'ils engendraient. Lorsque je débarquais chez elle, j'ignorais toujours comment j'allais la trouver. Allait-elle avoir la force de se lever, de marcher un peu ?

Pour rompre son isolement, elle n'avait trouvé comme solution qu'Internet et les tchats. Il lui était plus facile de parler à travers un écran à des inconnus que de se rendre au marché, lieu qu'elle affectionnait pourtant beaucoup avant sa maladie.

Même si ma fiche de poste stipulait : « entretien du domicile », j'aiderais Louise à continuer à vivre comme elle le faisait avant, sans honte, la tête haute. J'allais enfin pouvoir faire mon travail d'auxiliaire de vie sociale. Je m'étais donné des objectifs afin d'évaluer sa progression. La tâche serait longue et difficile, mais elle en valait la peine.

Le cancer équivaut à une double peine : non seulement il vous atteint physiquement, mais aussi socialement, émotionnellement, car il éloigne les amis. Il y a ceux qui vous évitent, comme s'ils craignaient la contamination ; il y a ceux qui redoutent de voir les effets dévastateurs de la maladie. On a du mal à mettre des mots sur le cancer, à parler sereinement de cette maladie ; autant on évoque la maladie d'Alzheimer (fréquemment en ironisant pour conjurer le sort sur le « elle perd la boule »), on parle de Parkinson à cause des tremblements qui inquiètent… mais comment aborder le cancer qui tue énormément ?

Le cancer tue, en effet. On éprouve des difficultés à parler ouvertement du cancer, on élude le plus souvent, de peur de nous porter la poisse, que la maladie ne nous touche à notre tour, nous ou les nôtres, rien qu'à prononcer son nom. J'ai toujours été abasourdie par le regard de l'autre sur cette maladie, et surtout lorsqu'elle concerne les femmes. En effet, on peut perdre ses cheveux quand on suit un protocole de chimiothérapie, mais la calvitie des femmes effraie, dérange, alors que celle des hommes est habituelle. Une femme chauve et sans sourcils se voit immédiatement étiquetée cancéreuse, rendant la maladie encore plus difficile à supporter pour la personne.

*

Louise était fatiguée, diminuée ; je l'aidais à marcher, à s'asseoir, mais j'étais déterminée à ne rien lâcher et à atteindre quelques objectifs simples pour commencer. J'aspirais à ce qu'un jour nous allions au marché ensemble. Car mon rôle, c'est aussi de rompre l'isolement.

J'intervenais vingt heures par semaine chez elle, j'y allais tous les jours, cela me permettait de suivre sa progression.

Au début, elle pleurait beaucoup, et la majeure partie de mon temps était consacrée à l'écouter. L'écouter me permettait aussi d'en apprendre plus sur sa vie, ce qu'elle aimait faire avant, comment elle imaginait la suite. La suite, justement, elle ne l'envisageait pas. Elle n'aspirait qu'à mourir pour ne plus souffrir.

Mais que signifiait « ne plus souffrir » pour Louise ? Ne plus souffrir des effets de la chimio et des douleurs physiques, ou ne plus souffrir de cet isolement et de cette image si détériorée d'elle-même ? C'est elle qui me donna la réponse : sa solitude lui pesait plus encore que tout le reste. Elle ne comprenait pas pourquoi ses amis semblaient l'avoir abandonnée à son tristc sort, et elle avait le sentiment de se battre seule.

*

Deux semaines déjà que je voyais Louise tous les jours. Les progrès étaient visibles : elle se levait de plus en plus. Pour permettre d'autres avancées, il fallait désormais prendre des décisions, et notamment réorganiser son intérieur. Chaque jour, en effet, elle se prenait les pieds dans le tapis à la sortie de sa chambre et se rattrapait au coin de la commode. Comment engager la conversation sur le sujet sans lui rappeler son état ? Avec empathie, diplomatie, en ayant une approche positive du changement et en insistant sur son caractère temporaire.

Elle accepta, un peu à contrecœur, mais consciente du fait que ces modifications lui permettraient de se déplacer mieux et en toute sécurité.

*

Les semaines, les mois s'écoulaient, ponctués par les rendez-vous à l'hôpital pour suivre le traitement de chimiothérapie, et les jours qui suivaient oscillant entre fatigue et nausées. Sa marche devenait plus assurée ; tous les jours, Louise et moi effectuions quelques pas dans la cour. Elle participait à mes activités : assise sur le banc, par exemple, elle me passait le linge à étendre. Mais mon objectif n'était pas encore atteint.

Louise avait décidé de ne pas porter de perruque mais un foulard. Elle ne supportait plus de voir son crâne si chauve. Face à son ordinateur, des photos étaient accrochées au mur. Celles d'une jolie femme aux cheveux couleur de blé. Celles des jours heureux. C'est pour cette raison que les sorties en dehors de la cour lui paraissaient impossibles : que diraient les gens de son foulard ? J'eus soudain l'idée saugrenue de lui demander si elle en avait un autre. Elle m'en sortit un du tiroir de la commode, et je me l'attachai sur le crâne. J'avais décidé que moi aussi je serais chauve, et que nous sortirions ainsi.

C'est la première fois que je vis Louise sourire. Elle se moquait allégrement de ma coiffe « œuf de Pâques »… mais qu'importe, le ridicule ne tuant pas, j'avais bien dans l'idée que nous sortirions ainsi toutes les deux. Après de féroces négociations, elle accepta enfin. Nous décidâmes d'aller au bout de sa rue et de revenir. Chaque fois que nous croisions quelqu'un, Louise me serrait le bras à me couper la circulation sanguine. Je posais alors ma main sur la sienne pour l'apaiser.

Sans s'en rendre compte, elle avait fait beaucoup plus de pas que d'habitude ; comme quoi, elle en avait les capacités. Il fallait poursuivre nos efforts ! Je ne savais pas quand, mais j'étais certaine d'une chose : je l'emmènerais au marché…

*

Un lundi, à mon arrivée, Louise était habillée et avait déjeuné. Quel plaisir de la voir en si bonne forme ! Elle s'était débrouillée seule ce matin-là. Il était peut-être temps de finaliser mon objectif.

— Louise, avez-vous besoin de courses au marché ?

— Oui, il me faudrait des fruits et des légumes…

— Quoi, comme fruits et légumes ?

— Oh, ce que tu trouves, tu connais mes goûts.

— Pas vraiment, Louise… Et choisir les meilleurs produits, vous savez que ce n'est pas mon fort…

Elle me stoppa net et me dit :

— Tu te moques de moi ? Tu as toujours bien acheté les fruits et les légumes !

— Certes, mais aujourd'hui, je préférerais que vous veniez avec moi. Et puis ça vous ouvrira l'appétit. Vous n'avez pas envie de choisir vous-même ce qui vous ferait plaisir à manger ?

— Si, si, bien sûr, mais ça veut dire qu'il faut que je t'accompagne au marché… C'est trop loin…

— Mais non, Louise, on marche depuis quelques jours dans la rue… et on s'arrêtera au besoin. Vous auriez le foulard que vous m'aviez prêté ?

— Pour quoi faire ?

— Pour aller au marché avec vous…

— Tu vas sortir comme ça ?

— Bien sûr ! Sauf si je vous fais honte…

Elle sortit le foulard du tiroir, c'est elle qui m'en coiffa, et nous partîmes toutes les deux, direction le marché. Elle me serrait toujours le bras, je posais encore ma main sur la sienne. Certes, il y eut bien quelques regards de passants sur nos coiffes, mais qu'importe, nous étions en chemin.

Le marché se profilait à l'horizon. Louise était terrifiée à l'idée de rencontrer des connaissances. Dès les premiers pas dans les ruelles étroites, une de ses amies l'interpella. Louise fit mine de ne pas entendre et continua d'avancer, mais la dame âgée nous rattrapa :

— Louise, comme ça fait plaisir de te voir ! Comment vas-tu ?

— Ça va… Tu vois, je commence à pouvoir aller au marché.

— Merveilleux ! Mais dis-moi, tu sais qu'à la chorale tu as toujours ta place ! Il faut que tu reviennes.

— Oui, je vais y penser.

— Non, cesse d'y penser, reviens ! Mais qu'avez-vous donc mis sur vos têtes ?

— Ce sont nos coiffes d'Arlésiennes ! répondit-elle non sans un certain humour.

À cette réponse, nous rîmes toutes les trois. J'avais gagné mon pari.

*

Il avait fallu six mois, mais Louise recommençait à vivre et savait dorénavant qu'elle n'était pas aussi seule qu'elle l'avait pensé. Cette visite du marché dura des heures. C'est moi finalement qui commençais à fatiguer d'être debout : Louise discutait à droite à gauche… Elle gagnait autant sur la maladie que sur l'image qu'elle avait d'elle-même. Quant à moi, j'avais fait mon métier dans toute sa noblesse.

Aujourd'hui, Louise est intenable, sort, bouge, participe de nouveau à la vie de la cité, n'a plus besoin de mon bras pour aller au marché. Je suis Anne-Sophie, elle est Louise, et notre histoire est liée par deux foulards colorés.

8

Une légère brise de révolte

J'étais revigorée, j'avais avec Louise réussi à exercer mon métier comme mes valeurs me le dictaient. Je slalomais cependant entre les peaux de banane qu'on me lançait. La direction de l'association voulut renouveler d'un coup tous mes allocataires. Évidemment, je m'y opposais ; mes collègues aussi : chambouler mon emploi du temps signifiait modifier le leur, car elles récupéreraient mes allocataires et moi les leurs.

Ma supérieure me reprochait mes dépassements de quelques minutes chez certains bénéficiaires, de déborder du cadre de mes tâches… Tout était bon à prendre, sujet à reproches. Elle avait encore en travers de la gorge ce diplôme obtenu sans son aide. Pour la convaincre qu'elle se trompait, je lui proposais régulièrement de m'accompagner, mais elle refusait systématiquement ma proposition.

Je décidai de ne plus l'écouter et je continuai à monter mon dossier sur les manquements de cette association au code du travail. Mes collègues étaient au courant et s'impatientaient. Mais il faut être patient, dans ces moments-là. La convention collective était devenue mon livre de chevet. Chacune de mes consœurs m'avait apporté ses plannings des trois dernières années, ses différents contrats et ses fiches de paie. Entre Cathy, qui n'avait pas eu sa majoration de 1,50 euro pour avoir travaillé un 1er mai, et ce depuis un an, Mathilde, qui avait enchaîné les CDD sans avoir été payée des primes de précarité, Véro, qui se battait pour le remboursement de ses kilomètres et ces plannings toujours donnés la veille du mois suivant, il y avait matière à plaidoirie. J'avais du pain sur la planche…

Pourquoi m'avaient-elles choisie comme porte-parole, je ne peux le dire. Mais c'était ainsi ; et l'étude de tous leurs documents sur trois ans allait me prendre du temps. Il fallait que je sois au point, et chaque soir, dossier après dossier, je relevais les infractions au code du travail ou à la convention collective.

Il y avait aussi un problème avec le comité d'entreprise. Mon employeur n'était pas équitable envers tous les employés, et le montant des chèques cadeaux pour Noël fondait comme neige au soleil. De 100 euros par employé, ils avaient baissé à 50. Une vague histoire de redressement URSSAF en guise d'explication, nous avait répondu la direction. Mais la véritable raison du redressement de 24 000 euros dont faisait l'objet le comité d'entreprise restait floue. Encore une fois, les employées payaient les manquements des dirigeants. C'est à ce moment-là que j'ai commencé à m'intéresser à la défense des salariés, mais je crois que j'ai toujours eu en moi cette envie d'en découdre, et, pour la première fois, on me donnait l'occasion d'exercer mon « talent ».

J'avais promis à mes collègues d'avoir étudié chaque cas pour la réunion mensuelle suivante. La tâche était titanesque, dans quoi m'étais-je engagée ? J'arpentais les rues du village la journée, et le soir, dès le repas terminé, j'analysais et j'analysais encore. Je comptabilisais dans chaque planning les jours de repos hebdomadaires non donnés, et ce sur deux ans. Les chiffres étaient effarants ! Un inspecteur du travail se délecterait du résultat, mais avant d'en arriver à ce stade, nous devions nous battre au niveau local.

*

La fameuse réunion suivante arriva. J'avais mon paquet de dossiers sous le bras, la convention collective, mes notes, j'étais prête. Notre chef de service commençait juste à prendre la parole quand je levai le doigt.

Comme une sorte de déclaration liminaire, je commençai à exposer certains soucis et demandes au nom de mes dix collègues et de moi-même : cela faisait des mois que nous souhaitions les plannings en amont, nous avions bien conscience que la requête devait remonter dans les hautes sphères mais, dans les faits, elle avait du mal à redescendre.

Et j'enchaînai, au cas par cas, en pointant les erreurs, les jours de repos non donnés, etc.

La réaction de la chef de service fut laconique :

— Faites un courrier à la direction !

La réunion se poursuivit dans une ambiance tendue. Mes collègues n'avaient pas apprécié la réponse de notre supérieure. À la fin de la séance, nous nous retrouvâmes au bar, devant la mairie, et la décision fut prise de rédiger un courrier commun. Dans les jours qui suivirent, il fut envoyé en recommandé avec accusé de réception. Nous avons toutes signé sans exception. Il n'y avait plus qu'à attendre.

N'ayant pas eu de réponse à notre courrier, nous avons réitéré nos demandes lors de la réunion de service suivante. Notre chef de secteur ne savait pas où elles en étaient, et les décisions des hautes sphères, elle ne les connaissait pas… La colère montait, doucement mais sûrement. Nous ne pouvions pas rester à attendre, l'esclavagisme avait assez duré. Si la montagne ne venait pas à nous, alors nous irions à elle.

Nous avons donc rédigé une seconde lettre, précisant que, si nous restions sans réponse sous quinze jours, nous serions dans l'obligation d'informer les autorités compétentes.

Bizarrement, un courrier arriva sous huitaine, nous indiquant que la directrice se déplacerait lors de la prochaine réunion et nous proposerait un accord. C'était aussi simple que ça ? Nous n'étions pas dupes : si nos employeurs souhaitaient nous faire une proposition sans même discuter, c'était que notre dossier dérangeait et qu'il fallait éteindre le feu avant qu'il ne se propage. Si tous les salariés de l'association, soit 1 500 personnes, étaient concernés, beaucoup d'argent avait dû être économisé. Et pourquoi personne ne s'était-il intéressé à ce problème avant moi, notamment les délégués du personnel ? Que de zones d'ombre à explorer… Je demanderais à voir le cahier des délégués du personnel afin de savoir si d'autres collègues rencontraient des problèmes. Cela me donnerait déjà un premier baromètre de la situation. L'association existe depuis quarante ans, le cahier doit être aussi épais qu'un annuaire téléphonique, enfin, je l'imaginais.

J'envoyai donc le soir même un mail à ma directrice pour lui demander s'il était possible de consulter le cahier des DP lors de sa venue, nous avions des questions à y apposer. Elle me répondit par l'affirmative.

Entre l'argent public qui était détourné pour des enfants d'allocataires sous couvert de l'association, les formations qu'elle ne dispensait pas, ce redressement URSSAF que les employés payaient en ne bénéficiant plus de leurs 100 euros annuels en chèques cadeaux, le code du travail qui était largement oublié, la convention collective qui était dans leur esprit une notion bien vague, nos employeurs cumulaient les manquements.

Lors de la réunion suivante, la directrice était bien présente. Le cahier des délégués du personnel aussi. Mais quand je l'ouvris, surprise : il n'y avait pratiquement rien d'inscrit à l'intérieur. Quatre pages noircies, des demandes qui dataient de dix ans… Aucun salarié n'avait jamais rien réclamé ? J'inscrivis nos questions sur le cahier presque vierge et la directrice commença son discours. Elle proposa de nous payer les jours de repos non pris. Aucune négociation ; dans sa grande bonté, l'association préférait nous les payer que de nous les faire récupérer. Elle annonça parallèlement qu'elle n'était pas gestionnaire des paies, et que tout allait être régularisé. Les filles étaient contentes, mais je restais dubitative. Pourquoi était-ce si simple ? Nous avions poireauté deux mois et, par un coup de baguette magique, tout allait rentrer dans l'ordre ?

Au culot, et comme il me manquait quelques plannings, je demandai à la directrice si, dans le protocole de proposition qui allait nous être fait, les plannings seraient ajoutés, afin de vérifier le bon calcul des jours de congé. Elle répondit par l'affirmative.

Il n'y avait plus qu'à attendre…

9

Du Simenon

J'intervenais chez une dame, dont je tairai le nom par respect pour cette femme âgée qui mourut dans des conditions indignes. Appelons-la Solange. Son état de santé s'était largement dégradé, et la fin de vie approchait à grands pas. Elle souhaitait mourir chez elle, mais je doute qu'elle ait imaginé la façon dont cela se passerait. Elle ne pouvait plus vraiment manger ni s'hydrater, et une perfusion lui avait été posée. Très vite, les enfants décidèrent qu'il ne fallait pas s'acharner. Mais de quel acharnement s'agissait-il ? Elle n'avait pas été hospitalisée de force, sa volonté était respectée, elle ne subissait aucun traitement si ce n'était le minimum pour vivre.

Un jour, la perfusion fut donc retirée. Les patchs de morphine s'entassaient presque les uns sur les autres. Tombée dans un coma profond, Solange résistait, au grand dam de ses enfants dont certains commençaient déjà à se disputer tel ou tel meuble. Je ne suis pas là pour m'interposer dans les familles, mais comment ne pas être amère devant un tel comportement ?

Cctte femme allait mourir de déshydratation, sous hautes doses de morphine ; le corps médical en avait décidé ainsi, c'était la fin, quelques jours de plus ou de moins ne changeraient pas la finalité de l'histoire.

J'cus même la désagréable surprise de trouver sur la commode le certificat de décès déjà signé, auquel il ne manquait plus que la date et l'heure. Et pendant que ces imbéciles continuaient leur inventaire, je voyais la dame qui s'éteignait. Je m'étais occupée d'elle quelque temps, et j'étais avec elle dans cette chambre pour ne pas la laisser partir seule.

Je commençais à me demander si j'allais continuer ce métier. J'assistais à une euthanasie en bonne et due forme ! Mais qui s'interrogerait sur le décès de cette vieille femme malade dans un petit village au fin fond de la Camargue ? Qui se poserait des questions ? Personne !

Le certificat de décès stipulait : « mort naturelle ».

Mort naturelle ? La déshydratation entraîne la mort mais n'est en rien naturelle ! Et les patchs de morphine collés un peu partout sur son corps faisaient plutôt penser à une overdose. Mais comme les enfants ne demanderaient pas d'autopsie, l'affaire était d'ores et déjà pliée.

Des mots comme « assassinat » agressaient mes pensées, et je ne pouvais rien faire. Du moins pour le moment. Chaque chose en son temps.

D'un seul coup, il y eut un bruit terrible dans la maison. Je sortis de la chambre pour voir ce qu'il se passait. Les enfants retournaient les tiroirs à la recherche d'une copie du testament. Le paroxysme de l'horreur me sembla être atteint. Ils avaient étalé tous les papiers par terre, afin de mettre la main sur le document avant que d'autres membres de la famille n'arrivent.

Ils avaient fouillé toute la maison et n'avaient rien trouvé. Ils invectivaient leur mère, supputaient le partage inégal qu'elle avait dû faire, « la mégère », comme ils la nommaient à cet instant précis.

Je voyais l'argenterie disparaître, les bijoux s'envoler, les meubles être partagés… Et elle s'enfonçait… Je pensai qu'elle serait peut-être finalement mieux où elle irait.

*

Quand Solange est décédée, dans l'heure qui suivit, les présents avaient déménagé la moitié de la maison. Un camion stationnait dans la cour. Il avait été rempli puis était parti. Dans quelle direction ? Je l'ignorais. Solange s'en était allée, et ses meubles aussi.

Il était temps pour moi de quitter ces lieux où je ne reviendrais jamais, puisque le décès d'un allocataire signifie la clôture immédiate du dossier. Je lui dis au revoir, je présentai mes condoléances aux charognards et je sortis sans demander mon reste, après avoir refusé de faire la toilette mortuaire de cette dame, que les enfants m'avaient demandée afin d'économiser sur l'acte du thanatopracteur…

Arrivée sur la place du marché, je me suis assise et j'ai pleuré. Le spectacle auquel j'avais assisté m'avait fait prendre conscience de ce que pouvait être une famille dans certains cas. Mes illusions s'étaient envolées, mes rêves étaient devenus des cauchemars ; allais-je continuer ce métier ? Allais-je accepter d'être la spectatrice impuissante de l'amoralité ? Mémé, où sont toutes ces valeurs que tu m'as enseignées ?

*

Dix minutes s'étaient écoulées. Dix minutes de questions sans réponses, dix minutes durant lesquelles j'étais restée tétanisée par la tristesse. Je suis évidemment pour que nos aînés puissent mourir chez eux, mais pas dans ces conditions.

« Respire, reprends-toi. »

Je pris mon téléphone ; il fallait que je vomisse mon mal-être. J'appelai ma responsable de secteur :

— Oui, Anne-Sophie ?

— Mme X est décédée, elle a été assassinée.

— Assassinée ? Mais comment ça, assassinée ? Allons, Anne-Sophie…

— Comment appelez-vous le fait de laisser mourir quelqu'un de soif et en surdose de morphine ? Et que pensez-vous des enfants qui vident la maison le jour même et d'un certificat de décès signé alors que la personne est toujours en vie ?

— Anne-Sophie, vous êtes bouleversée, mais cela ne nous regarde pas…

— Mais ne pourrions-nous pas, je ne sais pas, porter plainte, au titre de citoyen ?

— Non, Anne-Sophie, nous ne nous mêlerons pas de cette histoire, ce serait votre parole contre celle de la famille.

— Vous plaisantez ?

— Pas du tout, Anne-Sophie, c'est ainsi, le dossier est clos.

— Le dossier est clos ? Où est passée votre humanité ?

— Bon, écoutez, Anne-Sophie, j'ai des appels en attente, je vous ai dit que nous ne nous mêlerions pas de cette histoire. Rentrez chez vous, maintenant.

Elle raccrocha sans même un au revoir. Je venais de prendre une nouvelle claque. Je suis restée assise encore un moment sur le banc, j'ignore combien de temps exactement, quand mon téléphone a sonné. Ma chef de service. Elle tombait à point nommé.

— Anne-Sophie, vous pouvez m'expliquer pourquoi vous êtes en retard chez Louise ?

— Excusez-moi, mais êtes-vous au courant ?

— De quoi ?

— De ce que je viens de vivre…

— Votre responsable de secteur m'a appris le décès de Mme X. C'est un dossier clos, désormais, et je vous saurais gré de vous rendre à votre prochaine intervention dans les plus brefs délais.

— Vous me sauriez gré ? À mon tour, je vous saurais gré de bien vouloir respecter mon deuil et mon humanité ! Ah ! Mais que suis-je bête, j'oubliais, vous, c'est plutôt chiffres, dossiers…

— Je ne vous permets pas de me parler ainsi, je suis votre supérieure !

— Supérieure ou non, je continuerai à dire ce que j'ai à dire, mais si vous trouvez que je dépasse les bornes, licenciez-moi pour insubordination ! Au moins, je n'aurai plus à subir ce que j'ai subi ce matin. Vous me rendriez un grand service !

— Anne-Sophie, vous rendez-vous à votre intervention ?

— Oui, bien sûr… Bonne journée, madame.

Je raccrochai. Amère, en colère. Abasourdie par tant d'indifférence, de cynisme. Mais cette conversation aurait au moins servi à une chose : me persuader de continuer à apporter ce que je pouvais à mes allocataires – du moins tant qu'ils seraient vivants.

10

Charles

Je me rendais rarement chez Charles, mais j'aimais beaucoup ce vieux monsieur atteint de la maladie d'Alzheimer. Il était veuf, grand, et portait des lunettes rafistolées avec du ruban adhésif. Il ne s'était jamais remis de la mort de son épouse. Un cancer du poumon lui avait enlevé son âme sœur trop tôt. Il en parlait régulièrement, les larmes aux yeux. Ses souvenirs concernant sa femme étaient intacts ; en revanche, il ne se rappelait plus son métier…

Dans sa chambre, l'urne funéraire contenant les cendres de sa bien-aimée était posée sur la table de chevet. Probablement une façon pour lui de continuer de dormir à ses côtés. C'était quant à moi mon premier face-à-face avec une urne, et pénétrer dans cette chambre, pour faire le lit et le ménage, m'avait mise mal à l'aise au début. Et puis, malheureusement je dirais, on s'habitue à l'objet, qui devient à la longue un bibelot comme un autre.

Ce n'est qu'en écrivant ces lignes, en me remémorant la chambre, les rideaux bleus, le grand lit, que je me rends compte que ce n'était finalement pas un objet comme un autre. *Elle* était à l'intérieur. Sa femme, sa moitié, son amour. Cette urne que j'essuyais à chacun de mes passages, cette photo que j'époussetais machinalement, cette rose éternelle sur laquelle je soufflais pour enlever la poussière et ces immortelles qui me taquinaient à ne jamais vouloir rester posées sur cette table, je m'y étais habituée. Et ce sentiment m'est insupportable aujourd'hui. On fait par réflexe, sans y penser, parce que c'est comme ça, et on oublie toute la symbolique et l'importance de l'objet. J'ai soudain la désagréable sensation de lui avoir manqué de respect.

*

Les souvenirs immédiats de Charles passaient comme des nuages dans le ciel par grand mistral, mais les plus anciens persistaient. Il ne se souvenait jamais de mon nom, il m'appelait « ma grande ». Mes interventions chez lui se cantonnaient à la préparation des repas. Charles passait son temps devant la télévision, devant France 2 plus exactement, puisqu'il ne savait plus comment changer de chaîne. Il oubliait même parfois qu'il avait une chambre et dormait la nuit sur le grand canapé, sans même s'être mis en pyjama. Et le lendemain matin, je le trouvais comme je l'avais laissé la veille au soir.

Charles était incapable de me dire si les infirmières venaient bien quotidiennement pour sa toilette, et j'avoue que je restais quelquefois dubitative quant à leur passage…

Un matin, je pris le cahier de liaison et y lus : « Douché ce jour. » Je me tournai vers Charles : il portait les mêmes vêtements que la veille, sa barbe n'avait pas été rasée, ses cheveux étaient toujours aussi gras. J'étais perplexe.

Mais il était l'heure de faire manger Charles, qui trépignait d'impatience. Le foyer-restaurant, organisme ou partenariat public-privé qui permettait aux personnes âgées de manger pour 6 euros, avait comme d'habitude rangé les barquettes du repas dans le réfrigérateur du garage ; je n'avais plus qu'à les lui faire réchauffer. Je l'associai à la mise du couvert ; Charles était heureux, riait, me parlait. Il chantonna aussi, Ray Ventura et ses Collégiens. Il dansa même ! Il était si beau et si heureux… Je l'appelais Charles le bienheureux.

Les tracas de la vie quotidienne glissaient sur lui. Douche ou pas douche, peu lui importait ; de toute façon, il ne se souvenait plus. Moi, en revanche, la question me taraudait. Je ne voulais pas accuser qui que ce soit, mais j'avais des doutes. Afin d'en avoir le cœur net, ce jour-là, je m'enquis de l'humidité des serviettes et des gants dans la salle de bains.

J'y trouvai deux serviettes sèches comme du bambou, et deux gants de toilette à la limite de la lyophilisation. Je cherchai dans la panière de linge sale au cas où les serviettes y auraient été jetées. Rien. Et mon opinion fut faite lorsque je constatai que la douche aussi était sèche.

Quand je descendis au rez-de-chaussée, je ne pus m'empêcher d'apposer un commentaire après le « Douché ce jour » : « Douché, parfait, l'eau était sèche probablement ! »

Je n'avais pas l'autorisation de laver Charles, ni aucun autre allocataire d'ailleurs, sous peine de poursuites pénales si jamais un accident arrivait ; c'était le rôle des infirmières. Je savais que mon commentaire déplairait fortement, mais qu'une infirmière se fasse payer un acte qu'elle n'effectuait pas me déplaisait tout autant. Il faut savoir que, plus on fait de toilettes, plus on gagne. Si vous y ajoutez le forfait kilométrique et le déplacement, c'est de l'argent facilement gagné.

C'était la première fois que j'étais confrontée à ce genre d'abus. La Sécurité sociale ne contrôlant pas si les actes sont effectués, tout est facturable. Toujours est-il que Charles n'avait pas eu sa toilette.

*

Charles n'avait pas d'enfant, c'était l'un de ses plus grands regrets. Il ne lui restait qu'un très vague cousin très éloigné et qui vivait loin, il était donc sous tutelle. Un juge gérait ses comptes, et nous devions passer par lui pour engager la moindre dépense, comme acheter des vêtements. Toutes les semaines, un délégué apportait le minimum syndical afin que nous puissions faire des courses pour le repas du soir qui était à la charge de Charles. Pour tenir le mois entier, aucune folie possible : nous devions choisir les produits premier prix.

La tutelle… En voilà, un mot barbare. Comment en une décision vous êtes dépossédé de votre vie. Vous n'existez plus, vous ne décidez plus, on décide pour vous. La tutelle de Charles avait été sollicitée sans son accord, sans qu'il ait pu signifier à quiconque que son esprit était toujours vif. On ne demande jamais l'avis de nos aînés lorsque la tutelle est mise en place. Les juges des tutelles sont souvent injoignables, impossible donc de faire face aux urgences. Et puis, plus un juge a de tutelles sous sa responsabilité, plus il est payé par l'État, donc plus il gagne d'argent. Mais que sait-il, ce juge, qui, je le rappelle, prendra désormais toutes les décisions inhérentes à la vie quotidienne de Charles, des besoins, des habitudes, des envies de ce dernier, alors qu'il ne se base que sur des diagnostics et ne se déplace jamais ?

Nos demandes de nouveaux vêtements pour Charles, qui avait grossi, de chaussettes neuves, parce que les anciennes étaient usées jusqu'à la trame, restaient lettre morte, tout comme l'intervention d'un plombier. Et lorsque Charles eut besoin d'une bonne pédicure, nous avons dû la payer avec l'argent de vie du mois, ce qui réduisit le budget nourriture !

Charles était un oublié, là-bas aussi, sûrement, un numéro de dossier.

*

Nous approchions de Noël, et j'avais envisagé de passer la soirée du 24 décembre avec lui. Cela sortait largement du champ de mes activités et allait à l'encontre du recul professionnel prôné par nos supérieurs. Mais ma décision était prise : j'intervenais justement chez lui ce soir-là, il serait ainsi moins seul. Charles aimait Noël ; nous avions décoré ensemble la maison. Comme un enfant qui attend la venue du Père Noël, il chantait Tino Rossi. Il me demandait sans cesse comment étaient les illuminations dans le village ; je lui proposai donc d'aller les voir par lui-même. Charles n'avait plus l'habitude de sortir, de peur de se perdre, et restait enfermé trois cent soixante-cinq jours par an chez lui. Très enthousiaste et rassuré par ma présence à ses côtés, il s'habilla, monta dans ma voiture, et nous prîmes la direction du village.

Ses yeux brillaient à chaque guirlande lumineuse. Des « Oh, c'est beau ! » se firent entendre tout le long de la balade.

Nous sommes passés à trois reprises devant les mêmes décorations, et Charles s'émerveillait de la même manière chaque fois, ayant oublié qu'il les avait déjà vues. Mais qu'importe, il était heureux.

Mon mari, mes enfants et moi avons ensuite passé la soirée du 24 en compagnie de Charles, chez lui. Nous avons préparé le repas ensemble : Charles a tartiné les toasts, les enfants ont décoré la table, mon époux et moi avons fait réchauffer ce qui avait été préparé à la maison. Nous avons écouté des chants de Noël, nous avons mangé, ri, chanté ; nous avons passé un réveillon différent, mais marquant. Charles s'en souviendrait-il ? Personne n'en savait rien, mais ce soir, il riait, les yeux encore éblouis par le spectacle des décorations.

Les heures avançaient vite, et il allait falloir rentrer. J'avais peur que Charles vive mal notre départ. Nous avons rangé ensemble, et nous avons expliqué à Charles que nous devions rentrer chez nous. Il en avait bien conscience. Nous avons eu droit à une bise, mes enfants lui ont fait un câlin.

Il est resté sur le pas de la porte quand nous sommes montés en voiture. Il nous a recommandé d'être prudents sur la route, un peu comme si nous faisions partie de sa famille, il nous a regardés un instant et a fermé sa porte à clef. C'était une habitude qu'il n'oubliait pas. Qu'a-t-il fait ensuite, je l'ignore, mais ma famille et moi étions un peu tristes de le laisser.

*

Cette décision de passer du temps avec lui sortait largement du cadre professionnel ; je le savais, ma famille aussi. Mais le plus important était que nous ayons apporté du bonheur à ce vieux monsieur seul. Il ne m'avait pas fallu beaucoup argumenter auprès de mon mari et de mes enfants pour les convaincre de m'accompagner dans ce projet. Ils me connaissent, et si je leur demande d'être là pour une personne âgée, ils le seront. Sans hésitation.

Ce soir-là, les enfants ont aussi pu appréhender la difficulté de vieillir, de vivre avec la maladie, le handicap. Ils ont compris quelle chance ils avaient eue de vivre avec une grand-mère en pleine forme et avec toute sa tête. Je suis persuadée que c'est en changeant le regard des générations futures sur la vieillesse que les choses avanceront, que nous deviendrons solidaires les uns des autres. Noël ne se résume pas à une fête commerciale, c'est aussi une occasion de se retrouver en famille dans la joie et le partage. Et ce soir-là, nous étions la famille de Charles.

*

Je pensais qu'il ne se souviendrait pas de ce 24 décembre. Je me trompais : chaque fois que je retournais chez lui, Charles me disait :

— Dis, tu te souviens du Noël qu'on a fait ensemble ? Ils étaient gentils, les gosses. On a bien ri, dis, tu t'en souviens ?

— Oui, Charles, je m'en souviens.

Dix minutes plus tard :

— Dis, tu te souviens du Noël qu'on a fait ensemble ? Ils étaient gentils, les gosses. On a bien ri, on a bien mangé, tu t'en souviens ?

Avec le sourire, je répondais chaque fois la même chose :

— Oui, Charles, je m'en souviens…

Charles était un homme gentil qui oubliait, mais finalement, pas tant que cela.

11

Neuf mois plus tard

Depuis que nous avions pointé les dysfonctionnements et les manquements de l'association envers le code du travail, nous n'avions pas encore lu la moindre ligne de protocole d'accord pour régulariser les situations. Entre-temps, j'avais été désignée responsable de section syndicale et, tout auréolée de ce nouveau statut, j'imaginais bien faire avancer les débats. Je m'étais engagée auprès de mes collègues à mener ce dossier jusqu'au bout, et je les voyais perdre patience. Il fallait maintenant prendre le taureau par les cornes.

Les mails que j'envoyais ne recevaient plus de réponse, si ce n'est un laconique « On s'en occupe ». J'avais donc décidé qu'il serait maintenant judicieux de monter d'un cran : si la directrice ne voulait pas entendre raison, j'allais demander que le président de l'association prenne une décision.

Voici le courrier que j'adressai à la direction :

« Madame la directrice,

« Depuis maintenant neuf mois, nous en sommes

toujours au même point concernant les infractions que vous avez commises au regard de la convention collective et du code du travail. Par la présente, le collectif des auxiliaires de vie vous demande instamment lors de la prochaine réunion mensuelle la présence de notre président afin de débattre sur les régularisations que vous avez à faire en vertu des articles tant… et tant… du code du travail et de la convention collective. Sans réponse favorable de votre part sous quarante-huit heures, nous nous verrons dans l'obligation de porter collectivement cette affaire devant le conseil des prud'hommes, et il nous semble que, dans l'intérêt de tous, ce n'est pas souhaitable.

« Recevez, Madame la directrice, mes sincères salutations. »

Le lendemain en ouvrant ma boîte mail, je découvris ceci :

« Madame,

« J'ai pris note de votre demande et sachez que notre président sera donc présent à la prochaine réunion mensuelle qui se tiendra le 28 dans les locaux de la mairie comme habituellement.

« Veuillez agréer mes respectueuses salutations. »

Nous avions enfin une réponse constructive. Ce mail redonna un peu de force aux filles qui espéraient voir enfin le bout du tunnel.

*

Le jour de la grande réunion arriva, et pour une fois nous étions toutes à l'heure. Un vieux monsieur aux cheveux gris et en costume, la directrice et notre chef de service étaient présents. L'homme s'assit en bout de table et prit la parole. Il commença à nous expliquer la genèse de l'association, nous rappelant au passage que sa dernière visite dans le village remontait à quarante ans en arrière, quand il avait créé l'association et qu'il était venu proposer ses services à la mairie. L'homme était gentil ; nous avions le sentiment qu'il venait d'être informé des problèmes qui agitaient notre groupe. Il s'offusqua des manquements de sa propre association, lui qui avait été partie prenante dans la mise en place de la convention collective.

Nous attendions sagement qu'il termine son discours et ses compliments sur notre travail, insistant sur l'importance de notre métier dans l'accompagnement des personnes âgées restées à leur domicile. Il ne parla évidemment pas du tarif horaire qu'il facturait aux mêmes personnes âgées ; bien sûr, nos salaires étaient trop bas, mais c'était le salaire conventionnel, et il ne pouvait y déroger.

En réalité, rien ne l'empêchait de mieux payer ses employés, me dis-je en moi-même. Mais ce discours, nous le connaissions déjà par cœur.

Au bout d'une heure, la directrice sortit de son sac un paquet de dossiers. Chacune de nous reçut un protocole d'accord à signer, dans lequel la direction s'était chargée de compter les jours de repos non pris et de calculer ainsi le manque à gagner. Nous n'aurions qu'une année de rétroactivité, nous en avions demandé deux. Mais au moins le dossier avançait. Nous avons chacune lu ce qui était énoncé, et chacune de nous marqua un temps d'arrêt sur l'article suivant :

Article 6 – Clause de confidentialité

Madame Untel, en signant le présent protocole, s'engage à respecter une clause de confidentialité du présent accord. Dans le cas où Madame Untel ne saurait respecter cette clause, l'association se donne le droit de poursuivre la salariée devant le conseil des prud'hommes.

Nos employeurs nous demandaient noir sur blanc de ne pas divulguer cet accord. Pourquoi ? Très vite, nous avons compris que, si nous ébruitions ce que nous avions obtenu, d'autres collègues exigeraient le même traitement. Si le procédé existait chez nous, il devait en être de même à Marseille, par exemple. Or, dans une ville de cette taille, ce n'était pas dix salariés qui pouvaient potentiellement demander réparation, mais peut-être mille. Les finances de l'association en prendraient un coup.

Nous avons collectivement refusé de signer le protocole avec cette clause de confidentialité. L'union faisant la force, la direction accepta de supprimer l'article. Elle nous pressait de signer ; répétant que c'était la meilleure offre qu'elle pouvait nous faire. Nous avions tant le sentiment qu'on cherchait à acheter notre silence qu'aucune de nous n'avait l'intention de parapher le document sur un coin de table. Ils nous avaient fait attendre neuf mois, nous n'étions plus à quelques jours près.

Nous avons signifié à la direction que nous allions d'abord vérifier le comptage, puisque tous les plannings étaient agrafés au document. Notre chef de service avait subitement perdu l'assurance et la hauteur que nous lui connaissions. Une fois la réunion terminée, comme à notre habitude, nous nous sommes retrouvées au troquet d'en face et avons acté que je relirais nos protocoles pour traquer d'éventuelles erreurs. Je n'en trouvai au final que peu, que je corrigeai sur chaque document. J'appelai ensuite toutes mes collègues pour que chacune vienne récupérer son dossier le lendemain à la maison. Pour fêter notre victoire, j'avais mis au frais une bouteille de rosé et préparé quelques gâteaux.

Le lendemain soir, toutes étaient présentes, et toutes savaient exactement combien elles auraient en plus sur leur paie ce mois-là. Mathilde avait retrouvé ses 10 % de précarité sur tous ses contrats à durée déterminée, Cathy avait récupéré son 1er mai, et tout était rentré dans l'ordre. Elles n'y avaient pas forcément toutes cru au départ, mais nous avions gagné. Juste parce que l'enquiquineuse que j'étais avait décidé de plonger son nez dans les plannings. L'attente avait duré neuf mois, mais nous y étions parvenues car nous avions été solidaires.

Cependant, notre combat avait laissé des traces chez la partie adverse. La direction avait précisément compris que nous étions soudées et instaura dorénavant que les réunions mensuelles ne seraient plus groupées, mais par deux. Nous avions désormais chacune des heures de passage. Ils ne parvinrent cependant pas à nous diviser : seule, par deux ou en groupe, nous faisions bloc. Notre chef de service se lassa quand elle se rendit compte que les réunions par deux prenaient beaucoup plus de temps qu'en groupe. Finalement, l'ancienne méthode fut réintroduite, avec une modification de taille : à chaque réunion, maintenant, sans même le demander, le cahier des délégués du personnel était posé sur la table. Au cas où nous aurions à y poser une question.

Comme quoi, lorsque le combat est juste, il ne faut jamais abandonner.

12

Mensonge d'État

Cela faisait maintenant trois ans que j'exerçais comme auxiliaire de vie. J'en avais vu, vécu, des absurdités. Je voyais mes collègues dépérir, leurs salaires ne leur permettant pas de vivre décemment. Certes, le Sud est un lieu où le soleil se paie cher, mais j'avais rencontré des aides à domicile qui venaient de toute la France, et leur pouvoir d'achat était aussi squelettique que le nôtre. Les entreprises ou les associations pour lesquelles elles travaillaient les rémunéraient au lance-pierre. Les burn-out et les accidents de travail étaient fréquents chez les filles de notre village, et certaines, dont l'âge avançait, se fatiguaient.

Depuis longtemps, l'État souhaite favoriser le maintien au domicile des personnes âgées. Cette solution peut être envisageable pour nos aînés, mais encore faut-il que les moyens financiers adéquats soient alloués. Je dirais que nous ne maintenons pas nos personnes âgées au domicile, nous les soutenons avec le peu de moyens mis à notre disposition. J'entends par là que, si l'État n'augmente pas le montant des allocations personnalisées d'autonomie, le reste à charge pour nos aînés entame de façon insupportable le montant de leur retraite.

Pour mesurer le taux de dépendance, les professionnels de la gérontologie ont établi une grille, dite AGGIR (Autonomie, Gérontologie, Groupes Iso-Ressources), qui détermine des groupes GIR (Groupes Iso-Ressources). Encore une histoire de cases dans lesquelles il faut entrer… Suivant le taux de dépendance déterminé par cette grille, l'État vous alloue une somme qui vous permet de bénéficier d'un certain nombre d'heures de présence au domicile en passant par une association évidemment agréée par le conseil général. Voilà pour la théorie. La pratique est tout autre.

Reprenons le cas de Georgette. En étant reconnue comme appartenant au GIR 1, c'est-à-dire le groupe le plus dépendant, l'État lui octroyait généreusement une somme qui permettait en tout et pour tout sur le mois 60 heures de présence. 60 heures équivalent à environ deux heures par jour, puisque Georgette avait besoin d'une présence quotidienne. Comment voulez-vous prendre correctement soin de quelqu'un de très dépendant en n'étant présent que deux heures par jour ? Il faut bien comprendre que nos aînés sont seuls quand les aides à domicile ne sont pas là. Totalement seuls.

Georgette représentait un temps plein à elle seule, soit 151,67 heures ; elle devait donc supporter à sa charge 151,67 heures moins les 60 heures de l'État, soit 91,67 heures ; l'heure en semaine étant facturée plus de 20 euros, le montant mensuel qu'elle payait à l'association pour laquelle je travaillais était donc déjà très élevé. Et je ne parle même pas du tarif horaire des dimanches et jours fériés : il montait à 33 euros. Donc, si elle n'avait pas eu les moyens de payer, elle n'aurait eu aucune aide à domicile ces jours-là. Ce qui signifie même pas de repas !

Continuons nos comptes : la retraite de Georgette avoisinait les 800 euros par mois. Même en ajoutant la maigre pension de réversion de son époux, la somme totale ne couvrait absolument pas les factures de l'association.

Alors nombreux sont ceux qui, pour pouvoir régler ce qu'ils doivent, cèdent ce qu'ils possèdent, toute la richesse d'une vie de travail qu'ils souhaitaient transmettre à leurs enfants et petits-enfants.

Mais quand nos aînés n'ont pas de biens, n'ont rien d'autre que leur retraite, ils sont obligés de s'en tenir à l'enveloppe. Je considère dès lors que, d'une part, l'État les abandonne et que, d'autre part, certaines associations abusent en pratiquant des tarifs d'intervention démesurés. Alors, bien sûr, les arguments sont toujours les mêmes : les employés coûtent cher, les frais de fonctionnement de l'association sont élevés… Les frais de fonctionnement sont une notion très floue et, à ce jour encore, malgré mes recherches sur le sujet, j'ai du mal à comprendre : quand je vois la voiture de notre président, les frais de bouche des cadres, les locaux situés dans les beaux quartiers de Marseille, j'ai le sentiment étrange et pénétrant qu'on nous prend pour des cons. Nous, ce sont évidemment nos aînés, mais aussi toutes les ouvrières du torchon à poussière et de l'aspirateur.

Dans notre département, les Bouches-du-Rhône, il y avait une assistante sociale pour tout le service APA (Allocation personnalisée d'autonomie) du conseil général… Une ! Elle avait pour mission de visiter nos aînés et de fixer le nombre d'heures d'intervention en fonction de la fameuse grille AGGIR. Elle aussi déplorait le manque de moyens. D'abord, il pouvait se passer des mois entre l'envoi d'un dossier et l'évaluation de l'assistante sociale, tant il y avait de demandes et trop peu de personnel pour les traiter. Ensuite, on lui demandait presque d'octroyer le strict minimum suivant la classification de la dépendance. En attendant que l'Administration tranche, la personne âgée restait seule, sans aucune aide. Il n'y avait pas de référé dans ce domaine, c'était chacun son tour, et les urgences des situations n'étaient pas prises en compte. Alors quand l'État nous serine qu'il faut garder au maximum ses aînés au domicile, nous sommes d'accord, évidemment, mais avec quels moyens ?

*

Il m'est arrivé une ou deux fois d'être le témoin de pratiques allant à l'encontre du respect de la dignité de nos aînés.

Un matin vers 7 h 30, alors que j'arrivais chez un allocataire, je croisai un homme, sacoche à la main, qui cherchait un certain M. X.

Médecin du conseil général, il passait à l'improviste pour contrôler l'état de mon bénéficiaire. Suspicion d'accointance avec le généraliste… Nos anciens sont donc pour notre collectivité de potentiels fraudeurs. Comme la Sécu qui vous contrôle parce que vous êtes en arrêt maladie, lui venait vérifier si l'état de santé était bien en adéquation avec la déclaration.

Sans aucun ménagement, le médecin commença son interrogatoire à peine entré dans la maison.

— Bonjour, je suis le docteur, je viens voir comment vous allez. Vous pouvez vous laver seul ?

— Non, voyez, j'ai du mal à me lever.

— Vous marchez pourtant avec un déambulateur, vous pouvez donc vous déplacer jusqu'à la salle de bains…

— Difficilement, docteur.

— Te, te, te ! vous pouvez marcher. Et puis, si la position debout vous fatigue, mettez une chaise devant le lavabo pour vous laver. Faut pas se laisser aller comme ça…

Voyant que les choses allaient probablement mal tourner, je pris la parole :

— Docteur, je vous assure que les quelques pas qu'il fait dans la maison avec le déambulateur l'épuisent, il ne peut ni se déplacer facilement ni se laver seul, d'ailleurs les infirmières passent une fois par jour…

— Vous, je ne vous ai rien demandé, allez donc prendre l'air.

Charmant… Son attitude confortait mes craintes : l'Administration cherchait la petite bête, et dans ce combat inégal, M. X perdrait sans aucun doute. Le médecin continua son interrogatoire :

— Levez les bras.

— Je ne peux pas faire plus haut, docteur.

— OK. L'autre.

M. X tenta tant bien que mal de soulever son bras qui semblait peser une tonne, sans grand résultat.

— C'est tout ce que je peux faire, s'excusa presque l'octogénaire.

— Allez, encore un peu, je suis sûr que vous pouvez y arriver.

— Non, docteur, j'ai mal, je ne peux vraiment pas plus…

— OK, oui, ben, c'est de l'arthrose, rien de bien surprenant à votre âge. Vous avez votre dossier médical ?

— Mon quoi ?

— Votre dossier médical. Vous devez bien avoir quelque chose ? Vous êtes malade ? Vous prenez des médicaments ?

— Docteur, je ne sais pas, je ne sais pas de quoi vous me parlez.

Je pris l'initiative de présenter l'ordonnance et le pilulier, auquel le médecin jeta brièvement un œil.

— Quel jour sommes-nous ?

— Mardi.

— Non, nous sommes jeudi. Quel mois ? Quelle année ?

— Je ne sais pas, docteur… Est-ce que je vous offre un café ?

— Non merci, j'en ai terminé. Vous aurez de mes nouvelles d'ici dix jours.

— Merci, docteur, d'être passé me voir… C'est gentil…

L'entretien avait duré en tout et pour tout quinze minutes, et le médecin sortit en claquant la porte sans même dire au revoir. J'étais outrée par le comportement de cet homme. Ce vieux monsieur avait subi un interrogatoire en règle, avait été traité sans ménagement et avait répondu comme il avait pu avec toute sa sincérité. Et quand il avait tenté d'évoquer sa vie privée, le médecin l'avait coupé net : il n'était pas là pour discuter, mais pour contrôler. Mon allocataire n'avait pas compris ce qui s'était joué sous ses yeux, il n'avait pas conscience que cet homme avait entre ses mains son avenir. Lui avait toute confiance en un médecin : quand on est âgé et que le docteur vous parle, c'est rassurant. Nos aînés ont gardé l'image du médecin de famille, qui écoute et qui est bon. Or nous étions aux antipodes du gentil praticien de campagne. Qui n'avait d'ailleurs, tout docteur qu'il était, ni pris la tension, ni sorti le moindre stéthoscope. Aucun véritable examen médical n'avait été fait, la décision serait basée uniquement sur cet interrogatoire succinct et sur les capacités de mon allocataire à se mobiliser.

Un contrôle technique sur un être humain, rien de plus.

*

En attendant que les dossiers APA soient traités, parfois j'arrivais à trouver quelques subterfuges. Dans des cas de suite d'hospitalisation, notamment. Certaines mutuelles ont un service qui permet en cas de retour au domicile d'accorder des heures d'aide. Assez peu, dans les faits : quand l'un de mes bénéficiaires est rentré chez lui suite à une fracture du col du fémur, le maximum d'heures que j'ai pu obtenir fut douze. Douze heures sur un mois… Et il avait souscrit une excellente mutuelle !

Dans ces cas-là, on espère que le dossier APA sera traité, mais là encore c'est la grande inconnue. Alors, que faire, en attendant ? Laisser cette dame ou ce monsieur seul, sans aide ni ressources ? L'État refuse de prendre en considération le caractère d'urgence de la situation. Pourtant, urgence il y a, et pas seulement dans ces situations particulières : si une demande d'aide au domicile est faite, c'est que la personne en a besoin.

Ce n'est pas un luxe qu'elle s'octroie sur le dos du contribuable, mais une question de survie.

J'en arrive à me dire que non seulement l'État ne remplit pas son devoir, mais aussi qu'il y a une non-assistance à personne en danger. Il laisse alors le champ libre aux associations d'aide à domicile qui se frottent les mains devant ce juteux marché qui leur tend les bras. Notre population est vieillissante, ce n'est pas une découverte, et aucune mesure pour anticiper l'augmentation du nombre de personnes âgées dépendantes n'a été envisagée. On s'indigne tous, dans les médias ou ailleurs, du nombre de décès pendant une canicule. Il faut malheureusement ce genre d'événement pour que nos gouvernants prennent enfin leurs responsabilités. De vagues plans vont être mis sur la table, à grand renfort d'effets d'annonce. C'est un leurre : aucun de ceux annoncés n'a été suivi d'effets. La situation devient catastrophique. Il faut agir, et vite.

*

Claude était une dame de quatre-vingts ans, veuve, qui ne pouvait plus se lever. Elle vivait donc alitée trois cent soixante-cinq jours par an. Diabétique, polypathologique. Elle avait toute sa tête et n'aspirait qu'à une chose : mourir. Quelle vie était-ce pour elle d'être allongée ainsi toute l'année ? Elle bénéficiait comme tous les autres du passage des infirmières matin et soir pour la toilette, et, entre les deux, elle baignait dans ses excréments, comme les autres, sans que cela dérange quiconque.

De plus, Claude avait une très maigre retraite ; il lui était impossible d'augmenter le nombre des heures de présence chez elle en faisant appel à une aide à domicile de l'association. Et si elle demandait l'intervention d'une aide à domicile le dimanche ou les jours fériés, les heures seraient prises sur son quota de la semaine. Claude ne bénéficiait que de deux heures et demie de présence par jour ; rogner était inconcevable, tant sa dépendance était grande.

L'intervenante venait une demi-heure le matin pour lui préparer son petit déjeuner et le lui servir, une heure le midi pour le déjeuner et une heure le soir pour le dîner. Elle devait aussi se rendre à la pharmacie pour récupérer les médicaments, s'occuper du linge, des courses… Le reste de la journée, Claude était seule, complètement seule chez elle, dans son lit. Que se passait-il si un vomissement, une diarrhée, un malaise la prenait ? C'est ce qui arriva ce jour-là. Quand je reçus son appel, il était 14 heures.

— Allô, Anne-Sophie, c'est Claude, j'ai vomi, j'ai vomi, venez m'aider…

Par chance, j'étais chez une autre allocataire pas loin de chez elle. Je lui ai demandé si je pouvais m'absenter quelques instants, et heureusement elle accepta.

Quand je suis arrivée chez Claude, il était hors de question de la laisser dans l'état où je venais de la trouver. J'entrepris donc de la déshabiller, de la laver, de refaire le lit. Je le rappelle, je n'ai pas le droit de faire une toilette. Pourtant, ce jour-là, je n'ai pas voulu attendre que les infirmières arrivent dans la toute fin d'après-midi pour que Claude soit propre.

Alors, dites-moi, monsieur le Président, où sont les moyens humains que l'État nous a promis ? Je ne tire aucune gloire à avoir aidé Claude, parce que, en l'aidant, j'avais abandonné mon allocataire, qui elle aussi avait besoin de moi. Mon employeur n'a d'ailleurs jamais été informé de mon intervention chez Claude. Il m'aurait adressé un avertissement. Et si ma bénéficiaire avait refusé que je quitte son domicile ? Elle en avait le droit, après tout, ses heures, c'étaient les siennes et non celles d'une autre. Que serait devenue Claude ?

Le maintien des personnes à domicile a ses limites, et l'État compte sur le dévouement des soignants, leur citoyenneté, leur altruisme, leur humanité, pour pallier ses manques. Nous avons tous un jour été attendris par une vieille dame à l'entrée d'un passage clouté qui hésite à s'engager, nous avons tous au moins une fois proposé notre bras pour l'aider à traverser. C'est de cela que l'État abuse, et c'est une honte.

Malgré tout, rien n'ébranlait mes convictions d'être utile, rien n'ébranlait ma vocation ; j'étais une femme de terrain. Certes, je me débattais avec un État aveugle et sourd ; certes, le bénévolat était une pathologie chronique chez moi, mais le souvenir de Mémé, qui prenait le journal ou du pain pour une dame âgée malade incapable de se déplacer, est si vif encore dans mon esprit. Je devais suivre son exemple.

Donc, souvent, je passais à la pharmacie récupérer les médicaments de plusieurs allocataires et ne serait-ce que cinq minutes chez eux pour les déposer. Ce n'étaient que cinq minutes de présence hors de mon temps de travail, mais pour eux cinq minutes précieuses durant lesquelles quelqu'un avait pensé à eux.

C'est aussi la quintessence de mon métier et la substantifique moelle de mon savoir-être.

13
Berthe

J'étais rarement en contact avec les aidants familiaux, comme nous les nommons vulgairement. Je ne l'étais que si le mari ou l'épouse du bénéficiaire se trouvait encore en vie. La plupart de mes allocataires étaient veufs ou veuves. Sauf Berthe. Elle avait encore son mari, un homme crasseux, rustre, particulièrement égoïste. Pour ajouter au portrait, il était radin, à tel point qu'il ne commandait au foyer qu'un seul repas (pour Berthe) qu'il partageait entre eux deux. Berthe ne parlait pas, ne se plaignait jamais ; elle passait ses journées dans son fauteuil roulant, seule. Parfois, il lui avait allumé la télévision, parfois non. Lui était autonome, et sa femme était comme le trophée de chasse posé sur le meuble. Je me suis souvent demandé s'il n'était pas plus attaché à ce renard empaillé qu'à son épouse.

Leur maison était grande et prenait l'eau. La chambre de Berthe avait été installée au rez-de-chaussée, lui avait gardé la grande pièce à l'étage. Je venais deux fois par semaine ; les tâches étaient claires : le lundi, je nettoyais le bas, et le vendredi, c'était l'antre de l'ogre. Je préférais mille fois le lundi, je pouvais ainsi être quelques instants aux côtés de Berthe. Et puis, l'étage était chaque vendredi aussi crasseux que la semaine précédente ; le mari avait l'habitude de ne prendre qu'un bain par semaine ; la baignoire était à décaper à l'huile de coude pour qu'elle retrouve une blancheur toute relative. Je vous passe la description des toilettes, d'autant que le monsieur ignorait à quoi servait la balayette… La chambre était sombre, les volets toujours fermés, et une puanteur tenace aux produits ménagers prenait à la gorge. J'aérais autant que possible, mais rien n'y faisait, l'odeur nauséabonde restait. Le lundi, la poubelle vomissait les changes sales, et l'odeur d'urine empestait la chambre de Berthe.

*

Ce lundi-là, quand j'arrivai à 14 heures, Berthe était couchée. Était-elle malade ? Par terre gisaient des selles, Berthe pleurait. J'allai voir son mari, visiblement affairé dans son garage.

— Alphonse, que se passe-t-il ? Pourquoi Berthe est-elle couchée, est-elle malade ?

— Non, elle m'a emmerdé à table, je l'ai foutue au lit.

— Comment ça, « foutue au lit » ?

— Elle est punie. Je l'ai empoignée, et *basta*, elle est dans son lit, qu'elle le veuille ou non.

— Mais Alphonse, elle souhaitait peut-être aller aux toilettes, il y a des selles partout dans la chambre par terre…

— Ce n'est pas mon problème, elle n'a qu'à pas m'emmerder. Toute ma vie, elle m'a fait chier avec ses dépressions ! Et puis t'es bien là pour nettoyer, non ? Alors va faire ton travail et ne me fais pas chier.

Je retournai dans la chambre de Berthe. Elle avait les doigts et les ongles pleins de selles. Les draps étaient maculés d'excréments. Pour être un minimum au propre, elle les avait balancées par-dessus son lit. L'état de cette pauvre femme me souleva le cœur. Même si je savais que son mari allait me passer un savon, je décidai de la lever et de la nettoyer. Quand je la soulevai, je vis qu'elle baignait dans ses urines. Elle grelottait. La priorité était de la laver et de changer ses vêtements. Et s'il râlait, je lui dirais tout le bien que je pensais de sa façon de traiter son épouse, au risque d'être recadrée par mes employeurs. Le « on ne se mêle pas de la vie privée de nos bénéficiaires », à ce moment précis, était le cadet de mes soucis.

Laisser Berthe dans l'état dans lequel je l'avais trouvée aurait été pour moi de la non-assistance à personne en danger. Or il fallait se rendre à l'évidence : Berthe était vraiment en danger avec son bougre de mari.

Pourtant, je savais qu'elle l'avait épaulé durant toute sa vie ; elle avait travaillé sans compter ses heures à la boutique qu'il tenait, lui avait fait quatre enfants. Mais évidemment, il n'avait pas dû la déclarer, et elle touchait une retraite à l'image de son corps. Squelettique.

Seul le chien avait grâce aux yeux de cet homme, chien qui par ailleurs pissait allégrement partout sans être puni, lui.

Je m'interrogeais souvent sur la bonne façon de procéder avec Berthe. Devrais-je rédiger un certificat d'aggravation pour qu'elle bénéficie de plus d'heures de présence ? Mais à qui serviraient-elles, au final ? Alphonse voyait les aides à domicile comme ses femmes de ménage à lui. Quand il décidait que nous devions balayer la cour, il fallait s'exécuter, et rapidement. Pourtant, Berthe ne voyait jamais la cour, personne ne l'y emmenait.

J'avais donc fait toute la toilette de Berthe ; elle était au propre, elle souriait. Nos aînés aphasiques n'ont plus la capacité de nous remercier, leurs mercis se lisent dans leurs regards. Je me souviendrai du sien longtemps. Je l'emmenai dans le salon, puis j'allai nettoyer sa chambre. Ouvrir d'abord les volets, aérer, ramasser les selles par terre, sortir la poubelle, défaire le lit et lui mettre de nouveaux draps. J'ai astiqué la chambre de Berthe de fond en comble. Ça sentait bon le propre. J'ai poursuivi par la cuisine où Alphonse avait abusé de la friture… Je trouvai aussi deux flaques d'urine laissées par le chien contre les chaises. J'avais par dépit laissé tomber le nettoyage de la hotte, qui méritait plus d'aller directement à la déchetterie que d'être astiquée. Je continuai le ménage dans le couloir, et je terminai par le salon. Berthe était là, telle que je l'avais laissée, à moitié endormie. Elle était si pâle, si frêle… Je vis qu'elle avait froid. J'ajoutai donc un châle sur ses épaules. Mais comment ne pas avoir froid, quand on passe la majeure partie de son temps assise dans un fauteuil roulant ? Elle était seule, et pourtant elle avait encore son mari.

J'étais en train de récurer quand Alphonse rentra :

— Qui t'a dit de la lever ?

— Alphonse, je ne pouvais pas faire autrement, vous ne pouvez pas la laisser dans un état pareil.

— Ça ne te regarde pas, pourquoi l'as-tu levée ?

— Pour nettoyer la chambre et son lit, Alphonse, d'ailleurs, voici les draps qui sont à laver ainsi que ses vêtements.

— Ça attendra, j'ai fait une machine il y a une semaine, je ne vais pas en refaire une pour ça... et puis, c'est toi qui paies la lessive et l'eau ? C'est malin, il va falloir que je lui donne un goûter, alors que si tu ne l'avais pas levée, je n'aurais pas eu à le faire !

J'étais abasourdie par tant de méchanceté. Le mari gesticulait dans tous les sens et piétinait avec ses chaussures crottées le sol encore humide après mon passage. Le chien en profita pour se soulager contre le meuble en bois. Et au milieu de ce moment ubuesque, Berthe, sans dire un mot, grelottait.

— Alphonse, je viens de nettoyer, pourriez-vous s'il vous plaît avoir la gentillesse d'attendre que le sol soit sec avant de *pataler* dedans ?

— Ton travail, c'est bien le ménage ?

— Non pas tout à fait, donc si vous souhaitez que la maison reste propre, attendez que le sol sèche, s'il vous plaît.

— Je suis chez moi, je fais ce que je veux, et puis tu repasseras derrière moi.

Je ne suis bien sûr pas repassée derrière lui. Je ne pensais qu'à Berthe.

Il arrive que nous soyons confrontées à des aidants familiaux épuisés, ce que je comprends. Ce n'était pas le cas avec Alphonse : Berthe était maltraitée par son mari. Elle avait subi toute sa vie la maltraitance conjugale, pourquoi sa pathologie aurait-elle changé quoi que ce soit ? Le plus dur dans ces moments-là, c'est lorsque la porte du domicile se referme. Que faire ? Alerter ? Mon métier, c'est aussi d'alerter. Mais je serais seule sur ce coup-là. « On ne se mêle pas des histoires de famille » était le maître mot de mes employeurs.

Sauf que je considérais que, dans ce cas précis, nous étions face à un cas flagrant de maltraitance. Alors, en mon âme et conscience, en tant que citoyenne, j'ai dénoncé. Personne n'a jamais voulu m'écouter. C'était ma parole contre la sienne. Berthe ne parlait pas, ne pouvait pas raconter, ne pouvait pas confirmer. Mon droit d'alerte s'est étouffé dans le fauteuil roulant d'une vieille dame terrorisée. Circulez, il n'y a rien à voir…

Je sus par un appel de ma chef de service qu'Alphonse l'avait contactée à mon départ pour se plaindre de mon comportement. J'avais été insolente avec lui, je devais lui présenter des excuses. Il en était hors de question ; je ne m'excuserais pas. En revanche, je continuerais à m'occuper au mieux de Berthe lors de mes interventions. J'en profitai pour demander à ma grande chef d'informer ce rustre qu'à partir de ce jour ses toilettes resteraient dans l'état dans lequel il les mettait. Je refusais désormais de récurer son antre d'ours mal léché.

14

La curatelle renforcée

Louise aimait surfer sur le Net en espérant y rencontrer l'homme de sa vie. Sa solitude sentimentale lui pesait. Elle refusait ses soixante-quatorze ans, son cancer, la perte de ses cheveux. Même si elle recommençait à sortir et à marcher dans le village, quand elle rentrait chez elle, la maison était désespérément vide. Elle n'avait trouvé que ce moyen, le badinage par Internet, pour se revaloriser. Et puis, derrière un écran, c'est toujours plus simple. Elle était abonnée à des sites comme Badoo, Meetic, et passait la majeure partie de son temps à discuter avec des hommes plus jeunes qu'elle. Sa photo de profil montrait une femme blonde et pétillante, femme qu'elle était encore dix ans avant sa maladie. Elle s'était rajeunie de quelques années, pensant qu'elle trouverait plus facilement l'âme sœur. Elle était assez discrète sur ses conversations jusqu'au jour où, tout heureuse, elle me dit :

— Ça y est, j'ai trouvé un homme qui m'aime, il va passer me voir ici.

— Merveilleux, Louise, mais depuis combien de temps le connaissez-vous ?

— Oh, cela fait un mois que nous discutons, il me dit être amoureux de moi et que nous allons vivre ensemble.

— C'est tout le bonheur que je vous souhaite, Louise…

— En revanche, il est commercial, coincé en Côte-d'Ivoire, en attendant qu'on lui redonne son passeport.

Voilà le pot aux roses… J'entrepris donc, avec toute la délicatesse possible, de mettre Louise en garde, en lui expliquant qu'il existait tout un tas de petits malfrats qui profitaient de la solitude des femmes pour leur extorquer de l'argent. Louise se vexa : son Bertrand, elle l'avait vu en webcam, il n'était pas de ceux-là, j'avais tort. Et puis, de quoi je me mêlais ? Elle était heureuse, je n'allais pas gâcher son bonheur avec mes recommandations de prudence.

Elle en était persuadée, elle vivrait avec Bertrand et ne serait plus seule.

Je n'entendis plus parler du soupirant pendant quelques semaines, et je n'osais la questionner de peur d'être rabrouée. Louise était radieuse, c'était le principal.

*

Un mardi matin, j'arrivai comme à mon habitude vers 10 heures, et je trouvai Louise prostrée, pleurant sur le canapé.

— J'ai fait une bêtise… Je ne sais pas maintenant comment je vais m'en sortir, me dit-elle.

— Que se passe-t-il ?

— Vous savez, Bertrand…

— Oui…

— Il m'a fait envoyer un chèque que j'ai mis sur mon compte bancaire, et quand j'ai vu que le chèque était encaissé, j'ai retiré l'argent et lui ai envoyé par Western Union pour qu'il récupère son passeport…

— Et ?

— Et le chèque était en fait un chèque volé, je suis à découvert de 3 000 euros. Mais comment vais-je faire ?

La colère montait en moi, tant envers Louise qui n'avait pas écouté mes recommandations qu'envers ces arnaqueurs zélés qui profitent de la détresse des femmes.

Louise avait explosé son autorisation de découvert ; donc plus moyen de payer le loyer, plus de carte bancaire, plus de chéquier, on lui coupait les vivres. Il fallait dans l'urgence trouver une parade. Je n'avais qu'une solution : appeler l'assistante sociale du conseil départemental pour analyser la situation. Même si elle répétait souvent qu'elle n'avait que peu de moyens d'agir, elle aurait probablement des solutions d'urgence. Il y avait aussi le recours au Secours populaire et autres organisations de ce type qui fourniraient le minimum alimentaire et paieraient quelques factures. Mais toutes ces solutions ne seraient que provisoires, et il lui faudrait du temps pour remonter la pente.

Système D oblige, en attendant que l'assistante sociale vienne nous proposer des recours envisageables, Louise bénéficierait donc de colis alimentaires d'urgence. Il fallait malgré tout être vigilante, son diabète ne lui permettant pas d'accepter tout et n'importe quoi.

Nous attendîmes une semaine la visite de l'assistante sociale. Il fallut expliquer de nouveau la situation dramatique dans laquelle se trouvait cette dame âgée qui, en cherchant l'âme sœur, avait été dupée par un homme peu scrupuleux. L'espoir de ne pas finir sa vie seule l'avait fait rêver, et le rêve avait viré au cauchemar.

L'assistante sociale trouva des solutions pour que Louise puisse se nourrir : dorénavant, le foyer lui servirait ses repas, et le conseil général prendrait en charge les sommes jusqu'à ce que sa situation financière s'améliore. De plus, le nombre des heures d'accompagnement fut augmenté afin qu'elle ne soit pas seule et qu'elle ne tombe pas dans une dépression qui aurait pu aggraver sa pathologie.

Il fallait aussi porter plainte, mais contre qui ? L'homme avait bien sûr usé d'une fausse identité. L'assistante sociale lui proposa de l'accompagner dans le dépôt de sa plainte, demandant ainsi qu'une protection judiciaire soit mise en place. Louise accepta. Elle ne connaissait rien à la justice et imaginait qu'un avocat la prendrait sous son aile et qu'elle serait reconnue comme victime. Elle pensait ainsi guérir du deuil de cet amour pour lequel elle avait tout donné. Son argent, sa dignité, sa sincérité.

Dans les jours qui suivirent, Louise m'indiqua qu'un médecin expert était passé la voir. Un médecin expert de quoi ?

— Ne vous alarmez pas, Anne-Sophie, il a été très gentil, il m'a demandé de raconter mon histoire et de lui sortir mon dossier médical. Nous avons bien discuté, ne vous inquiétez pas, je pense que c'est pour m'aider avec la plainte que j'ai déposée.

Son assurance ne me rassura qu'à moitié.

Au bout de trois semaines, un recommandé arriva. Quel ne fut pas le choc quand nous avons lu la lettre ! Un juge, sur rapport du médecin expert, venait d'ordonner que Louise soit mise sous curatelle renforcée. Le gentil médecin expert était en fait venu diagnostiquer non pas l'état physique de Louise, mais bien son état psychologique.

La réalité me sautait au visage : que signifiait donc cette expression barbare de « curatelle renforcée » ? Et comment un juge pouvait-il prendre une telle décision sans même convoquer la personne concernée ? Louise n'avait été entendue par personne, hormis ce médecin. Tout avait été ourdi dans son dos.

À la lecture du document, je compris peu à peu les tenants et les aboutissants de la procédure. Dorénavant, un mandataire à la protection des majeurs allait décider pour elle. Concernant Louise, c'était double peine, le juge ayant estimé que le cancer dont souffrait la vieille dame pouvait évidemment expliquer qu'elle se soit fait berner de la sorte.

Louise ne comprenait pas tout ce que lui imposait maintenant d'être sous curatelle renforcée, mais elle avait bien compris que cela ne présageait rien de bon.

*

Deux jours plus tard, une mandataire judiciaire vint à son domicile. Louise souhaita que je sois présente. J'assistai donc ma bénéficiaire comme je le pus. La sentence tomba : Louise ne pouvait plus détenir de compte bancaire, ses achats devraient désormais se faire avec l'autorisation du mandataire, qui recevrait ses relevés de compte. Louise était en liquidation judiciaire.

Elle lui avait dans sa grande bonté accordé 50 euros d'argent de vie par semaine. Mais que fait-on avec 50 euros ? Terminé, le poisson frais, les fruits et légumes du marché, les compléments alimentaires. Après d'âpres négociations, finalement, la mandataire lui octroya 80 euros d'argent de vie. Ni plus ni moins.

Il fallait qu'elle fasse avec, c'était une décision du juge, de gré ou de force elle devait accepter de ne plus avoir le libre choix de ses achats. Elle était redevenue une malade du cancer, diabétique et de surcroît perdant la boule.

Nous avions la possibilité de faire appel de cette décision, ce que Louise fit. Mais, durant un an de procédure, elle eut la sensation de n'être rien ni personne. Un an !

Ne nous méprenons pas : ces mesures sont importantes pour des situations bien spécifiques, mais, dans le cas de Louise, qui avait juste fait une bêtise, était-il nécessaire de lui faire subir cette humiliation supplémentaire ? Avait-on vraiment pris le temps de l'écouter ? Non. Une décision arbitraire avait été prise, mais combien de décisions comme celle-ci le sont chaque jour ? Combien de personnes sont mises sous curatelle renforcée, ou sous tutelle, sans même être écoutées ?

15

La réalité

Cela faisait maintenant quelques années que je m'efforçais d'apporter un accompagnement de qualité, une empathie sans bornes et même de l'amour aux aînés dont je m'occupais. J'ose les appeler mes aînés ; ce n'était évidemment pas les miens, mais je les considérais chacun comme s'ils avaient été un de mes grands-parents. Peut-être que cela fut ma première erreur. Je m'étais engagée dans cette voie en espérant changer le cours de leur vie. J'avais sûrement pour eux trop d'amour, et leur départ était un peu comme si je perdais de nouveau ma grand-mère ou mon grand-père. Je n'avais pas réussi à me protéger contre des sentiments que je n'avais pas demandés. Avais-je vraiment voulu me protéger ? Je ne sais pas, je n'avais pas vraiment lutté. Pourquoi l'aurais-je fait ?

Or la réalité me rattrapa plus vite que je ne l'aurais cru.

Cette réalité perfide qui s'insinue un peu plus chaque jour, et qui vous plombe à chaque nouvel incident.

Ma détermination était malmenée, je commençais à mesurer les limites de mon travail.

J'étais persuadée que je changerais les choses, j'avais cette conviction si ancrée en moi… Je faisais de mon mieux, mais c'était compter sans le temps qui passe et qui les emporte. C'était ne pas avoir pris conscience que j'avais les pieds et les mains liés concernant les aides de l'État. C'était sans compter sur cet employeur qui n'avait toujours pas compris que mettre en place une sectorisation nous évitait une fatigue supplémentaire. De manière insidieuse, je débutais ma descente aux enfers.

Chaque été, je troquais mon vélo et mon véhicule contre mes jambes. J'allais ainsi beaucoup plus vite entre chaque intervention, vu le nombre de touristes qui débarquaient et saturaient le réseau routier. Je perdais un temps infini à la seule caisse ouverte du seul supermarché du village, pris d'assaut par les nouveaux arrivants en villégiature. Quand on passe de deux mille cinq cents à vingt-cinq mille habitants en quelques jours, plus moyen d'être à l'heure à chaque intervention. Mes journées devenaient harassantes, je marchais sous ce soleil tête baissée, comme si je portais sur mes épaules le poids de tous les bénéficiaires dont je m'étais occupée et qui avaient disparu. Peut-être étais-je une mauvaise auxiliaire de vie sociale parce que je n'avais pas su prendre le fameux recul nécessaire ? Mais comment s'habitue-t-on à la mort ? Je n'ai jamais réussi.

On peut bien se répéter « Il ou elle a bien vécu, il ou elle avait une vie ». On se console en se convainquant qu'il était vieux ou qu'elle était vieille, et c'est dans la logique des choses qu'une personne âgée décède plutôt qu'un enfant. Certes ! Mais je ne m'y habituais pas. J'allais à chaque enterrement, j'avais moi aussi besoin de faire mon deuil, de fermer le livre de notre histoire et non le dossier. C'était ma façon de les remercier de m'avoir apporté des rires, des sourires, des savoirs, et quelquefois des larmes. Les larmes nous servent à comprendre que nous sommes humains ; quand je n'en aurai plus, c'est que je devrai changer de métier.

Un ancien qui part, c'est une histoire qui s'envole. Parfois, j'en voulais à cette vie qui n'épargne personne. J'en voulais à ces enfants qui ne venaient pas rendre visite à leurs parents, j'en voulais à la terre entière. Je rapportais chaque jour à la maison mes colères, mes peines. J'avais pourtant fait un pari avec moi-même : j'étais censée laisser de l'autre côté du portail ma journée de travail ; sauf que je n'ai jamais vraiment trouvé comment y arriver. En surface, je donnais le change, à l'intérieur, je souffrais.

*

Je souffrais de mon intervention du matin quand j'arrivais chez Claude.

— Bonjour, Claude, bien dormi ?

— Oui, je veux mourir, j'en peux plus !

Je souffrais de mon intervention chez Claude en enchaînant avec Louise.

— Bonjour, Louise, comment allez-vous ce matin ?

— Je veux mourir j'en peux plus, Anne-Sophie, de ces effets de la chimio.

Je souffrais de mon intervention chez Louise en retrouvant Robert…

— Bonjour, Robert, comment allez-vous ce matin ?

— Je veux mourir…

Je souffrais de mon intervention chez Robert en saluant Lucette.

— Bonjour, Lucette, regardez comme il fait beau aujourd'hui.

— Oh, je m'en moque, je veux mourir pour retrouver mon mari qui me manque…

Et toutes les interventions étaient du même acabit.

Alors, le soir, quand mon époux me demandait comment s'était déroulée ma journée en voyant mes yeux rougis, je répondais :

— Pas terrible…

Je m'écroulais dans ses bras, et je pleurais les larmes que j'avais su garder toute la journée en moi. J'avais essayé d'apporter à tous mes allocataires un peu de présence, d'atténuer leur solitude, mais quand nos aînés n'aspirent qu'à partir parce qu'ils sont seuls, que leur dire ? Combien de nuits n'ai-je pas dormi en pensant à eux, combien de minutes supplémentaires suis-je restée chez les uns et les autres pour sécher une larme, combien de fois me suis-je sentie si inutile, tant leur mal-être était profond ?

J'avais pendant un temps trouvé un exutoire certes bruyant mais ô combien déstressant. Je me mettais au piano, ou plutôt je tabassais chaque touche. Je passais ma colère sur Chopin, je passais mes tristesses sur Bach et je retrouvais le sourire avec la *Méthode rose*. J'oubliais l'espace d'un instant ces idées qui m'obsédaient. Quand le piano ne fut plus suffisant, je me soûlais de musique, mais cela ne dura pas longtemps non plus. J'avertissais tout le quartier que je n'allais pas bien, tant les musiques que j'écoutais étaient tristes ct pesantes.

Alors je me suis mise à écrire et à écrire encore. Écrire ma colère, écrire mes peines, écrire mes journées… Je remplissais des pages et des pages. Je vomissais mes maux, et j'en espérais guérir. Malheureusement, même l'écriture ne m'a plus suffi. Je n'avais plus de mots, pourtant mes maux persistaient.

La bouteille de rosé dans le frigo me faisait de plus en plus de l'œil. Un verre ne tue personne. C'est quand on commence à se dire qu'un deuxième verre, ce n'est pas si grave, puis qu'un troisième permettra de s'endormir que les choses se compliquent. S'enivrer pour oublier. Voilà, je l'avais trouvée, ma solution, je m'enivrais, j'oubliais. Le vin n'était qu'un placebo qui me permettait d'accepter, de rire le soir, mais surtout de passer une nuit sans être réveillée par mes aînés qui venaient me hanter.

Et, plus le temps passait, plus mes besoins en vin augmentaient. J'avalais les verres aussi vite que je le pouvais. Il fallait que ça aille vite. Je lavais mes journées avec ce rosé absorbé en trop grandes quantités. Mais j'étais propre, comme si rien ne s'était produit, mes sentiments étaient partis quand j'avais tiré la chasse d'eau.

J'étais devenue quasi alcoolique pour tenir. Je n'en avais même pas conscience. Si rien n'arrivait, je risquais de sombrer.

J'appris plus tard que nombre de mes collègues avaient trouvé le même remède à leur mal-être. Elles ne supportaient plus les atermoiements d'un employeur qui nous exploitait, et cherchaient un sens à leur métier. Quelle était la finalité de nos échanges avec nos bénéficiaires, quelle fin pour les histoires que nous écrivions avec eux ? Nous la connaissions toutes, la fin, c'était la mort et la fermeture du dossier. Est-ce que je me pardonnais de boire parce que mes collègues en faisaient autant ? Sûrement. J'étais devenue comme elles. Je n'étais pas plus forte qu'elles, je n'allais pas changer le cours des événements. Donc, de deux choses l'une : ou je démissionnais et je trouvais un autre emploi, ou je devais rentrer dans le rang et faire abstraction de mes sentiments.

Quand un de nos allocataires mourait, c'était bien plus qu'un dossier qui se fermait dans nos esprits, et nous étions seules face à nous-mêmes, sans aucune aide psychologique de notre employeur. Dans notre village, apprendre le décès d'une personne âgée dont nous nous sommes occupées, c'est passer devant la maison régulièrement parce qu'elle est sur notre chemin, et voir les volets fermés ; ce sont ces souvenirs qui reviennent, des mots échangés et la bise du matin. C'est prendre chaque jour en pleine figure notre impuissance face au temps et à l'Administration,

Nous sommes tous et toutes à la fois des éphémères et des immortelles, comme ces fleurs que nous déposons sur les tombes de nos absents.

16

Le pot-au-feu

J'ai souvent été témoin de situations tragiques chez des personnes âgées dans le besoin, et dont la dépendance était telle que les heures d'allocation personnalisée d'autonomie allouées par l'État ne suffisaient pas. Mais j'ai aussi connu des personnes âgées, dépendantes, multipathologiques, qui m'ont fait vivre l'horreur.

Je ne parle pas de ce vieux monsieur qui m'avait mise dehors *manu militari* pour trois minutes de retard, alors que j'avais accepté de remplacer la prestataire habituelle au pied levé. Je reviendrai en revanche sur le cas d'Élisabeth. Elle avait écumé tout le personnel, plus personne ne souhaitait aller chez elle. Mes collègues n'avaient pas supporté sa méchanceté ni son manque de respect pour leur travail. J'avais pensé alors qu'elles manquaient de patience. Comment pouvait-on avoir des jugements si tranchés sur les gens en faisant notre métier ? J'imaginais qu'un comportement particulier en entraînait *de facto* un autre. J'avais eu de sérieux doutes concernant le professionnalisme de mes camarades.

J'interviendrais donc chez Élisabeth. Au passage, notez que je parcourais douze kilomètres jusque chez elle, et que l'association s'arrangeait pour qu'il n'y ait pas d'interventions à suivre ; ainsi les vingt-quatre kilomètres aller-retour étaient à mes frais.

Lorsque j'arrivai chez Élisabeth pour la première fois, elle était encore couchée. La maison était minuscule, comme le sont celles des hameaux de Camargue. Au mur, des tableaux partout, j'avais la sensation d'étouffer. Elle m'interpella et me dit d'une voix désagréable :

— Ah, c'est vous, la nouvelle ! C'est mon mari qui les a tous peints. Vous connaissiez mon mari ? C'était un peintre connu.

— Non, mais racontez-moi, j'aime la peinture et les arts, je ne demande qu'à apprendre.

À peine le temps de la saluer, de me présenter, notre discussion sur l'art pictural avait commencé. Cela me convenait assez bien ; si ce sujet était un point qui nous permettrait de nous entendre, autant en profiter. La maison était crasseuse, sentait à la fois les excréments de chat et une indescriptible odeur de vieux. Les murs avaient dû être blancs à l'origine ; désormais, leur couleur oscillait entre le beige sale et le marron clair douteux. Je n'osais lever les yeux tant les toiles d'araignées au plafond étaient nombreuses.

Je me demandais bien qui était venu faire le ménage pour la dernière fois. Dans l'évier gisaient assiettes, casseroles, couverts, recouverts d'une couche de graisse qui laissait présager de l'état de la plaque chauffante. J'étais un peu abasourdie : par quel bout allais-je commencer ? Il y avait tellement à faire.

Élisabeth se leva. La petite bonne femme squelettique se déplaça avec difficulté jusqu'à la table et se laissa tomber sur la chaise de tout son maigre poids. Elle m'ordonna de lui servir son petit déjeuner. Je ne savais pas ce qu'elle souhaitait, alors elle me dit sur un ton autoritaire :

— Du café, du beurre, du pain et de la confiture, comme tout le monde. Ce n'est pas compliqué, tout de même !

Je commençais à comprendre pourquoi mes collègues ne souhaitaient plus intervenir chez elle, elle était d'une antipathie que même son visage laissait transparaître. Mais qu'à cela ne tienne, je réussirais à l'amadouer.

Je débutais le ménage de cet endroit insalubre quand elle entreprit de me questionner.

— Vous êtes mariée ? Vous avez des enfants ?

— Oui, j'ai deux enfants, et je suis mariée.

— Deux ingrats alors, et sûrement un mari qui vous trompe…

— Pardon ?

— Vous croyez qu'à mon âge, nous sommes encore naïves ? Quel âge ont vos enfants ?

— Quatorze et neuf ans.

— Garçon ? Fille ?

— Un garçon, une fille.

— Ah, le choix du roi. Et vous qu'avez-vous fait comme études ?

Je lui exposai mon curriculum vitæ quand elle me coupa la parole :

— Tiens, une qui n'est pas trop stupide, ça change !

J'étais interloquée. Elle avait une bien piètre opinion de ses auxiliaires de vie sociale qui venaient deux fois par semaine rompre sa solitude et nettoyer son capharnaüm. Je continuai à frotter en y mettant toute la vigueur possible, si bien que même l'éponge rendit l'âme. Élisabeth se leva pour aller s'asseoir dans son grand fauteuil en face de la grande télévision, prit son programme télé et se mit à en faire les mots croisés. Je l'entendais lire les définitions :

— En six lettres, interjection de dépit…

Je faillis lui crier « crotte ! », mais je préférai me taire. Je fulminais ! Le chat de la maison s'amusait visiblement à parsemer ses excréments où bon lui semblait, et je ramassais des crottes séchées partout dans l'escalier. À l'étage en mezzanine, il avait dû uriner dans un certain nombre d'endroits tant l'odeur vous prenait à la gorge. Pliée entre sol et plafond, je l'entendis m'interpeller :

— Et vos parents, que faisaient-ils ?

Après mon curriculum vitæ, c'était mon pedigree que je devais exposer. Allais-je être confirmée, comme ces chiens de race que l'on emmène à une exposition canine ? Est-ce que ma lignée allait lui seoir ? Quand je lui expliquai que mes parents étaient enseignants, ainsi que ma grand-mère, je sentis que j'avais passé d'un seul coup le premier palier. Certes, je n'étais sûrement pas à ses yeux le plus beau chien de l'exposition, mais, au moins, comme elle me le dit très calmement :

— Bon, il y a peut-être un peu d'espoir avec vous d'avoir d'autres discussions que la pluie et le beau temps. Donnez-moi s'il vous plaît le livre de Baudelaire qui est dans ma bibliothèque, enfin, si vous connaissez un peu Baudelaire.

— « Spleen et Idéal », oui, je connais.

— Et Lamartine, vous connaissez ?

— Oui, aussi…

— Quel est votre auteur préféré ?

— Je n'en ai pas, j'aime bien Pascal, Montaigne… Je dirais peut-être que j'ai une préférence pour La Fontaine.

Voilà qu'elle se lança dans une tirade :

— « Selon que vous serez puissant ou misérable, / Les jugements de cour vous rendront blanc ou noir… »

— « Les animaux malades de la peste », répondis-je du tac au tac.

— C'est cela…

Je sentais que j'entrais peu à peu dans son monde, et j'espérais qu'elle en serait plus agréable. Mais mon espoir fut de courte durée. Elle avait ce don de s'intéresser à vous pour mieux vous tacler ensuite.

— Remettez-vous au travail, au lieu de rêvasser de littérature…

Je repris mes torchons, aspirateur et balais, et continuai donc ce pour quoi finalement j'étais payée. Elle avait raison, je n'étais pas là pour parler littérature, mais bien pour nettoyer son antre puant.

Alors que je m'attardais sur les murs de la cuisine, je remarquai qu'elle avait pris l'initiative de les repeindre : en y étalant de la pâtée pour chat ! Ce ne pouvait être qu'un acte volontaire, même en ouvrant les boîtes avec violence les projections n'auraient pas fait autant de dégâts. Il fallut donc gratter. Je mis un temps infini pour essayer de rendre cette demeure à peu près propre, et encore, propre est un grand mot. Je dirais un peu moins sale. La vétusté du lieu et l'obstination d'Élisabeth à embêter ses auxiliaires de vie en le salissant volontairement rendaient le travail de ménage ô combien difficile. Au bout de deux heures, elle m'interpella de nouveau :

— Vous devez me préparer mon repas pour ce midi, je souhaite un pot-au-feu.

— Je peux vous le préparer, mais vu le temps de cuisson, il ne pourra être prêt pour votre déjeuner, il ne me reste qu'une heure d'intervention. J'aurais commencé par cela si vous me l'aviez indiqué avant, c'est dommage.

— Préparez-le, je surveillerai la cuisson, et tant que vous y êtes, jetez-vous dedans, vous ferez le lard…

Cette dernière remarque me mit hors de moi. Je faillis lui répondre que, si j'étais à ses yeux un ersatz de lard, elle aurait parfaitement tenu le rôle de l'os à moelle, mais je m'abstins.

Je pensais que, chaque mercredi et chaque samedi, j'allais devoir supporter cette méchanceté gratuite, et j'intervenais chez Élisabeth avec peu d'envie. Un de ses jeux favoris était de laisser entrer les canards, qui ne se gênaient pas pour déposer leurs colis fécaux dès que le sol était lessivé…

Pour tenter de l'attendrir, comme j'avais appris qu'elle aimait les moules crues à peine vinaigrées pour l'apéritif, je m'arrêtais régulièrement lui en prendre quelques-unes. Je me disais que peut-être mes attentions l'adouciraient, avec le temps. Au contraire : celles-ci étaient devenues un dû, et si par malheur j'oubliais les moules, elle boudait.

— Bon, puisque je n'ai pas mes moules, je ne mangerai rien. Si, tenez, donnez-moi ce bout de saucisse crue.

— Mais Élisabeth, vous n'allez pas la manger crue, je peux vous la préparer.

— Vous m'emmerdez ! Donnez-moi mon bout de saucisse.

Elle suçota son morceau de saucisse et cracha ce qu'elle ne pouvait mastiquer par terre. Après ses repas, on aurait pu nourrir une armée de cochons, entre la viande mâchouillée et les légumes bien écrasés que l'on découvrait sous la chaise.

Elle était si aigrie que même ses enfants ne venaient plus la voir depuis la mort de son mari, sous peine de repartir en larmes tant elle avait été odieuse, et tant les reproches pleuvaient.

Il est difficile de vieillir, d'autant plus quand on est seule, éloignée de la cité, et qu'on a été quelqu'un. La renommée de son époux en tant que peintre lui avait permis de rencontrer des personnes importantes, et Élisabeth essayait à sa façon de sauvegarder son statut de femme bourgeoise, de femme de… alors qu'en réalité elle était seule.

17

J'ai honte

Depuis que j'ai commencé à écrire ces pages, je fais revivre Georgette, Louise, Juan, Charles et tant d'autres ; pourtant, j'ai honte.

L'association avait un nouveau dossier à me confier. On m'envoyait toujours comme cobaye pour tester la gentillesse ou la méchanceté de nos aînés ; j'héritais donc de ce nouveau cas. C'était une demoiselle qui habitait près de chez Claude. Atteinte d'un cancer du poumon, elle avait refusé les traitements, vu son âge.

Quand j'arrivai, une grande dame m'ouvrit, le sourire aux lèvres. Son regard bleu reste encore gravé dans ma mémoire. Sa première phrase fut :

— Vous prenez un café avec moi ?

— Oui, si vous le souhaitez, merci beaucoup, je m'appelle Anne-Sophie.

— Je sais, j'ai vu que c'était vous qui veniez aujourd'hui, je suis ravie de faire votre connaissance. Après, je vous ferai visiter la maison, mais vous savez, ne vous embêtez pas trop avec le ménage, je ne salis pas beaucoup. Et puis, vous savez – que je suis bête, vous ne pouvez pas savoir ! –, je n'ai pas de famille, je préfère une présence que de vous voir frotter !

Nous avons partagé un café, et elle me raconta son histoire. Ancienne institutrice, elle me rappelait Mémé. Elle avait le même regard d'un bleu profond et envoûtant que ma grand-mère. Elle avait aussi comme elle cet accent bourgeois, qu'à leurs âges on n'expose plus. Je retrouvai chez elle les mêmes recommandations que chez Mémé.

Je regardai ma montre discrètement. J'avais deux heures d'intervention programmées, j'aspirais tout de même à lui faire un peu de ménage. Mais elle en avait décidé autrement. À cet instant, j'avais mauvaise conscience. J'avais le sentiment d'être payée à ne rien faire. Pourtant, je reprochais souvent de ne pouvoir faire de l'humain tant nous étions considérées comme des femmes de ménage ; finalement, à ce moment précis, j'exerçais mon métier. À force de me sentir considérée comme une femme de ménage, je me rendais compte que je m'étais conditionnée à sauter sur les torchons, la serpillière, le seau dès la porte d'entrée franchie. Je savais cependant que l'humain est la quintessence de notre profession, et là, quand, pour une fois, une personne me considérait autrement qu'en professionnelle du récurage, je culpabilisais.

Elle me fit visiter les lieux. Nous arrivâmes dans la salle à manger, où les volets étaient clos. Elle me dit :

— Ne faites pas le ménage ici, je n'y viens jamais, et puis la maison est bien trop grande pour moi. Voilà mon quartier général !

Son quartier général était une pièce au rez-de-chaussée, où elle dormait dans un clic-clac, face à une télévision. Le long du mur, près du convertible, une immense bibliothèque. Ellc m'expliqua que son domicile se réduisait à son coin « couchage et lecture », à la cuisine et à la salle de bains. Le soleil éclairait et illuminait ce clic-clac au sommier défoncé et réchauffait la chambrée. Les rayons apportaient de façon surprenante à cette pièce l'espoir d'un bel été ; pas celui d'une rémission. Je la regardais se chauffer le dos au soleil tout en continuant à m'expliquer sa vie et sa vocation d'institutrice.

Je m'attardais sur cette bibliothèque quelques minutes, un véritable écrin de savoir. J'y retrouvais les lectures classiques de ma grand-mère. De Pagnol à Victor Hugo, en passant par Tolstoï.

— Vous aimez lire ?

— Oui, j'adore lire.

— Vous pouvez m'emprunter un livre si vous le souhaitez, mais n'oubliez pas de me le rapporter. Bon, assez parlé de moi, parlez-moi de vous.

Je lui déroulai mon pedigree : ma mère prof, mon père prof, ma grand-mère institutrice. Elle sourit.

— Je comprends mieux maintenant pourquoi quand je vous parlais de mes élèves, vous aviez un sourire. Vous devez avoir des anecdotes avec votre grand-mère, racontez-moi, vous, enfant…

— Oui, j'en ai tant ! Une me revient ! Mémé me l'a répétée maintes et maintes fois, et toujours elle riait aux éclats.

— Vous voulez me la raconter ?

— Avec plaisir. Quand ma grand-mère enseignait, elle avait un appartement de fonction au-dessus de sa classe, et il fallait descendre le grand escalier en bois pour arriver dans la cour de l'école. Lorsque j'étais petite, je filais dans la chambre qui donnait sur le grand portail de l'école, et si une élève arrivait, je courais le lui dire en criant : « Mémé, mémé, y a un z'élève. » Alors elle me laissait dévaler l'escalier et je devenais la responsable de l'ouverture du grand portail vert. Je tournais la grosse clef en fer forgé, et elle me rejoignait. À mes côtés, Mémé sentait bien ma grande fierté à me tenir là avec elle ! Je restais le temps de la récréation, puis je remontais dans l'appartement avec mon arrière-grand-mère pendant que Mémé faisait classe. Je guettais à la fenêtre le moindre son à l'extérieur qui m'indiquait la récréation. Je dévalais de nouveau l'escalier et sur mon petit tricycle jaune je jouais avec tous ces grands « z'élèves ».

La vieille dame souriait. Peut-être m'imaginait-elle petite, je ne sais pas. Son visage affichait cette forme de bienveillance et de gentillesse que je retrouvais dans les yeux bleus de Mémé. Elle continua à me raconter ces années où elle avait pris plaisir à enseigner aux enfants à lire, à écrire et à compter… C'était, pour elle, les mener sur le chemin de leur liberté.

— Ma grand-mère me racontait la même chose concernant ses élèves. La demi-heure de morale, les encriers, les plumes et les buvards, lui dis-je.

— Cela a bien changé de nos jours, je suis contente de ne plus être institutrice.

— Ma grand-mère disait la même chose que vous !

— Quel âge avait votre grand-mère ?

— Quatre-vingt-cinq ans…

— Nous sommes de la même génération. Où enseignait-elle ?

— Dans le Jura, à Foucherans.

— Vous êtes jurassienne ? Quel beau département ! Mais alors, pardon, l'hiver est froid !

— Oui, c'est vrai ! Dites-moi, voulez-vous tout de même que je vous fasse votre lit, que je change vos draps ?

— Pensez-vous ! Je me recoucherai dedans ce soir, à quoi bon, il sera à refaire demain. Laissez…

— Je peux peut-être au moins faire un brin de ménage dans la cuisine, la salle de bains et les toilettes.

— D'accord, si vous tenez vraiment à nettoyer, allez-y, mais j'aimerais que nous continuions à discuter, je peux vous accompagner ?

J'acceptai avec plaisir. Je voyais son souffle lui manquer, elle fatiguait vite. Alors elle s'assit, respira un peu dans son masque à oxygène et reprit notre discussion sur cette société dans laquelle elle ne trouvait plus sa place. Que lui répondre ? Qu'elle se trompait ? Je refusais de lui mentir.

La société actuelle, avec ses chamboulements et son modernisme, oublie ses aînés. La solitude qu'ils subissent aujourd'hui n'existait pas du temps où, dans les villages, chacun prenait soin de son voisin. Or, si nous prenions un peu de temps pour les écouter, nous nous rendrions compte qu'il est toujours captivant et constructif d'avoir leur vision de la société dans laquelle nous vivons.

Elle ne me disait pas : « C'était mieux avant », elle constatait, simplement. Elle se souvenait de la guerre, elle me racontait comment elle l'avait vécue. Je crois que c'est ce qui me plaît le plus dans mon métier : apprendre à voir les événements autrement, pas comme on nous l'enseigne à l'école ou dans nos livres. Grâce à mes discussions avec mes allocataires, spectateurs de l'époque, je vivais l'Histoire.

Par exemple : dans quel livre lirez-vous que, dans le Jura, ma grand-mère, âgée d'une dizaine d'années, agitait un mouchoir blanc à la fenêtre de la maison pour prévenir les résistants cachés dans la montagne que la voie était libre et qu'ils pouvaient venir chercher quelques subsides de nourriture ? Quel livre m'apprendra la terreur que j'ai vue dans ses yeux quand elle m'expliqua comment, petite fille sous l'occupation allemande, elle se rendait au collège à vélo, chaque jour, qu'il neige, qu'il pleuve ou qu'il vente ? Elle passait régulièrement devant les Allemands et, la peur au ventre, elle pédalait chaque fois un peu plus vite.

*

Je suis intervenue quelques mois chez cette dame. Je n'y ai pas fait beaucoup de ménage ; parfois, nous prenions un livre et nous discutions philosophie, oxymores et litotes, alexandrins et hémistiches, accord du participe passé et compléments circonstanciés. Parfois, nous nous asseyions sur la terrasse devant la maison et nous buvions juste un café et prenions le soleil. Elle s'émerveillait toujours de la beauté de mère Nature. Nous attendions le passage des flamants roses, nous échangions. Elle avait ses moments de doute, ses moments d'angoisse. Elle n'avait jamais été dans le déni de sa maladie, elle savait que sa mort arriverait tôt ou tard, mais ce qui l'inquiétait, c'était de souffrir. Pourtant, elle souffrait déjà beaucoup, elle maigrissait à vue d'œil, le souffle de plus en plus court, ses forces de plus en plus faibles. Si, au début de mes interventions, elle marchait seule, au fil des semaines, la canne devint un outil indispensable pour qu'elle fasse quelques pas.

Je l'ai accompagnée un certain temps, puis une collègue a pris ma suite. Je me suis insurgée contre ce changement ; même si je savais que je pouvais arriver un jour et la trouver décédée, je voulais continuer. Mon employeur, sur un coup de tête, me volait la relation si privilégiée que nous avions toutes les deux mise en place. Avec elle, j'avais le sentiment de retourner à l'école, elle était ma maîtresse et j'étais son élève. Elle se sentait valorisée malgré la maladie, lorsque nous revisitions La Fontaine ou rejouions Molière ! Nous chantions ces chansons désuètes d'artistes ringards et, le temps de quelques heures, elle riait.

J'avais oublié encore une fois le fameux « recul nécessaire » que me rabâchait mon employeur ; j'aimais cette femme parce que, parfois, elle me rappelait les règles d'orthographe et de grammaire si précieuses à ses yeux, comme le faisait Mémé.

Alors pourquoi ai-je honte aujourd'hui ? J'ai passé de si bons moments avec elle, je devrais être heureuse d'avoir exercé auprès d'elle mon métier comme j'aimais le pratiquer.

Elle est morte un mois après ma dernière intervention. Je n'ai pas eu le temps de repasser la voir, pourtant je le lui avais promis. Je ne suis pas allée non plus à son enterrement ; j'étais en vacances à ce moment-là. Alors oui, j'ai honte, parce que je n'ai pu lui dire ni merci ni au revoir.

Et parce que j'ai beau chercher au plus profond de ma mémoire, je ne me souviens même plus de son prénom.

18

Tatie Danielle

J'avais poursuivi mes interventions chez Élisabeth. Elle était toujours aussi odieuse, mais je m'étais habituée à ce qu'elle me manque de respect. C'est assez surprenant comme l'être humain, pour conserver son emploi, est capable de faire abstraction de soi et de se laisser maltraiter, même pour un salaire de misère.

Je lui trouvais des excuses, aussi : son âge, l'isolement… C'est lorsque nous sommes confrontés à ces conditions de travail particulières que l'on comprend ce qu'est le savoir-être essentiel à notre métier. Dans d'autres circonstances, jamais je n'aurais accepté que l'on me parle ainsi, jamais je n'aurais accepté d'être humiliée à ce point.

*

Il n'était pas prévu que j'intervienne ce jour, quand ma collègue m'a appelée. Elle devait partir assurer une autre intervention et Élisabeth n'allait pas bien : elle se plaignait de douleurs abdominales et de nausées.

C'était un mercredi après-midi, je ne travaillais jamais ce jour-là, pour essayer de passer un peu de temps avec mes enfants. Pourtant, en quelques minutes, j'avais oublié les méchancetés, les canards qu'elle laissait entrer et déféquer quand je venais de terminer le ménage… un peu comme ces contractions d'accouchement dont vous ne vous souvenez plus dès lors que votre enfant est posé sur votre ventre.

Mon époux m'emmena en voiture, et j'arrivai chez Tatie Danielle. Les infirmières n'avaient rien noté de spécial dans le cahier des transmissions que je consultai à peine entrée. Pourtant, Élisabeth n'allait pas bien, pas bien du tout. Elle avait du mal à parler tant la douleur était vive, et elle était livide. Je n'avais aucune compétence particulière pour poser un diagnostic, je connaissais juste la pathologie cardiaque d'Élisabeth et j'imaginais bien que ce qui lui arrivait n'était pas de l'ordre du normal. Je me décidai donc à appeler un médecin.

Dans les cinq minutes qui suivirent, le praticien était là. C'était mon médecin de famille. Ni une ni deux, mise en place de l'électrocardiogramme. Il n'était pas bon, et c'était ce que j'avais supputé : Élisabeth faisait une crise cardiaque. Le médecin s'affaira autour d'elle et, pendant que je préparais son sac, appela le 15. Mais le SAMU est à Arles, soit à quarante kilomètres. Nous espérions qu'ils se dépêcheraient. Régulièrement, je jetais un œil à Élisabeth, dont l'état ne semblait pas se dégrader. Il lui fallait des sous-vêtements, des pyjamas, des chaussettes, ses lunettes, ses appareils auditifs, ses ordonnances, sa carte Vitale (à ne surtout pas oublier) et quelques livres.

Le SAMU arriva presque quarante-cinq minutes après l'appel du médecin. L'appartement étant minuscule, le brancard eut des difficultés à entrer. Placée sous oxygène, Élisabeth était apeurée. Voir toutes ces blouses blanches qui s'affairent autour de vous, c'est très impressionnant. Je lui pris la main. C'est la première fois que je vis dans son regard de la reconnaissance. Elle était touchante et me fit de la peine.

Comment garder nos distances avec les personnes dont nous nous occupons dans ces moments-là, quand la mort peut nous frapper à chaque instant ? Elle qui me répétait souvent qu'elle voulait mourir était effrayée par ce qui lui arrivait.

Les pompiers l'installèrent dans l'ambulance dont on me refusa l'accès. Mais le médecin m'appela et me dit :

— Elle veut vous parler, venez.

À cet instant précis, l'angoisse monta : et si elle souhaitait me parler parce qu'elle savait que peut-être nous ne nous reverrions plus ? Aurais-je développé une forme de syndrome de Stockholm ? Tenais-je plus à elle que je l'aurais imaginé ? Je montai dans l'ambulance le cœur noué, et je sentais les larmes arriver.

Élisabeth souleva son masque à oxygène et me dit :

— Anne-Sophie, est-ce que vous pourrez vous occuper de mon chat tant que je ne serai pas là ?

— Oui, Élisabeth.

— Merci.

Et elle remit son masque. C'était donc de son chat qu'elle voulait me parler. J'en souris aujourd'hui, moi qui avais imaginé tant de choses avant de grimper dans ce camion… Elle voulait juste que je m'occupe de son chat. Sacrée Élisabeth !

Une fois l'ambulance partie, je retournai chez elle faire un brin de ménage et trouver le chat. Il s'était caché, tous ces intrus dans la maison l'avaient effrayé ; d'humeur peu sociable, c'en était trop pour la pauvre bête. J'arrivai tant bien que mal à l'attraper, mais je me demandais ce que j'allais en faire. Je ne pourrais pas venir tous les jours le nourrir ; mais j'avais fait une promesse.

Je n'avais pas non plus anticipé que mon époux m'avait déposée et que je me trouvais à douze kilomètres du village. Deux solutions s'offraient à moi : attendre 21 heures qu'il sorte du travail ou rentrer à pied. Je choisis la seconde option : je mis non sans mal le chat en cage, et je pris le chemin du village où j'arrivai trois heures et demie après mon départ de chez Élisabeth. J'en avais profité pour prendre le temps d'observer cette Camargue que je ne voyais habituellement qu'en voiture, et j'avais croisé des ragondins, des hérons et des avocettes qui m'offrirent l'honneur de leur envol.

J'eus le soir même des nouvelles d'Élisabeth : tout allait bien. Ses enfants m'appelèrent également le soir même pour me remercier. Je n'avais pourtant fait que mon travail, sauf que, cette fois, je n'avais pas accompagné une personne âgée en fin de vie, je la lui avais sauvée.

19

Solange et Félix

Il était assez rare que je puisse m'occuper d'un couple. Cette fois-ci, j'entrais dans l'intimité d'un couple non marié mais vivant conjointement depuis plus de trente ans. J'allais être spectatrice de cet amour dont nous rêvons tous, un amour qui dure contre vents et marée, un amour où finalement la tendresse est le maître mot de la relation.

Ils habitaient un petit appartement dans une des HLM du village. Le logement était propre, mais situé au premier étage. Or Félix avait fait un accident vasculaire cérébral et était devenu hémiplégique. L'étage, même peu élevé, n'était pas du tout adapté à son handicap. De nombreuses demandes furent faites auprès du service de l'habitat pour que le couple bénéficie d'un appartement au rez-de-chaussée, invoquant ses pathologies. Les logements du rez-de-chaussée avaient un jardinet, étaient plus spacieux, et pour un loyer identique. Félix aurait ainsi pu prendre le soleil, installé confortablement dans un fauteuil roulant.

Mais les requêtes demeurèrent lettre morte. Même si des appartements étaient vides, la réponse était constamment négative. Je me suis longtemps posé la question de l'humanité de ces bureaucrates qui ne parviennent pas à comprendre que cette demande ne relevait pas du caprice mais bel et bien d'une véritable nécessité. Le lieu de vie tient une place essentielle dans l'existence d'un individu ; quand on ne se sent pas bien chez soi, comment aller bien psychologiquement ? Solange et Félix étaient condamnés à vivre au premier étage pour des raisons aussi fallacieuses qu'écœurantes : ils n'avaient pas le bras assez long, et leur réclamation n'était pas soutenue par le maire. Et leur situation me révolte d'autant plus que certains logements, loués à l'année, servent de résidence secondaire à des bénéficiaires peu scrupuleux et sont donc fermés la plupart du temps.

*

Félix et Solange se sont rencontrés dans le village. Solange y venait en vacances et Félix était artiste. La Lyonnaise a abandonné son travail, sa famille pour vivre avec cet homme qui la faisait rêver. Félix, à l'époque, n'était pas au mieux : séparé de son épouse, il avait trouvé refuge dans l'alcool et était devenu un pilier de bar abonné aux retours difficiles à son domicile. Solange l'avait sorti de cette addiction, porté, et, ensemble, ils avaient décidé d'ouvrir une galerie dans le village. Évidemment, les œuvres de Félix seraient mises à l'honneur, mais pas seulement. D'autres artistes exposeraient.

Je me souviendrai toujours de cette boutique, éclectique, qui détonnait au milieu de celles de souvenirs ou de vêtements. Sur le trottoir, une grande vitrine rectangulaire protégeait des bijoux. Pas l'éternelle croix de Camargue à 20 euros si elle est plaquée or, ou 15 si elle est en acier ; les bijoux présents dans cette grande vitrine étaient soit des créations artisanales, soit des collections particulières de Charles Jourdan. Combien de fois, enfant puis adolescente, je m'étais arrêtée devant cette petite échoppe… Et voici que je retrouvais ces commerçants que je connaissais bien, âgés, en retraite et dépendants. Ce ne fut pas un moment facile ; mes souvenirs d'enfance m'avaient laissé en mémoire des adultes vaillants. Ces réminiscences me faisaient mal. Je les avais gardées intactes dans mon esprit, je voyais désormais la réalité de la maladie et de la dépendance.

Félix ne peignait plus, mais ne se levait plus seul non plus. Sur la petite étagère de la chambre traînaient pinceaux, peinture à l'huile, encre de Chine et porte-plume. La présence de ce matériel était à la fois pour lui un besoin, mais aussi un mal qui le rongeait. Solange dormait à côté de lui dans cette chambre minuscule, dans un petit lit. Elle ne l'aurait abandonné pour rien au monde. Elle lui servait son petit déjeuner, l'aidait à déjeuner et à dîner. Solange était cependant trop âgée pour prendre en charge les soins de son mari ; elle le voyait souvent bien sale, puisque comme chez toutes les personnes dépendantes les infirmières ne passaient que deux fois par jour, et attendait avec impatience les auxiliaires de vie sociale pour essayer de le rendre présentable.

Je n'avais pas le droit de changer Félix. Alors, que faire ? Humainement, il m'était impossible de le laisser ainsi. Je l'ai changé souvent, j'ai régulièrement utilisé les gants de toilette et pris le temps de lui laver les cheveux à la bassine, de le raser et de couper cette grosse barbe touffue qui l'empêchait de rester propre quand il buvait son café au lait.

Quelle vie avaient-ils tous les deux ? Les enfants vivaient loin, les seules visites qu'ils recevaient étaient les infirmières toujours pressées, les auxiliaires de vie deux heures par jour, deux fois par semaine. Solange s'épuisait, son moral déclinait. À plus de quatre-vingts ans, s'occuper de son compagnon comme elle le faisait était un sacerdoce. Elle avait sacrifié sa vie pour son peintre camarguais, voilà qu'elle continuait au péril de sa propre santé.

La santé de Félix était meilleure que celle de Solange. Elle avait de gros problèmes circulatoires, ses jambes parfois étaient si dures et si gonflées qu'elle ne pouvait plus marcher. Mais elle n'avait jamais oublié de lui servir ses repas ; elle mettait le temps qu'il fallait, accrochée à sa canne, grimaçant de douleur, mais elle continuait de prendre soin de son époux et s'oubliait elle-même.

Et puis, un jour, elle chuta dans l'escalier et fut hospitalisée. Qu'allait-il se passer pour son époux ? L'hôpital ne l'accepterait pas, il n'avait pas de pathologie nécessitant une hospitalisation. Avec mes collègues, nous avions donc pris la décision d'intervenir bénévolement auprès de Félix. Nous nous succéderions jour et nuit afin qu'il ne soit jamais seul. C'est cela, notre travail, prendre soin de l'autre, quelles que soient les circonstances et sans en attendre d'émoluments. Nous savions aussi que Solange et Félix n'avaient pas les moyens de payer l'association pour une prise en charge vingt-quatre heures sur vingt-quatre. C'était donc à nous de nous dévouer.

*

Solange s'en sortit avec quelques contusions et blessures superficielles. Elle était restée quelques jours à l'hôpital, puis avait regagné son domicile.

Pourtant, lorsqu'elle rentra chez elle, elle n'était plus la même. Souvent fatiguée, ses assoupissements étaient récurrents, la mémoire lui faisait défaut. Les infirmières venaient dorénavant pour eux deux. Solange avait des pansements à changer régulièrement : en tombant, elle s'était écorchée au niveau d'une veine, et comme sa circulation était de plus en plus mauvaise, la blessure se sclérosait. À chaque intervention de l'infirmière, Solange serrait les dents et s'accrochait au gros fauteuil en cuir. J'assistais impuissante à ce douloureux spectacle, ma main dans celle de Solange. Mon soutien n'apportait que peu de réconfort à la vieille dame, et ces images me hantent.

Félix, lui, allait bien, semblable à lui-même, mais Solange peinait de plus en plus. Malgré tout, elle se remit peu à peu à l'aquarelle ; quand le cerveau est occupé, la douleur se fait plus silencieuse l'espace d'un instant. Elle n'allait plus faire les courses et tombait régulièrement dans l'appartement, mais elle refusait d'être hospitalisée, pour ne pas laisser Félix seul. C'étaient donc nous, les auxiliaires de vie, qui allions chercher ses provisions. Les courses se résumaient souvent à ce dont Félix avait envie : pain au lait, café, confiture, jus de pomme. Entre les lignes, deux bouteilles de vin.

Mais depuis que le portage des repas avait été mis en place par le foyer, le réfrigérateur ne désemplissait pas. Il fallait bien se rendre à l'évidence, ils mangeaient très peu. Que faire ? Les forcer, à leur âge ? Impossible. Et qui étions-nous pour leur faire la morale ? Quand on est en fin de vie, n'a-t-on pas le droit de faire et de choisir ? Parce que, oui, Solange était en fin de vie, même si elle se levait, même si elle parlait, quand la porte était fermée je savais que ces deux heures où elle avait donné le change l'avaient exténuée.

Pendant quelques mois, je continuai de faire les courses. Je me rendis vite compte que Solange était tombée dans l'alcoolisme. De deux bouteilles de vin, on était passés à quatre. Que dire, là encore ? Observer, tout d'abord. Comment lui dire qu'elle était ivre régulièrement et que cette ivresse n'était pas compatible avec le traitement qu'elle prenait ? Fallait-il avertir son fils, ma supérieure ? Arrêter de lui acheter du vin ? De quel droit ?

Mémé aussi buvait à la fin de sa vie, elle aimait ce breuvage qui l'emmenait dans des siestes qui réparaient le peu de sommeil qu'elle trouvait la nuit. Le médecin lui avait pourtant dit lors d'une analyse de sang que ses gamma-GT, qui souvent signent l'atteinte hépatique, étaient élevées et lui avait demandé si elle buvait. Elle avait fait comme si elle n'avait pas compris.

— Solange, buvez-vous de l'alcool ?

— Oui.

— Et de l'eau ?

— Sachez, monsieur, que chez moi l'eau n'est qu'à usage externe…

Oui, Solange, comme Mémé, buvait. Pour oublier la douleur du changement de pansement, pour oublier cette vie de dévouement, pour dormir.

Son fils fut averti de l'addiction de sa mère. À quel moment en arrive-t-on à non-assistance à personne en danger et privation de liberté ? La frontière est si subtile. Nous reçûmes l'ordre de ne plus acheter de vin, qui fut remplacé par de la bière sans alcool. Est-ce que cela a changé quelque chose ? Non, rien. Solange trouvait le moyen de se procurer de l'alcool, en demandant à une voisine par exemple. Je n'allais pas ameuter tous les voisins pour leur expliquer que la vieille dame du premier était alcoolique et qu'ils devaient refuser d'aller lui chercher à boire au cas où elle les solliciterait. J'aurais dans ce cas pu être accusée d'avoir brisé le secret professionnel.

Voilà en quoi mon métier est difficile.

Solange est retombée quelques mois plus tard. La gravité de la chute ne lui permit pas de rentrer chez elle. Félix fut accepté dans la même chambre que sa femme, en séjour de longue durée. Lorsque je suis allée leur rendre visite à l'hôpital, Solange ne m'a pas reconnue, Félix, quant à lui, était pareil à lui-même. Solange décéda peu de temps après mon passage, je n'ai plus jamais eu de nouvelles de Félix.

Solange avait été ce que l'on appelle un aidant familial, qui, souvent, s'épuise plus vite que le malade et décède de fatigue. Sans formation aucune, munis de leur seul amour, ils s'usent la santé et le moral. En un an de soins, tout individu aidant familial prend dix ans.

Je dédie donc ce texte à « mes amoureux de Peynet », Solange et Félix, et à tous ces aidants familiaux que l'État abandonne.

20

Burn-out

Cela faisait maintenant quatre ans que je naviguais de domicile en domicile et que j'enterrais les uns après les autres mes bénéficiaires. J'avais pourtant choisi ce métier par conviction, mais peut-être était-ce en fait par utopie, je ne sais pas. J'avais espéré apporter plus de temps, moins d'isolement, des plaisirs à mes allocataires. Mais il y a une chose à laquelle je n'avais finalement jamais véritablement pensé : la mort.

Comment ai-je pu à ce point me tromper ? J'avais vu les limites de mon métier avec cette administration lourde qui ne comprenait rien à l'urgence, avec certaines de ces associations d'aide à domicile qui utilisaient la précarité féminine à des fins qui me choquaient. Je me persuadais que mon métier leur apportait un brin de bonheur, comme on apporte du muguet un 1er mai. Mais j'avais refusé d'ouvrir les yeux sur le fait que chaque lien que je nouerais, chaque histoire que je vivrais avec mes bénéficiaires se terminerait inéluctablement par leur disparition, qui arrivait un jour ou l'autre, sans prévenir et en faisant souffrir.

Nous ne sommes pas tous égaux face à la mort. J'ai rarement été confrontée à une mort sereine et paisible, comme un dernier endormissement tranquille après une vie bien remplie. Parfois, la mort s'obstine en douleurs, elle s'acharne en maladies plus difficiles à supporter les unes que les autres.

En quatre ans, j'avais perdu dix-sept allocataires. J'écris et je me rends compte que je parle de *ma* perte. Mais ces personnes ne m'appartenaient pas, elles appartenaient à leurs familles. Pourtant, elles étaient toutes devenues une partie de ma famille. Chacun pouvait m'appeler à n'importe quelle l'heure du jour ou de la nuit. Pourquoi ? Je l'ignore. C'était une évidence. Quand on travaille avec des personnes âgées, il est impossible de ne pas faire le parallèle avec sa propre vie et ses proches.

Ces personnes m'ont transmis beaucoup, m'ont appris à relativiser, m'ont fait grandir, m'ont donné des recommandations de prudence que seuls nos aînés peuvent nous transmettre.

J'avais réussi jusqu'alors à trouver mon salut dans un livre de Roland Barthes, *Fragments d'un discours amoureux*, grâce auquel je transposais mes situations de deuil en situations amoureuses. « Ne pas scénariser » : je connais ce chapitre par cœur. J'en étais même arrivée à me dire que la mort n'était qu'un changement d'état et que je ne devais pas scénariser les souvenirs quand je passerais devant le domicile de mes absents.

Mais voilà, Roland Barthes ne me suffisait plus, j'avais beau essayer de ne pas me souvenir des bénéficiaires, je n'y arrivais pas. Leurs visages, leurs voix, leurs sourires, leurs souffrances me hantent encore.

J'en voulais à la vie. C'est surprenant, pour quelqu'un qui cherchait à arrêter le temps. Je n'acceptais plus cette mort qui venait terminer ces histoires de vie. Chaque jour, en allant travailler, j'avais une boule au ventre, espérant que personne n'ait chuté ou qu'aucune pathologie n'ait emporté qui que ce soit. Cette hantise du décès ne me permettait plus de faire mon travail sereinement. La solitude au domicile face à ces urgences, le manque de soutien de la part de nos supérieurs, je n'en pouvais plus. Je ne supportais plus de fermer un dossier parce que la mort était survenue.

Il était donc grand temps d'arrêter avant que ce métier ne me dégoûte. J'ai demandé à mon employeur une rupture conventionnelle, qui n'a pas permis une séparation en bons termes, mais je me libérais. J'ai fait une pause quelque temps, je me suis posé beaucoup de questions. Arrêter, continuer, accepter, souffrir… J'ai posé mes maux en mots. J'ai écrit chacune des histoires vécues avec mes bénéficiaires sur quelques feuilles blanches. Je ne les ai jamais oubliés, et c'est bien grâce à eux aujourd'hui que ce livre existe.

Alors je n'ai qu'un seul mot à leur dire à tous : merci.

21

Pause

J'ai tenté de faire une pause. J'avais besoin de me retrouver. Mais être soignant, c'est une seconde nature, vous occuper des autres vous manque. En revanche, le soignant est incapable de s'occuper correctement de lui-même. Durant cette période, je déambulais dans le village, perdue, et je continuais de passer devant les maisons vides des bénéficiaires décédés, comme j'aurais été de chapelle en chapelle, me recueillant devant chaque autel. Je vivais le souvenir de mes allocataires disparus et je déprimais.

Mémé étant partie elle aussi, je devais opérer un retour aux sources, sans quoi je ne pourrais, je le savais, continuer de vivre. Il devint impératif pour moi de retourner dans ma région natale, la Franche-Comté.

Plus facile à dire qu'à faire… Il fallait d'abord trouver un travail. Pas question de changer de voie : ce serait auprès des personnes âgées. Je recommencerais à prendre soin d'eux, je ne savais faire que cela. C'est inexplicable, mais ainsi : mon cœur guidait ma raison. Je soignerais encore et toujours nos aînés, sachant pertinemment que j'en souffrirais. Tout le monde m'a mise en garde, mais personne n'a pu me faire entendre raison : c'était mon métier…

Je postulai donc un peu partout dans la région de ma grand-mère, je passai quelques entretiens. Le dernier fut dans son village. Je fus embauchée pour un essai de quelques heures dès le lendemain matin. Une jeune femme charmante, qui serait mon binôme, m'accueillit et m'expliqua mes attributions : quelques toilettes assez simples, pendant qu'elle prendrait en charge les plus lourdes. Quelques jours plus tard, la directrice de Foucherans m'appela : j'étais engagée au centre d'hébergement pour personnes âgées dépendantes du village. J'aurais pu choisir un poste ailleurs, mais je pris celui-ci sans hésiter. Je devais commencer le 22 décembre, nous étions le 17 ; il ne me restait que trois jours pour organiser notre déménagement…

Nous emménageâmes dans le Jura le 21 décembre. Mon époux serait au chômage, nous le savions ; nous espérions qu'il retrouve un travail rapidement. Pas dans son domaine de compétences – il n'y a pas de port dans le Jura ! –, mais il était prêt à me suivre dans l'aventure.

Les enfants, eux, étaient contents de quitter le Sud et ne nous demanderaient jamais d'y retourner. Emma, la cadette, qui était déscolarisée, voudrait même reprendre ses études dans une école publique ; ce fut notre plus belle victoire. Alexandre, l'aîné, étudierait dans le lycée où feu son grand-père enseignait.

Le lendemain de notre emménagement éclair, je devais commencer mon travail dans le village où j'ai mes plus beaux souvenirs d'enfance et où ma grand-mère a laissé une trace dans les esprits ; elle aura été une excellente directrice d'école primaire. À ce moment précis, je ne sais pas si c'est le lieu ou la nouvelle expérience qui me plaît. Et, même si je suis déjà épuisée par le déménagement ; demain, je serai en forme.

*

Foucherans, village où ma grand-mère était directrice de l'école primaire, où mon grand-père tenait la station-service, et où j'ai passé des vacances merveilleuses. Était-ce un signe que Mémé m'adressait ? Je ne le saurai jamais, mais je ne pouvais pas trouver meilleur endroit pour me reconstruire professionnellement et me rapprocher des moments heureux de ma vie, gravés pour toujours dans la cour des tilleuls de l'école où elle enseignait.

J'avais abandonné mes autels, je pourrais enfin commencer mes deuils.

22

22 décembre 2016, 7 heures

Ma tenue est déjà prête, mon nom imprimé sur ma blouse : « Anne-Sophie, AMP ». J'étais fière de ce sigle : AMP. J'étais enfin reconnue comme aide médico-psychologique. C'était écrit. Après un accueil chaleureux de mes collègues, je pris mes fonctions : la gestion du rez-de-chaussée, soit quatorze résidents. J'avais bien fait quelques heures d'essai avant d'être engagée, mais je ne me souvenais pas de tout. Surtout, j'avais espéré être doublée les premiers temps ; ce n'était visiblement pas prévu. La moitié des résidents étaient autonomes – j'entends par autonomes qu'ils arrivaient à se mobiliser ; pour les autres, c'était toilettes alitées.

Je sortis mon chariot de soin et celui de linge. À 11 h 30, tous les résidents devaient être prêts pour se rendre en salle de restauration. Par où allais-je commencer ? L'angoisse de ne pas être dans les temps m'étreignit.

*

Je frappai à la première porte et j'entrai dans la chambre. La dame dormait paisiblement, j'allais devoir la réveiller. Qui aime être réveillé quand il dort profondément ? J'avais beau y aller avec délicatesse, les seuls mots qui sortaient de la bouche de la résidente étaient :

— Foutez-moi la paix, bon Dieu ! Je veux dormir ! Je n'ai pas envie de me lever, revenez plus tard !

Voilà à quoi ressembla ma première prise en charge…

Je décidai de la laisser sommeiller encore un peu ; finalement, à sa place, aurais-je aimé que l'on me réveille, me manipule, me pose sur les toilettes, me lave sans mon consentement ? Sûrement pas. C'est là que commence la bienveillance. Écouter l'autre et respecter ce qu'il demande.

J'allai donc frapper à une autre porte ; cette fois, la dame était assise sur son lit. Soulagement… Il lui fallait sa canne pour marcher, je la lui donnai.

— Vous êtes nouvelle ? me demanda-t-elle.

— Oui, madame. Avez-vous bien dormi ?

— Oh, à mon âge, vous savez, on dort comme on peut.

— Souhaitez-vous aller à la salle de bains maintenant, ainsi, vous serez prête, ou préférez-vous être préparée après votre petit déjeuner ?

— Comme vous êtes là, allons-y, parce que après je ne sais pas à quelle heure vous allez revenir.

Cette phrase m'avait laissée un peu perplexe, mais je comprendrais vite pourquoi elle avait tenu ces propos.

— Que souhaitez-vous mettre comme vêtements aujourd'hui ?

— Oh, ceux d'hier, ils ne sont pas sales.

— On va quand même changer les sous-vêtements, vous ne croyez pas ?

— Si vous voulez, mais comme je mets des petites protections, il n'y a pas de raison que je les aie tachés. Ma fille vient me voir aujourd'hui, je suis contente.

— Raison de plus. Douche, alors ?

— Vous me proposez une douche ?

— Oui... Si vous ne voulez pas, ce n'est pas grave.

— C'est pas que je ne veux pas, mais ce n'est pas le jour de ma douche. Il y a des jours de douche, vous savez... ça se voit que vous êtes nouvelle.

— Ah, excusez-moi, effectivement, je ne savais pas. Mais si vous le souhaitez, je prends le temps de vous donner une douche.

— C'est le luxe, ce matin ! Je veux bien, merci.

7 h 45. La dame était nue dans la salle de bains, je transpirais à grosses gouttes, et elle avait froid.

— Je vous lave les cheveux ? lui proposai-je.

— Les cheveux ?

— Oui, voulez-vous que je vous lave les cheveux ?

— Non, je vous remercie. Comme personne n'a jamais le temps de le faire, j'ai pris rendez-vous avec la coiffeuse de l'établissement.

— C'est un service payant ?

— Ben oui, ma petite !

— Si vous le souhaitez, je vous lave la tête, vous économisez la coiffeuse.

— Non, laissez, j'ai rendez-vous dans deux jours, ça tiendra bien jusque-là.

— Comme vous voulez.

L'eau coulait sur le corps de la dame ; je la sentais détendue. Je me dépêchai de la laver, pour qu'elle ait le moins froid possible. Au fur et à mesure que je lui apposais des serviettes de toilette pour la sécher, elle me demandait de bien la frictionner.

— Plus fort, j'aime quand ça frotte. Vous pouvez bien me frotter le dos ?

Je m'exécutai. Puis direction l'habillage. Accrochée au lavabo, tout en se regardant dans la glace, la dame me dit :

— Ça fait du bien, une bonne douche, merci.

— Mais de rien, avec plaisir.

— Vous allez rester dans l'établissement ?

— Oui, pourquoi cette question ?

— Oh, ma petite, on en voit tellement qui arrivent et qui partent que je vous demande.

Sa question ne me surprenait pas tant que cela : je connaissais, et pour cause, les difficultés de ce métier, même si je n'en avais perçu alors que les contours.

— Non, je compte rester, lui répondis-je en la regardant dans les yeux.

— Tant mieux, me dit-elle avec un sourire.

Les soins de toilette achevés, je l'accompagnai vers sa table afin qu'elle prenne son petit déjeuner. Je vérifiai que les draps n'étaient pas souillés, refis le lit au carré, comme j'avais appris à l'école hôtelière, et je pris congé en lui souhaitant bon appétit.

Une heure s'était écoulée entre ma prise de poste et la fin de mon intervention auprès de cette dame. Je m'affolais : j'allais prendre du retard, je n'aurais jamais terminé à l'heure ! J'étais en période d'essai, il fallait que je tienne le coup et que je m'active.

Mais comment s'active-t-on ?

23

22 décembre 2016, 8 heures

Je retournai voir ma marmotte afin d'essayer de la lever et de l'installer à la table pour déjeuner. Je fus reçue de la même façon. Je tentai ma chance en frappant à une autre porte. Je savais que la dame était mobilisable avec de l'aide, mais je voulais au moins lui mettre ses bas de contention et l'installer pour le petit déjeuner. Elle aussi dormait paisiblement.

— Bonjour, c'est Anne-Sophie, dis-je à mi-voix. Le petit déjeuner va être servi, je vous aide à vous lever ?

Là encore, impossible. Je n'avais pas beaucoup de succès ce matin, mon premier jour s'annonçait des plus compliqué. Je devais encore prendre soin de treize résidents. Une lumière rouge s'alluma au-dessus d'une porte dans le couloir. Une dame avait besoin de moi.

Je frappai. Quand j'entrai, celle-ci était assise dans son grand fauteuil.

— Bonjour, je suis Anne-Sophie, vous avez sonné ?

— Vous êtes nouvelle ?

— Oui, madame. Vous avez bien dormi ?

— Vous allez rester ?

— Oui, pourquoi ?

— Oh, ici, on en voit tellement des différentes que je me renseigne.

— J'aimerais rester, mais je suis en période d'essai.

— Est-ce que vous pourriez me laver les pieds, me mettre ma crème et mes bas de contention ? Pour le reste de ma toilette, je me débrouille.

— Oui, bien sûr, madame.

Dans la salle de bains, je remplis une bassine, pris un gant propre et du savon, mis des gants et commençai.

— Si vous le souhaitez, plongez vos pieds dans la bassine, cela peut vous faire du bien.

— Oh oui, merci. Ça fait un moment que je n'avais pas senti l'eau comme cela. Vous savez, j'ai été résistante pendant la guerre.

— Vraiment ?

— Oui, et j'ai même écrit mes mémoires.

— Vous les avez fait éditer ?

— Oh... à quoi bon ?

— C'est dommage. C'est important, les témoignages, pour les générations qui suivent.

— Vous avez raison...

Tout en discutant de ses écrits et en l'écoutant me raconter sa vie, je lui lavai les pieds. C'est surprenant comme un simple lavage de pieds peut détendre une personne... J'apposai ensuite la crème, tout en m'inquiétant du temps que me prendrait le fait de mettre les bas de contention.

Ils décidèrent de ne pas me taquiner et je pus les lui enfiler. Réfection du lit en ayant préalablement vérifié que les draps n'étaient pas tachés, et je pris congé. La dame m'interpella :

— Vous auriez deux petites serviettes à me prêter et deux gants s'il vous plaît ?

— Oui, bien sûr, avez-vous aussi besoin de protections ?

— Oui, s'il vous plaît, trois bleues et une violette.

8 h 30. Je n'avais plus que douze résidents à lever.

Je m'apprêtais à m'occuper des personnes que l'on dit lourdes quand le chariot des petits déjeuners arriva. Entre celles qui n'avaient pas voulu se réveiller et celles que je n'avais pas encore vues, j'étais loin d'avoir préparé tous mes patients. L'angoisse montait.

*

9 heures.

On n'installe pas à la va-vite des résidents alités pour manger. On les installe de telle façon qu'ils soient à leur aise pour déjeuner, et qu'il n'y ait aucun risque de fausse route. On les cale avec des coussins, des polochons, on fait ce que l'on peut avec le matériel mis à disposition en espérant qu'ils ne glissent pas, et on espère que tout ira bien. On leur met une serviette aussi, on essaie de limiter les dégâts pour ne pas avoir à tout changer après.

J'entrai ensuite chez une dame dont je me rappelais que la toilette était un moment compliqué pour elle. J'étais seule et j'allais devoir me débrouiller.

— Bonjour, je suis Anne-Sophie, on va faire la toilette ?

Soudain, la dame se mit à pleurer. De peur, d'angoisse, je ne saurais le dire. Mais l'heure tournait, et je n'avais pas le temps de parlementer, elle devait s'exécuter. N'est-ce pas là qu'une forme de prise en charge dans l'indignité commence ?

L'odeur de la chambre ne laissait pas de doute possible, l'état des ongles de la résidente non plus : la protection était souillée.

— Madame, il faut que nous fassions votre toilette, vous ne devez pas être à l'aise, nous allons y aller doucement, d'accord ?

— Non…

— Regardez, je commence par vous mettre vos bas de contention, tout doucement. Dépliez vos jambes, que je ne vous fasse pas mal.

Elle pleurait, criait, refusait de déplier ses jambes. Mettre des bas de contention est déjà compliqué quand la personne se laisse faire, alors imaginez quand elle se débat !

Après quinze minutes de lutte et une fois les bas enfilés, je cherchai ma bassine d'eau, mes deux gants de toilette (un pour le buste et un pour les parties intimes), mes deux serviettes de toilette, et j'enfilai mes gants. Un véritable combat entre la résidente et moi allait alors s'engager. Tandis que j'essayais de la déshabiller en lui parlant doucement, elle m'enfonçait ses ongles sales partout où elle le pouvait, tentant de repousser ma main. Enlever sa chemise de nuit se révéla pire que tout : elle refusa de plier les bras, les plaquant le long de son corps. Je n'allais tout de même pas la découper ! J'essayais avec douceur, encore et encore, mais rien n'y faisait.

Quand soudain la dame se mit à chanter. Alors que je l'accompagnais, les tensions s'apaisèrent. Elle était moins réfractaire. Je chantonnai avec elle, elle se débattait moins. Puis, tout à coup, son humeur changea, elle pleura de nouveau, s'énerva quand je voulus lui laver les mains et surtout ses ongles noircis par les selles. Avait-elle mal ?

Finalement, après de longues minutes, j'arrivai à la sécher. Je lui proposai de m'aider à l'habiller. Elle accepta, mais continua de s'opposer à chacun de mes gestes. L'installation du soutien-gorge fut le point d'orgue de notre affrontement. Elle se coucha sur le dos et refusa de bouger… Entre deux pleurs, deux cris, deux pincements ou deux morsures, elle chantait. J'étais épuisée. Je réussis enfin à la vêtir en haut et changeai l'eau de la bassine pour m'occuper des parties intimes.

Ma collègue entra et posa son petit déjeuner sur la table. Encore une pression supplémentaire pour moi, le café froid n'est pas digeste.

— On va faire la toilette du bas, lui dis-je en me munissant de mon gant de toilette. Vous êtes d'accord ?

— Non…

— Mais vous ne pouvez pas rester comme ça, insistai-je, vous devez être mal à l'aise.

— Oui… répondit-elle en sanglotant.

— On va se mettre sur le côté, je vais y aller tout doucement. Si je vous fais mal, vous me le dites, d'accord ?

— Non… « Qu'est-ce qu'on attend pour faire la fête, qu'est-ce qu'on attend pour être heureux… »

Elle se remit à chanter, des larmes dans les yeux.

Je pris sa main et j'accompagnai son mouvement pour la basculer sur le côté. Elle s'accrocha à la barrière du lit.

Ses jambes étaient recroquevillées ; enlever ce slip sali fut une épreuve.

Malgré un énième refus de la dame, je commençai à la nettoyer. Elle se raidit au fur et à mesure et urina sur le lit. Roulage des draps, installation de serviettes de toilette pour protéger ce qui était encore propre. J'avais encore ses parties intimes à nettoyer.

Je dégoulinai de chaud, la toilette n'était pas terminée. Honnêtement, à ce moment précis, je n'en pouvais plus. Mon enthousiasme en avait pris un sacré coup derrière les oreilles. Il me restait onze personnes, et je me débattais depuis quarante-cinq minutes avec cette dame. J'avais mal au cœur d'être obligée de me battre pour exécuter ma tâche, même si je me rassurais en me répétant que c'était pour son bien.

La toilette se poursuivait dans les larmes et les cris. Je la rinçai, l'essuyai, et j'installai la protection propre. Afin de bien essuyer son entrejambe et les plis de l'aine, sans quoi les rougeurs arriveraient vite, je devais la mettre de nouveau sur le dos.

Les genoux pliés, je l'essuyai tant bien que mal ; elle hurlait, m'insultait. Sa main gauche agrippa mes cheveux, elle en garderait d'ailleurs une petite poignée.

Il était 9 h 50. Je repensais aux deux résidentes qui n'avaient pas voulu se lever, et à leurs petits déjeuners qui refroidissaient sur la table.

J'habillai tant bien que mal la dame, qui avait adopté la position fœtale. Dix minutes plus tard, tout le bas était enfilé. Il fallait maintenant l'asseoir sur le bord de son lit et l'aider à passer sur son fauteuil roulant.

Interdiction d'utiliser le verticaliseur, qui permet le transfert assis-debout, avec cette dame : elle était tellement crispée qu'elle partait en arrière et l'appareil avec. Quant au lève-malade, il n'avait plus de batterie. Et aucune collègue ne répondit à mon appel à l'aide.

Force était de constater que ce serait seule que j'effectuerais ce transfert.

La voilà assise sur le bord du lit, les pieds sur le sol. Tout est en place.

— Je vais vous installer dans votre fauteuil, vous allez m'aider ? Le petit déjeuner est servi.

— Le petit déjeuner est servi ?

— Oui, regardez sur la table. Vous allez pousser sur vos jambes et je vous aide, d'accord ? N'ayez pas peur, je suis là, je vous tiens.

— Non !

Les cris et les hurlements reprirent. Les boutons de ma blouse sautaient les uns après les autres sous les assauts de la dame. Note pour plus tard : plus de queue-de-cheval…

J'aurais tant aimé prendre plus de temps avec elle, ne pas avoir à la contrarier, mais j'avais largement dépassé les limites. Dès que je sentis qu'elle s'appuyait un peu sur ses jambes, je fis le transfert. Elle se laissa tomber comme un poids mort et elle m'embarqua dans le fauteuil. Une douleur dans le dos me coupa le souffle, mais ça passerait…

Enfin, elle était à table. Je courus, vérifiai qu'elle prenait bien son traitement, vidai ma bassine, la désinfectai, nettoyai les gants, courus encore chercher des draps propres et du produit désinfectant pour le lit. Puis direction mes bacs à linge, la poubelle pour jeter la protection souillée.

Au suivant.

24

22 décembre 2016, 10 heures

Je sortis de la chambre épuisée. Épuisée de m'être battue contre mon énervement et contre cette résidente apeurée. C'est alors qu'une dame aux cheveux d'un joli blanc m'interpella :

— Bonjour, mon petit, dites, est-ce que vous me feriez mon lit ?

— Oui, bien sûr. Souhaitez-vous que je vous aide pour la toilette ?

— Oh non, non, mon petit, je me débrouille, j'ai juste besoin que vous me fassiez mon lit.

— Vous souhaitez que nous changions les draps ?

— Oh, pensez-vous ! Cela fait dix jours que je les ai.

— Dix jours ?

— Oui.

— Changeons-les, puisque je suis là.

— Mais vous n'avez pas le temps, ma pauvre !

— Venez…

Je mentais, la dame avait raison. Elle souriait. Elle avait ce visage des grands-mères russes, avec ses fossettes rosées. Très élégante, fine et grande, bien coiffée.

Je revois ses beaux yeux bleus et son fauteuil crapaud à côté de la fenêtre où elle s'endormait les après-midi.

— Merci. Vous êtes nouvelle ?

— Oui.

— Vous allez rester ?

Toujours la même question…

— Oui, j'y compte bien.

— Parfait, alors nous nous reverrons.

10 h 10, il me restait toujours onze résidents. Je pensai à mes deux dames du fond du couloir qui n'étaient pas levées. J'étais décidée à aller les voir, et cette fois-ci, je serais ferme. Une lumière rouge s'afficha. Je me rendis auprès de la résidente.

— Bonjour, vous avez sonné, vous avez besoin de quelque chose ?

— Oui, pourriez-vous m'installer le bassin ? J'ai besoin, s'il vous plaît.

— Bien sûr.

Ce soin était devenu naturel chez elle ; sa pudeur, elle en avait fait le deuil, sa dépendance aussi. Elle avait besoin du bassin, et elle discutait avec moi comme si elle buvait son thé.

— Vous êtes nouvelle.

— Oui, je m'appelle Anne-Sophie.

— Et vous allez rester ?

— J'y compte bien.

— C'est bien. Vous savez, moi, j'ai perdu ma fille. Elle est morte d'un cancer. Regardez, elle est en photo sur l'étagère. Et moi je suis encore là. C'était à moi de mourir, pas à ma fille.

Elle se mit à pleurer. J'eus envie de la consoler, de la prendre dans mes bras, mais ç'aurait été outrepasser mes fonctions. Manquer de ce fameux recul professionnel.

Alors je l'ai écoutée. Je n'avais pas le temps, mais je le pris.

— Vous êtes bien installée ? lui demandai-je avant de partir.

— Oui, parfait, vous pouvez aller vous occuper de quelqu'un d'autre, je vous rappelle quand j'ai terminé.

— Ça va aller, vous êtes sûre ?

— Mais oui, ma petite, j'ai l'habitude.

L'habitude. Comment ce mot « habitude » peut-il être utilisé par nos aînés quand on les installe sur un bassin, une fois leurs changes ôtés ? Le confort est sommaire. Leur nudité exposée. Leur dignité envolée. De quelle manière arrive-t-on à s'habituer ?

Quand je sortis de la chambre, je retournai voir la première dame ; elle dormait encore. Le petit déjeuner était évidemment froid ; les médicaments étaient posés sur la table, et, vu l'heure, il était temps qu'elle les prenne. Je m'approchai d'elle. Elle était toute chaude, emmitouflée dans sa couette. C'est beau de voir un ancien dormir, j'aurais pu rester des heures à l'observer. Son visage était serein, pas de douleur, et sûrement de jolis rêves.

Si elle n'était pas en EHPAD, probablement aurait-elle dormi toute la matinée, se serait levée quand elle l'aurait décidé, aurait pris son petit déjeuner à midi. Là, ce n'était pas possible. Il y a des règles, dans un EHPAD, des horaires, et les rythmes biologiques sont rarement respectés.

Comment la réveiller ? Si j'ouvrais les volets pour laisser passer la lumière, pas sûre qu'elle apprécierait. Je me rapprochai donc et lui caressai la joue.

— Madame Trapot, c'est Anne-Sophie, il faut vous réveiller, votre petit déjeuner est servi.

— Mmmmm…

— On va se réveiller doucement, je vais ouvrir les volets, vous êtes d'accord ?

— Mmmmm…

— Vous avez bien dormi ?

— Mmmmmm…

— On va se lever, je vais vous aider. Désolée, j'ai les mains froides.

Je relevai la couette et lui enfilai ses bas.

— Vous m'emmerdez, je veux dormir !

— Je sais, mais il faut vous lever, le petit déjeuner est servi et il est 10 h 20, je vais vous aider.

— Je ne veux pas me lever.

— Je sais, mais nous n'avons pas le choix, vous n'allez pas rester au lit toute la journée ?

— Merde !

— Allez, venez, je vais vous aider.

Alors qu'elle était encore à moitié endormie, je la pris dans mes bras et j'accompagnai son mouvement pour l'asseoir sur le bord du lit. Elle était toute molle. Il fallait la tenir avec douceur, et continuer de la motiver.

— Je vais tomber…

— Mais non, je suis là, je vous tiens.

Je me plaçai devant elle et la chaussai. Elle se laissait partir en avant, elle somnolait.

J'approchai le déambulateur, en redoutant déjà les quelques mètres vers la salle de bains. Je l'aidai à empoigner l'accessoire indispensable à ses déplacements et lui donnai une légère impulsion pour qu'elle puisse se mettre debout. Elle se laissa encore partir en avant. Elle aurait préféré dormir, et je n'avais pas d'autre choix que de la lever. Je culpabilisai.

— On va s'installer aux toilettes, venez.

Je la déshabillai, j'enlevai la protection souillée et je restai encore à côté d'elle.

— Je vais tomber !

— Mais non, je suis là.

— Sale pute ! Je ne vous aime pas.

— Nous allons apprendre à nous connaître.

— Espèce de connasse, fous-moi la paix, je vais tomber !

— Mais non, je suis là, je vous tiens.

— Ferme ta gueule ! Et puis tu me fais mal.

— Où est-ce que je vous fais mal ?

— Nulle part ! C'était pour t'emmerder.

— On va faire votre toilette, alors, vous êtes d'accord ?

— Non, va-t'en !

— Je ne peux pas vous laisser comme cela.

— Dégage, je te dis, salope !

J'allais encore être obligée de la contraindre. Si j'avais respecté son rythme biologique, peut-être aurais-je évité toutes ces insultes. Lui en vouloir, lui en tenir rigueur ? Non ! Elle était âgée, et je n'aurais sûrement pas été heureuse moi non plus, même à mon âge, que l'on m'oblige à me lever.

Je l'installai sur le banc dans la douche, tirai la chasse d'eau et commençai à la déshabiller. Elle continuait de se laisser tomber en avant. Était-ce du cinéma ou un véritable manque d'équilibre ? Je l'ignorais.

— Donnez-moi votre main. La température de l'eau vous convient ?

— C'est trop froid !

— Et ainsi ?

— C'est encore trop froid.

— Comme cela, alors ?

— C'est trop chaud !

Cinq bonnes minutes de perdues pour trouver la température qui lui seyait. Et l'heure qui tournait…

Les invectives fusaient, je ne les entendais pas. Je faisais mon travail. Plus je lui parlais, plus elle m'insultait.

Je changeai de gant pour la toilette du bas. Il fallait qu'elle se lève pour que je puisse laver ses parties intimes. Je craignais qu'elle ne tombe. Et ce que je redoutais arriva : elle se redressa quand je le lui demandai mais se laissa partir en avant, manquant de justesse de se fracasser le front contre le mur. Enfin, je la séchai, posai la serviette sur le petit banc pour qu'elle s'y asseye. Je terminai d'enfiler le slip filet et le change, la jupe et ces satanés bas de contention. Il fallait trouver des astuces pour éviter aux résidents un maximum de mobilisation.

Mon téléphone se mit à sonner. La dame sur le bassin avait terminé. Je ne pouvais pas abandonner ma résidente sur le banc de la salle de bains à moitié habillée.

— Je vais tomber… me dit encore celle-ci tandis que je la relevais.

— Mais non, je suis là.

— Je tombe…

— Je suis là, ne vous inquiétez pas.

En fait, j'étais très inquiète. Et si elle tombait, comment la rattraper ?

Je l'installai dans son fauteuil roulant. Un coup de peigne, un peu de parfum. Mon téléphone sonnait toujours. Je culpabilisai de plus belle. Au bout du compte, la résidente récalcitrante était enfin à sa table de petit déjeuner. Le café était froid, je dus courir à l'autre bout du couloir pour le réchauffer au micro-ondes. Et mon téléphone sonnait toujours.

Les médicaments, le linge sale, les poubelles, je filai m'occuper de la résidente installée sur le bassin depuis maintenant une demi-heure. Le lit attendrait, je reviendrais.

25

Course contre la montre

Plus qu'une heure pour que tous les résidents dont j'avais la charge soient prêts à aller en salle de restauration, et il ne me restait que des toilettes alitées. Je savais qu'elles me prendraient du temps, je ne serais donc pas à l'heure. Et aucune collègue pour venir m'assister. Moi qui avais espéré que ce serait différent de l'aide à domicile, je me sentais aussi seule que lorsque j'étais auxiliaire de vie sociale. J'apprendrais à mes dépens, avec le temps, ce qu'était une équipe, et combien la réalité était loin de l'image idéalisée que je m'en étais faite.

— Je suis désolée, je n'ai pu venir avant, m'excusai-je auprès de la dame sur son bassin.

— Oh, ce n'est pas grave, j'ai l'habitude… répéta-t-elle

Comment peut-on avoir l'habitude de rester de très longues, trop longues minutes sur un morceau de plastique inconfortable qui vous laisserait des marques ?

— Je vais vous faire votre toilette, tant que je suis là, vous êtes d'accord ?

— Oui, allons-y.

Quand je lui enlevai le bassin, comme je l'avais craint, la dame avait des marques. La culpabilité m'étreignit. C'était ma faute, j'aurais dû répondre dès son premier appel. Mais je n'avais pas le temps pour m'étendre sur mes états d'âme ; ma résidente était polyhandicapée, et le temps pressait. Je commençai le déshabillage.

— Ça va, je ne vous fais pas mal ?

— Oh non, vous pouvez y aller. D'où venez-vous ?

— Je suis franc-comtoise, née à Besançon.

— Ah, vous connaissez le Jura, alors ?

— Oui.

Nous fîmes doucement connaissance, tandis que je la tournais et la retournais pour pouvoir pratiquer une toilette la plus complète possible. On a beau y mettre un maximum de douceur, l'individu, avec ces manipulations qui deviennent peu à peu des automatismes, n'est-il pas réduit à un corps ? Mes collègues avaient-elles les mêmes réticences que moi ?

La toilette devrait être un moment de détente pour les résidents, elle se résumait à de la technicité et à des tours de grand huit sans lot à la clef. C'était donc à moi de trouver des astuces pour éviter au maximum de la bringuebaler dans tous les sens : lorsque la dame était sur le dos, je lui installais le slip filet avec la protection et la jupe. On remontait le tout, en s'assurant qu'il n'y avait pas de plis dans l'entrejambe, je la basculais d'un côté pour passer les fesses, et de l'autre pour que l'avant passe aussi. Ces deux actions, anodines quand on est valide, deviennent fastidieuses quand on a plus de quatre-vingts ans et que l'on est paralysé.

Une fois habillée, la dame souhaita rester couchée ; on aurait été fatiguée à moins.

— Revenez me chercher pour aller manger, je vais me reposer un peu en attendant, si cela ne vous dérange pas.

— Non, pas du tout. Avez-vous besoin de quelque chose ? demandai-je en approchant sa table, sa sonnette et son téléphone.

— Non, ça ira, merci, me répondit-elle.

*

Sortie de la chambre de cette résidente, il me restait trente minutes pour encore deux toilettes alitées, et je n'avais toujours pas réveillé la deuxième dame du fond du couloir.

Youpi ! Quand j'entrai dans sa chambre, celle-ci était levée et attablée, et elle avait pris son petit déjeuner et ses médicaments. Je lui proposai de se rendre aux toilettes.

— Tu es qui, toi ? me demanda-t-elle, sur la défensive.

— Je suis Anne-Sophie, je viens vous aider à aller aux toilettes. Vous venez avec moi ?

— Tu veux me tuer, c'est ça ? On m'a mise ici pour me tuer…

— Mais non, suivez-moi, je vous emmène juste aux toilettes. Votre chemise de nuit est trempée, vous devez avoir froid.

— Je vous connais, vous, les blouses blanches, vous croyez que je suis folle, c'est ça, hein ?

— Bien sûr que non, mais vous avez besoin de vous changer. Vous verrez, cela vous fera du bien.

— Du bien ? Arrête tes conneries ! Moi, c'est chez moi que je serais bien.

— Vous habitiez où ?

— Ben, pas loin, quelle question !

— Donnez-moi la main, vous allez me raconter votre histoire et nous allons faire connaissance.

Finalement, elle me tendit ses deux mains et, accrochée à mon bras, franchit les trois mètres qui nous séparaient de la salle de bains en cinq bonnes minutes. Elle sentait si fort l'urine qu'un seul choix s'imposait : une douche. J'étais dans le jus, je n'aurais jamais terminé à temps, mais tant pis, j'aurais pris soin de nos aînés.

La crainte me vint cependant : j'étais en période d'essai, est-ce que mon efficacité toute relative au vu du temps qui m'est concédé me desservirait ?

À cet instant, j'eus envie de pleurer. Je n'y arriverais jamais. Les agents de service tentèrent de me rassurer. Mais j'avais du mal à contenir les larmes qui commençaient à perler au coin de mes paupières. Inspirer, expirer et repartir. Il me restait deux toilettes lourdes à faire en quinze minutes. C'était impossible. Pour couronner le tout, mon téléphone sonna. Ma gentille résidente avait de nouveau besoin du bassin. Déshabillage, installation du bassin. Je la laissai faire ce qu'elle avait à faire en espérant qu'elle ne me rappelle pas trop vite.

*

11 h 20.

Je frappai à la porte d'un monsieur. Il avait déjeuné, comme il avait pu : les draps avaient reçu la moitié de son café au lait…

— Bonjour, monsieur, vous avez bien dormi ?

Poser cette question à cette heure-ci m'apparut soudain grotesque.

— Oui, très bien.

— On va aller à la toilette, vous êtes d'accord ?

— Oh oui, alors !

Le verticaliseur était rechargé, j'avais anticipé et l'avais emporté dans la chambre.

— Bien, alors vous allez m'aider, on va s'asseoir sur le bord du lit.

— Oh oui, oui !

Malgré toute sa bonne volonté, le monsieur était lourd et ne put que très peu être utile à l'opération. Mon dos en prit un coup, mais le résident fut assis. Imaginez-vous un homme de quatre-vingts kilos qui se tient à deux petites poignées comme celles d'une trottinette, et que vous devez pousser jusqu'à la salle d'eau. Les roulettes sont aussi larges que celles d'un chariot de supermarché. Pas de direction assistée. Il faut éviter les murs, les coins de meuble, pour que le résident n'y laisse pas un coude.

Je lui baissai son pyjama, son slip filet, et j'enlevai la protection pour l'installer sur la chaise percée. Mais son sphincter ne put attendre, et ses selles tombèrent sur le sol. Ce n'était pas sa faute, bien sûr, mais les larmes perlèrent de nouveau. En plus de le doucher, il faudrait que je nettoie le sol. Garder son calme, l'installer sur la chaise. Je devais laver le sol souillé pour pouvoir accéder à la douche avec l'appareil. Une seule solution : enlever le plus gros avec ce que je pouvais et passer la douche. L'odeur était pestilentielle. Pour autant, le monsieur était de bonne humeur.

*

11 h 30, la lingère frappa.

— Ton linge est là ?

— Oui, je suis désolée, je n'ai pas eu le temps de le descendre, je suis très en retard.

— Je le prends.

— Merci beaucoup.

Première étape de la toilette : le rasage. Je soufflai, il avait un très bon rasoir électrique. Du temps de gagné. C'est tout de même terrible de commencer à imaginer comment gagner du temps…

Le résident était d'une grande gentillesse et obtempérait sans rechigner. Je lui lavai le dos, le buste, le visage et les cheveux. Sous l'effet de l'eau chaude, les gens se détendent et parlent. Lui me parla de tout et de rien, ses propos n'étaient pas toujours cohérents, mais qu'importe, je répondais. Mon téléphone sonna. La séance bassin était terminée. Je me trouvais encore confrontée au dilemme de laisser ce monsieur sans surveillance sur cette chaise percée, où il risquait l'accident, ou d'éviter d'autres marques à ma résidente.

Je décidai de finir la toilette du monsieur, mais je devais activer le mouvement. Comment faire encore plus vite ?

Une fois le haut lavé et habillé, je repris l'engin de malheur pour entreprendre la toilette des parties intimes en position semi-debout quand mon téléphone sonna de nouveau. Ce n'était pas la même chambre. Je n'avais pas d'autre choix que de terminer sa toilette, et j'étais donc obligée à ce stade d'imposer à l'autre résidente de la non-traitance. La colère montait ; ce n'était pas cela, mon métier.

Il fallait que je me dépêche pour que la station à moitié debout ne le fatigue pas plus. La toilette du bas se ferait donc au lavabo. Tout en évitant autant que faire se peut de mouiller le haut, je le nettoyai. Il fatiguait, je me dépêchai un peu plus. Je le séchai, j'installai la protection propre. Mon téléphone bipa encore ; mon Dieu que cet appareil me stressait ! Direction le fauteuil roulant. Là aussi, des précautions sont à prendre pour que la personne ne glisse pas. Installation des appuie-pieds, un joli pull, un coup de peigne et un soupçon de parfum. Il me sourit. Je m'occuperai de son lit plus tard, pas le temps.

Cela montait à trois le nombre de lits non faits.

*

J'allai ensuite voir ma résidente sur le bassin. Je savais que cette intervention me prendrait moins de temps que la deuxième, une dame qui voulait que je lui fasse sa toilette. Il était 11 h 45, et elle ne m'avait pas encore vue de la matinée…

En lui enlevant son bassin, j'avais prié pour qu'il n'y ait pas de selles. Raté. Je devais, en plus du nettoyage du bassin, renouveler la toilette intime de la résidente. Certaines collègues la font à la mousse nettoyante, je considère que nos aînés ne sont ni des tapis ni des moquettes, et que le savon est plus approprié. Certes, cela prend plus de temps, mais la finalité est une meilleure prise en soin.

J'en profitai pour l'installer dans son fauteuil roulant. Là encore, grand moment de solitude : porter une dame parce qu'elle ne supporte pas les engins, viser le fond du fauteuil, et surtout, vérifier que la jupe soit bien au milieu. Pour de nombreuses personnes âgées, la préoccupation majeure est l'élégance, et j'aimais cette idée. Un coup de peigne, quelques gouttes de parfum, elle était prête pour aller manger.

Je ferais son lit plus tard.

Et de quatre.

26

11 h 50 : dernière toilette de la matinée

Je frappai et j'entrai dans la dernière chambre. Je m'excusai platement de mon retard.

— Ne vous alarmez pas, j'ai l'habitude.

Encore cette satanée formule… J'étais mal à l'aise, j'avais chaud, je n'avais pas réussi à boucler toutes mes tâches en temps et en heure, et je m'inquiétais pour ma période d'essai. Je n'avais qu'une seule envie : me sauver en courant et pleurer dans un coin.

Mémé, aide-moi à tenir, s'il te plaît !

Je m'en voulais d'avoir laissé cette gentille dame si longtemps dans sa protection souillée. Je lui crémai les jambes, et je lui enfilai ses bas de contention. Je cachais mes larmes, mais j'avais la gorge nouée et je n'arrivais pas à parler. J'étais frappée de plein fouet par la culpabilisation qui envahit le soignant qui ne peut accomplir son travail en lui donnant du sens, c'est-à-dire en prenant l'individu dans sa globalité et non comme une somme d'actes à enchaîner dans le moins de temps possible.

— Vous êtes nouvelle ?

— Oui.

— C'est bien, je vais vous aider et vous dire comment on me fait ma toilette.

— Je suis encore désolée pour le retard.

— Oh, ce n'est pas grave, ils m'attendront bien pour manger, et puis je n'ai pas très faim.

La dame me demanda de l'installer sur sa chaise percée, elle était autonome concernant la toilette du haut. Je l'aidai donc à s'asseoir sur le bord du lit, lui enfilai des chaussons et lui passai les sangles du verticaliseur. Elle râla de douleur ; à la vue de ses jambes gonflées, je compris vite qu'il faudrait que le transfert ne soit pas long. Les roulettes de l'appareil étaient toujours aussi peu dociles, et je tenais à bout de bras une personne qui devait peser près du quintal. Je l'installai sur la chaise, la rapprochai du lavabo. Elle souhaita ses sous-vêtements, son caraco, et me dit :

— Je vous rappelle quand j'ai terminé, vous devez encore avoir des choses à faire, ne vous inquiétez pas pour moi.

J'avais effectivement quatre lits en instance. Je profitai de sa proposition qui tombait on ne peut mieux pour rattraper mon retard. Enfin, c'est ce que je pensais. Je me mis à faire les lits quand une petite voix au fond du couloir m'interpella :

— Mademoiselle, vous savez quand l'aide-soignante viendra s'occuper de ma toilette ?

Ma culpabilité fut à son comble, j'avais oublié cette résidente.

— Je viens maintenant si vous le souhaitez.

— Oh, merci, vous êtes gentille.

Non, je n'étais pas gentille, je l'avais oubliée. Heureusement pour moi, elle était presque autonome et pouvait, avec mon aide, faire seule sa toilette au lavabo. Même si ce n'est pas ce que je préfère, c'est toujours mieux que rien. Dix minutes à ses côtés, un peu de parfum, et la voilà partie, canne à la main, vers la salle de restauration. Je n'aurai pas vraiment eu le temps de discuter avec elle, mais j'aurai été efficace. Mon téléphone sonna : ma résidente précédente avait terminé.

*

De retour dans la chambre de la dame, je lui agrafai son soutien-gorge, l'aidai à enfiler son tee-shirt, et l'éloignai du lavabo. Il me restait toute la toilette intime à faire. Je la rattachai au verticaliseur, et, comme pour les autres, j'en profitai pour préenfiler le bas. Je l'apprendrais à ses dépens, mais cette résidente souffrait d'une pathologie qui nécessitait une intervention rapide après un passage aux toilettes.

Savon, gant, séchage, attention aux plis. Mes gestes étaient devenus automatiques. Je ne sais même pas si je lui ai parlé, je ne voyais que l'heure qui tournait. Quelqu'un frappa à la porte. Une collègue. Enfin ! C'est à cette heure-ci que l'on venait me demander si j'avais besoin d'aide, alors que toutes avaient pu prendre leur pause de 10 heures ? C'était probablement le traitement que l'on réservait aux nouvelles. Elle me proposa d'emmener des résidents dans la salle à manger. La tête dans le fessier de la dame, évidemment que j'apprécierais qu'elle emmène des résidents !

La toilette terminée, et après un passage toujours éprouvant et périlleux par le verticaliseur, je l'installai bien au fond de son fauteuil. Elle me demanda son foulard, son sac à main et un peu de parfum. Je la conduisis enfin jusqu'à la salle de restauration.

*

Je devais terminer à midi, il était presque 13 heures. J'avais encore ma poubelle à sortir et deux lits à faire. Je me suis acquittée de toutes ces tâches et, une fois dans les vestiaires, je me suis mise à pleurer. En attendant l'heure de la reprise, soit 14 h 30, je suis allée me reposer de cette matinée infernale.

*

Les jours qui suivraient, je serais toujours au même étage. Pourtant, sur le planning, il était bien noté que je devais passer dans les autres étages, mais mes collègues en avaient décidé autrement. Je pris cette délicate attention comme une sorte de bizutage. J'ai donc travaillé durant quatre jours consécutifs au rez-de-chaussée ; je me suis sentie coupable, inutile, incapable, jusqu'à l'écœurement, mais j'ai continué, parce que même si chaque jour je débauchais en retard, chaque jour j'avais pris soin des résidents avec le temps que l'on avait bien voulu m'accorder.

J'apprendrais plus tard que personne ne voulait travailler au rez-de-chaussée… C'est beau, une équipe !

27

Jour de repos

Ce premier jour m'avait épuisée. J'étais à la fois en colère et triste, et je ruminais. J'étais partie en pleurs, écœurée de ne pas m'être sentie à la hauteur des tâches qui m'incombaient, et avec le sentiment d'avoir été abandonnée à mon triste sort. Sous prétexte que j'avais fait mon essai au rez-de-chaussée, soit quatre heures en tout et pour tout, j'étais pour mes nouvelles collègues une professionnelle de cet étage. J'avais été lâchée dans le grand bain sans bouée. Elles ne m'avaient que très peu adressé la parole, juste pour me demander quelle mouche m'avait piquée d'avoir quitté le sud de la France pour le Jura.

Je comprenais mieux pourquoi les nouvelles recrues ne voulaient pas rester, on ne pouvait pas dire que l'accueil dans l'établissement était des plus chaleureux. Personne ne m'a expliqué les tâches à effectuer dans la journée. Elles exécutaient leur routine en m'ignorant gentiment. Alors j'ai suivi, j'ai observé, j'ai pris des notes. Après tout, elles n'étaient que des collègues.

J'avais tenté dc me rassurer en me persuadant qu'elles n'avaient probablement pas eu le temps ; or je les avais vues prendre une pause-café à 10 heures sans même me proposer de les accompagner. J'aurais décliné l'invitation, certes, mais j'aurais été contente qu'elles pensent à moi.

*

À la maison, tous ces désagréments me hantaient. J'avais quitté l'aide à domicile pour ne plus me sentir seule, et je retrouvais la même situation au sein d'un établissement.

Je repensais à un épisode en particulier. Je devais rapporter les plateaux des petits déjeuners des résidents qui n'avaient pas terminé au moment du ramassage de ceux-ci. J'avais déjà fini en retard, j'avais amené les résidents dans la salle de restauration quand, du fond de la pièce, j'entendis une serveuse peu encline à être agréable m'apostropher :

— Hé ! Toi !

En claquant des doigts, comme on appellerait un chien. Je me retournai.

— Oui, toi, là-bas, les plateaux, ce n'est pas moi qui vais aller les chercher, tu les rapportes.

La serveuse m'avait interpellée devant tout le monde. Je sentis la honte rosir mes joues. J'avais galéré toute la matinée, et je prenais cette réflexion comme un énième manquement : j'avais oublié les plateaux.

Je n'ai rien rétorqué, je ne me suis pas plainte du comportement des autres. J'avalai la pilule, mais après plusieurs verres d'eau. Mon métier, pourtant, je le connaissais ; aujourd'hui, je me sentais nullc.

De retour à la maison, j'avais devant moi des sacs de linge à ranger, des cartons à déballer. Je n'avais pas le courage de m'y mettre. Il allait pourtant bien falloir, les enfants n'allaient pas piocher dans des sacs-poubelle pour trouver leurs vêtements ! Et puis, il faudrait que je me traîne jusqu'au supermarché acheter des produits frais ; jusqu'à maintenant, seuls des sandwichs rythmaient nos repas. Le camping, c'est sympathique, mais pas trop longtemps.

Pour couronner le tout, nous n'avions pas d'eau chaude, le ballon avait lâché faute d'avoir été détartré. Le plombier, en cette période de fêtes, était débordé. Moi qui rêvais d'un bain pour évacuer les douleurs et la pression, c'était raté.

*

En ce 23 décembre, jour de congé, je n'avais pas vraiment réussi à me reposer. J'avais vainement tenté d'oublier la veille, à part quelques instants dans le regard de mes enfants. Mais le répit serait de courte durée.

Demain, j'y retournerai ; demain, je ferai de mon mieux ; demain, j'essaierai de ne pas penser ; demain, j'essaierai d'être un automate pour terminer à l'heure et ne rien oublier.

Je m'accrocherai ; au diable les collègues, j'étais là pour prendre soin de nos anciens.

28

La magie de Noël

En cette veille de Noël, j'étais toujours affectée au même étage – décidément, on ne me ferait pas de cadeaux, même les 24 et 25 décembre. Je n'en pouvais plus, de ce rez-de-chaussée ! Je l'avais même déjà en horreur.

La façade de l'établissement était jolie, les illuminations donnaient vraiment le sentiment que Noël approchait. À l'intérieur, un sapin trônait, des décorations avaient été installées un peu partout dans la salle de restauration. Le reste du bâtiment, en revanche, était identique à lui-même, et les couloirs étaient toujours aussi blancs. La vitrine était soignée, elle plairait aux familles, mais les coulisses étaient moins clinquantes. Et les tâches à effectuer au pas de charge, Noël ou pas Noël, identiques à n'importe quel autre jour.

Aujourd'hui, par exemple, il n'y avait plus de gants à usage unique, je serais dans l'obligation de prendre des gants de toilette classiques. En cas de selles, ça s'annoncerait coton… Il n'y avait plus non plus de protections bleues, il faudrait donc mettre à tout le monde des violettes, celles de la nuit, plus absorbantes et disgracieuses. Nos aînés se promèneraient donc en cette veille de Noël avec des fessiers rebondis. Et tant pis pour ceux qui souhaitaient rester discrets sur le port des changes.

Combien de fois nous avons manqué de matériel, combien de fois la réserve fut vide, je ne compte même plus…

Malgré la présence de haut-parleurs dans chaque couloir, aucun chant de Noël n'était diffusé dans l'établissement. Les seules notes qui résonneraient seraient les mêmes que d'habitude : les bruits métalliques des chariots qui s'entrechoquent, des poubelles qu'on vide, des infirmières pressées, le chuintement des chaussons des aînés sur le carrelage.

Je me consolai en me disant que ce soir, une fois à la maison, des chants de Noël m'accueilleraient, le sapin serait illuminé, et ma famille me cajolerait. Mais nos aînés ? Ceux qui étaient sans famille resteraient seuls dans leur lit ce soir, à la même heure que d'habitude. Rien ne changerait, ce serait finalement une journée comme une autre. Certains dans l'après-midi seraient installés devant la télévision ; les goûters seraient distribués, les changes et les mises en pyjama effectués.

Il régnait ainsi une ambiance assez lourde dans l'EHPAD. Aucune effervescence, aucune joie dans les regards. Seules les décorations nous rappelaient que nous étions la veille de Noël. À 20 heures, tous les résidents seraient couchés. Où sont passés les repas en famille ou entre amis ? Où sont passés ces moments privilégiés où ces femmes passaient des heures dans leur cuisine pour préparer la veillée ? Qui irait à la messe de minuit ? Personne. Certains espéraient avec angoisse que leurs proches viennent les voir le lendemain, sans en avoir la certitude.

Je savais déjà que les couchers seraient ardus, chargés en émotion et tristesse. Et comme je n'aurais pas plus de temps à leur accorder, je partirais le cœur blessé. Comment réconforter un sage seul pendant ces fêtes ?

*

Le dîner de ce soir était fidèle aux autres jours : l'éternelle soupe, un friand au fromage difforme et trois feuilles de salade pour l'accompagner, un carré de Vache qui rit pour la majorité, et pour quelques-uns un morceau de fromage à la coupe ; enfin, une orange en dessert. L'orange, pour certains résidents, c'était leur madeleine de Proust. Quand ils étaient enfants, ils en recevaient parfois une en guise de cadeau de Noël.

Le repas se termina à 19 h 15. La morosité gagna la salle. Ce soir, pas d'embouteillages aux ascenseurs, un silence bruyant pesait sur chacun. Les résidents regagnaient leurs chambres, le regard bas. J'étais triste ; j'aurais tant voulu les emmener tous chez moi afin qu'ils ne se sentent pas si seuls ! J'aurais tant voulu leur offrir un réveillon comme nous en avions savouré un avec Charles. Mais c'était impossible, et j'en avais le cœur lourd.

J'entrai dans la première chambre. Robert était triste. Sa femme et ses enfants lui manquaient. Pendant que je le déshabillais, quelques larmes perlèrent sur ses joues burinées par l'âge. Je tentai de le réconforter.

— Robert, demain, votre épouse vient vous voir, vos enfants aussi, il y a juste une nuit à passer…

— Je sais, ma petite, mais nous faisions de grandes tablées pour la veillée de Noël… Et regarde-moi : ce soir, je suis seul dans cette chambre. Je suis un vieux con !

— Mais non, Robert…

— Si, regarde, je ne suis même plus capable de me déshabiller seul !

— Robert, je suis juste là pour vous accompagner, vous êtes encore très autonome. Votre canne à la main, vous poussez le fauteuil de votre voisin pour qu'il aille en salle de restauration !

— C'est normal, ça, ma petite, il faut toujours savoir aider les autres.

Je l'accompagnai vers son lit, il s'allongea.

— Dis, ma petite, tu pourrais me mettre ma radio sur moi ?

— Oui, bien sûr, mais elle risque de tomber quand vous dormirez.

— On va l'attacher.

J'enlevai la ceinture du pantalon de Robert et l'attachai à la barrière du lit. Robert aurait son poste pour seule compagnie ce soir. Quand je sortis, il m'apostropha :

— Dis, ma petite, si demain, ma femme ne vient pas, tu m'aideras à lui téléphoner ?

— Elle viendra, Robert, ne vous inquiétez pas. Mais au besoin nous l'appellerons ensemble, je vous le promets.

— T'es bien gentille, toi. Tu vas retrouver ta famille ce soir ? Vous ferez une grande fête ?

— Oui, Robert, je vais retrouver ma famille, mais nous ne ferons pas une grande fête. Je travaille demain, je serai là pour m'occuper de vous.

— T'as des enfants, ma petite ?

— Oui, deux. Un garçon et une fille.

— Moi aussi j'ai des enfants, mais il y en a que je ne vois plus. Tu sais, ils n'ont pas apprécié que je divorce et que j'épouse ma femme actuelle.

— Ne vous tourmentez pas, Robert, essayez de dormir pour être bien en forme demain quand tous viendront vous voir, d'accord ?

— Tu seras là demain ?

— Oui, et je viendrai m'occuper de vous, promis.

— Salut, ma petite, à demain alors.

— À demain, Robert, bonne nuit, reposez-vous.

J'avais passé beaucoup de temps avec lui, et j'avais encore du monde à coucher. Et dans chaque chambre où j'irais, la tristesse serait palpable.

*

Je suis rentrée en retard ce soir-là, comme d'habitude. À mon arrivée, la table était mise, le sapin scintillait, les enfants étaient pressés d'ouvrir leurs cadeaux disposés au pied de l'arbre. Des chants de Noël retentirent dans la maison.

J'étais là sans être vraiment là. Il me faudrait un moment pour réaliser que c'était la veillée de Noël ; j'étais rentrée, il allait falloir en profiter.

*

25 décembre, 7 heures. J'arrivai dans l'établissement. La première collègue que je croisai avait mis un serre-tête avec des cornes de renne ; une petite coquetterie qui me fit du bien. J'aurais pu y penser pour

égayer cette journée. L'année prochaine. Les transmissions furent encore faites au pas de charge ; une seule infirmière aujourd'hui, nous étions donc autorisées à distribuer les médicaments. C'est une tâche supplémentaire qui ne prend pas vraiment de temps mais qui s'ajoute tout de même à celles déjà fort nombreuses du matin. Je sortis mes chariots. Troisième jour de bagne. Souffler un grand coup… C'était parti.

Je finirais mes toilettes à l'heure ce matin, mon linge serait descendu à temps, mes poubelles seraient sorties, et tous mes lits seraient faits. Je commençais à apprivoiser mon parcours du combattant, mais j'étais sur les rotules. Je me battais toujours avec certains, je n'oubliais plus la chambre du fond et j'arrivais même à m'occuper de deux résidents en même temps. Tout est question d'organisation, et certes aussi un peu de leur bon vouloir.

Aujourd'hui, les tenues de mes résidents seraient différentes, j'y tenais. Les belles jupes que l'on sort peu seraient dépoussiérées, les jolis caracos mis et les pantalons à pinces enfilés. Ce monsieur, par exemple, avait beau être dans son fauteuil roulant, j'aimais le voir habillé avec son pull noir col roulé et son pantalon en velours bleu marine côtelé. Concours d'élégance aujourd'hui à l'étage !

Depuis 10 heures, des chants de Noël résonnaient dans les couloirs. Enfin… La salle de restauration aussi était différente : la mise en place ressemblait à celle d'un beau restaurant gastronomique ; j'espérais que le contenu des assiettes suivrait le même chemin. Contrairement à la veille, il régnait dans l'établissement une ambiance de fête. Les familles arrivèrent pour déjeuner avec leurs aînés ; des résidents étaient partis en vadrouille fêter Noël au domicile de leurs enfants.

La femme de Robert était là, j'eus droit à un clin d'œil, je souris.

Et puis il y avait ceux qui étaient seuls, ceux qui voyaient les enfants et petits-enfants venir souhaiter un joyeux Noël à Mamie ou Papi, avec un cadeau. Eux n'auraient rien aujourd'hui.

Pourquoi ne pas mettre plus d'ambiance dans cette salle, pourquoi ne pas chanter ? J'étais à la table des aidés quand je commençai à pousser la chansonnette ; au début discrètement, et de plus en plus fort. Du « Minuit chrétien », au « Il est né le divin enfant », Tino Rossi n'avait qu'à bien se tenir, une véritable chorale se mit en ordre de notes. Je crois que l'air qui eut le plus de succès, c'est « Noël blanc ». Les voix montèrent, les sourires apparurent. Les familles aussi chantaient. Je passai pour une extraterrestre auprès de mes collègues serveurs ; le ridicule ne tue pas, et puis rien ne les empêchait de venir se joindre à nous.

C'était la première fois que le repas ne se réduisait pas à des bruits de fourchettes dans les assiettes depuis que j'avais pris mon poste dans l'établissement. Voilà comment je considérais mon métier : être la pierre angulaire du bien-être de nos aînés, et, ce midi, j'avais réussi.

L'après-midi, les résidents seraient placés devant la télévision ; merci aux programmateurs des chaînes de télé, Noël est souvent l'occasion de revoir de vieux films, comme les éternels *Sissi*, ou *Violettes impériales*. Ce jour-là, ils ont regardé, si mes souvenirs sont bons, *La Route fleurie*, avec Georges Guétary. Tous connaissaient les chansons de cette opérette.

L'établissement vivait, même si nos prescriptions de travail étaient les mêmes qu'hier, même si nous courions toujours dans les couloirs ; l'ambiance était familiale, enfin je pouvais prendre le temps de discuter. Robert était heureux. Il s'était isolé avec son épouse, il voulait en profiter, il était très amoureux de cette femme aux cheveux gris et aux yeux si bleus…

Je me suis dit que, au vu du succès des chants en plein repas, il faudrait refaire la même chose de temps en temps. Par exemple, si je travaillais le 1er janvier, peut-être aimeraient-ils regarder et écouter le concert du Nouvel An retransmis tous les ans depuis Vienne ? Chez ma grand-mère, nous ne manquions jamais cette retransmission qui finissait chaque fois par *La Marche de Radetzky*. Je me pris à rêver. Pourquoi pas, finalement ?

*

Ce soir-là, les couchers ont été moins difficiles, tous avaient passé une bonne journée. Les angoisses de nos aînés seraient moins présentes, beaucoup me parleraient de ce repas de midi en chansons, et je me prendrais à sourire avec certains résidents.

Il était temps de rejoindre mon mari et mes enfants. Je ne les avais pas vus se lever ce matin, il était tard, ils m'attendaient. Mais j'avais, moi aussi, passé un joyeux Noël.

29

Un dimanche de janvier

La nouvelle année débuta comme se termina la précédente : au rez-de-chaussée, de 7 heures à 18 heures cette fois-ci. J'avais commencé à prendre mes marques, je finissais à l'heure, et j'essayais autant que faire se peut de passer du temps avec les résidents. J'avais réussi à mettre en place les toilettes respectant au maximum leur dignité, même si, fondamentalement, j'aurais aimé rester plus longtemps avec eux.

Aujourd'hui, pendant l'heure du repas, je m'occuperais de la table des assistés, ceux qui ont besoin d'aide pour manger, couper les aliments, se servir de l'eau ou du vin. La table des humiliés, en quelque sorte, regroupés au même endroit. Pour des raisons pratiques, certes, mais ils s'en trouvaient stigmatisés.

D'autant que le regard des autonomes n'est pas le même sur plus dépendants qu'eux. Peut-être la crainte un jour de changer de place et de se voir à cette table de la honte.

En plus de couper les aliments, je fis le service. Il faut savoir s'entraider, c'est bien cela, la définition d'une équipe, n'est-ce pas ? L'entraide entre collègues, dans ces établissements, est obligatoire. Par chance, on ne m'avait pas encore demandé de tondre les pelouses ou de planter des fleurs, mais qui sait, il ne faut jamais dire jamais.

Une dizaine de personnes déjeunaient à cette table ; entre celles qui mangeaient mixé, celles qui mangeaient avec leurs doigts, celles qui ne pouvaient pas couper leur viande, et le service à faire, je ne chômai pas. Le temps des repas devrait être un moment d'échange, il devrait y avoir du bruit, or chacun avalait sa ration en silence, peu discutaient. C'était aussi triste qu'un déjeuner de famille où personne ne s'apprécie vraiment, mais se retrouve par obligation.

Dans les assiettes, un morceau de viande en sauce avec une purée qui aurait remplacé aisément les joints d'une vieille baignoire. La cuillère tient debout dans cet ersatz que je nomme « enduit de pomme de terre ». Quant au mixé servi, sans couleur, sans odeur particulière ni présentation améliorée, il est loin d'être appétissant. J'ai l'impression d'être dans la cantine d'un camp militaire, à la seule différence que la ration est servie par des gens en tenue de serveur et les tables agrémentées de nappes.

Les quantités de nourriture étaient limitées, juste un fond d'assiette, parfois. Certes, nos aînés ont moins d'appétit, mais certains ont gardé un bon coup de fourchette, et je suis persuadée qu'en sortant de table ils ont encore faim. J'en ai même vu mettre dans leur sac ce que leurs camarades de table n'avaient pas mangé.

Mais vers 15 heures, ils avaient du gâteau, le même morceau depuis cinq ans.

Le repas terminé, c'était la course à celui qui retournerait dans sa chambre en premier. C'étaient les doigts qui se levaient tous en même temps pour réclamer son déambulateur ; c'étaient des voix qui vous interpellaient pour vous demander de les remonter en chambre. C'étaient les plus autonomes qui couraient vers les ascenseurs…

Cette salle de restauration, qui finalement était si calme, devenait soudain une fourmilière. On se serait cru sur les autoroutes du sud de la France un week-end de chassé-croisé entre juilletistes et aoûtiens, avec les mêmes embouteillages, voire les mêmes disputes !

C'est alors que le personnel doit user de toute sa ruse pour que tout le monde regagne sa chambre : car arriver à faire entrer deux fauteuils roulants et un déambulateur dans un ascenseur, c'est faisable. Si en plus vous êtes parvenue à ce que tout ce petit monde descende au même étage, bingo ; sinon il faut les ranger par ordre d'arrêt. Un véritable jeu de Tetris…

Il ne faut pas oublier de conserver un peu d'espace pour soi car ils ne montent pas seuls. Coincée entre la roue d'un fauteuil et la poignée d'un déambulateur, mon fessier était souvent bien maltraité.

Ce jeu d'arcade grandeur nature se produisait donc deux fois par jour et se passait relativement bien, au final. Sauf quand Arlette se trouvait dans les parages. Arlette, sa passion, c'était l'ascenseur. Toute la journée, elle se promenait entre les étages et appuyait sur tous les boutons. Sa petite manie n'était pas si dérangeante en journée, mais aux moments critiques, c'était plus problématique. Quand, après plusieurs tentatives, l'ascenseur arrivait enfin, deux possibilités : soit Arlette descendait et, comme sur l'autoroute, prenait la voie à contresens au milieu des résidents impatients ; soit elle avait déjà appuyé sur les boutons et, le temps que la porte s'ouvre, était déjà repartie. Tout le monde râlait, bien sûr. Mais Arlette, elle, s'en fichait et n'en faisait qu'à sa tête.

*

Aujourd'hui, c'était à moi d'animer la session d'activité de l'après-midi qui débutait à 15 heures. 14 h 45, tout le monde ayant regagné sa chambre, seuls redescendaient ceux qui, autonomes, souhaitaient participer à l'animation. Je devais ensuite faire le tour des chambres pour demander aux autres s'ils souhaitaient venir. Direction l'ascenseur. Encore une fois. Les néophytes se demanderont sûrement à quoi sert de remonter les gens dans leur chambre si une heure après il faut les redescendre. Tout simplement pour leur permettre d'aller aux toilettes et de changer leurs protections.

15 h 15. L'assistance était enfin installée. Dans la salle à manger trônait le piano d'une résidente. J'avais annoncé un après-midi musique, et donc je m'apprêtais à leur jouer quelques morceaux. Ce n'était pas du travail, mais du plaisir, autant pour eux que pour moi. Alors que je jouais un nocturne de Chopin, M. Lamotte se mit à pleurer à chaudes larmes. Gênée, je stoppai le morceau et m'approchai de lui. Visiblement, la musique lui rappelait des souvenirs, l'émotion que j'avais à jouer se transmettait. Mais il souhaita que je continue.

Les morceaux s'enchaînèrent ; certains aînés fredonnaient. Même si le classique avait encore beaucoup de succès, les morceaux chantés leur permettaient d'être acteurs et non plus seulement spectateurs. « Le Temps des cerises », « Volare », « Les copains d'abord », même un « Alléluia »… Yann Tiersen n'eut pas beaucoup de succès, Elton John encore moins. Je revins donc à du classique, l'*Adagio d'Albinoni*, que certains connaissaient et entonnèrent. Micheline me demanda la « Lettre à Élise », que j'entrepris, et les chants fusèrent. Mais les chariots des goûters arrivaient déjà, et j'allais devoir les servir.

Les regards posés sur la part de gâteau montraient toute la lassitude des résidents devant la monotonie de ce qui leur était apporté. Chocolat chaud, thé, café ou sirop à l'eau. Penser à donner les yaourts fortifiants à ceux qui en avaient besoin. Je m'attardai à faire manger ceux qui ne se nourrissaient plus seuls tandis que les autres, qui avaient déjà terminé leur collation, ne comprenaient pas pourquoi la musique ne reprenait pas.

Vint le temps de débarrasser les tables et de faire la vaisselle. Car oui, j'étais de corvée de vaisselle, comme mes autres collègues dans les étages supérieurs.

Il était 16 h 30, la musique n'avait toujours pas repris. Déjà les collègues arrivaient et emmenaient certains résidents pour les mettre en pyjama. La salle se vidait. Seuls les autonomes restaient, acteurs privilégiés des prochains morceaux que je jouerais.

17 h 15, rangement de la salle pour dresser les tables en vue du dîner. J'avais passé pour la première fois un merveilleux après-midi. J'avais vu des sourires, entendu des voix qui s'élevaient, des personnes âgées réjouies. Dorénavant, je serais la « musicienne » ;

c'est du moins ainsi que certains me nommeraient. Ce surnom me plut : si la musique pouvait leur permettre de me voir autrement que comme celle qui chaque jour les voyait nus, je serais heureuse.

17 h 45. Il était l'heure d'effectuer mes transmissions et de signer mes soins. Est-ce que j'ai donné une douche, est-ce que la prise de médicament du matin a bien été faite, etc. C'était aussi l'occasion de mettre des observations que je jugeais importantes. Aujourd'hui, rien à signaler.

En fait, si, j'avais bien quelque chose à signaler, mais je ne le marquerais pas : j'étais là depuis 7 heures, il était 18 h 10, et je n'avais pas eu le temps de prendre ma pause.

30

L'aile droite

Cela faisait maintenant quelques semaines que j'étais dans l'établissement ; je commençais à prendre mes marques. Je ne connaissais pas encore le nom de tous les résidents. Mais j'avais enfin mis les pieds dans les autres étages.

Le premier n'était qu'un long couloir, qui donnait l'impression d'être entre le hall 1 et le hall 2 de la gare de Lyon, à Paris ; à la seule différence qu'il y avait des portes sur les côtés. Les rituels du matin restaient les mêmes qu'au rez-de-chaussée : sortir les chariots, faire les toilettes, regarder sa montre. J'aimais bien être dans l'aile droite, j'ignore pourquoi. Peut-être parce que j'arrivais à avoir plus d'échanges avec les résidents de ce côté-ci du couloir. Et puis, il y avait Georgette, la reine de la chanson. Cette gentille dame était toujours de bonne humeur et chantait du matin au soir, et bien sûr durant la toilette. Elle m'appelait son Opaline ; non qu'elle ne se souvenait pas de mon nom, il était inscrit sur ma blouse. Mais en moins gros que celui de l'établissement…

Il y avait aussi Serge, Christiane et Arlette la voyageuse.

Les couloirs se réveillaient, les yeux étaient parfois difficiles à ouvrir, les articulations à dérouiller, les protections étaient pleines, et parfois les lits trempés.

La course contre la montre était lancée : chariots à vider, poubelles à sortir, et les bacs de linge pleins à craquer.

Combien de toilettes, ce matin, une dizaine ? Bien plus ! Nous étions encore en sous-effectif, et aucune remplaçante ne viendrait nous épauler. Alors pas question de donner les douches aujourd'hui, sauf cas de force majeure. Qu'est-ce, un cas de force majeure, quand il s'agit de personnes âgées dépendantes pour la plupart ?

Ce matin, combien de chevelures ne seraient pas lavées, combien de dents pas nettoyées !… Le temps me manquait, il fallait prioriser les soins. Quinze, seize toilettes en quatre heures ; mes prescriptions de travail étaient telles que j'allais encore culpabiliser.

J'appris une nouvelle règle, celle des trois F : figure, fesses, fauteuil. Cette règle est la définition même de la prise en soin que l'on nous impose, sans prendre en compte l'humain ni la dignité. Je travaillais en mode dégradé, c'était récurrent. Le sous-effectif est une pathologie contre laquelle aucun traitement n'a été trouvé.

La matinée était passée, la course dans les couloirs ne se stopperait que vers midi. Et encore !

*

Pour le déjeuner, j'ai été affectée au club. Pas un club de bridge au décor cosy, pas un club de jazz à l'ambiance joyeuse, non. C'est un espace avec des tables et des chaises, avec au mur une télévision, et un coin cuisine avec évier et micro-ondes, au milieu du couloir. Souvenez-vous : il y a la table des résidents à accompagner dans la prise des repas ; ce sont les personnes âgées encore plus dépendantes qui sont au club, celles que l'on cache pour ne pas gâcher la vitrine. En effet, il arrive que des familles partagent le repas avec leurs parents dans la salle de restauration ; avoir en face d'elles une dame hémiplégique, qui bave quand vous lui donnez la becquée, une autre avec sa poche à uriner bien visible à côté d'elle, couperait probablement l'appétit de ces invités de marque… Cette dépendance-là, qui veut la voir ? Ces résidents ne sourient pas, ou pas vraiment, ne tiennent pas de propos cohérents, ne marchent pas seuls, n'ont pas de belles dents. Cette dépendance est laide, elle fait peur, elle terrifie. Alors le club, ce sont ceux que l'on ne veut pas montrer. Et que l'on ne descendra pas forcément aux animations.

Ce midi-là ils étaient onze, pratiquement tous en fauteuil roulant avec handicap. Sur onze, cinq auxquels il fallait donner à manger comme à des bébés, et six à surveiller et à aider au besoin.

Je devais récupérer deux chariots : celui isotherme avec leur nourriture dédiée et celui où sont rangés la vaisselle sale et les médicaments. Avant de remonter, bien vérifier si le cuisinier sait compter jusqu'à onze. Parce que, une fois en haut, plus le temps de redescendre chercher une assiette, un plat ou quoi que ce soit d'autre. Au marqueur blanc, il était stipulé à même le chariot qu'il devrait être « redescendu à 13 h 15 pour le midi et 19 h 15 pour le soir ».

Je pestais régulièrement contre ce chariot de distribution de repas, j'avais l'impression de pousser un réfrigérateur : pas de poignée, de minuscules roulettes, et aucune prise pour le diriger. Plus haut que moi, je conduisais à vue la pile d'assiettes que j'entendais claquer les unes contre les autres sans les voir, le pichet de vin tempétueux. Arrivée devant l'ascenseur, j'attendis. Certains résidents l'empruntaient encore, je patientai. Finalement, le moment de la bagarre arriva.

En effet, passer le seuil de l'ascenseur nécessite de soulever un peu le chariot, qui fait son poids. Sans cette manœuvre, les roulettes se bloquent dans ses rails. Une fois à l'intérieur, je me retrouvai au second, où des résidents voulaient descendre. Mais comme je prenais toute la place avec mes deux engins, ils s'inclinèrent. À l'étage souhaité, deuxième bagarre. Sortir l'engin sans renverser le vin, sans que les assiettes tombent. Je me dépêchai : il était 12 h 15, dans une heure, les deux chariots devraient être redescendus, sous peine d'essuyer les remarques de ceux ou celles qui faisaient la plonge.

Aidée d'une collègue, je commençai à donner la becquée, assise entre deux résidents, une cuillère dans chaque main. Le chronomètre était lancé. Attendre qu'ils déglutissent était la moindre des choses, mais le temps filait, le temps courait. Étais-je une aide médico-psychologique ou une éleveuse de canards ? La question peut paraître saugrenue, mais à cet instant précis, n'étais-je pas en train de faire du gavage ? Avaient-ils le temps de prendre plaisir à manger ? Le repas – qui devrait être un moment de convivialité – est en fait une course contre la montre. Et cette dame qui n'arrivait pas à avaler, qui mâchait du mixé avec ses gencives, qui ne parlait pas, bavait et recrachait chaque cuillerée, qu'en penser ? Qu'elle n'avait pas faim ? Ce serait la solution de facilité. Qu'elle n'aimait pas ? Plus probable.

En guise de fromage, toujours et encore ces éternels triangles de Vache qui rit. En manger sans pain, à la cuillère, ce doit être un peu écœurant, à la longue…

Mais lorsque je servis le dessert, stupéfaction ! Des poires ! Non seulement il faudrait les éplucher, mais elles étaient aussi dures que des morceaux de bois. Comment les manger lorsqu'on n'a plus de dents ? Ma collègue et moi tentâmes de les écraser, mais les fourchettes rendirent l'âme. Nous n'avions plus beaucoup de solutions : compotes, pour tout le monde, les mêmes depuis des années.

L'œil sur la pendule. Il était déjà 13 h 13. L'une de nous se dévoua pour descendre le chariot qui devrait être en bas deux minutes plus tard, l'autre continuerait la distribution. Nous prendrions du retard sur les changes de 14 heures, mais peu importe, le retard est une notion si vague et si abstraite que nous en avions perdu toute définition concrète.

Le repas terminé, c'était le retour des embouteillages dans les couloirs. Entre déambulateurs et fauteuils roulants qui n'avançaient pas, il fallait slalomer.

— Madame, vous pouvez m'aider s'il vous plaît à faire avancer mon fauteuil, je suis fatiguée, me demanda une résidente tandis que j'en poussais déjà un.

— Je ne peux pas, je suis désolée, vous n'êtes plus très loin de votre chambre, encore un léger effort.

C'est alors qu'elle se mit à pleurer. Si je lui disais de m'attendre, elle bloquerait les couloirs. Je garai donc ma résidente, j'aidai l'autre dame et je la conduisis jusqu'à sa chambre.

— Oh merci, vous êtes gentille… je voudrais aller aux toilettes, vous pouvez m'aider ?

Je bouillonnais intérieurement. Mais impossible pour moi de refuser. Je calai le fauteuil contre la barre de sécurité des toilettes, la levai, baissai le slip filet, j'enlevai la protection que je jetai, et je l'accompagnai dans sa rotation. Je n'avais en revanche pas le temps d'attendre qu'elle ait terminé, mon autre dame était toujours garée dans un coin du couloir et elle avait besoin d'être changée et couchée, elle était fatiguée.

— Je vais m'occuper de la dame, et je reviens, vous ne bougez pas, vous m'attendez, d'accord ?

— Oui, d'accord, vous êtes gentille.

Un sourire, et je me sauvai. Non, je ne suis pas gentille, j'ai juste pris sur moi pour ne pas m'énerver, mais au fond j'étais furieuse. D'être obligée de m'occuper de deux personnes à la fois, de ne pas pouvoir faire mon travail correctement.

Mon téléphone sonna. Chambre 200. La dame avait terminé de se soulager. Ma collègue et moi – la résidente avait si mal partout qu'il valait mieux être deux – avions bientôt fini avec la résidente dépendante et mon téléphone sonna de nouveau. Elle s'impatientait.

— J'ai terminé, j'ai fait caca, me dit en ces termes la dame que je trouvais comme je l'avais laissée.

— Je vais vous nettoyer. On prend la barre, on se lève ?

— J'ai mal aux genoux.

— Je vais me dépêcher, promis ; pour que vous ne soyez pas trop longtemps debout.

Mais ce n'est pas vraiment ce qu'il s'est passé : la dame en avait partout, sur elle, sur ses vêtements. Partout.

Mon téléphone sonna encore. Chambre 205. La personne attendrait.

Lorsque j'expliquai à la dame que je devais la laver, elle se mit à pleurer. De honte. Je pris ses mains pour la réconforter et filai chercher un slip filet dans le chariot, en croisant les doigts pour qu'il reste sa taille.

À mon retour, la dame pleurait toujours. Je me mis alors à son niveau, accroupie devant elle. Mes mains dans les siennes, nous nous sommes regardées.

— Angèle, il n'y a rien de grave, ça peut arriver, vous allez m'aider, et ni vu ni connu.

— Je suis vieille, ma petite, tu sais.

— Oui, je sais, Angèle, c'est pourquoi vous devez avoir plein d'histoires à raconter. Vous savez ce que l'on va faire ? Pendant que je fais votre toilette, vous me parlez de vous, d'accord ?

— Oh, ma petite, moi, tu sais, j'attends de mourir.

— Et vos enfants, Angèle ? S'ils vous entendaient, que diraient-ils ?

— Oh, ils sont grands, mes enfants.

— Ce n'est pas une raison, ils passent vous voir, ils ont encore besoin de vous.

Rien n'y faisait, elle continuait de pleurer. Alors je fis un geste interdit : je la pris dans mes bras. Oui, j'étais en train de réconforter une vieille dame à moitié nue et assise sur les toilettes ; c'est aussi cela, mon métier. Et je recommencerais encore et encore.

Les pleurs se sont calmés.

J'ai fait sa toilette aussi doucement et rapidement que j'ai pu. Doucement et rapidement, n'est-ce pas une association surprenante ? Rapidité et délicatesse sont-elles compatibles ? Je ne sais pas, mais j'essayais en tout cas de m'y astreindre. J'installai la protection en remontant le slip filet. Mon téléphone sonna. Chambre 207. Je remontai la jupe, afin de la mettre en place, j'agrippai le fauteuil, et je donnai une légère impulsion à Angèle pour qu'elle se redresse l'espace de quelques secondes afin de positionner le fauteuil. Elle se laissa tomber dedans.

— Que ça fait du bien de s'asseoir.

— Vous voyez, cela n'a pas pris longtemps. Je vous installe dans votre gros fauteuil pour la sieste ?

— Oui, vous êtes gentille.

J'enlevai mes gants, direction le fauteuil crapaud coincé entre la fenêtre et le lit. Là, dilemme : soit c'était le fauteuil roulant qui passait, soit c'était moi. Il allait pourtant bien falloir que j'accompagne Angèle dans sa rotation. Là aussi, parfois je bouillonnais : mais qui a pensé à l'agencement des chambres ?

Approcher au maximum le fauteuil roulant près de l'autre, en laissant tout de même à Angèle la place de se tourner sans qu'elle se prenne les pieds dans les pédales ; pour cela, se mettre en face d'Angèle et, à reculons, faire avancer le fauteuil dans ce minuscule couloir. Assez vite, se positionner sur le côté pour que la résidente soit au plus près du crapaud. Lui donner une impulsion pour qu'elle se lève et accompagner sa rotation en la maintenant. Avec de la chance, vous resterez debout si elle ne se laisse pas trop tomber dans l'objet suscité.

La praticabilité dans un EHPAD est une notion subsidiaire à laquelle les directeurs pensent rarement pour améliorer le travail des soignants et le bien-être des résidents.

Mon téléphone sonna encore. Chambre 218. Trois chambres qui avaient besoin de quelque chose, et déjà une demi-heure que j'étais avec Angèle. Ma journée s'achevait à 15 h 30, il était 14 h 45. Avec un sourire, après m'être assurée qu'elle ne manquerait de rien, je lui souhaitai un bon après-midi et pris congé.

Au moment où je passai la porte, je croisai ma responsable, perchée sur ses talons hauts et ultra-maquillée.

— Anne-Sophie, on ne sort pas des chambres avec des gants.

Vivement 15 h 30…

31

Concours de tricot

Au rez-de-chaussée vivait Fantine. Grande, les cheveux blancs coupés au carré, elle était complètement autonome. Elle se promenait régulièrement dans les couloirs. Sa passion, le tricot. Parfois, il arrivait que je retrouve une aiguille quelque part. Il n'y avait qu'une personne qui pouvait l'avoir perdue. Les après-midi, elle s'asseyait sur le canapé vers l'entrée et elle tricotait. Elle ne tricotait pas des vêtements, mais de petits carrés de laine, qu'ensuite elle cousait ensemble, faisant ainsi une couverture qu'elle donnerait aux associations pour que les SDF aient quelque chose de chaud quand ils dormiraient dehors en plein hiver.

Elle était rarement de mauvaise humeur et toujours partante pour les animations pliage de serviettes ou l'épluchage de pommes de terre. Je ne l'ai jamais vue à une activité qui ne serait pas utile à l'établissement. Elle avait ce besoin de se rendre indispensable, Fantine. Elle vivait dans l'établissement depuis des années. Elle n'avait pas de famille qui venait la voir et était sous tutelle. Elle n'avait plus de biens, elle avait vendu sa maison pour pouvoir se payer un EHPAD, où probablement elle devait se sentir moins seule que chez elle. Il ne lui restait que quelques meubles en souvenir de sa vie passée.

Elle ne supportait pas la douche ; de son temps, la douche était un luxe, elle n'en voulait pas. Certains résidents l'évitaient, les bourgeoises, en particulier, qui la trouvaient négligée. Mais elle se moquait de tous ces quolibets, elle était « nature », comme on dit, et parlait avec tous ceux qui voulaient bien engager la conversation.

Parfois, elle perdait la clef de sa chambre ; on la voyait chercher partout. Elle la retrouvait généralement entre ses pelotes de laine. Je l'aimais bien, Fantine ; elle avait le don de vous remettre le sourire aux lèvres quand vous n'étiez pas bien. Qu'avait-elle fait dans sa vie ? Je suis incapable de le dire, elle restait discrète. Je ne l'imaginais pas avoir eu un travail à responsabilités, je la pensais plutôt ouvrière. C'est du moins ce que me laissait croire son sens de l'humain et de l'aide à l'autre si ancré en elle.

Non pas que je considère généralement que les personnes âgées ayant occupé jadis des postes à responsabilités aient moins d'humanité que celles qui ont été ouvrières, par exemple, mais tout de même, dans l'établissement, il y avait une fracture entre ceux qui avaient mis les mains dans le cambouis et les autres. Leurs besoins, leurs demandes étaient différents. Leur patience aussi. Il y avait également le camp des femmes qui n'avaient jamais occupé de poste salarié et qui avaient élevé leurs enfants en attendant que leurs maris rapportent la paie. Elles étaient un mix des deux autres catégories, à la fois bourgeoises et aidantes.

Mais revenons à Fantine.

Un jour, le psychologue des lieux lui annonça qu'elle n'avait plus les moyens de payer l'établissement et qu'elle allait devoir envisager un autre mode d'hébergement. Fantine ne pouvait l'accepter ; elle voulait rester ici, elle y avait ses habitudes, ses repères, ses quelques connaissances. Elle s'y opposa donc formellement. Elle menaça de fuguer, de se suicider s'il le fallait. L'affaire sembla donc en rester là.

Les jours, les semaines passèrent. Un autre jour, le même psychologue, en passant par un couloir où il était sûr de croiser Fantine, la stoppa. Voilà que la discussion s'engageait. Il l'avait inscrite à un concours de tricot qui aurait lieu deux jours plus tard ! N'était-ce pas merveilleux ? Elle, la Pénélope de l'EHPAD, se sentit valorisée, revigorée, et le tricot, elle s'y connaissait. Elle gagnerait.

*

Le jour J est enfin arrivé, Fantine était prête ; dans son sac, des pelotes de laine, des aiguilles, des culottes au cas où il y aurait un petit souci. Un taxi l'attendait devant l'établissement. Quel luxe ! Elle dit « à ce soir » avec fierté à ses copains résidents et partit vers le lieu du concours.

Sauf que, ce jour-là, là-bas il n'y avait pas de concours de tricot. Elle avait simplement été virée. Elle se retrouvait seule avec son petit sac, ses pelotes et trois culottes dans un nouvel EHPAD dont elle ignorait tout. Ses meubles suivraient le lendemain par camion. Je n'ose imaginer le choc pour elle. C'en fut également un pour nous : les soignants n'avaient pas été informés de cette décision. Tout avait été organisé en petit comité.

Nous étions pourtant en période de trêve hivernale. La chambre des résidents dans un EHPAD privé à but lucratif est un endroit privé, un peu comme un logement loué à des locataires qui paient leur loyer. Mais en l'occurence, pas de trêve hivernale, pas d'avis d'expulsion par un magistrat. Les juges sont ceux qui décident. Fantine n'allait pas se retourner contre eux, elle était trop seule. Et l'EHPAD qui l'accueillait, était-il complice de la supercherie ? Non, il ne l'était pas. Mais comment faire machine arrière une fois le pot aux roses découvert ? Impossible.

Tout ne se résume donc qu'à l'argent ? Comment une telle situation peut-elle advenir ?

Parce que ces aînés sous tutelle, sous curatelle renforcée, finalement peu importe le terme, ne sont plus considérés comme faisant partie intégrante de la cité, parce qu'on leur a volé et leurs biens et leurs vies, parce qu'aux yeux de chacun ils n'existent même plus tant les regards que l'on porte sur eux ne sont que des zéros qui s'alignent sur des chèques.

Fantine avait toute sa tête, elle n'avait juste plus assez d'argent pour se payer un EHPAD privé à but lucratif où elle se sentait bien, où elle ne dérangeait personne.

Après cette mascarade, je n'oublierai jamais que je travaille pour des actionnaires, pas pour des philanthropes.

32

La douche

Définition : moment rarement offert aux résidents.

Les douches sont un soin de la vie quotidienne, chacun de nous en prend généralement au moins une chaque jour. Dans mon établissement, il existait un protocole de douches, à l'image de ceux de soins et du nombre de changes mis par jour, qui déterminait qui était douché quel jour : ce monsieur, c'était le mercredi et le dimanche par exemple, cette dame, le jeudi, etc. Tout était programmé, et aucune dérogation possible. Que la personne ait transpiré ou non, qu'elle ait juste besoin de se délasser sous les jets, si ce n'était pas le jour, c'était non. C'est cela aussi, la hiérarchisation des soins.

*

Nous étions en sous-effectif depuis longtemps, les douches n'avaient pas été données depuis quelques semaines. La culpabilité nous rongeait, mais comment faire ? Quand vous avez plus de dix, onze, douze toilettes à assumer, seul l'essentiel est traité. L'intime. Les cheveux sont subsidiaires, pour nos directeurs.

Ce jour-là, débordées, comme d'habitude, mes collègues ont fait ce qu'elles ont pu. La directrice en pleine réunion leur avait clairement expliqué que la prochaine fois que le cas se présenterait, il faudrait faire la toilette des gens qui avaient de la famille en visite, parce que celle-ci pourrait s'offusquer de voir ses parents encore alités à midi. Elle comprendrait alors que les résidents baignent dans leurs changes depuis la veille. Il faudrait donc privilégier certains au détriment d'autres. Les sans-famille n'avaient donc pas le droit au même traitement ?

Les familles n'étaient pas dupes mais n'osaient vraiment s'exprimer, sous peine de s'entendre dire : « Mais si vous n'êtes pas satisfait, trouvez un autre établissement. »

C'était la réponse facile, il y a tant de proches dans le désarroi qui ne trouvent pas de place pour leurs aînés.

Ce jour-là, donc, une fille rendant visite à sa maman observa que les cheveux de celle-ci n'avaient pas croisé de shampoing depuis longtemps. Ils tenaient presque en l'air sans gel. En fait, cela faisait environ trois semaines que les douches n'avaient pas été données. Pourquoi ? Pas assez de personnel. La fille descendit donc voir la directrice pour obtenir des explications. Celle-ci lui répondit que, en effet, l'établissement était en sous-effectif et qu'il fonctionnait en mode dégradé. Mais qu'elle pouvait tout à fait prendre rendez-vous pour sa maman chez la coiffeuse qui venait toutes les semaines à l'EHPAD, payante évidemment.

Est-ce aux résidents de pallier les dysfonctionnements de l'établissement ? Les douches sont de la responsabilité des soignants ; si la direction faisait son travail, dès que le sous-effectif est acté, il devrait être comblé.

Ce manque de volonté de remplacer le personnel absent a pour conséquences des soins minimes, une dignité assassinée sur l'autel de la rentabilité, et des soignants qui s'épuisent tant physiquement que moralement.

Les plaquettes de promotion de nos établissements privés à but lucratif sont attractives, chaque lieu met le paquet sur la communication, mais quand il s'agit de remplacer des soignants absents… Je me demande même parfois si cette situation ne les arrange pas. Moins de soignants, c'est moins de salaires à payer, donc plus de dividendes pour les actionnaires.

Dans notre pays, nous sommes beaucoup plus touchés par la cause animale que par la vieillesse. Chacun s'offusque, moi la première, des mauvais traitements infligés à ces pauvres bêtes qui ne sont que le défouloir de déglingués du cerveau. On est abasourdis par les vidéos de L214 sur les traitements des animaux dans les abattoirs, nous ne pouvons rester insensibles à cette maltraitance gratuite. Mais quand des associations viendront-elles filmer incognito au cœur des EHPAD ? Quand y aura-t-il des L214 dans nos établissements afin d'en dénoncer les conditions d'accueil ?

Pour réglementer la cause animale, nos dirigeants promulguent des lois. Ainsi, nos amis les animaux ne sont plus considérés comme des bibelots qui décorent la maison. Mais qu'en est-il de nos aînés ? Des lois existent, pourquoi ne sont-elles pas respectées ? Qui s'offusque aujourd'hui du mode de fonctionnement des EHPAD ? Faut-il que nos aînés soient attachés à un arbre sur une aire d'autoroute par une famille qui part en vacances pour que les consciences se réveillent ? La vieillesse est le reflet de notre dégénérescence future, malheureusement l'« âgisme » règne. On court après le temps et la jeunesse éternelle, mais aujourd'hui, à cinquante ans, sur le marché du travail, vous êtes mis au rebut. Les savoirs ne se transmettent plus, ne se partagent plus, ils se périment.

La vieillesse fait peur, elle inquiète. Qui veut voir son reflet dans trente ou quarante ans ? Personne. Comme si devenir vieux et dépendant était contagieux.

Aujourd'hui, il existe la Société protectrice des animaux, et tant mieux. À quand une Société protectrice de l'homme âgé ?

33

Les stagiaires

Définition : personnel gratuit généralement jeune, taillable et corvéable à merci.

Il n'est pas rare que dans l'établissement nous recevions des stagiaires. Ce sont souvent des jeunes filles mineures qui préparent le bac « accompagnement, service et soins à la personne », et que nous devons épauler. Elles ont l'obligation de faire un stage dans un EHPAD. Je ne suis pas certaine que ce soit la meilleure façon de leur donner envie de continuer… Il m'est arrivé de superviser deux stagiaires, pas en même temps heureusement. Deux jeunes filles utopistes, pleines de rêves et d'enthousiasme. Pour ne pas les dégoûter du métier d'aide-soignante avant même qu'elles aient commencé, il m'a fallu sourire plus que j'en avais envie, m'armer d'un langage positif et essayer de ne pas courir dans les couloirs.

*

Le premier jour, j'ai eu Jessica avec moi. Par chance, je n'étais pas en charge du rez-de-chaussée, sinon la tâche que je m'étais fixée d'être souriante pour vanter les belles valeurs de mon métier aurait été bien mal engagée.

Nous étions au premier étage, que j'aime bien, j'allais pouvoir transmettre mon enthousiasme. Jessica n'avait pas le droit de faire des toilettes, mais elle était prévenante et faisait les lits. Je me dis pourtant que si ses trois semaines de stage n'étaient réduites qu'à cette activité, elle allait vite s'ennuyer. J'ai aussi été stagiaire, et je me suis toujours promis que je ne ferais pas subir à d'autres ce que j'avais subi. Je lui proposai donc de faire, sous surveillance, une toilette simple à une dame autonome qui se tiendrait au lavabo. Elle était un peu apeurée, non pas que la vision de la nudité l'effrayât, mais elle craignait de mal s'y prendre. Je lui expliquai donc pourquoi utiliser deux gants de toilette, deux serviettes, lui rappelai de mettre ses gants en latex. La jeune stagiaire se débrouilla très bien ; elle habilla la dame, la coiffa, et la raccompagna vers sa table. Tout s'était bien passé, Jessica était contente. Comme je ne considère pas les stagiaires comme de la main-d'œuvre corvéable, je fis le lit. C'était aussi une façon de lui montrer que nous étions sur un pied d'égalité au niveau des tâches à effectuer, ingrates ou non.

Rien n'est finalement ingrat dans mon travail. N'en déplaise à ceux qui m'étiquettent « torche-cul de petits vieux ». Combien de fois l'ai-je entendue, cette expression sur mon métier… Souvent je réponds bêtement : « Tu seras bien content ou contente d'avoir des gens comme moi qui viendront te torcher le cul au moment de ta vie où tu seras vieux, incontinent et dépendant. »

Généralement, la discussion en reste là (spéciale dédicace à ma génitrice).

Mais revenons à Jessica. Elle se donnait, suivait le rythme soutenu que je lui imposais. Elle allait maintenant m'aider à faire les toilettes alitées, ce serait plus simple pour moi pour les mobilisations. D'elle-même, elle préparait la bassine, les deux gants, les deux serviettes et le savon. Les résidents avaient l'air de l'apprécier, elle était discrète, elle s'intéressait à eux. À tel point que, ce matin-là, les toilettes furent terminées en avance. Que faire ? J'aurais pu aller voir mes collègues et leur proposer notre aide. L'idée m'a traversé l'esprit. Mais l'avaient-elles jamais fait pour moi ? Je décidai d'emmener Jessica savourer une pause de cinq minutes, avant, ensuite, d'aller voir les autres.

En remontant dans les étages, je vis qu'une collègue était dans « le jus ». Il lui restait beaucoup de toilettes. Une ou deux de plus, ce n'est pas un drame, nous avons alors pris la décision de l'aider. Et c'était l'occasion, pour une fois, de respecter le calendrier des douches. Jessica me demanda si elle pouvait la donner à cette dame ; aucun problème pour nous. Elle avait compris le système du nombre de protections et alla chercher les changes dans le chariot. Slip filet, quelle taille ? Elle se prit pour référence en comparant les culottes à son bassin ; je souris : pour cette dame, c'était du double XL.

Nous sommes retournées dans la chambre. Jessica commença à la déshabiller, en ayant préparé aussi les vêtements qu'elle allait lui mettre. Soudain, elle leva les yeux vers moi.

— Je crois que j'ai oublié quelque chose.

— Ah bon, et quoi donc ?

— Des gants en latex.

Je souris de nouveau et sortis de ma poche une paire à sa taille.

— Merci beaucoup.

— Ne t'inquiète pas, ça viendra.

La douche se passa bien. Je lui rappelai de bien essuyer les plis afin qu'aucune mycose ne vienne allégrement coloniser la peau de ses résidents.

Toute la journée s'est déroulée ainsi. Avant de partir, Jessica m'a remerciée. Je fus assez surprise ; personne, à part les résidents, ne m'avait jamais remerciée de quoi que ce soit, dans cet établissement.

*

Les jours passaient, et Jessica prenait de plus en plus d'assurance. Elle commençait aussi à voir les failles du système. Malgré mon discours résolument positif, elle n'était pas dupe. Elle voyait bien que certaines fois nous n'avions pas le temps d'accomplir notre travail correctement. Je trouvais toujours quelques arguments spécieux pour lui prouver le contraire, mais au fond elle n'avait pas tort.

Le moindre aléa, le moindre grain de sable vient bloquer la machine, et ce sont les résidents qui en pâtissent. Si les grains de sable s'accumulent dans une journée, et que c'est la dune du Pilat que nous avons en face de nous, il est évident que les horaires de travail ne seront pas respectés et que les heures supplémentaires non payées vont s'accumuler.

Arriva le jour que je redoutais. Jessica était dans l'établissement depuis deux semaines et demie. Comme il manquait du personnel, la direction avait décidé de l'envoyer seule se substituer au personnel absent de l'étage. C'est illégal : elle ferait des toilettes, serait dans l'obligation de se servir du matériel sans aucune surveillance. Ce jour-là, Jessica viendrait me voir très souvent pour me demander de l'aide. Je finis par lui dire de s'occuper d'abord des toilettes simples, nous ferions les lourdes à deux.

Quand je la retrouvais, elle était en nage, elle n'en pouvait plus. Elle s'est effondrée sur une chaise, en pleurs.

— Non mais tu te rends compte ! me dit-elle, visiblement en colère. On me met sur un étage comme si j'étais du personnel, j'ai encore à apprendre !

— Jessica, tu t'es très bien débrouillée, allez, viens, on va continuer ensemble, on va y arriver.

— Je suis dégoûtée !

— Mais non, ma grande, ne t'inquiète pas, tout va bien.

Une fois ses larmes séchées, nous avons commencé les toilettes lourdes. Ce que je voulais au maximum éviter était donc arrivé. Non par ma faute, mais par celle d'une direction qui n'avait rien trouvé de mieux que de l'envoyer seule dans un étage.

Pour son dernier jour, nous avons demandé à notre directrice de faire un geste vis-à-vis de Jessica. Elle est ressortie du bureau avec un panier garni. Les restes de Noël. Nous avions espéré des chèques cadeaux pour qu'elle se fasse plaisir : raté.

Lorsqu'elle est venue me dire au revoir, j'ai eu de la peine de la voir partir, mais c'est ainsi. Elle a égayé mon travail par sa jeunesse et par ses sourires – si rares sur le visage des soignants de nos jours.

*

Quelque temps plus tard, j'aurais une autre stagiaire, mais elle, on la perdra : après son bac, elle a préféré changer de voie. Je me souviens que, manquant de temps, j'ai rempli son dossier, assise par terre pendant qu'elle douchait une dame, pour que je puisse la surveiller. Je ne pouvais pas lui mettre de mauvaises appréciations ; d'abord parce qu'elle ne les méritait pas, ensuite parce que je n'avais pas véritablement pu m'occuper d'elle comme je l'aurais souhaité.

Mes collègues ont quant à elles eu la lourde tâche d'apprendre le métier à une personne en réinsertion professionnelle. Ce cursus est plus difficile : en effet, dans ce cas, pas de rapport à remplir, la stagiaire est jugée par un professionnel qui se déplace un jour déterminé à l'avance pour une mise en situation professionnelle. La dame en question n'a pas réussi cette évaluation. Pas parce qu'elle n'était pas compétente, non ; simplement parce que personne n'a eu le temps de lui montrer tous les gestes à effectuer, ceux que l'on vous apprend à l'école.

Tous ces gestes essentiels que même nous, soignants diplômés, n'arrivons plus à faire.

34

Escarres

Dans un EHPAD, le souci majeur, outre le personnel manquant, c'est l'escarre. Qu'est-ce qu'une escarre ? C'est la destruction locale plus ou moins importante d'un tissu, due à une diminution de l'irrigation sanguine à la suite d'un processus ischémique. Plus simplement, c'est une rougeur qui apparaît sur les points d'appui, principalement chez les personnes alitées. Elle se loge le plus souvent aux talons, aux coudes, au scrotum, vers les fessiers. Si la rougeur n'est pas soignée à temps, les tissus se nécrosent et l'escarre se creuse très rapidement.

Pour éviter la course contre l'escarre, il existe des soins de prévention : massage des talons, changements de position réguliers pour les personnes qui restent trop alitées. Encore faudrait-il que nous puissions effectuer ces gestes. Faute de temps, les soins de prévention passent souvent à la trappe. Alors pourquoi s'étonner de ces escarres qui se multiplient dans des établissements ?

*

Je m'occupais de Charles, au rez-de-chaussée. Il avait déjà une escarre qui s'était bien formée au niveau du fessier. Même si les pansements étaient régulièrement faits, elle se creusait à la vitesse grand V. Impossible d'arrêter cette nécrose qui, comme la gangrène, le rongeait. D'ailleurs, l'odeur d'une escarre est très particulière, c'est une odeur de tissus morts.

Celle de Charles était mal placée, sous la fesse droite : les protections recouvraient aux trois quarts le pansement de selles et d'urine. Je continuais à utiliser le verticaliseur pour lui faire sa toilette, ainsi il allait sur la chaise percée pour ses besoins plutôt que de les faire dans ses protections. J'espérais éviter ainsi que le pansement ne soit trop souillé. Mais quand vous êtes dans votre protection toute la nuit, que vous êtes incontinent, c'est un vœu pieux. Or je ne suis pas habilitée à refaire le pansement, c'est du ressort de l'infirmière. Je commençais donc sa toilette, et quand j'avais terminé, je devais biper l'infirmière de garde, et j'attendais (comme Charles d'ailleurs…). Je l'avais harnaché pour qu'il puisse tenir à peu près debout le temps qu'elle nettoie et pose un nouveau pansement. Combien de minutes avons-nous parfois attendu !… En écrivant cela, la moutarde me monte au nez.

Malgré les soins, l'escarre ne s'améliorait pas, elle était même en voie ascendante. Jusqu'au jour où j'aurais pu entrer le poing dans la plaie. Charles ne disait rien pendant les soins, pourtant je n'imagine pas qu'il n'ait pas eu mal.

*

Quelques semaines plus tard, sa santé déclina ; il avait de la fièvre. Impossible de savoir d'où venait l'infection. Après une courte hospitalisation, le diagnostic de l'hôpital fut sans appel : Charles était dénutri et déshydraté ; l'escarre ne guérirait jamais si on le laissait ainsi. Pourtant, elle avait bien réduit, et sa fièvre avait baissé. Mais, même s'il allait mieux, tout le monde imaginait Charles en fin de vie.

L'hôpital avait prescrit des produits particuliers pour le traitement de l'escarre, qui n'ont jamais été commandés, et, en quelques jours, celle-ci repartit de plus belle. Sa femme, qui passait tous les jours déjeuner, dîner avec lui pour être sûre qu'il mange, n'en a jamais rien su.

Charles ne se levait plus, les toilettes se faisaient désormais alitées. Nous avions besoin d'être deux. Nous le changions de position toutes les deux heures, mais rien n'y faisait, l'escarre empirait, et Charles dépérissait. Il m'est arrivé une fois de prendre son épouse dans mes bras tant son désarroi était grand face à ce mari qu'elle avait connu si fort et qui était aujourd'hui tellement affaibli. La famille se battait pour le bien-être de Charles ; elle fut considérée comme faisant partie de celles qui dérangent. Ce que certains, ici, détestaient. Manque d'empathie, mépris des soignants et des familles m'ont toujours sidérée. Quand vous étiez une famille qui ne rentrait pas dans le cadre, il y avait dans cet établissement des personnes qui vous ignoraient, parfois vous engueulaient… ou qui ne répondaient jamais à vos interrogations.

Il avait été prescrit par l'hôpital que des patchs de morphine soient appliqués à Charles une heure avant les soins de l'escarre, pour endormir la douleur. Un jour, sa fille était venue voir son père à l'improviste en fin de matinée. Elle se trouvait dans la chambre quand l'infirmière arriva. Celle-ci lui demanda de sortir afin qu'elle refasse le pansement. Sa fille, outrée, refusa : l'infirmière allait prodiguer les soins sans avoir préalablement mis le patch de morphine. Charles aurait souffert le martyre ! Et la famille, au vu de son expérience, était en droit de se demander combien de fois cette situation s'était produite.

Charles a continué à dépérir, lentement, et l'escarre s'est aggravée. Il faisait des allers-retours hôpital-EHPAD. Il oscillait entre sursaut de vie et rechute rapide. Sa fille se battra pourtant pour trouver un autre établissement où le placer ; sans succès. Elle ne pouvait continuer d'être le témoin impuissant de la déchéance de son père. Elle souhaitait que sa prise en soin et sa mort, si elle devait survenir, soient dignes.

*

Les familles sont prises en otage par nombre d'établissements. Elles portent déjà le poids de la culpabilité d'avoir dû placer leurs proches, et quand elles dénoncent de mauvais traitements, parce qu'elles ne veulent pas être complices, elles sont souvent condamnées à subir les décisions arbitraires des directions, seules maîtres à bord. Comment peuvent-elles faire leur deuil quand, comme Charles, leur parent décède dans de grandes souffrances ? Comment ne pas avoir en tête ce visage où la douleur se mêle à l'impuissance ?

Quand je pense à Charles, aujourd'hui, je le revois sur le verticaliseur. C'était la trottinette qui le menait jusqu'aux toilettes. Lui voulait analyser les mécanismes ; je souhaitais juste qu'il ne bouge pas trop pour que je puisse le déplacer sans risque. Il était beau, élégant. Sa femme me racontait que, peu de temps avant d'arriver dans l'établissement, il faisait encore de longues marches, seul. Je l'imagine sur un fond de Yiruma, lui et cette nature qu'il aimait tant. Il avait un regard et un sourire que je garderai profondément en moi.

35

Les couchers

Définition : acte purement technique d'un transfert d'une position quelconque à une position allongée en un temps imparti de maximum quatre minutes.

Ce soir-là, je travaillais jusqu'à 20 heures. Ma collègue et moi avions tout le pan gauche du premier étage à coucher. Il était 19 h 15. Nous disposions donc de quarante-cinq minutes pour prendre en charge plus d'une dizaine de résidents et donner les médicaments du soir. Soit, si je voulais terminer à l'heure, accorder à chacun quatre minutes en moyenne. C'est peu, quatre minutes.

À vos marques, prêtes, partez !

Nous commencions toujours par les chambres du fond, un chariot de change à proximité, les médicaments dans leur rack positionné sur la poubelle. Coucher un résident, ce n'est pas seulement l'accompagner dans son lit, le border et lui raconter une histoire. Coucher un résident, c'est l'emmener aux W-C, le déshabiller, lui faire une toilette intime, lui installer la protection, l'accompagner jusqu'à son lit, disposer le coussin à sa guise et les aménagements qu'il aime pour la nuit, lui donner ses médicaments, et enfin sortir en lui souhaitant une bonne nuit. Certains vous attendent pour les accompagner, d'autres ont pris les devants en se rendant déjà aux toilettes et en se déshabillant, mais c'est assez rare.

Marceline était la première résidente sur ma liste, cent cinquante kilos à la pesée. Elle s'était déjà mise en pyjama, était allée faire ses besoins, il ne me restait plus que la toilette intime, la mise en place du change et l'aide au coucher.

Tant bien que mal, j'arrivai à remonter le slip en maille un peu trop petit pour elle – il n'y en avait plus à sa taille –, puis la protection, en évitant tout pli à l'entrejambe.

— Je suis en colère, ce soir, m'annonça Marceline tandis que je plaçais le filet sur ses cheveux.

— Ah bon, pourquoi ?

— Tu l'as vue, la mère Machin ? Elle était assistante sociale, et c'est elle qui m'a placée chez les bonnes sœurs parce que mes parents étaient pauvres et qu'elle avait considéré qu'ils n'avaient pas les moyens de s'occuper de moi. Tu l'as vue, la salope ? Et voilà que maintenant je supporte de la voir tous les jours, cette vieille peau.

— Calmez-vous, Marceline, ne vous occupez pas d'elle.

— Attends qu'elle passe à côté de moi, elle va voir…

— Mais non, Marceline, ce ne serait pas correct. Allez, on va se tourner pour s'allonger, d'accord ?

J'attrapai ses jambes et tentai de lui donner assez d'élan pour qu'elle soit bien au milieu du lit. J'avais si mal au dos… Une fois installée, je lui souhaitai bonne nuit.

— À demain, Marceline, passez une bonne nuit.

— À demain… Tu vas t'occuper de la salope ?

— Non, ce n'est pas mon étage, Marceline, allez, reposez-vous.

Je sortis et frappai à la chambre d'à côté. Évelyne était allée aux toilettes mais n'arrivait pas à s'essuyer. Les fesses à l'air, elle avait plus de selles sur les mains qu'il n'y en avait sur le papier. Une toilette s'imposait. Et comme elle s'était levée sans avoir terminé, le sol était jonché d'excréments dans lesquels en plus elle avait marché… Les chaussons étaient donc à laver.

— Évelyne, venez, je vais vous nettoyer. On va enlever les chaussons, je vous en donne une autre paire.

— Ah bon, pourquoi ?

— Parce que je ne peux pas vous laisser vous coucher dans cet état.

— Mais je suis propre !

— Vous serez plus à l'aise après la toilette, croyez-moi.

Et me voilà à la laver au lavabo. Plus je passais sur son anus, plus des selles sortaient. Je lui proposai donc de se rasseoir sur les toilettes, et de terminer.

— Mais j'ai terminé !

— Je n'en suis pas sûre, vous ne voulez pas réessayer ?

— Non, puisque je vous dis que j'ai terminé !

Quinze minutes à me battre avec son sphincter. J'arrivai enfin à ce qu'elle soit propre. Installation du slip filet, de la protection, et je l'accompagnai jusqu'au lit. Je n'eus pas vraiment le temps de nettoyer son dentier qui trempait dans le petit réceptacle prévu à cet effet. Elle se coucha, je lui donnai son cachet, lui souhaitai bonne nuit et j'allai frapper à la porte d'à côté. La dame dormait déjà, elle n'avait pas eu le courage de m'attendre ; j'en informerais mes collègues de nuit.

Porte suivante, Henriette. Henriette me touchait particulièrement. Je savais que je passerais du temps avec elle ; chaque soir, elle paniquait, et des crises d'asthme montaient. Il fallait prendre le temps de discuter un peu pour la réconforter.

Quand je suis entrée, elle était assise sur son lit et pleurait. Je m'assis à côté d'elle.

— Henriette, qu'est-ce qui ne va pas ?

— Oh, ma petite, je n'arrive même pas à enlever mes bas…

— Je vais vous aider, ne vous inquiétez pas.

— C'est moche, la vieillesse, tu vois.

— Non, ce n'est pas moche, c'est une étape de la vie, un jour je serai comme vous.

— Je ne te le souhaite pas, ma petite. Tu as des enfants ?

Cela faisait dix fois qu'elle me posait la question depuis que j'étais dans l'établissement, et je lui répondais la même chose, en lui ôtant ses bas, à chaque expression de sa douleur d'être dépendante.

— Oui, j'en ai deux.

— Garçon, fille ?

— Un garçon de seize ans et une fille de onze.

— Et tu es là à aider une vieille à cette heure plutôt que d'être avec eux ? Tu sais, il faut en profiter, des enfants, ça pousse vite.

— Je les verrai ce soir, ne vous inquiétez pas.

Je lui enfilai sa chemise de nuit, lui installai le slip filet et la protection. Assise sur le lit, elle commença à manquer de souffle, et paniqua.

— Henriette, je vais aller vous chercher un verre d'eau fraîche. Avez-vous fait vos pulvérisations ce soir ?

— Oui, mais cela ne fonctionne pas !

— Attendez-moi, je reviens.

Je courus à la fontaine et lui rapportai ce verre d'eau fraîche qui pourrait lui faire du bien.

— Vous êtes gentille, Anne-Sophie. Je n'ai pas de nouvelles de mes enfants, je ne sais même pas quand ils vont passer me voir…

— Vous avez essayé de les joindre ?

— Oh non, je n'ose pas, je ne veux pas les déranger.

Ses larmes coulaient toujours.

— Henriette, appelez-les demain, et vous verrez.

— Oui, tu as raison, j'essayerai.

Elle m'a prise dans ses bras. Le câlin dura quelques minutes. Elle en avait besoin. Puis elle se mit dans son lit.

— Tu seras là demain ?

— Oui, Henriette, je serai là. Je passerai vous voir, vous me direz si vous avez pu joindre vos enfants, d'accord ?

— Oui d'accord, merci, Anne-Sophie.

— Bonne nuit, Henriette, à demain.

— À demain.

Il était pratiquement 20 heures, et il me restait des gens à coucher. Je finirais encore en retard ce soir.

Chambre suivante. Tout était à faire. La dame m'attendait dans son fauteuil, elle n'avait pas pu aller aux toilettes seule. Je l'installai donc, j'en profitai pour la déshabiller, et en attendant qu'elle termine, j'allai m'occuper de la résidente d'à côté. Je savais que le coucher était rapide avec elle, il fallait juste lui enlever ses bas de contention, lui installer des talonnettes après avoir massé quelques instants ses talons, et le tour était joué.

Quand je revins dans la chambre, la première dame était toujours assise sur la cuvette. J'enchaînai un peu mécaniquement les gestes quotidiens, et bientôt la résidente se retrouva en pyjama, assise sur son lit, prête à se coucher.

Au moment où j'ôtai ses chaussons, elle se mit à pleurer.

Est-ce que la nuit est porteuse d'angoisse ? Est-ce la peur que la mort les touche dans leur sommeil ? Est-ce que la journée s'était mal passée ? Sont-ils tout simplement comme ces bébés qui, quand le jour tombe, pleurent sans raison apparente ? Je ne sais pas, mais c'est récurrent, et les pleurs touchent plus les femmes que les hommes.

Je discutai avec elle en la manipulant, elle pleurait toujours. Comme pour Henriette, je m'assis à ses côtés.

— Dites-moi ce qui ne va pas.

— Je ne sais pas, j'ai peur…

— Vous avez peur de quoi ?

— Je ne sais pas. Vous êtes là demain ?

— Oui, demain, je suis là.

Elle pose sa main sur ma joue et esquisse un sourire.

— Vous viendrez vous occuper de moi ?

— Cela dépend à quel étage je serai affectée, mais, de toute façon, nous nous verrons dans la journée.

— Oh non ! Je ne vais pas encore avoir une nouvelle !

— Mais non, ne vous inquiétez pas. Vous prenez votre cachet. Tenez, un verre d'eau.

Je lui relevai la tête, et elle s'exécuta. Je lui installai draps et couverture et fis exprès de me tromper en voulant remonter la barrière du lit. Je savais qu'elle aimait quand je faisais des bêtises, elle en sourit.

— Je perds la tête, décidément, fis-je mine de me plaindre.

— Oh, à ton âge, quand même…

— Si, si, vous n'auriez pas été alerte, je me trompais.

— Je sais que tu me fais marcher.

Ses larmes avaient disparu.

— Je vous souhaite une bonne nuit.

— Oui, bonne nuit, Anne-Sophie. C'est bien ça, ton prénom ?

— Oui, c'est bien mon prénom.

— Alors à demain.

— Oui, à demain. Bonne nuit.

Et je continuai et continuai encore. Ce soir, j'aurai fini les couchers à 20 h 45, sans avoir eu le temps de faire mes transmissions. C'est une faute professionnelle. Si j'y allais maintenant, je ne serais pas partie avant 21 h 30. Les ordinateurs fonctionnaient quand ils en avaient envie, c'était aussi une des joies de mon établissement. Tant pis, j'embarquai mes poubelles et me dirigeai vers le vestiaire. Ma collègue d'étage était déjà partie sans me dire au revoir ; c'était fréquent, l'envie de rentrer chez soi devenait plus forte que tout, je n'en prenais même plus ombrage.

Ce soir-là, quand je rentrerais, mes enfants seraient probablement couchés, mais j'aurais essayé d'apporter plus de quatre minutes à chacun des résidents afin qu'ils ne se sentent pas jetés comme des objets dans leur lit.

36

Passage en caisse

Ce titre veut tout dire et ne rien dire, si je ne l'explique pas. Dans les EHPAD, des médecins coordinateurs sont présents, mais ils n'ont pas le droit de prescrire. Ils ne sont pas là tous les jours, et, la nuit, il n'y a aucune infirmière. Il arrive même que, la nuit, du personnel non diplômé se retrouve en charge de la totalité de l'établissement. Dans mon EHPAD, deux personnes étaient présentes la nuit pour soixante-dix-sept résidents, qui devaient gérer les urgences, les décès ou tout autre problème susceptible de survenir.

Alors si le médecin coordinateur ne s'occupe pas des résidents, il est légitime de se poser la question de qui les soigne. C'est généralement leur médecin traitant. Je ne veux pas faire de ce que j'ai vu une généralité, mais, tout de même, ce à quoi j'ai assisté se révèle assez effarant.

*

Quand une personne âgée ne va pas bien, l'infirmière appelle son médecin, qui viendra quand il le pourra. Parfois, cela peut prendre deux jours, il est probablement débordé. C'est ainsi que Serge, qui avait les jambes en sang, aussi dures que du bois, et qui ne pouvait plus marcher, aurait la visite de son praticien plusieurs jours après l'appel. Or, il peut s'en passer, des choses, en quelques jours ! Les infirmières ont fait ses pansements tous les jours, mais tous les jours il a souffert tant les plaies suppuraient. Serge est donc resté assis dans son gros fauteuil, n'osant s'absenter de sa chambre au cas où le généraliste apparaîtrait. Car, oui, le médecin de Serge, s'il ne trouvait pas le patient dans sa chambre quand il venait, ne perdait pas son temps à le chercher, il repartait.

J'ai vu quelques médecins rendre visite à leurs patients, prendre le temps de discuter avec eux et renouveler leurs ordonnances. Ceux-là existent mais sont, disons-le ouvertement, rares.

Il y a des médecins que j'appelle « les supermarchés du médicament ». Ceux-là se dirigent directement dans le bureau des infirmières, jettent un œil à l'état de santé de leurs patients, prescrivent à l'identique, mettent les cartes Vitale dans le lecteur et repartent. Ils ne sont allés voir personne, n'ont pas pris de tension, ni même dit un mot pour savoir comment se portaient leurs malades. Rien. *A contrario*, j'ai toujours vu les kinés s'occuper des résidents. Ils restent pour les faire marcher dans les couloirs, prennent du temps avec eux.

Une chose est certaine : qu'ils soient débordés ou non, les médecins n'oublient jamais de passer la carte Vitale. Quand vous avez quatre ou cinq patients dans la même maison de retraite, où la visite est facturée au minimum 33 euros, le déplacement est rentable. Et s'ils cumulent plusieurs établissements… Combien de fois ai-je vu ces situations ? Trop. J'en viens à douter de la vocation de ces praticiens-là.

Où est le suivi ? Où est l'intérêt qu'ils portent à leurs patients âgés ? Peut-être leur demanderai-je un jour, au risque de me faire rabrouer. Parce que, non, le médecin commerçant ne supporte pas qu'on lui adresse la parole ni qu'on remette en cause sa façon de pratiquer.

Décidément, nous ne faisons pas partie du même monde.

37

Les équipes

Nous étions fin janvier. La vie continuait dans l'établissement entre les aléas, les journées à rallonge sans pause, les décès. J'avais beaucoup remplacé ce mois-ci, particulièrement les week-ends. Ma feuille de paie m'indiquait 196 heures de travail. Même moi je n'arrivais pas à y croire. J'aurais pu dire non à tous ces remplacements, mais je n'avais pas voulu. Pourtant, je regretterais quelquefois d'avoir apporté mon aide.

*

Ce dimanche-là, la directrice m'a appelée vers 9 heures. Je n'avais eu que le samedi pour me reposer. Je sautai dans mes habits, tel un pompier qui partirait au feu, et j'arrivai vers 9 h 30.

Après avoir salué le personnel présent, je montai vers les étages. Personne. Deuxième étage, pas plus de monde dans les couloirs. Retour au premier, j'aperçus une collègue que je ne connaissais pas.

— Salut, je viens vous donner un coup de main, où manque-t-il quelqu'un ?

— Salut… Tu n'as qu'à prendre ce côté-là.

— OK. Il y a déjà des toilettes de faites ?

— Je n'en sais rien…

Et elle est partie. Quel accueil ! Je me retrouvais comme une imbécile au milieu de ce couloir que je connaissais, mais où j'avais le sentiment d'être une étrangère. Il me fallut quelques instants pour réaliser : je venais de laisser ma famille un dimanche de repos pour recevoir un accueil aussi peu sympathique. Je n'étais pas là pour être reçue comme le Messie, mais un « merci » m'aurait fait du bien ! La compétition entre les équipes, je la prenais en pleine figure à cet instant précis. Mais comme j'aspirais à ce que cette journée se passe bien, je démarrai les toilettes.

Je frappai à une première chambre. Une dame attendait. Je me suis vite rendu compte que c'était tout ce pan de l'étage qui attendait. Combien de toilettes à faire ? Surtout ne pas compter. Je terminerais quand je terminerais. J'avais deux heures, je ferais de mon mieux, comme d'habitude.

Je pris les chambres dans l'ordre. En sortant de chez Georges, je tombai sur Yvette dans le couloir. Je n'étais pas encore passée pour sa toilette, et Yvette avait décidé de se préparer seule. Mais elle avait un peu perdu la tête, Yvette, et appelait seins nus, dans le couloir, son soutien-gorge à la main. Elle était perdue et cherchait sa chambre. Je la raccompagnai, ne pouvant décemment pas la laisser se promener dans les couloirs dans cette tenue. Elle refusa que je la lave, elle l'avait déjà fait, me dit-elle. Je doutais qu'elle se soit vraiment lavée, mais je n'allais pas la brusquer.

J'agrafai son soutien-gorge et lui trouvai un haut pour aller avec ce pantalon sale qu'elle ne voulait absolument pas changer.

Son pantalon n'était pas sale, je n'y connaissais rien, me rabroua-t-elle. Et puis elle ne l'avait mis que ce matin. Cela faisait trois jours que mes collègues et moi tentions de lui changer sans succès. Si j'avais eu plus de temps, j'aurais sûrement essayé de l'apprivoiser pour qu'elle accepte le changement, mais aujourd'hui je ne pouvais pas. Elle me remercia, et je repartis dans le couloir.

Toutes les lumières d'appel en haut de chaque chambre étaient allumées et transformaient le couloir en une longue guirlande de Noël ! Sauf que nous n'étions pas à Noël, et que tous les résidents sans exception avaient besoin de quelque chose en même temps. Je soufflai et j'entrai dans une chambre en souriant.

— Bonjour, vous avez sonné ?

— C'est à cette heure-ci que vous arrivez pour ma toilette ?

— Je ne suis là que pour remplacer une collègue absente, d'où le retard. On y va ?

— Un peu, oui, qu'on y va ! Vous avez vu l'heure ? Décidément…

Et ce serait ce même discours chaque fois que je pénétrerais dans une chambre. Je ramènerais Yvette deux fois dans la sienne entre deux déposes de poubelles ou de linge, et je la rhabillerais, car je la retrouverais dans ce long couloir seins nus appelant quelqu'un pour l'aider. Aujourd'hui, la règle des trois F prenait tout son sens. J'étais dans l'obligation d'infliger à chaque résident une prise en soin qui ne me plaisait pas, qui n'avait pas de sens ce matin, qui manquait d'humain.

Je luttais contre le temps qui fondait comme neige au soleil. J'étais encore loin du sommet de mon Everest de travail.

Et durant toute cette sale journée, personne ne viendrait m'aider, je ne verrais aucune collègue.

Une idée me hantait : j'avais laissé ma famille un dimanche de repos pour assister une équipe qui risquait fort de m'abandonner à mon triste sort et pour venir effectuer un travail qui ne serait pas abouti.

*

À midi, je n'avais pas terminé mes toilettes. Je voyais quelques collègues qui venaient chercher les résidents pour aller en salle de restauration. Moi, je pataugeais entre eau savonneuse, urine et selles. Mes gestes étaient devenus des automatismes, je ne réfléchissais plus. Je frappais, j'entrais, j'emmenais la personne dans la salle de bains : déshabillage, toilette, rhabillage, et au suivant. Je n'avais refait aucun lit, on verrait plus tard.

Une leçon à retenir : ne jamais se dire « on verra plus tard » dans un EHPAD, parce que vous n'êtes jamais disponible. Je ne sais plus à quel moment j'ai refait les lits, mais je les ai refaits. Toutes mes collègues se connaissaient, je n'en connaissais aucune, et elles me l'ont bien fait sentir. J'étais le pion qui était allé là où elles ne voulaient pas se rendre. J'ai donc aidé la table de la honte pour le déjeuner.

Le repas terminé, je commençai à remonter les résidents pour le change de 14 heures, et je ne vis personne. Entre celles qui étaient parties en pause et celles qui s'étaient mises en binôme, je me retrouvais seule. Totalement seule ; aucune solidarité entre équipes, aucun regard bienveillant, aucune parole amie. Cette équipe ne travaillait pas comme la mienne, je fis donc ce qui me parut être à faire et comme notre équipe l'aurait fait. Je sentais les larmes me monter aux yeux ; je ne m'étais jamais sentie aussi mal à l'aise. J'avais envie de rentrer chez moi, de retrouver les miens.

Il doit exister, j'en suis sûre, de vraies équipes, fortes et solidaires, dans lesquelles chaque personne se sent investie de sa mission mais aussi de celle du groupe entier. Mais, personnellement, je n'en connais pas. D'abord parce que, dans mon établissement, les équipes sont majoritairement féminines, et, je dois bien l'admettre, cumulent les poncifs que l'on prête aux femmes : les moqueries sur les physiques, les messes basses, les colportages et autres bavardages sont monnaie courante. Certaines, les fausses bonnes copines, ne vous adressent la parole que lorsqu'elles sont dans le jus. Les vraies bonnes copines, en revanche, celles qui mangent ensemble à l'extérieur, qui font tout à deux, ne vous adressent pas un regard, et attention à vous si vous tentez d'interférer dans ces couples fusionnels ! La plupart, dans votre dos, critiquent vos pratiques : vous en faites trop ou n'en faites pas assez, vous êtes trop rapide ou trop lente, vous ne levez le petit doigt pour personne ou vous passez votre vie dans le bureau de la direction… J'en passe et des meilleures. Il y a celles qui vous apprennent votre métier, qui vous observent et qui, au moindre manquement, vous attendent au tournant. Il y a celles qui sont souvent en pause alors que vous croulez sous la charge de travail. Il y a celles qui ne prennent pas de gants avec les résidents. Il y a enfin celles qui font leur travail et qui rentrent chez elles. Bref, il y a une multitude d'individualités. Pas d'équipes soudées.

Mais revenons à ma solitude de ce jour-là. Je devais partir à 18 heures, j'étais donc d'animation l'après-midi. Je me suis débrouillée pour aller chercher les résidents volontaires un par un, aucune de mes collègues n'est venue m'aider. J'avais dans l'idée de proposer à nos aînés encore du piano. Je n'avais apporté aucune partition, j'ai joué de tête. Pour certains morceaux, mes doigts se positionnaient automatiquement sur le clavier. Enfin un moment où j'étais bien.

Était-ce vraiment pour les résidents que je m'étais mise au piano, ou pour moi-même ? Peu importait, au fond, j'allais pouvoir leur apporter un peu de douceur, de réconfort, sans regarder ma montre ni avoir à appliquer une règle quelconque.

À 15 heures, je commençai à jouer. Quelques têtes apparurent dans l'encadrement de la porte. C'étaient mes collègues. Je tenais ma revanche. À 16 heures, goûter.

C'était à moi de le servir. Mais quelle ne fut pas ma surprise lorsque je vis deux collègues s'avancer et me dire :

— Continue à jouer, on donne le goûter, c'est trop beau.

Le concert a duré jusqu'à 17 h 30. Deux heures et demie d'humanité, comme une parenthèse enchantée. Très vite, la routine a repris le dessus : je fis mes transmissions, je me changeai et je rentrai enfin chez moi.

Ce soir-là, j'avais mal à mon travail.

38

À la lumière d'une ombre

Ce jour-là, j'étais affectée à l'unité protégée. Étant une aide-soignante spécialisée dans les troubles cognitifs et le handicap, j'allais enfin pouvoir exercer mon métier dans sa totalité. L'unité protégée devrait être un cocon pour des résidents atteints de maladies neurodégénératives comme Alzheimer ; en réalité, c'était un fourre-tout de pathologies. Sur les quatorze personnes que comptait l'unité, seules quelques-unes déambulaient, les autres étaient polyhandicapées dans des fauteuils roulants.

Comme chaque matin, ce fut la course aux toilettes. Je fus frappée, mordue, parce que j'étais obligée de réveiller les résidents sans tenir compte de leur rythme biologique afin qu'à 9 h 30 ils aient tous pris leurs médicaments. Quelques jours plus tôt, j'avais entendu notre commerciale dire à une famille qui venait visiter l'unité : « Ici, vous voyez, nous faisons des animations, aujourd'hui, par exemple c'est après-midi crêpes. Ici, vous verrez, votre maman sera bien prise en charge, on est dans l'obligation de respecter les rythmes biologiques de nos résidents, c'est un point d'honneur dans notre cahier des charges… » J'avais failli m'étouffer. On ne vend pas la réalité aux familles dans le désarroi qui cherchent le meilleur pour leur proche. On les endort avec des arguments spécieux, la plaquette est jolie, les paroles sont rassurantes ; mais la réalité est tout autre.

Chez nous, dans l'unité protégée, les résidents sont pris en charge comme nous le pouvons avec les moyens que l'on nous donne. Et, comme partout ailleurs, le temps nous manque cruellement.

Le matin, il faut descendre les chariots de petits déjeuners et les servir sans l'aide de personne. Ensuite, cap sur les toilettes. Notre cadre a eu la riche idée de ne pas répartir les produits d'hygiène et de les mettre tous dans une seule pièce. Malheur à vous si vous oubliez quelque chose ! Rien n'est véritablement réfléchi, tout est décidé par les directeurs qui n'enfilent jamais une blouse et pensent avoir la science infuse.

*

Ce matin-là, vers 11 heures, la cadre, toujours perchée sur ses talons, nous a rejointes. Il nous restait, je crois, cinq ou six toilettes à faire, quand elle me dit :

— Anne-Sophie, vous n'avez pas écrit le menu sur le tableau, pas mis la météo ni quelles animations vous avez faites ce matin.

Les bras chargés de linge, je restai soufflée par sa hiérarchie des priorités. Alors que je lui répondais que la seule animation de la journée avait été les toilettes, elle poursuivit sur le même ton :

— Oui, mais c'est important pour les familles de voir que nous inscrivons des choses au tableau, et puis ça ne vous prend pas longtemps… Au fait, avez-vous nourri Alois ?

Alois, le chat de l'unité protégée. Pourquoi Alois ? Parce que Alois Alzheimer. On ne manque pas d'humour, en unité protégée… Ce chat n'est pas gentil, il pisse absolument partout et peut attaquer n'importe quand. Il y a aussi une cage avec des perruches ; avec le chat, c'est un savant mélange, il n'y a pas à dire… Quand ce ne sont pas les résidents qui, agacés par le bruit des perruches, font voltiger la cage à travers l'unité. L'endroit est vivant, c'est un fait. On y arrive avec beaucoup d'entrain, on en ressort sur les rotules.

Ce jour-là, j'étais en charge de l'animation. Comme d'habitude, la seule chose qui me vint, ce fut la musique. J'avais apporté mon violon quelques jours avant, les résidents avaient apprécié : sur leurs visages, souvent figés, étaient apparus des sourires, certains s'étaient dandinés dans leurs fauteuils, tandis que d'autres avaient frappé dans leurs mains.

Aujourd'hui, ce serait piano. Comme on s'en souvient, l'instrument qui meublait la grande salle à manger appartenait à une résidente de l'unité. Elsa. Elsa était belle et d'une grande élégance. De surcroît, au premier regard, tout chez elle vous paraissait aller parfaitement. Elle avait peu de rides, voire pas du tout, elle était fine, ses cheveux étaient noirs de jais, pas un seul fil blanc. Ses vêtements étaient classiques, elle avait du charisme, de la classe. Mais Elsa n'était que l'ombre d'elle-même, elle avait tout oublié. Elle parlait très peu, si ce n'est pour être dans l'opposition, et il lui arrivait d'être violente – sa pathologie générait ce genre de comportement. La plupart du temps, elle était discrète, assise sur sa chaise. Elle marchait à tout petits pas et avait besoin d'une main pour avancer. Besoin d'une main qui lui donnerait confiance en elle, comme on le ferait pour un enfant qui apprend.

À l'heure de l'animation, j'avais une idée en tête. J'approcherais Elsa du piano. Depuis combien de temps n'avait-elle pas touché un clavier ? Mes collègues m'ont toujours dit qu'à son arrivée c'était elle qui faisait résonner les cordes de l'instrument, qui était alors dans sa chambre. Pourquoi lui avait-on enlevé, je ne le saurai jamais. Mais je sais la douleur d'un musicien auquel on ôte son instrument. Enlevez-nous nos instruments, nous sommes aphasiques.

Je commençai par Bach, puis ce fameux nocturne de Chopin qui fait trembler d'émotion. Elsa, à côté de moi, se mit à chantonner, puis chanta de plus en plus fort. Sa voix recouvrait maintenant les notes. Cette fois-ci, c'était sur moi que le nocturne faisait de l'effet : Elsa chantait, et moi je pleurais.

Le morceau terminé, je lui tendis le livret des partitions pour qu'elle choisisse un morceau. Elle désigna un menuet de Bach.

— Elsa, il n'est pas évident, celui-ci.

— Ah non, il n'est pas évident.

Alors elle tourna les pages, trouva un morceau. Et plutôt que de me rendre la partition, elle se mit à jouer de la main droite. Elsa était une ombre dans la lumière, ce jour-là elle avait retrouvé son instrument.

Ma collègue était bouche bée. Et je ne pus retenir mes larmes.

Non, ce n'est pas vrai, Elsa n'avait pas tout oublié…

39

Tout va bien

Martine était une oubliée. Elle ne parlait pas, elle suivait nos demandes sans broncher, même quand elle était mal réveillée. Martine n'était pas difficile, mangeait ce qu'on lui proposait, restait des heures assise dans le petit salon sans mot dire, seule. Elle ne participait jamais aux animations parce qu'elle était tellement discrète que personne ne l'y emmenait. Qu'avait-elle fait dans sa vie ? Je l'ignorais.

Quelquefois, son mari passait la voir ; il semblait plus âgé qu'elle, mais je ne pouvais donner d'âge à Martine. Quand je la regardais, j'avais le sentiment de voir une fillette dans un corps d'adulte. Hormis le diabète, je ne lui connaissais aucune pathologie. En décrivant Martine, je me rends compte qu'il y a des aînés que nous ne voyons plus. À part sa toilette, lui distribuer son repas, quand avais-je vraiment pris le temps de discuter avec elle ? Jamais.

Elle était facile, et il y en avait si peu parmi les résidents que ceux qui l'étaient devenaient des fantômes errant dans les couloirs. Leurs vies se résumaient à nous voir passer à côté d'eux en courant.

*

J'ai toujours été surprise par la chambre de Martine. Souvent les résidents apportent meubles, livres, télévision, photos et tout autre souvenir qui les relient à leurs vies avant l'EHPAD. Dans sa pièce, il n'y avait rien. Sa chambre était à l'image d'une cellule monastique : un lit, une table, une chaise et un fauteuil. Elle ne vivait pas dans l'opulence de biens, elle n'en avait pas. Dans son armoire, quelques vêtements qui se battaient en duel, point.

Finalement, Martine était devenue, à l'image de son lieu de vie, un rien ; une dame âgée sans histoire, sans paroles, sans biens, une dame âgée fantôme.

*

Mais, depuis quelques jours, Martine faisait parler d'elle. Non pas qu'elle se soit rebellée, qu'elle se soit mise à parler : elle se grattait. Nous avions avisé les infirmières de son état. Martine n'était pas une priorité, personne ne se déplaçait vraiment pour constater tous ces petits boutons. La semaine est passée ainsi, quand une infirmière remplaçante se déplaça enfin. Alerte rouge ! Branle-bas de combat ! Suspicion de gale.

Depuis une semaine, nous n'avions pas pris de précautions particulières quand nous nous occupions de Martine, et si la gale se confirmait, nous avions toutes de grandes chances d'être contaminées, et de la rapporter triomphalement dans nos demeures sans le savoir.

*

Dans un EHPAD, les mots comme mort, décès relèvent du normal ; en revanche, gastro, grippe, gale font souffler un vent de panique. La différence dans les consciences entre des pathologies particulières et la fin de vie, c'est factuel. L'habitude, probablement ! Je m'habitue à la mort qui plane chaque jour, je suis touchée quand un résident part, mais je ne me fais pas aux pathologies moins communes.

*

Dorénavant, ce serait blouse et gants obligatoires avant d'entrer dans la chambre de Martine ; tous ses vêtements seraient mis dans des sacs-poubelle et vaporisés de produits antiacariens. Les draps aussi. Même Martine. Désinfection complète.

Le surlendemain, un expert en dermatologie passerait. Nous resterions donc vigilants, et Martine serait confinée dans sa chambre, quarantaine obligatoire, tant que le diagnostic ne serait pas posé. En attendant, tous les soignants se grattaient, c'en était devenu psychologique.

C'est son époux qui dut payer la prise en charge de la possible maladie de sa femme. Tout rapporte, dans un EHPAD, même la gale. Il se saignait déjà aux quatre veines pour la maintenir dans l'établissement, ce surcoût de 75 euros par mois était une somme astronomique pour le couple.

Quelques jours plus tard, une première collègue fut renvoyée chez elle. Elle était contaminée. Impossible de travailler dans ces conditions. Le lendemain, une collègue de nuit se vit aussi renvoyée chez elle, même diagnostic.

Les jours, les semaines passèrent, et Martine ne voyait vraiment plus personne. Plus personne ne voulait entrer dans sa chambre. D'ailleurs, dans le couloir, la couleur était affichée : devant la porte était posté un portemanteau avec la seule et unique blouse que nous devions enfiler, et sur une chaise, une boîte de gants. Il ne manquait plus qu'une pancarte « Attention, gale », et on aurait eu toute la panoplie du manque de respect de la pathologie.

Martine aurait bien aimé sortir de sa chambre et déjeuner avec les autres. Interdit. Errer dans les couloirs ? Interdit !

Un jour où nous manquions de personnel, stupeur de l'équipe : notre collègue renvoyée chez elle pour cause de suspicion de gale était là. Elle portait une blouse.

— Mais qu'est-ce que tu fais ici, tu es guérie ?

— Ils m'ont appelée ce matin, il manque du monde, ils m'ont donc demandé de remplacer.

— Et tu n'as pas refusé ?

— J'ai besoin de manger.

Que répondre à cet argument ? Rien.

40

L'or gris

Une entrée dans l'établissement se profilait. Depuis des semaines, nous demandions que les entrées soient moins lourdes ; cela signifie que nous souhaitions, pour le respect de la dignité des résidents, que des personnes plus autonomes soient acceptées. Le monsieur attendu serait logé en définitive au rez-de-chaussée, la partie du bâtiment la plus difficile à gérer pour nous ! Cela voulait dire plus de difficulté pour les soignants. Mais surtout plus de profit pour la direction. Pourquoi était-il plus rentable d'accepter des résidents lourdement handicapés dans l'établissement dans lequel je travaillais, à but lucratif ? Parce que chaque personne âgée perçoit l'allocation personnalisée d'autonomie, versée par les conseils généraux. Plus la dépendance est élevée, plus la somme est importante. Elle n'est pas d'un montant fixe, mais calculée selon la grille AGGIR (voir p. 89). En moyenne, un GIR 4 percevra une pension de 300 euros, un GIR 1, 600 euros.

On comprend donc mieux pourquoi il est plus juteux d'accepter des personnes en grave perte d'autonomie.

Ces sommes s'ajoutent au reste à charge que le résident doit payer. Dans cet établissement, ils déboursent en moyenne 2 700 euros par mois. Une somme rondelette, pour le moins. Et lorsqu'on sait que les résidents ou leurs familles, pour payer l'hébergement de fin de vie, soit vendent la maison acquise à la sueur de leur front, soit vident les comptes d'épargne, et espèrent secrètement que la mort les touchera assez tôt pour que leurs enfants ne soient pas obligés de payer pour eux…

L'établissement vend du rêve en plaquettes colorées et mise sur son caractère privé. Mais il faut savoir que la prise en charge est exactement la même que dans un établissement public. Ce n'est pas parce que nos aînés paient plus cher que le soin sera de meilleure qualité. Pourquoi ?

En France, les Agences régionales de santé (ARS), tous les cinq ans, recalculaient le GMP (GIR moyen pondéré) et le PMP (pathos moyen pondéré) – qui sert à déterminer la prise en charge médicale nécessaire aux personnes âgées dont l'état de santé est dégradé – afin de doter l'établissement d'une enveloppe financière devant servir au paiement des salaires. Évidemment, on ne parle que des salaires des soignants diplômés ou non diplômés mais en voie d'acquisition des expériences. Si les GMP et PMP sont identiques dans un établissement comme celui où j'officie et dans une structure publique, il y aura le même nombre de soignants.

Plus les chiffres sont hauts, plus l'enveloppe est importante. Un établissement privé avec des dotations publiques, donc… c'est l'argent du contribuable, le vôtre, le mien, qui est distribué à des actionnaires, parce que, ne nous méprenons pas, il y a si peu de contrôles que bien des établissements peuvent faire ce qu'ils veulent de cette manne.

À partir du GMP et du PMP, l'ARS avait décidé qu'il fallait donc, dans mon établissement, dix-neuf soignants diplômés pour s'occuper de soixante-dix-sept résidents, même si l'autorisation d'ouverture du lieu avait été accordée pour soixante-quinze. C'est un détail, mais tout de même, un détail qui a son importance. Imaginez l'argent que génèrent deux résidents de plus.

Le profit n'a aucune morale : dans certains établissements du même type, l'indécence va jusqu'au rationnement des protections, souvent de qualité inférieure, pour économiser 10 centimes. Car c'est aussi l'enveloppe de soins qui paie les protections, les gants et le matériel indispensable à nos métiers. *Idem* pour l'alimentation : la plaquette promotionnelle et le site Internet promettent souvent des repas diversifiés, équilibrés. Or, en moyenne, dans ces établissements, les repas ne doivent pas coûter plus de 4 euros par jour. Je veux bien croire qu'ils font des commandes groupées et qu'ils bénéficient de tarifs préférentiels, mais je mets quiconque au défi d'établir un petit déjeuner, un déjeuner, un goûter et un dîner équilibrés pour 4 euros.

Et lorsque des économies sont faites et qu'il reste de l'argent public, qui assure que celui-ci est réinvesti pour nos aînés ? Personne.

Le problème étant posé, nos gouvernants s'insurgent tous du constat alarmant de l'état de dénutrition de nos seniors dans les EHPAD, des escarres qui se soignent mal et des pathologies qui s'accélèrent. Mais depuis combien de temps cela dure-t-il ?

*

Un soir, dans mon établissement, les fours étant en panne, le dîner de remplacement servi fut composé de raviolis en boîte. Cinq raviolis se battaient en moyenne au fond des assiettes. Les personnes âgées ne dirent mot. Pourtant, elles avaient faim, elles avaient vidé les corbeilles de pain. Mais elles firent contre mauvaise fortune bon cœur, demain on mangerait mieux. Et puis, la plupart avaient connu la guerre et le rationnement, alors elles s'adaptaient. La colère monta tout de même chez certains ; mais comment prendre l'initiative de dire quelque chose quand, pour toute réponse, vous recevriez les foudres du chef de cuisine ?

Le lendemain midi, les fours étant toujours en panne, ce fut chips et jambon blanc pour tout le monde ; pratique pour ceux qui n'ont pas de dents et qui doivent manger du mixé ! Le soir arriva et, dans l'assiette, comme la veille, cinq raviolis en boîte. C'en était trop : les résidents ont refusé de manger ce qu'il leur était proposé, et une grève des repas a débuté. Il ne faut pas s'imaginer que, parce qu'elles sont vieilles, ces personnes sont devenues idiotes ; elles savent très bien combien elles paient chaque mois et s'insurger quand le traitement qui leur est accordé devient indigne. Spectatrice de ce qu'il s'était passé, je me suis tout à coup sentie fière. Fière de leur détermination, fière de leur action solidaire, fière de voir que les résidents avaient encore l'envie de dire non.

*

Le cynisme de certains responsables d'établissements privés à but lucratif est sans limites – comme l'est l'appât du gain. La mort, ultime étape de la vie, est naturelle. Vous, moi allons mourir un jour. Nous ne pouvons mourir que si nous avons vécu. Notre mort, nous la souhaitons tous douce et sans souffrances. Mais personne n'a la même histoire quand l'heure a sonné, nous ne sommes pas égaux face à la Grande Faucheuse.

La mort est omniprésente dans les EHPAD, dont beaucoup ne rechignent contre aucun profit : ainsi, des établissements ont des contrats non écrits avec des entreprises de pompes funèbres. Quand le résident décède, la direction utilise la souffrance, le désarroi des proches pour conseiller telle ou telle société capable d'organiser les funérailles. Elle souffre avec la famille, est dans l'empathie, la comprend. Même si cette dernière n'a jamais vraiment eu affaire à elle, ne l'a jamais vraiment croisée dans les couloirs, ce jour-là, elle aura les mots qui sauront réconforter, elle passera une main dans le dos pour mieux aider le parent qui, perdu, choisira peut-être l'entreprise qu'elle lui conseillera.

Les pompes funèbres sont d'ailleurs souvent installées à proximité des maisons de retraite, parfois juste en face. D'une certaine façon, la logique commerciale est respectée. Oui, mais pas seulement. À chaque début d'année, les patrons de ces sociétés apportent volontiers aux secrétaires et cadres des maisons de retraite des boîtes de chocolats – une couronne mortuaire n'aurait pas été du meilleur effet. Échanges de bons procédés, la mort est un commerce comme un autre. Et, en règle générale, plus un établissement envoie de clients à une entreprise, plus la commission est intéressante.

Mais la marchandisation, l'exploitation de la douleur des proches laissent un goût amer dans la bouche.

*

Voilà donc l'univers dans lequel je travaille, où la vieillesse est une marchandise. La soignante que je suis se débat chaque jour pour que le soin reste un acte humain et non un chiffre dans un bilan comptable. L'humain est une notion non quantifiable, mon métier ne devrait pas être régi par des politiques de rentabilité. La vieillesse ne rapporte rien à l'État ; au contraire, elle coûte. En se dédouanant de la prise en charge des personnes âgées, celui-ci ouvre grand la voie aux établissements privés qui ont toute la liberté de financiariser la vieillesse.

Mais nos aînés, qui ont cotisé toute leur vie, n'ont-ils pas droit à un peu de dignité ?

Les EHPAD sont vus comme des mouroirs, et c'est ce qu'ils sont. Combien de personnes âgées décèdent par manque de considération des directeurs et des médecins coordinateurs qui restent sourds aux paroles et doléances des soignants ? Pourtant, il faut en être convaincu, si aujourd'hui ces établissements tiennent encore debout, c'est grâce au dévouement de tant de petites mains.

Cela s'appelle l'or gris.

41

Nouvelle entrée au rez-de-chaussée

M. Ernst était le nouveau venu de l'établissement. Il avait eu un accident vasculaire cérébral et était paralysé du côté gauche. Il était aussi en traitement pour une bactérie multirésistante ; il fallait lui appliquer une pommade sur tout le corps après la toilette. En tant que personnel soignant, nous devions être encore plus vigilants. Ses vêtements, ses draps étaient placés dans des sacs hydrosolubles avant d'être lavés. Ses poubelles étaient déversées dans un grand carton et envoyées à un organisme particulier qui les traiterait.

Son arrivée pesait sur cet étage déjà chargé. Or, quelques jours plus tard, un autre monsieur fit son entrée dans cette aile de l'établissement. Lui était sondé ; sa prise en soins prendrait donc aussi beaucoup de temps.

Alors que nous réclamions plus de personnel pour ce niveau, la direction, en guise de réponse, nous ajoutait deux résidents lourds. Encore une preuve flagrante que la parole des soignants n'est jamais écoutée.

*

M. Ernst ressemblait à un SDF quand il est arrivé : barbe longue, cheveux gras, habits et corps sales. Autrefois, professeur de physique-chimie dans un lycée du sud-ouest de la France, il avait encore toute sa tête, seul son corps l'avait en partie abandonné. Ses tee-shirts étaient découpés dans le dos, la technique que des prédécesseurs avaient trouvée pour lui enfiler ses vêtements. Un dossier d'hospitalisation à domicile était fait, il se poursuivrait donc dans l'établissement. Les soins seraient effectués par des infirmières extérieures, mais pas les toilettes. Il avait des pansements un peu partout, était dans un triste état. Il n'était pas âgé, mais je n'étais pas convaincue, tant s'en faut, que son état s'améliorerait dans un EHPAD.

L'établissement décida que M. Ernst n'aurait droit ni à un verre de vin ni à ses cigarettes. Je connaissais pourtant des résidents autorisés à boire de l'alcool dans leur chambre ou à table, et qui s'endormaient avant même la fin du repas tant ils étaient alcoolisés. Alors pourquoi cet homme était-il traité différemment ? Il nous était formellement interdit de lui offrir une cigarette. Était-ce une prescription médicale ? Aucunement, juste une solution de facilité pour l'établissement. Comme le monsieur ne pouvait pas vraiment se déplacer seul, il fallait un soignant pour l'accompagner dehors. C'était donc du temps perdu, du temps où un soignant n'était pas rentable. Les EHPAD deviennent parfois des lieux de privation de liberté quand les résidents ne sont plus du tout autonomes.

Il a donc fallu sevrer M. Ernst du tabac. Il s'est mis à chiquer. Il ne chiquait pas du tabac, il ne mâchouillait pas des chewing-gums à la nicotine, non : il chiquait du carton ou du papier toilette ! Il fallait bien qu'il trouve un placebo. Quand je le voyais faire, j'allais lui chercher du pain, c'était toujours mieux que du carton. La direction n'avait pas l'air gênée que cet homme en soit réduit à cela. C'était ainsi, ils avaient décidé, lui devait s'y plier. Combien de fois nos voix se sont élevées, combien de fois nous avons été méprisées… On ne discute pas les ordres. Nous ne sommes pas là pour penser, nous sommes des techniciennes de la toilette, pas des technocrates qui « décisionnent » sur les mesures à prendre.

Je parlais intégrales, nombres complexes, logarithmes et fonctions exponentielles avec cet homme. Il me racontait ses élèves et la fin de sa vie professionnelle. Il ne devait pas être tendre, comme prof, il était cartésien et bien accroché à certaines idées reçues. Il n'avait pas sa langue dans sa poche et savait envoyer balader s'il n'était pas d'humeur. Mais il pouvait aussi être gentil et aidant lors de sa toilette alitée. Il se moquait complètement de son style, raillait parfois toutes ces vieilles dames endimanchées. Pour lui, la beauté, finalement, « ne se mangeait pas en salade », et comme il me le répétait souvent, citant Saint-Exupéry : « On ne voit bien qu'avec le cœur, l'essentiel est invisible pour les yeux. »

Un matin, quand je suis entrée pour m'occuper de lui, le choc, la stupéfaction. Ses petits yeux chafouins me regardaient, interrogateurs :

— Ben quoi, qu'est-ce que tu as, ce matin ?

— Il y a eu une bagarre cette nuit, dans cette chambre ?

— Non, pourquoi ?

— Pourquoi ? Mais qu'avez-vous fait, cette nuit ? Tout va bien ?

— Ben oui.

Du sol au plafond, des boulettes de papier toilette mastiquées et collées aux murs. Même la télévision en avait pris pour son grade ; c'était ce qui s'appelle avoir de la neige sur l'écran. Je souriais intérieurement. Il n'avait pas manqué de munitions. Je commençai à le déshabiller, il souriait.

— Vous allez avoir des difficultés à regarder la télévision, maintenant.

— Je me suis énervé hier soir.

— Comment cela, vous vous êtes énervé hier soir ? Contre quoi ?

— Contre ces politiciens, là ! Écoute, j'en ai vu un hier soir que je n'aime pas et me suis défoulé.

— Vous ne l'aimez vraiment pas ! Vous m'auriez dit le contraire, je ne vous aurais pas cru !

Je riais, il riait de ses petites bêtises. La toilette était détendue. Elle prenait toujours autant de temps, mais j'aimais cette ambiance de douceur. Ma collègue agent de nettoyage frappa à la porte et entra. Elle pâlit. Quand elle vit le carnage et la mise à mort de tous ces rouleaux de papier toilette, elle referma la porte en disant :

— Oh, mon Dieu, je reviens.

Quelques minutes plus tard, les infirmières de l'établissement, la maîtresse de maison, la secrétaire pénétrèrent dans la chambre pendant que je triais le linge. Il eut droit à une leçon de morale, à laquelle il répondit très calmement :

— Vous me faites chier.

Comment ne pas éclater de rire ? Je souris encore en écrivant cela, même si la scène est au fond bien triste.

*

C’est l’histoire de M. Ernst, ancien enseignant, obligé de chiquer du papier toilette ou du carton. C’est l’histoire de cet homme dont les libertés ont été sacrifiées aux décisions d’un établissement. C’est l’histoire de cet homme seul, têtu, sans famille, qui assumait ses actes, qui m’a souvent fait rire, et qui, si son bras gauche le lui permettait encore, serait probablement en train de nous jouer un morceau de la guitare qu’il gardait précieusement à côté de son lit.

42

« Ne vous inquiétez pas, il est très gentil. »

Ce jour-là, un nouveau résident faisait son entrée dans l'unité protégée. Jacques venait remplacer un monsieur que la direction avait d'autorité installé dans les étages supérieurs sans son consentement, ce qui l'avait d'ailleurs déboussolé un moment, car de ce fait il avait perdu tous ses repères. Il ne savait pas comment descendre manger, se trompait d'étage, ne retrouvait pas sa chambre, prenait des décisions incompréhensibles auxquelles nous devions nous plier.

L'homme qui avait pris sa place était grand, très grand, et charmant. Il marchait bien, avait l'air tout à fait normal ; ses réactions ne montraient aucune forme de troubles cognitifs. Il souriait fréquemment, dansait dès qu'il y avait de la musique. Le matin, il était souvent le premier debout ; il s'asseyait à une table, attendant que je lui serve son petit déjeuner. Tartine de pain confiture, café au lait et jus de fruits. Il était le premier à vouloir aider à la cuisine, il s'intéressait à ce que nous faisions. Il était gentil, si gentil…

Le temps passa ainsi quelques semaines, et puis son comportement commença à se dégrader. Il cherchait son épouse partout. Elle était décédée quelques mois plus tôt ; le lui avait-on dit ? Je l'ignorais. Dans sa chambre, pas de luxe, quelques photos en noir et blanc qui laissaient supposer qu'il avait été gymnaste dans un cirque ou ailleurs.

Ses demandes concernant son épouse devenaient chaque jour plus pressantes, et que lui répondre, sinon lui mentir ? Comme peu de famille venait le visiter, je trouvais des subterfuges, et souvent mes arguments le calmaient pour un temps. Il était sous traitement léger, pourtant je sentais bien que quelque chose clochait chez lui.

Son état psychique se détériora, ses yeux se firent méchants. Nos discussions devinrent plus difficiles à tenir, il ne pensait qu'à son épouse. Si je lui disais la vérité, comment la prendrait-il ? Je commençais à craindre ses réactions. À force de travailler dans l'unité protégée, je sentais quand un résident était proche de la rupture et que la crise approchait ; en ce qui concernait Jacques, je n'avais aucun repère. Alors je restais sur mes gardes.

Deux jours plus tard, à 7 heures du matin, j'étais de nouveau affectée à l'unité protégée. Jacques était déjà levé, comme à son habitude. J'aurais préféré qu'il dorme toujours, je me trouvais encore seule à cette heure et j'avais de moins en moins confiance en ses réactions. Dès qu'il me vit, il m'agressa :

— Tu étais où, cette nuit ?

— Bonjour, comment allez-vous ?

Ce n'était pas à moi qu'il parlait, mais à son épouse. Ses yeux en disaient long sur la colère qui l'animait. Pourvu que je réussisse à le calmer…

— Vous souhaitez déjeuner, vous voulez m'aider ?

— Tu étais où cette nuit ?

J'étais enfermée dans la petite cuisine ; il y avait donc une distance de sécurité entre lui et moi. Je détournai encore une fois la conversation.

— Je vous offre un café, vous en voulez un ?

— Oui, s'il te plaît.

— Je vous mets des tartines avec, vous voulez déjeuner ?

— Oui, j'ai faim.

— Allez vous asseoir, j'arrive.

— Je m'assieds où ?

— Où vous le souhaitez, vous avez toute la salle pour vous.

Il s'installa à sa place habituelle. Je terminai la préparation. Je n'étais pas sereine quand je lui apportai son plateau.

— Oh, c'est beau, merci, c'est gentil.

— Mais de rien, bon appétit.

Il s'était radouci, était doux comme un agneau. Depuis plusieurs jours, le ton de sa voix alternait entre méchanceté et douceur. J'avais le sentiment d'avoir deux hommes en face de moi. Pendant qu'il était affairé à manger, je m'occupai des autres résidents. L'unité protégée se réveillait doucement. Certains résidents le rejoignirent à table et s'assirent à côté de lui. Sa colère repartit de plus belle. Il revint furieux vers la cuisine.

— Dis-leur de foutre le camp ! On est chez nous, ici, c'est quoi, tous ces gens que tu as invités ?

— Ils prennent juste leur petit déjeuner.

— Oui, mais je suis chez moi, ici ! Qui t'a donné l'autorisation d'inviter tous ces gens ? Et puis c'est qui qui paie leur repas ? Non ! non ! non ! Vire-les-moi !

Il hurlait. Ma collègue arriva enfin ; nous serions deux à le gérer, ce serait plus simple. Du moins, c'était ce que je pensais. J'enchaînai rapidement avec sa toilette ; sans les autres résidents, peut-être se calmerait-il.

Arrivée dans la chambre, je proposai de le raser d'une voix la plus douce possible. Il fallait qu'il redescende en tension. Il se calma peu à peu. Il refusa de porter des protections, je n'insistai pas. Il m'aida très gentiment à faire son lit. Quand il était ainsi, c'était un homme merveilleux, souriant, amusant.

Je craignais le retour dans l'espace commun. Je l'accompagnai jusqu'à son fauteuil, où il s'assit tranquillement. Aux expressions de son visage, j'avais l'impression qu'il allait se rendormir. Un peu de répit en perspective.

Ma collègue et moi continuâmes les toilettes jusqu'au moment où sa colère reprit. Le calme n'avait pas duré longtemps. Peut-être une demi-heure. Désormais il entrait dans les autres chambres pour nous trouver.

J'étais avec une dame à moitié nue quand il pénétra avec fracas dans sa pièce.

— Pouvez-vous sortir, Jacques, s'il vous plaît ? Je termine avec cette dame et j'arrive.

— Non ! Tu fais quoi ? Et puis, les gens sont encore là.

— Vous êtes dans la chambre de cette dame et je suis en train de la laver, je vous promets, j'arrive. Sortez, s'il vous plaît.

Il sortit en claquant la porte. Il donnait des coups de pied dans chaque porte du couloir. Cinq minutes plus tard, il était de retour.

— Je t'ai dit de faire partir ces gens ! Tu fais quoi, bon Dieu ?

— Je termine avec cette dame, et promis, j'arrive.

— Je vais les tuer, tu sais, si tu les fous pas dehors !

— Je termine, j'arrive.

Il repartit en se tapant la tête contre les murs du couloir. J'ai été obligée de fermer à clef pour le respect de la résidente et de sa nudité. Jusqu'à ce que je sorte, il tambourinerait à la porte. Il invectiverait chaque résident qui passait à côté de lui. Ma collègue avait terminé avant moi, elle le prit en charge. Il était violent, dans ses mots, ses actes. Pas d'autre choix que d'appeler les infirmières pour qu'elles lui délivrent un « si besoin ». Nous n'arrivions pas à le calmer avec nos mots et notre douceur, seule une action chimique pourrait agir à ce stade.

Le médicament pris, il s'assit dans le grand fauteuil. Nous ne l'avons plus entendu jusqu'à midi, il a dormi. Mais l'heure du déjeuner approchait, et nous devions le réveiller. Fallait-il l'isoler pour qu'il ne voie pas les autres résidents ? Pas sûr que ce soit la bonne solution à long terme, si nous espérions qu'il finisse par s'intégrer. Je l'installai donc à une table où il n'y avait que des messieurs, et curieusement ils discutèrent. Les conversations n'avaient ni queue ni tête, entre Germain qui cherchait son cheval grimpé au poteau électrique, Henri qui n'entendait rien et qui faisait répéter la moindre phrase, et lui qui répondait à Germain qu'il était fou, qu'un cheval ne grimpait pas aux poteaux, mais tout se passait pour le mieux.

En revanche, à une autre table, Rosa hurlait et engueulait tout le monde. Tous les attablés étaient effrayés. Hugues, dans son coin, se mit à crier lui aussi sur Rosa.

— Mais tu vas la fermer, ta gueule !

Il allait falloir vite calmer tout ce petit monde. Certains s'étaient levés et avaient fui. Ils n'avaient que très peu mangé. Pendant que l'une de nous les rattrapait pour les remettre à table, l'autre continuait de donner la becquée à ceux qui n'étaient pas autonomes. Louisette riait toute seule et chantait. Rosa hurlait toujours. Hugues lui répondait de plus belle. Germain, Henri et Paul étaient au-dessus du poteau et voulaient désangler la pauvre bête.

J'avais mal au crâne.

Servir les desserts, le sucre apaisait. Il était 13 h 15, il fallait remonter les chariots, changer et coucher ceux qui avaient besoin de faire la sieste. Jacques était calme, je commençai par emmener les dames. Il resta assis sur sa chaise, sans broncher. La fille de Germain venait d'arriver et s'installa à côté de son père.

Quand je revins, Germain avait uriné par terre et craché ses glaires. Il fallait le changer.

— Germain, venez, on va se changer.

— Non, pourquoi ?

— Vous êtes trempé, je vous donne mes mains, venez, je vais vous aider.

Il se leva avec difficulté, mes mains dans les siennes. Il me les serrait si fort qu'il me faisait mal. Quand je lui demandai de relâcher mes doigts, il se rapprocha et voulut un câlin. Pas un de ces câlins qui réconfortent, non, un de ces câlins que lui aurait faits son épouse…

D'un seul coup, Jacques s'était levé. Je connaissais ces yeux.

— Où tu l'emmènes ?

— Je vais changer le monsieur.

— Menteuse ! Tu vas te faire sauter, hein ?

— Non, Jacques, je vais le changer.

— De toute façon, je suis sûre que tu me trompes.

Il était retombé dans sa paranoïa. La fille de Germain tenta d'empêcher Jacques de nous suivre dans la chambre, et une fois à l'intérieur je nous enfermai à clef. Jacques hurlait, insultait, frappait la porte.

La fille de Germain s'inquiéta de la sécurité dans cette unité. Je ne pouvais lui en tenir rigueur, malgré mes tentatives pour la rassurer. Son père n'était évidemment pas en sûreté avec Jacques dans le coin, pas plus que nous, d'ailleurs. Le personnel avait beau remonter les agissements aux cadres de l'établissement, personne ne faisait quoi que ce soit.

La fin de journée se passa difficilement, mais le repas du soir fut assez paisible. À l'heure des couchers, Jacques redevint agressif et défonça la porte de l'unité protégée. Nous étions quatre à le maintenir, sans succès. Il nous fit voler comme de simples ballons de baudruche et commença à tout casser. Quand les pompiers, appelés par une collègue, sont arrivés, Jacques s'était radouci. Malgré nos suppliques, les pompiers ont refusé de l'emmener. Il nous aurait presque fait passer pour des folles, tant il était doux comme un agneau.

Ce soir-là, je suis partie avec une heure et demie de retard. J'ai appris le lendemain matin, en lisant les transmissions, que Jacques avait remis ça quelques instants plus tard, qu'un second appel aux pompiers avait été donné, et que, cette fois-ci, ils l'avaient emmené : Jacques avait été interné en unité psychiatrique.

Entre-temps, il était rentré dans les chambres, avait frappé des résidents sans autre raison que parce qu'il se croyait chez lui. Le psychologue de l'établissement jamais n'apporta de réponse à son problème.

Ce cas illustre parfaitement la quête acharnée de profit : pour gagner de l'argent, certaines directions sont capables de mettre en danger la vie des soignants et des résidents. Triste constat.

43

A comme animations…

Le produit phare d'un EHPAD est la partie « animations » proposée à nos aînés. La brochure commerciale les promet diversifiées, adaptées aux pathologies. À la lire, l'EHPAD est un endroit où l'ennui n'existe pas – ne vous inquiétez pas, on s'occupe de tout ! La plaquette vante les projets de vie individualisés. Il y aurait même une animatrice dédiée aux activités, présente du lundi au vendredi, et le week-end les soignants prendraient le relais.

Mais, en réalité, rien n'est mis en place. Personne ne prend le temps de s'intéresser à la vie passée des résidents, à leurs véritables besoins. Nous, les aides-soignantes et les aides médico-psychologiques, connaissons à peine leurs pathologies, alors, leur projet de vie… !

Quand ils franchissent la porte de la maison de retraite, les gens ne sont plus rien, si ce n'est des vieux qui n'ont pas la possibilité de rester chez eux. Leur histoire n'existe plus, leurs finances sont pompées un peu plus chaque mois, seuls leurs corps portent les stigmates d'une vie plus ou moins rude. Nous, soignants, aussi empathiques que nous pouvons l'être, sommes complices de leur perte d'autonomie. Nous accélérons leur régression ! Comme nous savons que nous n'avons pas le temps de les emmener ne serait-ce qu'aux toilettes, alors que fait-on ? Dès leur entrée dans l'établissement, nous rendons les protections obligatoires, qu'ils soient incontinents ou non. Je ne me suis jamais mise à leur place depuis que je travaille dans l'établissement, mais aujourd'hui je me rends compte, en écrivant, qu'il faut faire une terrible abstraction de soi-même et de ce que l'on a été pour accepter d'être pris en charge de cette façon-là. Si, en plus, vous avez toute votre tête, quelle indignité vous subissez à vivre dorénavant avec des couches !

Mais revenons aux animations. Que va-t-on proposer, puisqu'on ne sait rien des résidents ? Et surtout à qui ? En règle générale, les animations sont proposées à ceux qui sont à peu près autonomes et à ceux qui ne font pas trop de bruit. Comme des élèves sages et d'autres turbulents, seuls les premiers participent aux grandes animations anti-ennui ; les seconds restent seuls dans leur chambre.

L'animation majeure dans mon établissement, c'est l'atelier lecture. Le matin, en petit comité, il s'agit de lire le journal. Lorsqu'elle a lieu aussi en unité protégée, l'animatrice pose le journal sur la table, feint de lire quelques articles, mais prend surtout le temps de boire son café en dénigrant ses collègues et la direction. Ici, pas d'oreilles qui traînent, du moins aucune ne se souviendra de ce qui a été dit. Ces matins-là, l'unité protégée devient le salon où l'on cause. Tout le monde, famille comprise, s'accorde à dire que l'organisation de l'établissement est à revoir pour une meilleure prestation ; mais personne ne dénonce quoi que ce soit une fois les portes sécurisées passées.

L'autre animation phare, c'est l'animation onglerie. Elle a lieu le matin aussi, et les dames apprécient. Pendant quelques instants, l'animatrice leur fait une beauté des mains. Parfois, elles ont même droit à l'application de vernis. C'est pratique, le vernis, ça cache les ongles sales que nous n'avons pas le temps de nettoyer correctement dans nos quinze minutes de toilette. Les familles n'y voient que du feu, si ce n'est que maman est coquette. Ma grand-mère m'a toujours dit : « L'important, ce n'est pas la propreté dessus, ma Sophie, l'important, c'est la propreté dessous ; imagine que tu aies un accident et que l'on soit dans l'obligation de te déshabiller, si ta culotte est sale, tu pouvais bien paraître propre en surface, imagine la honte… » Elles sentiront probablement dans la journée l'urine et les selles, mais l'honneur est sauf, les ongles sont peints.

Les directeurs attendent généralement beaucoup des bénévoles pour animer les après-midi. Chez nous, il y a un musicien qui vient deux fois par semaine. Une fois pour faire un immense jeu de société avec ceux qui ont encore la faculté de répondre, une seconde fois pour jouer de la guitare quelques heures sur de vieux rythmes désuets.

*

Cet après-midi-là, je devais aider à l'animation. Je chanterais des chansons, j'inviterais les plus autonomes à danser, d'autres frapperaient dans leurs mains. Voilà que M. Lamotte est arrivé, avec sa pathologie, des tremblements. Il manquait de tomber à chaque pas. Pour seule aide à la marche, il avait sa canne où était accroché un colson. Quand il ne pouvait vraiment plus avancer, il fallait mettre son pied devant le sien, ainsi, il devait passer par-dessus, et l'automatisme de la marche pouvait reprendre pour quelques instants. Il aimait la musique, mais aujourd'hui, il souhaitait danser. Vu sa pathologie, c'était risqué, mais comment lui refuser de danser s'il en avait besoin ?

Je préférai donc danser avec lui. Il ne boitait pas, était même stable, il me serrait contre lui, et parfois même réussissait à me soulever. Je devins alors une marionnette qu'il faisait valser à sa guise. Au changement de morceau, il avait trouvé une autre résidente pour tourner, une dame qui chantait tout le temps, dansait beaucoup avec son mari avant. Elle était moins aguerrie que lui mais semblait revigorée. Ses jambes, bizarrement, paraissaient moins fortes que celles de son cavalier, pourtant elle n'avait pas sa pathologie. Il fallait le faire ralentir, ils allaient finir par terre. Une autre musique, une autre cavalière, et tout l'après-midi M. Lamotte danserait. Il inviterait toutes les vieilles dames à pousser le pas du tango, du paso doble, sans jamais tomber et toujours avec le sourire.

L'heure du goûter approchait. Il n'avait pas envie de manger, but un verre et redemanda de la musique. Si un jour quelqu'un me dit que la musique ne peut être une thérapie, je l'emmènerai un dimanche dans mon établissement afin de lui prouver le contraire.

Le temps de quelques valses, et l'après-midi se termina. M. Lamotte avait repris sa canne et était redevenu cet homme qu'il ne supportait plus d'être. C'était en allemand qu'il m'expliquait son désarroi. Lui, l'homme cultivé, ne pouvait plus écrire, ne pouvait plus courir ; son corps avait lâché mais sa tête était intacte.

Certains lundis, il y a une animation gym douce. Elle est organisée par un intervenant extérieur. On se lance des ballons, on tape des pieds, on fait des mouvements avec les bras, on essaie de se dérouiller. Cette activité a vraiment peu de succès. Elle a au moins le mérite de changer de l'ordinaire !

Les sorties aussi sont considérées comme des animations. Elles sont assez rares dans l'établissement. La camionnette louée pour le transport permet aux aînés à mobilité réduite d'y participer. Il y a neuf places, donc neuf résidents qui partent ensemble. Sur soixante-dix-sept, c'est peu. Souvent, cette sortie est un repas, ou un repas spectacle. Ces animations ne sont pas gratuites, contrairement aux autres, donc seuls les plus aisés peuvent se permettre un tel écart. Où est l'égalité pour chacun ? Elle est inexistante.

Certaines animations pourraient être qualifiées d'utiles : pliage de serviettes, épluchage de pommes de terre ou de légumes pour la soupe du soir. Si j'avais mauvais esprit, je dirais volontiers que ce sont des heures normalement effectuées par du personnel que la direction n'aura pas à payer.

D'autres sont organisées en fonction des événements : animation confection de guirlandes de Noël, animation guirlandes de Pâques, animations guirlandes en tout genre…

Un samedi sur deux, l'animation attendue est celle du loto. Chez nous, une infirmière vient sur son temps personnel avec ses cartons, son boulier et ses pions. Si le nombre de participants est important, le manque de jetons est pallié par des grosses pâtes. Inlassablement, elle répète les numéros. Il faut apporter son aide à ceux qui n'entendent pas bien, à ceux qui en jouant déplacent leurs jetons et sont perdus. Je ne sais pas où elle déniche des lots, mais à chaque carton plein, nos aînés ont une petite breloque. Elle intervient bénévolement et ne coûte rien à la direction. Et, cerise sur le gâteau, nos aînés ne se sont pas ennuyés.

*

Voilà ce que sont les animations. Mais ne nous leurrons pas : l'animation la plus fréquente dans mon établissement, c'est d'être installé devant la télé tout l'après-midi. Les résidents sont laissés là, endormis et à moitié tombés de leur fauteuil, parce qu'ils ne sont pas assez réceptifs aux autres. Pour eux, pas de jeux ni de loto, et encore moins de sorties.

En parlant de sorties, quand les directions des EHPAD mettront-elles en place l'animation « devoir citoyen » ? Combien de nos aînés ont-ils la possibilité d'aller exprimer leurs votes ? Certes, certains signent des procurations à leurs familles, mais ce n'est pas la majorité. Ils n'ont pourtant pas perdu leur droit de vote ; mais personne n'est mis à leur disposition pour les accompagner, ce serait de la perte de temps et une rentabilité nulle. Mais ne serait-ce pas leur permettre d'être considérés comme citoyens de la cité prenant part aux échéances électorales en France ? Ne serait-ce pas leur permettre de garder une estime d'eux-mêmes ? Alors que la plupart se sont battus pour le droit de vote, ce ne serait que leur rendre justice. Les personnes âgées sont donc considérées non seulement comme des comptes en banque, mais surtout comme des exclus de la société.

44

Décès de Robert

Robert est tombé dans la nuit et a été retrouvé le matin par terre. Perdu, désorienté, il a été hospitalisé.

Tous les soirs et même parfois dans la journée, il avait besoin que je discute avec lui. Ses angoisses montaient, il lui fallait une présence. Je n'avais pas toujours le temps de m'occuper de lui dans ces moments-là, je ne pouvais répondre à chacune de ses demandes. Parfois, il m'envoyait promener, revenait vers moi en s'excusant. Je me souviens qu'il m'appelait « ma petite », ou « la pianiste ». Procédés mnémotechniques pour se souvenir de mon visage ou de ma voix. Il avait donné à chacune de nous un surnom, et nous l'acceptions. Parfois, il avait juste besoin que nous lui prenions la main pour le raccompagner dans sa chambre.

Il était un ancien agent de la SNCF, il ne se déplaçait jamais sans sa canne. Ses cheveux avaient la blancheur d'une pellicule de neige juste tombée.

Robert attendait toujours son copain de la chambre d'à côté, qu'il aidait en poussant son fauteuil roulant chaque midi et chaque soir en salle de restauration.

Il était comme cela, Robert répondait toujours présent, comme si son existence n'avait de but au sein de l'établissement que dans l'accompagnement aux autres. Souvent, il s'en oubliait lui-même et prenait des risques. Il aurait pu tomber maintes fois. Il refusait de l'entendre. Il s'était défini comme l'homme qui aide son prochain.

La solitude était sa plus grande angoisse. Quand la porte de sa chambre était fermée, il se sentait seul ; il errait souvent dans les couloirs, espérant que l'une de nous prenne le temps de venir le voir, et ne s'endormait jamais sans sa radio.

Robert, c'était le café de la collation de 16 heures ; Robert, c'était cette voix au fond du couloir qui vous appelait ; Robert, c'était un homme gentil.

Un jour, il est parti, et la radio s'est tue.

J'ai décidé que j'irais à son enterrement. Pourquoi ? Un besoin, un remède à ma mauvaise conscience de ne pas avoir répondu à ses demandes, je ne sais pas. Et puis j'avais lié des rapports particuliers avec son épouse.

Arrivée aux pompes funèbres, je trouvai le fameux « chalet », la chambre funéraire. Toute la famille était là, j'étais un peu gênée. Mais l'épouse de Robert s'approcha pour me remercier d'être venue. La direction des Opalines brillait par son absence, mais des soignants étaient présents.

La cérémonie fut sobre. J'en appris beaucoup sur la vie de Robert. C'était un amoureux de la nature ; il avait été trésorier d'une association reconnue d'utilité publique. Robert, c'était aussi les copains qu'on ne lâche jamais, un peu comme la chanson de Brassens. Robert, c'était le refuge en pleine montagne qu'il aimait garder. Les photos défilaient, j'étais admirative de l'homme que je ne connaissais finalement pas, moi qui n'avais vu que le vieux monsieur à la radio, la voix qui vous appelle au fond du couloir et qui sans cesse vous demande quelque chose.

J'en sus bien plus en quelques minutes qu'en des mois de travail à côté de lui. J'ai posé une immortelle sur son cercueil, parce que Robert, comme tous les autres, est un immortel dans mon cœur. Aujourd'hui, je sais qui était l'homme à la canne et aux cheveux blancs qui nous prenait la main pour se rassurer.

Ce n'est pas un adieu, Robert, ce n'est pas un au revoir, tu es dans la pièce voisine, juste dans la pièce voisine, il suffit de savoir regarder. On ne meurt véritablement jamais. Le corps qui renferme notre être n'est rien, l'important, ce sont les souvenirs que nous laissons.

N'est-ce pas, Mémé ?

45

Réunion de crise

Depuis des mois, nous travaillions en sous-effectif. Depuis des mois, je ne me reconnaissais plus. Était-ce bien cela, les soins que je voulais apporter à nos anciens ? J'avais beau faire le pitre, sourire, chanter, je me demandais, seule dans mon lit le soir, ce que j'avais vraiment apporté de concret à mes résidents, quand je repensais à ma journée. De la technicité, certes, mais où étaient passés l'empathie, l'humain ? Ah, « l'humain », ce beau mot que je ne cessais de répéter. J'acceptais des prescriptions de travail qui ne permettaient pas de le faire correctement. Ne devenais-je pas complice du système ?

Même en courant toute la journée, je voyais bien les dysfonctionnements. J'acceptais, pour gagner du temps, que les médicaments soient distribués par des filles non diplômées qui en cas d'erreur seraient pénalement responsables sans imaginer la gravité de ce qu'elles auraient fait, que les toilettes soient faites en trop peu de temps, donc de ne pas respecter la dignité des personnes dont je m'occupais. Il fallait que j'arrête avant de sombrer.

Ce qui me confortait dans mon constat, c'était que mes collègues avaient les mêmes soucis. Les burn-out se multipliaient dans l'équipe, les pleurs, les boules au ventre en arrivant au travail – notre quotidien. Il était temps de faire entendre nos voix, nous ne pouvions décemment plus être ces soignants qui souffraient. Pas pour nos petites personnes, non, pour eux, seulement pour eux.

Une réunion de crise fut mise en place le 28 mars. La cadre, toujours perchée sur ses talons hauts, allait enfin prendre la mesure du malaise. Nous étions remontées comme des coucous suisses.

— J'ai bien compris votre problématique, nous allons y remédier, nous annonça la cadre.

— Parfait, et comment ? demandai-je.

— Vous n'êtes pas sans savoir que nous avons du mal à recruter, que personne ne veut venir travailler dans notre établissement, argumenta-t-elle.

— Posez-vous les bonnes questions. Pourquoi, à votre avis ? Les salaires sont en moyenne à 1 250 euros pour une aide-soignante diplômée, qui travaille onze heures par jour, et, en plus, qui doit être présente deux week-ends par mois, lança une collègue.

— Ce n'est pas qu'une question de salaire, nous répondit la cadre.

— Cela en fait partie ! Et quand elles arrivent, elles repartent aussi vite, pourquoi ? Parce que nous n'avons pas la possibilité de les doublonner, qu'elles se retrouvent seules dans un étage sans savoir quoi que ce soit sur les résidents ! lança une autre.

Je me suis alors dit en moi-même qu'elles étaient un peu gonflées, elles m'avaient laissée seule pendant quatre jours… mais passons.

— Nous allons réorganiser les plannings.

— Réorganiser les plannings ? S'il manque des soignants, vous pouvez bien tourner les plannings dans tous les sens, cela ne résoudra rien. Ce qu'il faut, ce sont des équipes stables, et nous n'en avons pas, dit une troisième.

— C'est un peu votre faute aussi, osa la cadre. Vous ne savez pas garder les nouvelles, vous ne savez pas les accompagner.

Voilà que, de victimes, nous devenions accusées ! Et de ne pas pallier les manquements de notre hiérarchie, par-dessus le marché !

Le dialogue de sourds dura toute la réunion, qui fut au final une immense perte de temps. Et pendant que nous étions là à discutailler, nos aînés nous attendaient pour les changes. Encore une preuve flagrante de mépris, et pas tant envers nous qu'envers les résidents.

— Et comment fait-on quand la réserve de changes est vide, quand il n'y a plus de gants ?

— Un problème de livraison qui devrait être rapidement réglé.

— Soit. Mais serait-il possible d'avoir des gants adaptés à la taille de nos mains ? De mettre en place un pôle de remplacement quand des collègues ne viennent pas, pour éviter le sous-effectif ?

— Impossible.

— Prendre des intérimaires, alors, quand on est dans ces situations dégradées ?

— Nous n'avons pas les moyens de prendre des intérimaires.

— Pas les moyens ? Nos actionnaires sont la quatre centième fortune de France, et vous n'avez pas les moyens ? Si rien ne change, nous nous mettrons en grève.

Le mot était lâché.

La cadre posa son stylo et ricana. Elle ne nous prenait pas vraiment au sérieux ; nous allions lui faire comprendre à quel point nous étions déterminées.

Nous n'espérions rien en quittant la réunion. Dans l'établissement, rien ne se perdra (à part des collègues), rien ne se créera (pas de nouvelles recrues en vue), rien ne se transformera (peut-être nos plannings, et encore).

La grève a donc été décidée, elle allait commencer le lundi suivant. Pourtant, nous nous posions tant de questions. Qui prendrait en charge nos résidents ? Ce fut une décision difficile à voter, l'empathie se rappela à nos bons souvenirs. Elle n'est pas là juste à certains moments, vous ne pouvez pas la faire disparaître quand cela vous arrange, elle est accrochée en nous comme un coquillage à un rocher.

Mais nous n'avions plus le choix.

46

2 avril 2017 : le début de la fin

C'était le week-end d'avant-grève, combien serions-nous ? Combien d'appels les aides-soignantes de nuit auraient-elles reçus de collègues remplaçantes indiquant qu'elles ne viendraient pas ? Aujourd'hui, au lieu d'être huit, nous serions six à prendre en charge soixante-dix-sept résidents. La relève s'était faite rapidement, encore plus vite que d'habitude, pas de temps à perdre. Les yeux sur nos montres… à vos marques, prêtes, partez ! Vous avez quatre heures et demie…

La fourmilière se mit en ordre de marche comme tous les jours. Mais à six au lieu de huit, comment faire ? Et qui privilégier ? Nous avions eu une réunion de crise quelques jours auparavant : une collègue allait arriver, nous n'allions pas rester dans cet état. La matinée avançait, et personne ne venait, nous étions toujours six, et la tâche loin d'être terminée. Notre préavis faisait pourtant apparaître en premier lieu le manque de personnel ; nous étions certaines que la direction aurait tout mis en œuvre pour que nous ne partions pas en grève et, ce jour, qu'elle trouverait du personnel remplaçant.

Aujourd'hui encore plus qu'hier, je serais dans l'obligation de presser mes résidents, à peine un quart d'heure à leur accorder, un « Bonjour » furtif, et pas vraiment le temps de discuter. Par anticipation, pour économiser nos pas, les changes de la journée avaient été embarqués dès le matin.

Les résidents étaient mal réveillés, difficiles à lever, les articulations douloureuses, mais qu'importe, « Veuillez m'excuser, je n'ai pas le temps ce matin… Enfin, vous le savez, nous sommes en sous-effectif, votre voisin m'appelle déjà… »

Combien de toilettes et de lits aujourd'hui, onze, douze, treize, seize ? Combien de mots échangés ? Beaucoup moins ce matin. Et une alerte succédait à une autre : « Je reviens, bien sûr que je reviens, enfin… oui mais non, je reviendrai beaucoup plus tard, enfin peut être. » Au suivant !

Pas de douche en ce jour funeste, peut-être la semaine prochaine, aujourd'hui encore, je ne pourrai prendre soin de vous avec toute la dignité que vous méritez.

Je vous demande sincèrement de m'en excuser.

Aucune de nous ne se reconnaît dans son métier ; nous ne devrions pas être les architectes de cette productivité imposée. Nous devrions être la pierre angulaire de la fin de vie, cet accompagnement dont nous aurons tous besoin un jour pour apprivoiser les dernières années de l'existence dans la sérénité.

Lundi, nous serons en grève. Lundi, nous crierons que nos métiers sont tout autres et que « Le soin, c'est de l'humain, pas du chiffre ! ».

47

2018

À l'aube du dernier trimestre 2018 j'aurai connu toutes les phases émotionnelles qu'une personne normale peut connaître.

En quelques mois, se sont enchaînés dépression, haine, colère, petits rires (un peu), grandes joies (rarement), éclats de rire (jamais).

Je me remets de cette grève de cent dix-sept jours, mais personne ne me comprend. Pendant presque un an, je cours les plateaux télé, radio, ne voulant pas qu'un couvercle soit posé sur la grève de Foucherans qui a dénoncé ce que j'ai écrit tout au long de ce livre. Car c'est ma seule possibilité de guérir. Mais qui le comprend ? Je suis en fait passée du statut de curiosité à celui d'empêcheuse de tourner en rond.

Je me rappelle les trahisons des grands patriarches syndicaux, je me souviens de ces collègues qui ne me connaissent plus, je me retrouve seule, seule à espérer que les choses vont évoluer. Si seule dans mon essence de combattante.

Fuir, ne pas penser, accepter toutes les invitations des tribunes où je pourrai m'exprimer, ne pas oublier ce pour quoi nous nous sommes battues, et surtout ne pas oublier le nom du syndicat dont je fais partie, voici ma carte de visite. Et ce qui me fait devenir progressivement cette femme-sandwich qui porte à la fois l'importance de se syndiquer et le combat pour nos aînés.

À l'époque je réponds à tous les critères : je ne m'exprime pas trop mal dans les médias, je n'ai peur de rien, je suis une bonne élève, je connais mon sujet et, le mieux de tout, je suis une femme. Un constat qui m'effraie : mon genre, à cet instant, est la quintessence même des paroles d'un syndicat qui, finalement, me pressera. J'aurai en effet droit à des coups bas de certains membres du syndicat régional. Des hauts placés, pas la base, qui ne me soutiendront pas parce que je m'opposerai à leurs décisions à mes yeux parfois trop radicales ; parce que je prends trop de place, je suis un électron libre, une insoumise, parce que leur expérience n'est pas une valeur qui m'impressionne, moi qui ai celle d'une grève interminable.

Alors, face à tous, je suis seule, sans salaire, mais je continue à me battre pour la cause, pour toutes les mémés et les pépés ! Pourquoi sans salaire ? Depuis la grève, je suis en arrêt maladie, ma famille est la victime collatérale du conflit ; nous n'allons pas très bien. Entre les enfants qui me rappellent que je les ai oubliés et mon époux qui a mal supporté l'ensemble, il faut reconstruire le socle abandonné durant cent dix-sept jours intenses. Dans un contexte financier lourd puisque je ne perçois aucune indemnité journalière, n'ayant pas travaillé assez d'heures dans les trois mois précédant mon arrêt – évidemment, en grève, je ne pouvais prétendre aux indemnités versées par la Sécurité sociale à toute personne en arrêt maladie. À quelques jours de Noël, s'impose une vérité : si nous voulons manger, c'est au Secours populaire qu'il faut aller chercher de quoi nous offrir un repas. Pareil pour les cadeaux.

Comme Noël reste un moment particulier dans l'année, nous avons quand même eu un beau cadeau. Une amie nous a invités, et nous avons passé une veillée de Noël comme si nous étions en famille. Je tiens à la remercier encore, ici, de cet accueil et de ce geste magnifiques.

Finalement, cette grève résonne en moi comme un échec. Car, depuis, rien n'a changé. Nos personnes âgées sont toujours aussi maltraitées. Tout juste puis-je me réjouir d'avoir, avec mes camarades, marqué l'histoire des luttes jurassiennes, permis à la société de prendre un peu conscience de cette maltraitance institutionnelle. Mais concrètement, tout est pareil. Sur le terrain, les soignants sont en souffrance, les familles cadenassées dans leur parole, et l'État dans une logique illogique avec recours à des groupes privés, dont beaucoup n'ont comme mot d'ordre que la rentabilité.

Ayant vu les limites du syndicalisme, il me semble alors venu le temps de changer les choses. Mais comment ?

En modifiant les lois et en m'engageant en politique…

Ma résistance commence.

Composition et mise en pages
Nord Compo à Villeneuve-d'Ascq

Imprimé en France par

Maury Imprimeur
à Malesherbes (Loiret)
en décembre 2019

N° d'impression : 241814
Dépôt légal : décembre 2019
S29969/01

Je dédie cette année 2018 à Jeanine, Michèle et Lili.

*

Ce petit texte m'a été offert par ma fille le jour de mon anniversaire. Cela faisait plus de six mois que la grève était terminée, mais visiblement ce moment de nos vies l'avait marquée. Plus que je n'avais d'ailleurs pu l'imaginer. Elle aimait venir sur le piquet, faire flotter les drapeaux au bord de la route. J'avais bêtement pensé que c'était pour faire l'école buissonnière. Mais non, elle était devenue une combattante, elle aussi.

Pour en avoir longtemps discuté avec elle, elle avait écrit ce poème après avoir compris ce qu'était une lutte pour la justice. J'admire cette petite fille, tout comme j'admire mon fils et mon époux de me laisser mener ce combat et pour avoir subi, sans se plaindre, cette grève de cent dix-sept jours.

- Juste une femmme

Commme un gâteau sans farine,
Commme une rose sans épines,
Une grève sans parole?
Impossible !
Une femmme a été choisie,
Une qui saurait défendre ses collègues,
117 jours, elle a tenue,
Ses aînés, elle a défendu,
A la TV, elle est passée,
La grève est finie,
Pourtant les interviews se succèdent encore,
Commme un gâteau sans farine,
Commme une rose sans épines,
Une femmme,
A été choisie,
Pour défendre ses anciens,
Et grâce à elle,
Cette grève a été gagnée,
Par cette femm mme extraordinaire.

Table des matières